Peloubet's

NIV Bible Study Companion
2001–2002

Based on the International Bible Lessons
for Christian Teaching Uniform Series

James Reapsome

128th Annual Volume
Founded by Francis N. Peloubet

Cook Communications Ministries
Colorado Springs, Colorado/Paris, Ontario

Peloubet's
NIV Bible Study Companion

© 2001 Cook Communications
Ministries, 4050 Lee Vance View,
Colorado Springs, CO 80918, U.S.A.
All rights reserved. Printed in U.S.A.
May not be reproduced without
permission. Lessons based on
International Sunday School
Lessons: the International Bible
Lessons for Christian Teaching,
© 1998 by the Committee on the
Uniform Series.

Senior Editor
Doug Schmidt

Editor
Dan Lioy

Bible Editor
Jim Townsend, Ph.D.

Cover photography
© 1998 by Dan Stultz

Cover Design by
Jeffrey P. Barnes

Scripture quotations, unless other-
wise noted, are from THE HOLY
BIBLE, NEW INTERNATIONAL
VERSION, © 1973, 1978, 1984 by
International Bible Society. Used by
permission of Zondervan Publishing
House. All rights reserved.

ISBN: 0-7814-5613-4

Jesus' Ministry

Light for All People

The Power of the Gospel

Unit I: Justified by Faith

Unit II: Living by Faith

Unit III: No Other Gospel

Worship and Wisdom for Living

Unit I: Songs for Faithful Living

Unit II: Praise the Creator and Redeemer

Unit III: Words for the Wise

Use Peloubet's with Materials
from These Publishers

Sunday school materials from the following denominations and publishers follow International Sunday School Lesson outlines (sometimes known as Uniform Series). Because *Peloubet's NIV Bible Study Companion* follows the same outlines, you can use *Peloubet's* as an excellent teacher resource to supplement the materials from these publishing houses.

DENOMINATIONAL:

Advent Christian General Conference: *Adult*

American Baptist *(Judson Press): Adult*

United Holy Church of America: *Adult*

Church of God in Christ *(Church of God in Christ Publishing House): Adult*

Church of Christ Holiness: *Adult*

Church of God *(Warner Press): Adult*

Church of God by Faith: *Adult*

National Baptist Convention of America *(Boyd): All ages*

National Primitive Baptist Convention: *Adult*

Progressive National Baptist Convention: *Adult*

Presbyterian Church *(U.S.A.) (Bible Discovery Series—Presbyterian Publishing House or P.R.E.M.): Adult*

Southern Baptist *(Baptist Sunday School Board): All ages*

Union Gospel Press: *All ages*

United Holy Church of America: *Adult*

United Methodist *(Cokesbury): All ages*

NONDENOMINATIONAL:

Cook Communications Ministries: *Adult*

Echoes Literature: *Adult*

Standard Publishing: *Adult*

Urban Ministries: *All ages*

Jesus' Ministry

The First Miracle

DEVOTIONAL READING

Psalm 77:11-15

DAILY BIBLE READINGS

Monday September 3
Mark 4:35-41 Jesus Calms a Storm

Tuesday September 4
Matthew 14:22-27 Jesus Walks on Water

Wednesday September 5
Matthew 14:28-33 Peter's Doubt

Thursday September 6
Mark 8:1-13 The Feeding of 4,000

Friday September 7
Mark 8:14-21 The Disciples Do Not Understand

Saturday September 8
Matthew 8:18-27 Following Jesus through the Storm

Sunday September 9
Matthew 14:14-21 The Feeding of over 5,000

Scripture

Background Scripture: *John 2:1-11*

Scripture Lesson: *John 2:1-11*

Key Verse: *This, the first of his miraculous signs, Jesus performed in Cana of Galilee. He thus revealed his glory, and his disciples put their faith in him.* John 2:11.

Lesson Aim

To discover that trusting in Jesus fills our empty lives with joy and purpose.

Lesson Setting

Time: A.D. *27*

Place: *Cana of Galilee*

Lesson Outline

The First Miracle

  I. Jesus at the Wedding: John 2:1-2

 II. Mary's Request: John 2:3-4

III. Mary's Faith: John 2:5

IV. Jesus' Command: John 2:6-8

 V. The Master's Discovery: John 2:9-10

VI. The Disciples' Faith: John 2:11

Introduction for Adults

Topic: *Seeing Is Believing*

Social embarrassments come in all sizes, shapes, and colors. But rarely do they open doors for discussions about spiritual issues. This is because it's hard for people to make the connection between everyday life and God's will.

Nevertheless, seeing is believing when people observe how Christians handle not just social embarrassments but also the deeper issues of life. For instance, many people take notice when they see a person of faith finding the strength to endure trials, hardships, and sufferings.

Consider how extraordinary it is to witness Christians refusing to take revenge when others have wronged them (Prov. 20:22). It's also exceptional when a believer uses a gentle response to defuse a potentially explosive situation (15:1). Jesus' followers may not be able to turn water into wine, but they can lead people to faith in Christ by the way they follow His commands in ordinary situations.

Introduction for Youths

Topic: *Seeing Is Believing*

What does it take to believe in Jesus? Miracles? Visions? Facts? Testimonies of others? Generations raised on believing only hard data find it difficult to accept the reliability of other kinds of facts. In response, believers over the centuries have noted that Christianity appeals to the facts of history, which are clearly recognizable and available to everyone. This observation applies to the miracle of Jesus turning water into wine (the subject of this week's lesson).

Believing in Jesus is not a blind leap of faith into the dark void of ignorance. Rather, it is an intelligent decision that is informed by eyewitness accounts (1 Cor. 15:1-8). Jesus' original followers wrote about what He did so that we might trust in Him for eternal life (John 20:30-31). As Christ said to Thomas in verse 29, "blessed are those who have not seen and yet have believed."

Concepts for Children

Topic: *Jesus Changed Water into Wine*

1. Jesus, His followers, and His mother went to a wedding at Cana in Galilee.
2. When Jesus' mother noted that the wine was gone, Jesus told the servants to fill six stone jars with water.
3. Those at the wedding soon discovered that Jesus had turned the water into wine.
4. Jesus used this miracle to show His glory.
5. Jesus has the power to meet our every need.
6. We can depend on Jesus to fill our lives with meaning and joy.

The Lesson Commentary

I. JESUS AT THE WEDDING: JOHN 2:1-2

On the third day a wedding took place at Cana in Galilee. Jesus' mother was there, and Jesus and his disciples had also been invited to the wedding.

This week we begin a new quarter of lessons that focus on Jesus' ministry. The first unit of study (lessons one through five) considers two types of miracles that Jesus performed during His ministry—those involving nature and healing. From this material we will discover that God loves and cares for all people and that He has the power to meet their needs.

Our lesson for this week deals with Jesus turning water into wine. In the preceding chapter of John's Gospel, we learn that Christ is the living Word, that He eternally existed with the Father and the Spirit before time began, and that He came to earth as a human being so that the lost might be saved (1:1-18). As John the Baptist declared, Jesus is the Lamb of God "who takes away the sin of the world" (vs. 29). It's no wonder, then, that so many people would be willing to become His followers (vss. 35-51).

We read in 2:1 that Jesus performed His first miracle "at Cana in Galilee." The exact location of this village remains unknown, though some think it may have been about eight or nine miles northeast of Nazareth. The incident occurred on "the third day," which is a reference to the last narrated event—the calling of Philip and Nathanael (1:43).

Jesus, Mary, and the disciples had been invited to the wedding (2:2). The fact that these people all attended the event suggests that the wedding may have been for a close relative or family friend.

An examination of early Christian art suggests that the changing of water to wine stands as one of Christ's most popular miracles. For instance, of the 52 marble sarcophagi originally found in the catacombs of Rome and now preserved in the Museum of Saint John Lateran in Rome, not less than 16 have carved upon them a representation of Jesus at this wedding.

II. MARY'S REQUEST: JOHN 2:3-4

When the wine was gone, Jesus' mother said to him, "They have no more wine." "Dear woman, why do you involve me?" Jesus replied. "My time has not yet come."

In Jesus' day, wedding festivals could last up to a week. On such occasions, banquets would be prepared to accommodate many guests. The attendees would spend the time celebrating the new life to be enjoyed by the married couple. Archaeological evidence indicates that entire villages would be invited to a wedding celebration. Also, to refuse such an invitation was considered an insult.

Careful planning was needed to accommodate such a large crowd. This was imperative, for the strong unwritten rules of hospitality implied that it was humiliating to be caught in short supply of some necessary item. Yet, for some unknown reason, the bridegroom failed to provide enough wine for the duration of the festivities. Perhaps more guests came than he had anticipated, or perhaps they stayed longer than he had planned.

The wedding meal consisted of bread dipped in wine. Typically the guests would call for innumerable toasts. After that, more visiting, eating, and drinking would occur (though this was rarely an occasion for drunkenness). Wine diluted with water was the accepted beverage of the times, and people were accustomed to it. Because of a lack of water purification processes, this mixture was safer to drink than water alone.

Mary reported to Jesus that the wine had run out (John 2:3). It is clear from Jesus' response that Mary's statement implied more than a simple observation of fact. Implicit in her words was a request for Jesus to do something about the situation so that the bridegroom could avoid being socially embarrassed.

According to verse 11, Jesus had not yet performed any miracles. Thus, at this point in the account we can only speculate as to what Mary had observed in Jesus that would give her the idea He could somehow resolve the problem.

It's unlikely that Mary expected Jesus to send the people home, for that was not His prerogative. Mary probably didn't want Him to send His disciples into town to buy more wine, for they surely lacked the funds to do so. Some scholars think that Mary previously had seen Jesus on other occasions do many kind and helpful things for hurting people. Perhaps in the privacy of neighborhood life, Jesus was known as an extraordinary and caring person.

Regardless of what Mary may have been thinking, Jesus gave her a startling and provocative answer. He did not say either yes or no. Instead, He asked Mary why she had come to Him for help. Without waiting for her reply, Jesus identified His ultimate mission in life. His goal was to die on the cross in order to atone for the sins of the world (1:29).

Jesus was neither cruel nor harsh in His remarks to His mother. "Dear woman" (2:4) was a common term of address that implied no disrespect. We might say, for instance, "Dear lady." Yet, it is also clear that a gentle rebuke is contained in Jesus' response. He wanted Mary to think of Him not so much as the Son whom she had reared but rather as the Messiah of Israel.

Jesus used a social situation to point to a spiritual reality. In fact, the contrast between the wedding crisis and His mission could not have been more vivid. "Why do you involve me?" underscores Mary's desire that Jesus do something to help a family avoid social embarrassment. "My time has not yet come" stressed that Jesus' death was a more eternally relevant issue.

From what followed it's clear that Jesus had not offended Mary; otherwise, she would not have spoken as she did in verse 5. (Some scholars think Jesus reproved Mary in her hearing only, and that Mary afterward told the apostle John about it so that he could write it down.) Although Mary did not understand what Jesus was going to do, she nevertheless trusted Him to do what was right.

Despite the awkwardness of the situation, Jesus conducted Himself impeccably in the social affairs of His community. And though His mission was lofty, He was not above mingling with people on all levels, so that they might be drawn to Him in faith (2:11).

Jesus' response to Mary shows that the Savior knew and controlled His eternal future (10:17-18). Mary, in turn, submitted to Jesus' decision about how to handle the situation. Like Mary, we also should accept Jesus' way of doing things. For instance, when we bring our problems to Him, we should allow Him to do what He deems best.

III. MARY'S FAITH: JOHN 2:5

His mother said to the servants, "Do whatever he tells you."

Jesus' response did not cause Mary to lose heart. No doubt she cared for the bride and bridegroom, and no doubt she was encouraged by the fact that Jesus had not turned her away. Mary knew to whom she could go when she needed help. Therefore, she summoned great faith and ordered the servants at the feast to do whatever Jesus would tell them (John 2:5). The way Mary spoke to the servants suggests she was possibly a relative of the family or at least a close friend.

Mary was confident that Jesus would do the right thing, whatever it was. Also, Mary knew that Jesus' love and sympathy would lead Him to do something to relieve the family in difficulty. In this episode we discover the depth of Mary's relationship with Jesus.

As Christians, we put ourselves in the shoes of the servants. We are obliged to do whatever Jesus tells us to do. He makes no mistakes, and His commands are not burdensome (1 John 5:3). They are always built on His wisdom and love.

IV. JESUS' COMMAND: JOHN 2:6-8

Nearby stood six stone water jars, the kind used by the Jews for ceremonial washing, each holding from twenty to thirty gallons. Jesus said to the servants, "Fill the jars with water"; so they filled them to the brim. Then he told them, "Now draw some out and take it to the master of the banquet." They did so.

Jesus took action immediately. He told the servants to fill six stone jars with water (John 2:6-7). The jars normally kept the family's water supply fresh and cool. The vessels varied in size, which we can imagine from the gallons of water they held. The Jews used the water to wash their hands and vessels according to the Mosaic law's requirements. Apparently because of the number of wedding guests, the water in six jars had been used up, so they needed to be refilled.

The servants might have been puzzled by Jesus' unusual sounding command. Why take ordinary water to the master of ceremonies (vs. 8)? Despite whatever doubts the servants may have had, they did not complain. Instead, they did exactly what Jesus said. After the servants filled the jars to the top with water, they then dipped some out and took it to the person in charge of the festivities.

V. The Master's Discovery: John 2:9-10

And the master of the banquet tasted the water that had been turned into wine. He did not realize where it had come from, though the servants who had drawn the water knew. Then he called the bridegroom aside and said, "Everyone brings out the choice wine first and then the cheaper wine after the guests have had too much to drink; but you have saved the best till now."

Mary's faith was honored when Jesus did His first miracle at this humble peasant wedding. When the person in charge of the festivities tasted the water now turned into wine, he was so pleasantly surprised that he commended the bridegroom for his good taste (John 2:9).

The master of ceremonies noted that it was customary for the host (such as the bridegroom) to serve the best wine first and then later to bring out the less expensive wines. But the bridegroom was congratulated for the brilliant stroke of keeping the best wine until last (vs. 10).

Jesus' first miracle was experienced not so much as a miracle, but rather as a wonderful discovery. Only Jesus and the servants initially knew what had happened. Jesus evidently took no unusual action, such as touching the stone jars or commanding the water to turn into wine. Most likely, Jesus' mere thought brought about the attesting sign.

Jesus did not call for a pause in the festivities, and He did not summon everyone's attention. He also did not tell those present to gather around and see how He had changed water into wine. Rather, Jesus performed His miracle in a quiet and humble manner.

John 1:3 reveals that Jesus is the Creator of all things. In fact, acts of creation and transformation are part of His nature. We do not know how Jesus changed the water into wine at Cana in Galilee, only that He did it instantaneously and without fanfare. But we do know that Jesus used this miracle to validate His claim to be who He was incarnate (an assertion that would later lead to His crucifixion).

VI. The Disciples' Faith: John 2:11

This, the first of his miraculous signs, Jesus performed in Cana of Galilee. He thus revealed his glory, and his disciples put their faith in him.

All the miracles of Jesus were signs He performed to set forth His power so that people would trust in Him. It's true that Jesus healed and helped people in dire straits, and they were blessed in this way by His miracles; yet, in the end, Jesus' foremost goal was to relieve the deepest spiritual needs of people.

Jesus' changing the water into wine unveiled His glory (that is, His divine nature and power), and the disciples believed in Him (John 2:11). His glory was seen in two aspects at Cana—His love for the neighborhood people and His control over the elements of nature.

Discussion Questions

1. When the supply of wine ran out during the festivities, what did Mary do?
2. What was the nature of Jesus' response to Mary's statement?
3. Why do you think Mary submitted to Jesus' will in the matter?
4. How did Jesus' disciples respond to the miraculous sign He performed?
5. Why should we allow Jesus to deal with our problems as He sees best?

Contemporary Application

Jesus brought good news to a broken world. He announced that God's kingdom was at hand, and that all people should repent and believe in the Gospel (Mark 1:15). Jesus did so not from the isolation of a religious ghetto, but rather from the everyday world inhabited by ordinary people.

For instance, a neighborhood wedding provided the ideal setting for Jesus to show His love and power. Suddenly He was no longer just a carpenter from Nazareth (6:3). Rather, He was the Messiah of Israel, the one who inspired faith and obedience.

People today also need to see Jesus in this way. He is much more than a famous painting or statuesque religious figure. When we trust in Him, He remains ever present to help us through our ordeals. And regardless of the nature of our problems, He is there to watch over and strengthen us.

Clearly, then, our Savior is not confined to the sanctuary. Instead, He is present in every place of life. He wants us to find salvation and peace through faith in Him. And He calls us, as His followers, to declare the message of His love and care to the lost so that He can fill their empty lives with joy and purpose. What a wonderful gift we have to share with others!

Nature Miracles

DEVOTIONAL READING

John 6:28-40

DAILY BIBLE READINGS

Monday September 10
*Mark 2:1-12 Healed Because
of His Friends' Faith*

Tuesday September 11
*John 9:1-12 A Blind Man Is
Healed*

Wednesday September 12
*Mark 5:1-15 Healing the
Gerasene Demoniac*

Thursday September 13
*Mark 5:21-24, 35-43
Healing Jairus's Daughter*

Friday September 14
*Mark 5:25-34 The Faith
That Makes You Well*

Saturday September 15
*Mark 9:17-29 Healing That
Comes Only through Prayer*

Sunday September 16
*Mark 3:1-6 Healing a Man
with a Withered Hand*

Scripture

Background Scripture: *Matthew 8:23-27; 14:14-21*
Scripture Lesson: *Matthew 8:23-27; 14:14-21*
Key Verse: *The men were amazed and asked, "What kind of
man is this? Even the winds and the waves obey him!"*
Matthew 8:27.
Scripture Lesson for Children: *Matthew 14:13-21*
Key Verse for Children: *Jesus replied, "They do not need to
go away. You give them something to eat."* Matthew 14:16.

Lesson Aim

To recognize that Jesus has the ability to meet our
needs.

Lesson Setting

Time: A.D. *28–29*
Place: *Sea of Galilee and a remote area near Bethsaida,
northeast of the lake*

Lesson Outline

Nature Miracles
  I. Jesus Calming the Storm: Matthew 8:23-27
      A. *The Disciples' Fear: vss. 23-25*
      B. *The Savior's Rebuke: vs. 26*
      C. *The Disciples' Question: vs. 27*
  II. Jesus Feeding the 5,000:
      Matthew 14:14-21
      A. *The Compassion of Christ: vs. 14*
      B. *The Disciples' Problem: vs. 15*
      C. *The Savior's Solution: vss. 16-18*
      D. *The Multiplied Food: vss. 19-21*

Introduction for Adults

Topic: *Filling Our Needs*

Life is filled with hardships, many of which are unexpected and unavoidable. It's in these tough, overwhelming circumstances that Christian faith swings into action. We find that Jesus is loving, wise, powerful, and trustworthy. How exciting it is to discover that, even in life's darkest moments, the Lord is there to watch over and provide for us.

Christians sometimes say, "Oh, that wouldn't matter to God." Or, "It's too trivial to pray about." But we soon learn that nothing is inconsequential to God. He invites us to experience the great privilege of praying to Him about everything, not just major crises. In fact, we grow the most spiritually when we place all of our needs in His hands.

This week's study of the nature miracles that Jesus performed will bring us fresh insight concerning the ability He has to meet our needs. We will learn that nothing is impossible for Him to do for us (Luke 18:27).

Introduction for Youths

Topic: *Changing the Rules*

The teenager and his father returned to the car after fishing a couple of hours, only to discover that the car keys were nowhere to be found. They searched everywhere and finally the father said, "Let's pray and ask God to help us find those keys." So the two did just that, and in a matter of minutes the keys turned up.

Was this a minor miracle? Regardless of our response, the lesson is clear. Our faith in Jesus covers all areas of our lives. Faith is not confined to the church building, the Sunday worship services, or the youth meeting. Rather, God wants us to trust and obey Him in every circumstance of life.

Jesus encountered people at the point of their greatest needs. He used these incidents to teach His disciples to trust Him more. These were also opportunities for the crowds to hear His teaching and receive His healing touch. By studying the way Jesus ministered to others, we are encouraged to depend on Him more in our trying situations.

Concepts for Children

Topic: *Jesus Fed Hungry People*

1. A crowd followed Jesus, and He healed their sick.
2. When Jesus told His followers to feed the crowd, they said they had only five loaves and two fish.
3. After Jesus' followers handed out the food, the people ate until they were full, and 12 baskets of food were left.
4. Five thousand men plus women and children were fed.
5. Through this incident Jesus showed that He loves and cares for us.
6. We can depend on Jesus to meet our needs.

The Lesson Commentary

I. JESUS CALMING THE STORM: MATTHEW 8:23-27

A. The Disciples' Fear: vss. 23-25

Then he got into the boat and his disciples followed him. Without warning, a furious storm came up on the lake, so that the waves swept over the boat. But Jesus was sleeping. The disciples went and woke him, saying, "Lord, save us! We're going to drown!"

After Jesus finished giving the Sermon on the Mount (Matt. 5—7), He came down from the mountainside with large crowds following Him (8:1). The unfolding narrative reveals that Jesus healed a man with leprosy (vss. 2-4), restored to health the young servant of a Roman officer (vss. 5-13), and brought wellness to many other people, including Peter's mother-in-law (vss. 14-17).

When Jesus saw how large the crowd was growing, He told His disciples to cross to the east side of the Sea of Galilee (vs. 18). Perhaps while they were making preparations to depart, Jesus took the opportunity to teach some people about the cost of following Him (vss. 19-22). Jesus then got into a fishing boat and started across the lake with His disciples (vs. 23).

An ancient historian named Josephus noted that hundreds of boats could be found on the Sea of Galilee at any time. The vessel in which Jesus and His disciples rode was sufficiently large to hold them. They typically used oars and sails to cross the water. However, during a storm, the occupants would have taken down the sails to keep them from ripping and to make the vessel easier to control.

On this occasion a terrible storm suddenly swept down upon the boat and sent waves breaking into it (vs. 24). The reason for such gale-force winds is the surrounding landscape. The lake is about 700 feet below sea level, and is fed by rivers that have cut deep ravines surrounded by flat plains that are in turn hedged in by mountains. The ravines act like wind tunnels, gathering cooler air from the mountains as it crosses the plains. When the air mass runs into the hot lake shore, violent storms are whipped up without warning.

Despite the tempestuous situation, Jesus remained sound asleep, no doubt an indication of how tired He was from the day's strenuous ministry. This was a touching picture of His humanity. Clearly, Jesus shared in our humanity "so that by his death he might destroy him who holds the power of death—that is, the devil" (Heb. 2:14). Also, "he had to be made like his brothers in every way, in order that he might become a merciful and faithful high priest in service to God" (vs. 17).

Though several of the disciples were experienced fishermen, they were still terrified by the storm. Perhaps fearing that all was lost, they woke Jesus up and shouted, "Lord, save us! We're going to drown!" (Matt. 8:25). At this point they did not seem to know that Jesus could control the forces of nature. As the unfolding narrative reveals, the disciples would exchange their fear of the wind and the waves for wonder and awe over Jesus' deity and power.

B. The Savior's Rebuke: vs. 26

He replied, "You of little faith, why are you so afraid?" Then he got up and rebuked the winds and the waves, and it was completely calm.

Jesus responded to the disciples' panic stricken cry with a pointed rebuke. He charged them with having "little faith" (Matt. 8:26), that is, not enough faith to overcome their fear of drowning. They sufficiently trusted Him to cry out for help, but they did not have enough faith to ride out the storm.

Of course, we cannot be too hard on the disciples. After all, powerful storms can arouse the natural human instinct of fear, which God built into us for self-preservation; otherwise, we would wander recklessly into all kinds of danger.

Nevertheless, Jesus stressed that because of Him the disciples were in no danger of drowning. It's true that people of faith need to take an objective, sensible look at reality. But faith also factors in the Lord's supreme ability to help. Such faith pushes us to depend on the Savior in our time of greatest need.

This incident is analogous to the experience of parents with their young children. Many times children run to their parents in fear. Their parents, knowing the circumstances, assure their children that there is nothing for them to fear. Jesus expected more than this from His disciples when they faced serious danger. That's why He rebuked them for their lack of faith in Him.

Jesus next stood up in the boat and rebuked the winds and waves, and suddenly it was perfectly calm. Christ's divine power was clearly manifested in the fact that the storm ceased immediately. The terrible winds and the crashing waves simply disappeared as if there had never been a storm.

C. The Disciples' Question: vs. 27

The men were amazed and asked, "What kind of man is this? Even the winds and the waves obey him!"

The disciples were taken aback by what they had seen. In fact, they were so astonished that they wondered about Jesus' true identity. The miracle He had performed proved that He is God the Son. Interestingly, the Old Testament assigned such awesome powers to God (Pss. 89:9; 107:25-30).

Jesus performed many miracles during His earthly ministry, some of which are not recorded in the Gospels. His miracles were extraordinary expressions of God's power. When Christ performed a miracle, God directly altered, superseded, or counteracted some established pattern in the natural order.

The miracles of Jesus served several purposes. First, they confirmed His claim to be the Messiah. Second, they validated His assertion that He was sent by God and represented Him. Third, the miracles substantiated the credibility of the truths Jesus declared to the people of Israel. Fourth, they encouraged the doubtful to put their trust in Him. Fifth, the miracles demonstrated that the one who is love was willing to reach out to people with compassion and grace.

II. JESUS FEEDING THE 5,000: MATTHEW 14:14-21

A. The Compassion of Christ: vs. 14

When Jesus landed and saw a large crowd, he had compassion on them and healed their sick.

As Matthew 9—13 reveals, Jesus continued to teach the disciples and heal the infirmed. But despite His favorable reception among the general populace, Jesus experienced increasing opposition from Israel's religious leaders. Even the people from His hometown of Nazareth refused to accept His messianic claims.

There was confusion among the people concerning Jesus' identity. For instance, Herod Antipas superstitiously thought He was John the Baptist come back from the dead (14:1-2). Previously Herod had imprisoned and executed John, who had been popular among the people but despised by the religious establishment (vss. 3-12).

As soon as Jesus heard the news about John's death, the Savior went off by Himself in a boat to a remote area to be alone (vs. 13). But the crowds followed Him on foot from many villages and finally caught up with Him near Bethsaida (Luke 9:10), a town on the northeast shore of the Sea of Galilee.

Although Jesus desired quietness and solace, He did not ignore the people. Rather than becoming disappointed and upset, He had compassion on them and healed their sick (vs. 14). He responded in this way because of their desperate physical and spiritual needs. Jesus could not turn His back on them, for their compelling needs demanded a loving, merciful, and powerful response (Mark 6:34).

B. The Disciples' Problem: vs. 15

As evening approached, the disciples came to him and said, "This is a remote place, and it's already getting late. Send the crowds away, so they can go to the villages and buy themselves some food."

Christ's work went on all day, and it was now getting late (Matt. 14:15). His disciples, noting the time and desolateness of the place, proposed a straightforward solution to the problem—send the people home. Food was available nearby, so this seemed like the logical thing to do. In the thinking of the disciples, it was time to close up shop and retire for the day. On the surface this might appear to be a reasonable suggestion. However, it was not Jesus' preference.

C. The Savior's Solution: vss. 16-18

Jesus replied, "They do not need to go away. You give them something to eat." "We have here only five loaves of bread and two fish," they answered. "Bring them here to me," he said.

Despite the straightforward simplicity of the disciples' plan, Jesus rejected it. Instead, He told them to feed the crowd (Matt. 14:16). Verse 21 reveals that there were 5,000 men on hand, in addition to all the women and children.

We can only imagine how stunned Jesus' disciples were at His directive. They concluded they could not possibly feed so many people with their meager supply of food—five barley loaves of bread and two fish (vs. 17). We learn from John 6:9 that the bread and fish comprised a young boy's lunch.

Jesus was not put off by the apparent impossibility of feeding so huge a crowd with such slim provisions. That's why He asked for the bread and fish (Matt. 14:18). He would prefer to feed the people with what was available at the moment than send them away hungry.

The disciples had looked at the problem from a reasonable human perspective. But then when Jesus told them to feed the people, He put the disciples in an impossible dilemma. They were forced once again to rely on Him for the solution.

D. The Multiplied Food: vss. 19-21

And he directed the people to sit down on the grass. Taking the five loaves and the two fish and looking up to heaven, he gave thanks and broke the loaves. Then he gave them to the disciples, and the disciples gave them to the people. They all ate and were satisfied, and the disciples picked up twelve basketfuls of broken pieces that were left over. The number of those who ate was about five thousand men, besides women and children.

Jesus arranged for an orderly dispersal of food (Matt. 14:19). In Mark 6:39-40 we learn that Jesus had the people sit down in groups of 50 and 100, no doubt for convenience and fairness in the food distribution. The women and children probably sat by themselves according to prevailing local customs.

Jesus first took the loaves and fish. Then He offered a prayer of thanksgiving to God in heaven. Finally, Jesus broke the loaves and had the disciples give the food to the crowds. Everyone had enough to eat, and afterward the disciples picked up 12 full baskets of leftovers (Matt. 14:20). Clearly, the food was multiplied by the Lord's power to satisfy the vast crowd's hunger (vs. 21).

In addition to showing Jesus' creative power, this miracle also revealed the power of His love and mercy for people in need. Christ did it to bolster His claim to be God's Son and Israel's promised Messiah. John 6:14 reveals that the people realized a prophet had come among them. In fact, this miracle was so overwhelming that the people were ready to take Jesus by force and make Him their king. Thus He "withdrew again to a mountain by himself" (vs. 15).

This reminds us that at any time and in any circumstance the unsaved may try to milk God for all they can get for themselves. God sees human hearts, and He knows when people seek physical food and when they seek spiritual nourishment. Jesus fed all the people, regardless of how far they had come in their understanding of His messianic identity. But He refused to become a pawn of the crowds.

Discussion Questions

1. What was Jesus doing when the storm arose, and what was the disciples' response?
2. Why did Jesus rebuke the disciples for their lack of faith?
3. How did the disciples respond when Jesus calmed the storm?
4. How did Jesus show compassion to the vast, hungry crowd of people?
5. What did the feeding of so many people reveal about Jesus?

Contemporary Application

We have all faced severe storms in our lives. These might involve the loss of a job, the death of a loved one, or the onslaught of a frightening disease. Regardless of the nature of these trials, it is virtually impossible for us to avoid them. And they have a way of pushing us to the limits of our faith.

Whatever our needs, Jesus offers to meet them. The question we face is whether we have the courage to believe that He can help us. In other words, it's not a matter of what Jesus can do but rather of our willingness to trust Him every step of the way.

Our popular culture, of course, ridicules the idea that Jesus can make a difference in our storm-filled lives. In fact, when believers talk about the power of Christ to meet their needs, the lost often do not take them seriously. Our job is not to win over the skeptics by the sheer force of our intellectual arguments. Rather, we should encourage them to investigate for themselves the teachings, claims, and deeds of Jesus.

When people are honest enough to consider the facts objectively, many times they will change their minds about Jesus. The Spirit can move them to come to Jesus in faith, receive His forgiveness, and feed on His Word. Perhaps God might use us to invite people to take a fresh look at Jesus. We need not fear, for Jesus is here to help!

Healing Miracles

DEVOTIONAL READING

John 4:46-54

DAILY BIBLE READINGS

Monday September 17
*Matthew 11:25-30 The
Weary Can Come to Jesus*

Tuesday September 18
*Luke 7:11-17 A Son Is
Restored to His Mother*

Wednesday September 19
*Matthew 12:15-21 God's
Chosen Servant*

Thursday September 20
*Matthew 12:22-28 He Heals
by Whose Authority?*

Friday September 21
*Matthew 15:1-9 Breaking
the Tradition of the Elders*

Saturday September 22
*Matthew 15:10-20 The
Things That Defile a Person*

Sunday September 23
*Matthew 15:21-31 A
Woman of Great Faith*

Scripture

Background Scripture: *Mark 3:1-6; John 9:1-12*
Scripture Lesson: *Mark 3:1-6; John 9:1-12*
Key Verse: *[Jesus] said to the man, "Stretch out your hand."
He stretched it out, and his hand was completely restored.
Mark 3:5.*
Scripture Lesson for Children: *John 9:1-11*
Key Verse for Children: *As long as it is day, we must do the
work of him who sent me. Night is coming, when no one can
work. John 9:4.*

Lesson Aim

To discern the importance of ministering the love of
Jesus to those who are hurting.

Lesson Setting

Time: *A.D. 27 and 29*
Place: *Capernaum and Jerusalem*

Lesson Outline

Healing Miracles

  I. The Man with the Shriveled Hand: Mark 3:1-6
      A. *The Setting: vs. 1*
      B. *The Trap: vs. 2*
      C. *The Challenge: vss. 3-4*
      D. *The Demonstration: vss. 5-6*
  II. The Man Born Blind: John 9:1-12
      A. *The Theological Question: vss. 1-3*
      B. *The Opportunity: vss. 4-5*
      C. *The Healing: vss. 6-7*
      D. *The Neighbors: vss. 8-9*
      E. *The Testimony: vss. 10-12*

Introduction for Adults

Topic: *Restoring Wholeness*

We can be thankful for all of the medical help available today, especially when compared to the lack of such resources in Jesus' day. We can also be thankful that more and more people are seeing the connection between physical and spiritual wholeness. People with a balanced outlook on life and people with strong faith tend to be better candidates for wellness.

As Christians, we have many opportunities to give the reasons for our faith and hope. For instance, people want to know how we found wholeness, joy, and satisfaction in our lives. They need Christians like us to explain to them how and why Jesus gives a wholeness that lasts.

The accounts of Christ's healing miracles help us to relate the truth of the Gospel to our needs and those of others. Jesus' compassion, wisdom, love, and power move us. And His triumph over legalism and skepticism shows us the value of finding true peace and freedom through faith in Him. Every time we read these accounts, our hearts should be filled with gratitude toward God for sending His Son to save us and make us whole.

Introduction for Youths

Topic: *A Healing Word*

We rub shoulders every day with people who need forgiveness and healing. Perhaps they are like the man born blind (the focus of John 9:1-12). They have no idea that Jesus can help them. God can use us to tell them about Jesus.

The Lord may not use us to heal the sicknesses of others, but He can use us to bring them hope, encouragement, and love through the proclamation of the truth. We can invite the lost to read with us the accounts of Jesus recorded in the four Gospels, and we can offer to pray with and for them.

Along the way, we should pray that the lost will come to a saving knowledge of Christ. We can ask God to enable them to discover that Jesus is the only one who truly redeems and heals, not just now but also for eternity. They need to know that He is the greatest friend they can ever know!

Concepts for Children

Topic: *Jesus Healed a Man Who Was Blind*

1. Jesus and His followers saw a man who had been blind since birth.
2. Jesus said that the blindness was not caused by sin in either the man or his parents.
3. After Jesus made mud and put it on the man's eyes, Jesus told him to wash in the Pool of Siloam, and when the man did this, he was able to see.
4. Jesus wants us to show His love for others by helping them.
5. Jesus wants us to stand up for the truth even when others do not believe us.

The Lesson Commentary

I. THE MAN WITH THE SHRIVELED HAND: MARK 3:1-6

A. The Setting: vs. 1

Another time he went into the synagogue, and a man with a shriveled hand was there.

One Sabbath Jesus' disciples were accused of violating a religious law by picking grain. In defending them, Jesus used an Old Testament example to show that human needs are more important than man-made interpretations of the law (Mark 2:27). If anyone doubted Jesus' right to make pronouncements about Sabbath observance, He declared that He was "Lord even of the Sabbath" (vs. 28).

Undoubtedly the religious leaders were not pleased with Jesus' comments on the occasion of the first Sabbath conflict. But in the second one (3:1-6), we can see the religious leaders' hatred coming to the surface.

Jesus was in a synagogue during this episode, and one of those present was a man with a shriveled hand, perhaps the result of a birth defect or injury (vs. 1). The synagogue was the place where Jewish people gathered for worship. ("Synagogue" is a transliteration of a Greek word that means "to gather together.") Synagogues originated during the Babylonian captivity after Nebuchadnezzar's destruction of the Jerusalem temple in 586 B.C. In Christ's day, synagogues served as places of worship and instruction for the Jews.

B. The Trap: vs. 2

Some of them were looking for a reason to accuse Jesus, so they watched him closely to see if he would heal him on the Sabbath.

By this time, the religious leaders had turned against Jesus. They were jealous of His popularity, His miracles, and the authority in His words and deeds. Rather than point people to God, they made acquiring status in the community their foremost priority. And because the religious leaders refused to give up their coveted power, they also refused to acknowledge Jesus as the Messiah. Sadly, when He began to expose them as frauds, they began looking for ways to turn the people against Him.

The religious leaders knew that Jesus healed the sick. They thus hoped the man with the deformed hand would provide them with a reason for condemning the Savior (Mark 3:2). The charge of violating the Sabbath was something the religious leaders could bring before the Sanhedrin (the Jewish supreme court) and make stick against Jesus.

C. The Challenge: vss. 3-4

Jesus said to the man with the shriveled hand, "Stand up in front of everyone." Then Jesus asked them, "Which is lawful on the Sabbath: to do good or to do evil, to save life or to kill?" But they remained silent.

Genesis 2:2 reveals that when the Lord had finished Creation, "on the seventh day he rested from all his work." That rest was the model for the Sabbath. It is not known when the Hebrews began keeping the Sabbath. From Exodus 16:27, however, we know that they began before God gave the fourth commandment to require Sabbath observance.

In the four or five centuries before Christ, Jewish religious teachers debated at length what actions should and should not be permitted on the Sabbath. They formulated 39 articles prohibiting all kinds of agricultural, industrial, and domestic work. The religious traditions also prohibited any healing on the Sabbath, except when there was an immediate threat to life. This was based on the teachers' understanding that healing is work, and all work was prohibited on the Sabbath.

However, the teachers also developed ways of getting around their own rules. For instance, they taught that no one should travel more than 2,000 cubits (about 3,000 feet) on the Sabbath. But if people were to deposit food 2,000 cubits from home before the Sabbath, then on the Sabbath they could declare the spot a temporary residence and act as though they had not traveled up to that point. It's no wonder Christ felt He had to put the Sabbath back into perspective.

Jesus knew the thoughts of the religious leaders, but this did not deter Him from healing the man with the shriveled hand. The Savior first directed the man to come and stand in front of everyone (Mark 3:3). Jesus then asked His critics whether it was legal to do good deeds on the Sabbath (vs. 4).

The implication of Jesus' question is that we commit evil by failing to do whatever good we can in helping others. For instance, we are guilty of murder when we refuse to save a life we have the ability to rescue from danger. The legalists were so spiritually calloused that they refused to answer Jesus' question.

D. The Demonstration: vss. 5-6

He looked around at them in anger and, deeply distressed at their stubborn hearts, said to the man, "Stretch out your hand." He stretched it out, and his hand was completely restored. Then the Pharisees went out and began to plot with the Herodians how they might kill Jesus.

The religious leaders refused to acknowledge that even good could be done on the Sabbath. In their concern for the details of the law, they had forgotten mercy. They did not understand the kind of grace that prompted God to provide a Sabbath in the first place.

Jesus could have waited until the next day to heal the man, but He didn't. Jesus also could have healed the man secretly, but He didn't. Instead, He focused everyone's attention on the man by healing him publicly (Mark 3:5).

Once this was done, the Pharisees began to plot with the Herodians, who were supporters of Herod Antipas, the Roman-appointed ruler of Galilee. Both the Pharisees and the Herodians were determined that Jesus must die (vs. 6). The only questions were when and how.

Here we see a sad irony. Jesus did good on the Sabbath by healing a man with a deformed hand. But the Pharisees and Herodians did evil on the Sabbath by plotting to kill a man (the Savior).

II. THE MAN BORN BLIND: JOHN 9:1-12

A. The Theological Question: vss. 1-3

As he went along, he saw a man blind from birth. His disciples asked him, "Rabbi, who sinned, this man or his parents, that he was born blind?" "Neither this man nor his parents sinned," said Jesus, "but this happened so that the work of God might be displayed in his life."

The sixth sign miracle featured in John's Gospel reveals Jesus as the Light of the world (8:12; 9:5). He was also unique among the prophets in that none of them had cured blindness (9:30-33). Giving sight to the blind was a messianic activity foretold in the Old Testament (Isa. 29:18; 42:7), and it validated Jesus' claim to be the Son of God (John 20:30-31).

While Jesus and His disciples were walking along, they encountered a man who had been born blind (9:1). The disciples wondered whether the man's blindness was a result of his own sins or those of his parents (vs. 2).

Before we react too strongly to the disciples' question, it is helpful to note that their query reflected the mind-set of their Jewish peers. It was commonly believed that sin was the primary, if not exclusive, cause of all suffering or calamity. For instance, babies allegedly could be born with physical defects because of their parents' sins.

While sin may be the cause of some suffering, as clearly indicated in Scripture (John 5:14; 1 Cor. 11:30), it is not always the case necessarily (2 Cor. 12:7). Jesus reflected this view in His clear and direct response to the disciples' question. The Savior stated that the man's blindness was not due to his sin or his parents' sins. Rather, he had been born blind so that the power of God, as seen in the working of a miracle, could be displayed in the man (John 9:3).

B. The Opportunity: vss. 4-5

"As long as it is day, we must do the work of him who sent me. Night is coming, when no one can work. While I am in the world, I am the light of the world."

Jesus declared, "We must do the work of him who sent me" (John 9:4). God's work was about to be revealed, and Jesus immediately put Himself and His disciples in the place of being used by God for that purpose. It was not enough to be theologically correct about the cause of the man's blindness. More importantly, something had to be done about it.

Jesus explained that it was imperative for Him and His disciples to quickly carry out the tasks the Father had given them to do. The reason is that little time remained before night would fall and all the work would come to an end. Jesus was speaking metaphorically. The light of day was a reference to His continued presence on earth with His disciples. And the coming of night was a reference to the period of darkness that would ensue when Jesus was taken from His disciples by means of His crucifixion.

Jesus reassured His disciples, however, that while He was still on earth, He was the "light of the world" (vs. 5). He did not mean that He somehow ceased being the light once He ascended to heaven. Rather, Jesus meant the light of His presence shone most brightly among people when He was on earth doing His Father's will. The Savior would prove His claim by giving the blind man the ability to see.

C. The Healing: vss. 6-7

Having said this, he spit on the ground, made some mud with the saliva, and put it on the man's eyes. "Go," he told him, "wash in the Pool of Siloam" (this word means Sent). So the man went and washed, and came home seeing.

Jesus spit on the ground, made mud with the saliva, and smoothed the mud over the blind man's eyes (John 9:6). Just as God had originally made human beings out of the dust of the ground (Gen. 2:7), so too Jesus used clay to create a seeing pair of eyes for the blind man.

The Savior told the man to go and wash in the Pool of Siloam. Hezekiah originally built this reservoir southeast of Jerusalem. An underground tunnel carved out by the king's workers carried water to the pool from the Gihon Spring in the Kidron Valley. During times of siege, having clear access to water was imperative (2 Kings 20:20; 2 Chron. 32:30).

The man obeyed Jesus by washing in the pool. Though he left blind, the man came back able to see (John 9:7). A genuine miracle had indeed taken place!

D. The Neighbors: vss. 8-9

His neighbors and those who had formerly seen him begging asked, "Isn't this the same man who used to sit and beg?" Some claimed that he was. Others said, "No, he only looks like him." But he himself insisted, "I am the man."

The man's neighbors and others who had known him were flabbergasted to find him able to see (John 9:8). Some thought the man was the former blind beggar, while others thought he wasn't. In the midst of debate, the man kept insisting that he was the same person (vs. 9). (In Jesus' day, begging was the only means of support for those with a severe physical deformity like congenital blindness.)

E. The Testimony: vss. 10-12

"How then were your eyes opened?" they demanded. He replied, "The man they call Jesus made some mud and put it on my eyes. He told me to go to Siloam and wash. So I went and washed, and then I could see." "Where is this man?" they asked him. "I don't know," he said.

When questioned about his experience, the former blind beggar told those listening what Jesus had done for him (John 9:10-11). When asked where Jesus might be, the man said he didn't know (vs. 12). The religious leaders then questioned the man and eventually threw him out of the synagogue (vss. 13-34). Despite this, the man gained not only physical sight but also spiritual sight, for he recognized that Jesus is the Messiah (vss. 35-38).

Discussion Questions

1. Why were the religious leaders so intent on accusing Jesus of wrongdoing?
2. What did Jesus prove by healing the man with the shriveled hand on the Sabbath?
3. How did the religious leaders respond, and why in this way?
4. What was the nature of the theological question the disciples asked Jesus?
5. What truth about Himself did Jesus confirm in healing the man born blind?

Contemporary Application

When we read the accounts about the healing miracles of Jesus, we are stunned at the reactions of the religious leaders. One would think they would have rejoiced in His healings and gladly welcomed the truth He proclaimed. The tragic lesson here is that even religion can stand in the way of receiving Jesus by faith.

Of course, those who claim they are whole and able to see spiritually without Jesus are really blinded and infirmed by their sin. That's because they trust in their own reason and goodness rather than the Savior. They believe that following strict religious traditions will bring them eternal life. And they do not want to confess the truth about themselves, so they refuse to admit their need for spiritual health and sight by believing in Jesus.

At the same time, Christians should be careful lest they become calloused toward people who refuse to believe in Jesus. As the Savior did with the blind man, so too we should reach out to the lost with healing love, regardless of the reasons for their condition. We cannot rule out anyone as a candidate for God's kingdom. Often the spiritually blind find sight, not because of our persuasive and eloquent arguments, but rather because of God's and our tenderness, patience, and kindness.

A Mother's Faith

DEVOTIONAL READING

Luke 4:16-21

DAILY BIBLE READINGS

Monday September 24
John 9:13-17 Healed by a Sinner or a Prophet?

Tuesday September 25
John 9:18-25 I Once Was Blind, but Now I See

Wednesday September 26
John 9:26-41 Who Sees, and Who Is Blind?

Thursday September 27
John 11:1-16 Lazarus Dies

Friday September 28
John 11:17-27 Jesus Is the Resurrection

Saturday September 29
John 11:28-37 Mary Wishes Jesus Had Been There

Sunday September 30
John 11:38-44 The Dead Man Comes Out

Scripture

Background Scripture: *Matthew 15:21-31*
Scripture Lesson: *Matthew 15:21-31*
Key Verse: *Then Jesus answered, "Woman, you have great faith! Your request is granted." And her daughter was healed from that very hour.* Matthew 15:28.

Lesson Aim

To affirm the value of persistent, courageous faith.

Lesson Setting

Time: A.D. *29*
Place: *Tyre, Sidon, and Galilee*

Lesson Outline

A Mother's Faith

   I. The Woman of Great Faith: Matthew 15:21-28
      A. *The Woman's Plea: vss. 21-22*
      B. *The Woman's Persistence: vss. 23-27*
      C. *The Woman's Request Granted: vs. 28*
  II. The Healing of Many Others: Matthew 15:29-31
      A. *The Presence of Large Crowds: vss. 29-30*
      B. *The Amazement of the Crowds: vs. 31*

Introduction for Adults

Topic: *Persisting in Faith*

Faith is hard work, not a loopy feeling in the stomach. We don't feel faith; rather, we do faith. Faith demands courage and sacrifice. It transcends the boundaries of church buildings, services, and creeds, and it drives us to our knees to cry out to God for deliverance.

Faith is only as strong as its object. Public opinion polls show that people value faith, but faith in what? The economy? Their jobs? Their money? The power of the national government?

The account of the Canaanite woman shows us that the road to faith is paved with humility and confession. Her experience shows that the Lord Jesus Christ is the only valid object of faith. The woman knew Jesus was the answer, and she allowed nothing to stand in her way. That truly is saving faith!

Introduction for Youths

Topic: *Mothers Are Like That*

Mothers agonize when their children get sick. They also worry about their children getting into trouble. And Christian mothers pray that their children will trust in Jesus for salvation.

A teenage daughter was surprised to find her mother waiting for her when she came home late one night. Suddenly it dawned on the girl that her mother truly cared about her. The daughter asked, "Mom, you really do worry about me, don't you?"

Mothers love and care for their children. That's why they lie awake at night waiting for the car to pull into the garage. Christian mothers pray for the needs of their children. Such moms understand that there is more to provide for their children than food, shelter, and clothing. In addition, these mothers also seek to provide emotional and spiritual nourishment. How satisfying it must be when their children realize their mother's love for them.

Concepts for Children

Topic: *Jesus Grants a Mother's Request*

1. While Jesus and His followers were walking, a non-Jewish woman asked Jesus to heal her daughter.
2. At first Jesus did not do anything, but the woman kept following along and shouting.
3. The woman did not give up, and eventually Jesus honored her faith by healing her daughter.
4. Later on large numbers of people who were ill came to Jesus, and He healed them.
5. Jesus can do amazing things for us that no one else can do.
6. We can trust Jesus to watch over us and guide us in every situation.

The Lesson Commentary

I. THE WOMAN OF GREAT FAITH: MATTHEW 15:21-28

A. The Woman's Plea: vss. 21-22

Leaving that place, Jesus withdrew to the region of Tyre and Sidon. A Canaanite woman from that vicinity came to him, crying out, "Lord, Son of David, have mercy on me! My daughter is suffering terribly from demon-possession."

During Jesus' Galilean ministry, a delegation of Pharisees and teachers of the law traveled north from Jerusalem to interrogate Him. They asked why His followers did not wash their hands before eating. The leaders believed that refusing to do so made the disciples ceremonially unclean (Matt. 15:1-2). In Christ's response He stated that the religious leaders had elevated man-made rules above God's commands (vss. 3-9). Jesus then declared to a crowd that it is what springs from the hearts of people that defiles them, not what they eat (vss. 10-20).

After these events, Jesus desired to get away from the crowds so that He could focus on training His disciples. Thus He left Galilee and traveled 30 or 40 miles northwestward to the area of Tyre and Sidon, where He found a place to stay (vs. 21). Tyre and Sidon were Phoenician cities located on the coastal plain between the mountains of Lebanon and the Mediterranean Sea. Both cities were known for their maritime exploits and as centers of trade.

Though the time away was supposed to be a retreat, it didn't turn out that way. Jesus' reputation had preceded Him, and even in this Gentile region people came to hear His teachings and benefit from His miracles.

The woman whose daughter was demon possessed must have seen something in Jesus to make her believe He would help her (vs. 22). That faith was strengthened by compassion for her child. Because of the mother's faith in Jesus, she did what the residents of Jesus' hometown would not do: she presented her plea to Him for His help.

Matthew's Gospel says the woman was a "Canaanite," which was the Jewish way of referring to non-Jews living in Phoenicia in Jesus' day (Mark 7:26). The woman referred to Jesus as "Lord, Son of David" (Matt. 15:22), which suggests that she had some awareness of His messianic identity.

The woman explained that her daughter had a demon in her, and that it was severely tormenting her. Mark 7:26 says the woman kept begging Jesus to cast the demon out of her daughter. This underscores how desperate and helpless the woman felt.

B. The Woman's Persistence: vss. 23-27

Jesus did not answer a word. So his disciples came to him and urged him, "Send her away, for she keeps crying out after us." He answered, "I was sent only to the lost sheep of Israel." The woman came and knelt before him. "Lord, help me!" she said. He replied, "It is not right to take the children's bread and toss it to their dogs." "Yes, Lord," she said, "but even the dogs eat the crumbs that fall from their masters' table."

Despite the woman's persistent pleas for help, Jesus did not give her a reply (Matt. 15:23). Though Jesus meant all along to help the woman, He decided before doing so to test her faith. The disciples, however, were bothered by the woman's begging and urged Jesus to send her away. Sadly, they showed no compassion for her or sensitivity to her needs.

Jesus noted that the Father had sent Him to help the people of Israel—His lost sheep—not the Gentiles (vs. 24). Jesus did not say this to imply that Jews were the only ones to be saved; rather, they were to become the first agents through whom Jesus would extend His Gospel throughout the world (Rom. 1:16).

The woman was undeterred. She approached Jesus, knelt before Him in worship, and cried out, "Lord, help me" (Matt. 15:25). Jesus' statement in verse 26 describes a common domestic situation in which a family is eating dinner while small household dogs are begging for food. Jesus said the order in which the appetites should be satisfied is children first, dogs second.

This statement has a double meaning. On one level it refers to the focus of Jesus' mission. In this case, "children" are Jews, the "dogs" are Gentiles, and the "bread" is the Gospel. It's hardly likely, of course, that the woman understood this meaning of Jesus' words. More likely she understood them on a practical level.

The woman had interrupted Jesus' retreat with His disciples. For Jesus to help her, then, would have required Him to take His time and energy away from the disciples and give them to the woman. On this level of meaning, the "children" are the disciples, the "dogs" represent the woman, and the "bread" is Jesus' ministry.

The woman still was not put off by Jesus' reply to her request. She extended the Savior's analogy for her own purposes. The meal did not have to be interrupted and the children's bread be given to the dogs. All the dogs needed were a few crumbs dropped during the meal (vs. 27). In other words, the woman was saying that Jesus could quickly and easily fulfill her request, and then get back to teaching His disciples.

C. The Woman's Request Granted: vs. 28

Then Jesus answered, "Woman, you have great faith! Your request is granted." And her daughter was healed from that very hour.

The woman's answer pleased Jesus. He may even have laughed at the way she turned His statement to her own benefit. Then He rescued her daughter from the evil spirit (Matt. 15:28). Ironically, many Jews would lose God's blessing and salvation because they rejected Jesus, and many Gentiles would find salvation because they recognized and accepted Him.

The basic principle here is that people persist in faith because they know who Jesus is and that He will honor their commitment to Him. Christ's love and power are always available, but our desires are not always granted immediately. To test us, Jesus sometimes does not answer. His silence may seem unbearable. But then we should recall the Canaanite mother and keep coming back to Jesus in faith.

Like the woman from the vicinity of Tyre and Sidon, we should demonstrate boldness in seeking God's help. Often we are too easily discouraged from our spiritual pursuits. We need the humility to know we deserve nothing, but the determination to draw upon the riches of God's grace.

Commenting on the mother's faith, Martin Luther wrote: "This was a most beautiful and shining faith, and is a notable example, showing the method . . . of wrestling with God. For we ought not at the first blow immediately to cast away courage and all hope, but we must be urgent, we must be prayerful, we must seek and knock."

In this account, the mother was not perfect. Thankfully, Jesus does not demand perfection before we can place our faith in Him. The woman came to Jesus just as she was. She accepted her identity, and did not recoil at Jesus' words. We, too, should be willing to come to Jesus just as we are without any pretense.

II. THE HEALING OF MANY OTHERS: MATTHEW 15:29-31

A. The Presence of Large Crowds: vss. 29-30

Jesus left there and went along the Sea of Galilee. Then he went up on a mountainside and sat down. Great crowds came to him, bringing the lame, the blind, the crippled, the mute and many others, and laid them at his feet; and he healed them.

After leaving Tyre, Jesus traveled about 25 miles north to Sidon. He then headed southeast through the territory of Herod Philip. Jesus cut a wide path around the eastern shore of the Sea of Galilee and eventually ended up in the region of Decapolis (Mark 7:31).

Jesus may have taken this roundabout route in order to avoid the territory ruled by Herod Antipas. Herod thought Jesus was John the Baptist risen from the dead and thus intimated a hostile interest in Him (Matt. 14:1-2). This is also the place where many people wanted to take Jesus by force and make Him their king (John 6:14-15).

The events that followed in Matthew 15:29-30 occurred in the Decapolis. This was a confederation of 10 cities south of Galilee and mostly east of the Jordan River. The league of cities was formed to preserve Greek culture in the Semitic region shortly after (the Roman) Pompey's invasion of Palestine around 64 B.C. These cities were primarily Gentile strongholds.

After the journey, Jesus climbed a hill and sat down, most likely to rest and teach His disciples. These were critical days for them. As they traveled together, Jesus taught them who He was and what His plans were. They needed to absorb as much as they could, for serious trouble loomed ahead.

However, Jesus' presence could not remain a secret for long. A vast crowd brought Him a wide assortment of people with severe physical difficulties (such as lameness, blindness, crippledness, and muteness). When the infirmed were laid before Jesus, He healed all of them. What a powerful testimony to His compassion and mercy!

Why did Jesus want to withdraw when His mission was to proclaim the truth? He was well aware of the dangers of false enthusiasm. And He knew the crowds were looking for a miracle worker to deliver them from the Romans. Jesus also realized that His teaching and miracles had aroused intense hatred and opposition.

It's also important to understand that Jesus and His disciples occasionally needed rest. Jesus got tired, hungry, and thirsty just as we do. Rest times were not wasted moments, but rather opportunities for physical and spiritual rejuvenation.

Jesus, then, was well aware of the wounds and hurts of this huge crowd of suffering humanity. Although pressed to the utmost, Jesus never stopped loving and giving. Every healing was a message from God that His Son had come to save the lost. He truly is our merciful and great High Priest who can sympathize with our weaknesses, having endured great hardship and agony Himself (Heb. 2:14-16).

B. The Amazement of the Crowds: vs. 31

The people were amazed when they saw the mute speaking, the crippled made well, the lame walking and the blind seeing. And they praised the God of Israel.

The crowd erupted with amazement, for they had never seen anything like this before. Right before their eyes those who hadn't been able to talk were talking, the crippled were healed, the lame were walking around, and those who had been blind could see again. It's no wonder the crowds "praised the God of Israel" (Matt. 15:31).

Jesus performed miracles such as these to show that He had the power to forgive sins and give eternal salvation (9:1-8). They were signposts from heaven, declaring that God had intervened in human history for humanity's good.

The Canaanite mother's faith and the faith of the people brought to Jesus must have been significant sources of encouragement for the disciples. Jesus used these experiences to build their faith for the time when He would be gone and they would be His ambassadors to the world.

Discussion Questions

1. What malady plagued the daughter of the Canaanite woman?
2. How did Jesus initially respond to the woman's initial request? How did the disciples respond?
3. What was the woman's response when Jesus insisted on ministering the truth first to the Jews?
4. How did Jesus honor the woman's great faith?
5. How did Jesus respond to the large crowds of needy people?
6. What should be our response to those around us in great need?

Contemporary Application

The professor had carefully planned his daily schedule, and it looked as if every minute was accounted for. But then his friend asked him, "What about interruptions?" The professor muttered, "They are scheduled from 11:15 to 11:30!" It would be nice if we could schedule our interruptions, but life is not like that. Life is more like an earthquake that strikes unexpectedly at 3 A.M.

People interrupted Jesus at every turn. When He wanted to be alone with His disciples, a persistent mother found Him. And vast crowds brought the sick of every kind to Him for healing. Jesus never turned them aside, for He did not see them as interruptions, but rather as sheep without a shepherd (Matt. 9:36).

On some occasions we are more like the disciples, who disliked interruptions. They wanted Jesus to disperse all would-be inquirers. The disciples were more concerned about their own needs than helping others in desperate circumstances.

Admittedly, we need to schedule time for rest, recuperation, and spiritual refreshment. Nevertheless, we also need love, patience, and self-control when hurting people break into our lives. Because we know that God orders our lives, we can lay aside our plans, if necessary, to help those in need.

Too often, it seems, the church blindly follows its own agenda. There's no room in our programs for interruptions. Yet Jesus comes to us in the person of the one who has great needs. And He told us that when we do things for people in need, we are actually doing them for Him (25:34-40).

Raising of Lazarus

DEVOTIONAL READING

John 11:17-27

DAILY BIBLE READINGS

Monday October 1
  Matthew 13:24-30 The Parable of the Weeds among the Wheat

Tuesday October 2
  Matthew 13:36-43 The Parable of the Weeds Explained

Wednesday October 3
  Matthew 13:31-35, 44-46 What the Kingdom of Heaven Is Like

Thursday October 4
  Matthew 13:47-52 More Kingdom Parables

Friday October 5
  Mark 4:21-29 The Parable of the Growing Seed

Saturday October 6
  Matthew 13:1-13, 18-23 The Parable of the Sower

Sunday October 7
  Luke 15:1-10 He Told Them a Parable

Scripture

Background Scripture: *John 11:1-44*
Scripture Lesson: *John 11:1-6, 11-15, 38-44*
Key Verse: *Jesus said to her, "I am the resurrection and the life. He who believes in me will live, even though he dies; and whoever lives and believes in me will never die."*
John 11:25-26.

Lesson Aim

To affirm that Jesus has power over life and death.

Lesson Setting

Time: A.D. *30*
Place: *Bethany*

Lesson Outline

Raising of Lazarus
  I.   The Sickness of Lazarus: John 11:1-6
      A. *The Appeal to Jesus: vss. 1-3*
      B. *The Response of Jesus: vss. 4-6*
  II. The Explanation of Jesus: John 11:11-15
      A. *The Disciples' Confusion: vss. 11-13*
      B. *The Savior's Plain Statement: vss. 14-15*
  III. The Raising of Lazarus: John 11:38-44
      A. *The Objection: vss. 38-40*
      B. *The Prayer: vss. 41-42*
      C. *The Command: vss. 43-44*

Introduction for Adults

Topic: *Believing and Living*

Why does time seem to drag on when we're waiting for something important like a surgeon's report? Waiting often tests our faith in and commitment to God.

Consider Mary and Martha. Their patience was tested through days of waiting for Jesus. When He finally came, it looked as if it was too late, for their brother Lazarus had already died and was buried. Then the bereaved sisters told Jesus that had He come earlier, He could have prevented the tragedy from happening.

Like Mary and Martha, how many times we have said "If only" to God? "If only" is the antithesis of trust and obedience. If we live with regrets or harbor resentment against God, we cannot enjoy spiritual wellness.

Scripture tells us that God acts on our behalf according to His will, love, and wisdom (Rom. 8:28). Thus, it never pays to second-guess God's timing. This means Jesus never arrives too late to help us. We can rest assured that He will do what is best for us in His perfect will.

Introduction for Youths

Topic: *Alive Again!*

The restoring of Lazarus to life was the most powerful miracle of Jesus recorded in the Gospel of John. This close friend of the Savior had truly died. And Jesus, out of His great love for Lazarus, brought him back from the grave.

Perhaps the greatest miracle, however, is being born again. After all, before coming to faith in Christ, we were spiritually dead and condemned because of our sins. We obeyed Satan rather than God, and followed the passions of our evil nature rather than the desires of the Spirit (Eph. 2:1-3).

But because the Father is rich in mercy and loves us greatly, He gave us new life through faith in His Son. We have been identified with Jesus' death, burial, and resurrection. In fact, God sees us as being seated with Jesus in the heavenly realms (vss. 4-6). Now that is what it means to be alive again!

Concepts for Children

Topic: *Jesus Helped a Friend*

1. Lazarus, a close friend of Jesus, had died, and his friends were sad.
2. The sisters of Lazarus—Mary and Martha—wondered why it took so long for Jesus to come to them.
3. When Jesus finally came, He restored Lazarus to life.
4. From this miracle we see that Jesus has power over death; thus we do not need to be afraid of it.
5. When we trust in Jesus, He forgives our sins and gives us new life.
6. When our friends are ill or sad about the loss of someone they love, we can let them know about Jesus' love and power.

The Lesson Commentary

I. THE SICKNESS OF LAZARUS: JOHN 11:1-6

A. The Appeal to Jesus: vss. 1-3

Now a man named Lazarus was sick. He was from Bethany, the village of Mary and her sister Martha. This Mary, whose brother Lazarus now lay sick, was the same one who poured perfume on the Lord and wiped his feet with her hair. So the sisters sent word to Jesus, "Lord, the one you love is sick."

John 10:39-40 indicates that because of increasing hostility, Jesus went from the region of Judea into the less heavily populated area eastward across the Jordan River. Most likely this region was either Perea or Batanea, the general area in the tetrarchy of Philip.

Jesus' public ministry among the crowds was coming to an end, and He began to move into seclusion. From this time until His crucifixion, Jesus focused most of His attention on His disciples and others who were genuinely committed to Him.

As chapter 11 begins, the short time Jesus had spent in the east and northeast of the Sea of Galilee had already come to end. And as the prospect of suffering and death grew closer, Jesus returned to the area of Jerusalem. Though the religious establishment hated Jesus (10:39), His closest followers loved Him. Even rejection and scorn could not dim the glory of Christ as displayed through the restoring of Lazarus to life.

The Gospel of John had already presented six other miracles: turning water into wine (2:1-11), healing a royal official's son (4:46-54), restoring an invalid (5:1-15), multiplying the loaves and fishes (6:1-14), walking on the water (6:15-21), and curing a man born blind (9:1-12). The raising of Lazarus is the climactic and most dramatic sign in John's Gospel. Although Lazarus had been dead four days, with the process of decomposition having already started (11:39), Jesus brought him back to life.

According to verse 1, Lazarus lived in Bethany with his sisters, Mary and Martha. The village was located on the east side of the Mount of Olives along the road leading toward Jericho, about two miles from Jerusalem. Bethany was close enough to Jerusalem for Jesus and His disciples to be in danger, but sufficiently far away to avoid attracting unwelcome attention.

In 11:1 we find the first mention in John's Gospel of the family of Lazarus, Mary, and Martha. The sisters are also mentioned in Luke 10:38-42, and Mary's anointing of Jesus is recorded in John 12:1-8. In fact, in anticipation of the latter event, 11:2 says that Mary was the woman who poured the expensive perfume on Jesus' feet and wiped them with her hair.

Somehow Lazarus became ill, and his condition worsened to the point that Mary and Martha turned to Jesus for help (vs. 3). The sisters undoubtedly had seen Him perform many miracles. They thus were convinced of Jesus' ability to help Lazarus.

The message to Jesus most likely took about a day to reach Him. He, in turn, remained in Bethany two more days (vs. 6). And it probably took about a day for

Him and His disciples to reach Bethany. It may be that Lazarus died before the messenger reached Jesus. If so, this explains how Lazarus could have been in the grave for four days (vs. 17).

B. The Response of Jesus: vss. 4-6

When he heard this, Jesus said, "This sickness will not end in death. No, it is for God's glory so that God's Son may be glorified through it." Jesus loved Martha and her sister and Lazarus. Yet when he heard that Lazarus was sick, he stayed where he was two more days.

The disciples were party to the grim news from Bethany. They knew how much Mary, Martha, and Lazarus meant to Jesus. Perhaps sensing the disciples' concern, Jesus gave them an explanation that both reassured and puzzled them.

First, Jesus sought to allay His disciples' fears by noting that the illness would not "end in death" (John 11:4). Second, the Savior explained that both He and the Father would be glorified in this situation. When we look for reasons for illness, we can take comfort that above everything else the glory of God is the ultimate issue. We may not be able to understand how this works out in times of illness, but we can pray that regardless of the outcome, God will be glorified.

Third, Jesus did not rush off to Bethany in a panic. Instead, He stayed where He was for two more days (vs. 6). One reason for this delay is that Jesus operated according to the Father's timetable, not that of people. A second reason is that the delay would ensure Lazarus had been dead long enough to prevent others from either misinterpreting the miracle as a fraud or mere resuscitation.

II. THE EXPLANATION OF JESUS: JOHN 11:11-15

A. The Disciples' Confusion: vss. 11-13

After he had said this, he went on to tell them, "Our friend Lazarus has fallen asleep; but I am going there to wake him up." His disciples replied, "Lord, if he sleeps, he will get better." Jesus had been speaking of his death, but his disciples thought he meant natural sleep.

After two days had passed, Jesus decided that it was time to return to Judea (John 11:7). The disciples, however, objected, noting that their leaders were seeking to kill Him (vs. 8). Jesus assured His followers that He was doing God's will and thus would remain safe from all harm (vss. 9-10).

Jesus then explained that their friend Lazarus had "fallen asleep" (vs. 11). Christ was speaking euphemistically about death. He also stated that He was going to Bethany so that He could wake up Lazarus. The disciples took Jesus to mean that Lazarus was literally sleeping, and thus they were confused (vs. 13). In their minds, if Lazarus were sleeping, that meant he would also get better on his own (vs. 12).

B. The Savior's Plain Statement: vss. 14-15

So then he told them plainly, "Lazarus is dead, and for your sake I am glad I was not there, so that you may believe. But let us go to him."

Realizing His disciples' confusion, Jesus stated plainly that Lazarus had died (John 11:14). The Savior then explained that this incident would give His followers another opportunity to believe in Him (vs. 15).

If Jesus had been with Lazarus during the final moments of his life and healed him of his sickness, the opportunity for an even greater miracle would have been lost. Jesus intended to use the death of Lazarus as an occasion to demonstrate to the disciples and others His power over death.

This was not a trivial desire of Jesus. He knew that His closest followers needed their faith in Him clarified, matured, and strengthened. Consider, for example, the dialogue between Martha and Jesus, which is recorded in verses 17-27. Despite Jesus' statement that Lazarus would rise again, Martha failed to grasp what He was saying. Instead, she affirmed a more general theological truth about the resurrection of the righteous.

Even when Jesus declared Himself to be "the resurrection and the life" (vs. 25), Martha still could not quite understand what this meant for Lazarus. Though she affirmed Jesus' messiahship (vss. 26-27), she remained unaware of the fact that Jesus would restore Lazarus to life. Furthermore, Martha's sister Mary and their friends remained just as oblivious to the truth of what Jesus said He would do for Lazarus (vss. 28-37).

III. THE RAISING OF LAZARUS: JOHN 11:38-44

A. The Objection: vss. 38-40

Jesus, once more deeply moved, came to the tomb. It was a cave with a stone laid across the entrance. "Take away the stone," he said. "But, Lord," said Martha, the sister of the dead man, "by this time there is a bad odor, for he has been there four days." Then Jesus said, "Did I not tell you that if you believed, you would see the glory of God?"

John 11:33 says that at the sight of the wailing, Jesus was "deeply moved in spirit and troubled." On one level, the phrase suggests Jesus was touched with sympathy at the sight and perhaps indignant at the sorrow in death that sin has brought to the human condition.

On another level, though, the Savior seemed agitated by the unbelief of His closest followers. He had plainly stated that He would restore Lazarus to life. Yet Martha and Mary, instead of rejoicing over what Jesus was about to do, remained filled with despair over their brother's death. This attitude of unbelief and doubt is reflected in the statement made by some of the onlookers (recorded in vs. 37).

We can only imagine the emotions Jesus felt as He approached the tomb of Lazarus, a cave with a stone rolled across its entrance (vs. 38). In Jesus' day, people used caves carved in the limestone rock of a hillside as tombs. These graves were large enough for people to walk inside, and a tomb could hold several corpses.

Martha didn't understand why Jesus would want the stone removed from the tomb's entrance. She noted that after four days the smell from the decomposing corpse of Lazarus would be terrible (vs. 39). Jesus, ever patient in the midst of such confusion, stated once again that if Martha had faith, she would witness the glory of God (for example, in Jesus' restoring Lazarus to life; vs. 40).

Unlike the Egyptians, the Jews neither tightly wrapped the body of the deceased nor embalmed it. Instead, they loosely wrapped the body in linen cloth and added spice in the layers and folds. The aromatic spices helped to counteract (but not completely eliminate) the objectionable ordors resulting from the decomposition of the corpse.

B. The Prayer: vss. 41-42

So they took away the stone. Then Jesus looked up and said, "Father, I thank you that you have heard me. I knew that you always hear me, but I said this for the benefit of the people standing here, that they may believe that you sent me."

We can only imagine the bewilderment and skepticism among the onlookers. Though Jesus' command to remove the stone from the tomb of Lazarus seemed to go against common sense, it was done anyway (John 11:41).

Jesus' prayer, which is recorded in verses 41 and 42, is not so much a petition as it is an expression of thanksgiving to the Father. Jesus knew in advance that the Father would grant His request, and thus the Savior gave thanks for this. Jesus declared in the hearing of the onlookers that the Father always answered His requests. Jesus stated this openly, not for His own benefit, but rather for the sake of the onlookers. It was His desire that in seeing the miracle, they would believe His claim to be the Messiah.

In restoring Lazarus to life, Jesus would prove that He is the master of death. Ironically, though, this miracle would set in motion a series of events that would lead directly to His arrest and eventual execution. Yet even in Jesus' crucifixion, both He and the Father would be glorified (17:1, 5).

C. The Command: vss. 43-44

When he had said this, Jesus called in a loud voice, "Lazarus, come out!" The dead man came out, his hands and feet wrapped with strips of linen, and a cloth around his face. Jesus said to them, "Take off the grave clothes and let him go."

When Jesus had finished praying, He commanded Lazarus to come out of the tomb (John 11:43). In one sense this served as a preview of the power of Jesus that would be fully displayed in the final resurrection when all who have died will hear the voice of the Son and live (5:25, 28-29).

Lazarus, who had been unquestionably dead, came out of the tomb. His hands and feet were still wrapped with strips of burial cloth, and a separate cloth covered his face. Jesus then told the people to unwrap the graveclothes and headcloth from Lazarus and let him go (11:44).

Many of the onlookers, when they saw the miracle, put their faith in Jesus (vs. 45). In fact, Lazarus became something of a curiosity, for he drew numerous onlookers who wanted to see for themselves the person whom Jesus had brought back to life (12:9). It was this kind of notoriety that the religious leaders especially feared, for it was bound to have political repercussions. Thus, it was after the restoration of Lazarus to life that the religious elite finally determined to put Jesus to death (11:46-53).

Discussion Questions

1. What expectation did Mary and her sister Martha have when they sent word to Jesus about Lazarus being sick?
2. Why did Jesus delay for two days before making the trip to Bethany?
3. When Jesus said He would awaken Lazarus from his sleep, what did the disciples think the Savior meant (John 11:11-13)? What did He really mean?
4. In what ways was Jesus deeply moved by the unfolding events (vs. 38)?
5. Why did Jesus offer a prayer of thanksgiving to the Father (vss. 41-42)?
6. What implications does the restoring of Lazarus to life have for us as believers?

Contemporary Application

The raising of Lazarus called forth faith from Mary and Martha, and from many of the Jews who witnessed the miracle. Tragically, however, it angered the religious leaders and convinced them that Jesus had to be executed.

When people consider Jesus today, some are so impressed that they give themselves fully to Him in faith. Others, however, do not take Him and His miracles seriously. They do not believe that He is the one and only source of eternal life.

One of the great values of trusting in Jesus is finding Him to be a real person who invites us to cast all our cares upon Him. We know that He identifies with our sorrows. When we suffer the loss of a loved one, we know that Jesus understands how we feel.

Christians have a sure hope in the face of sickness and death, and people need to hear about our faith and hope. One of the best ways is to invite them to study the life of Jesus. He prayed that people would believe in Him because He restored Lazarus to life. When we invite people to consider the miracles that Jesus performed, we give them an opportunity to believe and be saved.

Purpose of Parables

DEVOTIONAL READING
Matthew 13:18-23

DAILY BIBLE READINGS

Monday October 8
Deuteronomy 15:7-11 Your Neighbor in Need

Tuesday October 9
Luke 18:18-25 Sell What You Have and Give It to the Poor

Wednesday October 10
Luke 9:57-62 Follow Now, and Don't Look Back

Thursday October 11
Luke 10:17-24 Things Hidden from the Wise

Friday October 12
Deuteronomy 6:4-9 Love God

Saturday October 13
Leviticus 19:13-18 Love Your Neighbor

Sunday October 14
Luke 10:25-37 Who Is My Neighbor?

Scripture

Background Scripture: *Matthew 13:1-35*
Scripture Lesson: *Matthew 13:1-13, 34-35*
Key Verse: *This is why I speak to them in parables: "Though seeing, they do not see; though hearing, they do not hear or understand." Matthew 13:13.*
Scripture Lesson for Children: *Matthew 13:1-8*
Key Verse for Children: *"Still other seed fell on good soil, where it produced a crop—a hundred, sixty or thirty times what was sown. He who has ears, let him hear."* Matthew 13:8-9.

Lesson Aim

To commit ourselves to being more responsive to God's Word.

Lesson Setting

Time: *A.D. 28*
Place: *The Sea of Galilee*

Lesson Outline

Purpose of Parables

I.   The Parable of the Sower: Matthew 13:1-9
   A. *The Setting: vss. 1-2*
   B. *The Story: vss. 3-9*
II. The Reasons for the Parables: Matthew 13:10-13
III. The Prophetic Fulfillment: Matthew 13:34-35

Introduction for Adults

Topic: *Hearing the Word*

The structure of the ear enables sound vibrations to pass from outside the head to the part of our brain that controls hearing. Sound waves cause the eardrum to vibrate, which then turns the sound waves into nerve impulses inside the cochlea. Twenty-four thousand fibers cause a vibration in the cells that make up the organ of Corti. These fibers send messages through the auditory nerve to the center of hearing in the brain.

God designed our ears so that we can hear sounds of infinite variety. God also designed our souls to hear what He has revealed through Jesus Christ. But just as physical problems can cause deafness, so too our spiritual ears can become plugged by selfishness, willful disobedience, and outright sin. Only by obeying Jesus can we discern what's really important in our lives.

Introduction for Youths

Topic: *Get the Message?*

While walking through a supermarket one day, a man listened to a mother scream at her child, "Do you hear me?" Children soon get immune to that cry, and by the time they are teenagers they learn to tune it out. Of course they hear, but they don't obey. That's why we say, "Listen to me!" when we really mean, "Obey me!"

Jesus made it clear that in His kingdom hearing equals obedience. We are not serious about following Him if we refuse to do what He commands. Of course, God keeps giving us ample reasons to hear and heed His Word. We have no excuses for being ignorant of what He wants us to do.

In worship, prayer, and Bible study, God says, "Listen to Me." When we do, He fills our lives with contentment, no matter what our circumstances might be.

Concepts for Children

Topic: *Jesus Taught about a Sower*

1. As a crowd gathered on the beach, Jesus sat in a boat and taught them using stories called parables.
2. In one parable Jesus told, He said that some seed fell on a path and was eaten by birds.
3. Some seed fell on a thin layer of soil, sprang up, and died in the hot sun.
4. Some seed fell among thorns and was choked out.
5. And some seed fell on good soil and produced a rich harvest.
6. God wants us to accept and obey His Word, and in this way bear a lot of spiritual fruit.

The Lesson Commentary

I. THE PARABLE OF THE SOWER: MATTHEW 13:1-9

A. The Setting: vss. 1-2

That same day Jesus went out of the house and sat by the lake. Such large crowds gathered around him that he got into a boat and sat in it, while all the people stood on the shore.

This week's biblical passage describes Jesus' teaching the multitudes by the seaside. Open-air gatherings in which He preached and taught the people were common for our Lord. For instance, Jesus preached to over 5,000 people in the wilderness (Matt. 14:15-21). These crowds showed the appeal that Jesus had on the masses.

Some think this open-air preaching shows a shift in Jesus' ministry. At first He taught in the Jewish synagogues. However, when the Pharisees and other religious leaders would not listen to His message, He left their houses of worship and preached to people on the village streets, beside the roads, and on the open plains. There "the large crowd listened to him with delight" (Mark 12:37), for He met the spiritual and physical needs of others whenever the opportunity presented itself.

After Jesus had taught in a nearby house, He went and sat by the lake (Matt. 13:1). He may have left to meditate or perhaps to relax from the stress of His ministry. However, no sooner had He reached the shore than a large crowd of people gathered around Him. The great number of individuals who stood on the shore made it necessary for Jesus to move into a boat so that He could teach (vs. 2).

B. The Story: vss. 3-9

Then he told them many things in parables, saying: "A farmer went out to sow his seed. As he was scattering the seed, some fell along the path, and the birds came and ate it up. Some fell on rocky places, where it did not have much soil. It sprang up quickly, because the soil was shallow. But when the sun came up, the plants were scorched, and they withered because they had no root. Other seed fell among thorns, which grew up and choked the plants. Still other seed fell on good soil, where it produced a crop—a hundred, sixty or thirty times what was sown. He who has ears, let him hear."

One way that Jesus taught His disciples was with parables (Matt. 13:3). A parable is essentially a comparison. It uses a brief story or illustration to help people understand a concept. Parables are effective because they appeal to the entire person, touching the emotions, challenging the mind, and igniting the imagination.

The parable of the sower tells the story of a man who went out to plant seeds in a field. The planting, cultivation, and harvesting of crops was a fundamental part of life in ancient Palestine. Since farmers often produced surplus food, other rural people had the freedom to pursue occupations and professions not directly related to farming (for example, quarrying and mining).

In ancient times farmers would first break up the hard soil by using wooden plows pulled by oxen or other animals. Additional workers would follow behind, carrying seed in a jar, basket, or pouch. They would grab handfuls of the seed and scatter it on the ground. Another method of sowing involved placing bags of seeds on animals. Holes in the bags permitted the seeds to drop out as the animals walked over the plowed ground.

After the seeds had been planted, the ground would be covered up to prevent such birds as ravens and crows from consuming them. One method was to have animals trample the seeds beneath the soil. Another method was to turn the seeds under the soil using wooden hoes.

Although the farmer in Jesus' story lavishly planted his crop, the different kinds of ground where the seeds fell determined how the plants would grow. Since the emphasis is not on the sower but on the different soils where the seeds fell, some have titled this story as the parable of the soils. Their point is that, although Jesus did not minimize the importance of Christian workers (sowers) in preaching and teaching God's Word, spiritual growth occurs when a person receives the Gospel and remains committed to it.

The parable lists four outcomes—three in which people don't remain committed and one in which a person does. First, some seeds fell by the wayside. Jewish farmers planted their crops in long, narrow rows. The ground between these rows was often used as walkways by persons going through the field. These paths became beaten and hardened over time. Seeds that fell on this ground were quickly eaten by birds (vs. 4).

Second, some seeds fell on stony ground. This was probably a mixture of soil and rocks with a hard layer of stone a few inches beneath the topsoil. When seeds fell on this surface, they began to grow. Yet when the roots of these plants penetrated the earth for nourishment, they ran into the hard rock. Unable to receive nutrients, the plants starved and withered in the scorching heat of the sun (vss. 5-6).

Third, some seeds fell among thorns. Much like those that fell on stony ground, they took root and began to grow. When weeds with thorns grew alongside the young sprouts, however, they were crowded out. This plot of thorns with their spreading roots made it impossible for the new plants to grow (vs. 7).

Fourth, some seeds fell on good soil, which was fertile and free from rocks and thorns. This was the ideal setting for crops to grow. Seeds planted here germinated and yielded phenomenal harvests of up to 100 times what had been sown. Thus we see the amazing ability of the seed to reproduce itself and bear fruit (vs. 8).

Jesus wanted the disciples and multitudes to hear and understand the parable (vs. 9). That's why in verses 18-23 He explained the meaning of the story. Like the seeds that the sower distributed in the field, the Gospel of Jesus Christ is freely distributed in the world. How we receive God's Word into our hearts can be compared to how the seeds took root in the different soils.

First, the wayside where some seeds fell is like a person who hears the Word but does not understand it. Paul called this person "the man without the Spirit" (1 Cor. 2:14) because he or she cannot discern spiritual things. To this person these things are foolishness. Thus this person is closed to the truth of Christ. Indeed, Satan has hardened his or her heart to the Gospel of salvation (Matt. 13:19).

Second, there are those who joyfully receive God's Word when they hear it, but quickly succumb to life's trials and tribulations (vss. 20-21). As long as they have little or no trouble in life, their commitment flourishes. These people are like the fair-weather crowd who serve God at their convenience when no sacrifice is required of them. Unlike the people Jesus described in this second example, we are to deny ourselves by making Him the highest priority in our lives (16:25).

Third, the soil where the seeds fell among thorns is like those individuals who hear the Word and receive it but are hindered in their spiritual growth by the cares of life and the deceitfulness of riches. For them, serving themselves takes precedence over serving God. They are so preoccupied with achieving status and obtaining personal gain in life that the Word is choked and unfruitful (13:22). We need to beware of the danger of grasping for worldly things and, in the process, losing our soul (Mark 8:36). Nothing is more important than our relationship with Jesus Christ.

Our last category is those who hear, believe, and act on God's Word. Their openness and willingness to obey the commandments of Christ bring blessings into their lives and make them a blessing to others. To different degrees, their good deeds bear much fruit for the Kingdom (Matt. 13:23). In addition, the fruit we bear will be a blessing for us as well.

When we hear and receive God's Word, faith comes alive in our hearts. The Spirit convicts us of our sins and then comes to dwell in us so that we can live godly lives. As a result, we are increasingly transformed into the image of Christ. Spiritual growth continues as we regularly pray, read the Bible, and fellowship with other believers.

Thus, God calls us to be not only hearers but also doers of His Word (Jas. 1:22). Jesus told His disciples that they were to be like salt that seasons and light that gives the brightness of God's love to the world (Matt. 5:13-16). Thus God uses us to work His divine purpose here on earth.

II. THE REASONS FOR THE PARABLES: MATTHEW 13:10-13

The disciples came to him and asked, "Why do you speak to the people in parables?" He replied, "The knowledge of the secrets of the kingdom of heaven has been given to you, but not to them. Whoever has will be given more, and he will have an abundance. Whoever does not have, even what he has will be taken from him. This is why I speak to them in parables: 'Though seeing, they do not see; though hearing, they do not hear or understand.'"

After Jesus finished telling the parable of the sower, His disciples asked why He favored telling stories to people (Matt. 13:10). In verses 11-13 we discover that those who want to do God's will must understand the principles of His kingdom. It was necessary, then, that Jesus speak with the greatest clarity. That is why He made extensive use of parables, such as the one about a farmer sowing seed.

Jesus used parables because He wanted to make the truth understandable to those who were ready to learn. But He had another reason for using this method of instruction. His followers were given an understanding of the mysteries of the Kingdom, while those who were not following Him were left in the dark.

At first glance it may appear that Jesus did not want unbelievers to believe. But that cannot be, for Jesus had just told a parable in which seed (the Gospel) is scattered indiscriminately, without regard to the character of the soil (the hearts of the people). It is clear that God wants everyone to come to repentance (2 Pet. 3:9).

Jesus told the parable of the sower in a company of believers and unbelievers. His disciples were devoted to Him, but His enemies hated Him. Parables were a way of revealing information to those whose eyes had been opened by faith, while concealing some of it from those blind to the truth. Jesus wanted to conceal truth from those people because they had already heard. Only by believing would they qualify to know the meaning of the parables.

III. THE PROPHETIC FULFILLMENT: MATTHEW 13:34-35

Jesus spoke all these things to the crowd in parables; he did not say anything to them without using a parable. So was fulfilled what was spoken through the prophet: "I will open my mouth in parables, I will utter things hidden since the creation of the world."

As Jesus taught the crowds, He spoke in parables (Matt. 13:34). However, when He was alone with His disciples, He would explain the meaning and significance of what He had taught (Mark 4:34).

Matthew 13:35 says that Jesus' use of parables was a fulfillment of Psalm 78:2. In this verse "parables" refers to stories that illustrate moral attitudes or spiritual principles. "Things hidden" refers to riddles or enigmas, which require explanation. Matthew quoted this verse because it anticipated one of the key teaching styles Jesus would use during His earthly ministry.

Discussion Questions

1. What do you think drew the crowd to Jesus?
2. Why do you think Jesus used parables as a means of revealing God's truths to His disciples?
3. For what reasons might the parable of the sower have been easy to remember in the minds of Jesus' hearers?
4. How does the Gospel of Christ take root in us?
5. What does it mean to bear fruit in our Christian living?

Contemporary Application

In the parable of the sower, Jesus challenged each of us to take a spiritual inventory of our lives. If we allow our daily worries and the desire to get ahead to rule us, we will produce little that's of eternal value. Are we open to the message of the Gospel? Do we consistently study the Bible? Do we put into practice what we learn? The answers to these questions determine whether we will be victorious or defeated in overcoming evil.

When Satan comes to attack us, he does not always come as a roaring lion, but often in a subtle and cunning way. In fact, Paul cautioned the Corinthian believers, saying that Satan can disguise himself as an angel of light (2 Cor. 11:14). Satan is like the thief who comes to steal, kill, and destroy (John 10:10). Indeed, in Mark's account of Jesus' parable of the sower, Jesus warned that Satan comes and tries to take the Word away from our hearts (Mark 4:15).

Therefore, Christians need to be alert and resist Satan at every occasion. When we resist the devil, he will flee from us (Jas. 4:7). But how do we resist? Paul exhorted believers to dress ourselves in the whole armor of God so that we may be able to stand against the schemes of the devil (Eph. 6:11). Our faith and hope in Christ must be sure. And we must not allow anything to hinder our spiritual growth. Using God's Word properly will help us do that.

Jesus, then, calls us to be good soil, receiving His seed—the Gospel—joyfully and with total commitment. We are to prayerfully listen to God's Word when it comes to us not only when we first hear the truth but also every time thereafter. We should have the same attitude as the psalmist who prayed, "Your word is a lamp to my feet and a light for my path" (Ps. 119:105).

It is sometimes difficult to discern God's truth in the midst of a world that often justifies immorality and sin as socially acceptable. In fact, we find the attitude of "everybody's doing it" all around us. Therefore, as Christians we need to continually commit ourselves to being increasingly responsive to the Bible. The Lord's bountiful goodness and spiritual blessings come to us when we hear and obey His Word.

The Good Samaritan

Scripture

Background Scripture: *Luke 10:25-37*
Scripture Lesson: *Luke 10:25-37*
Key Verse: *[Jesus asked,] "Which of these three do you think
was a neighbor to the man who fell into the hands of robbers?"
The expert in the law replied, "The one who had mercy on
him." Jesus told him, "Go and do likewise." Luke 10:36-37.*
Scripture Lesson for Children: *Luke 10:25-37*
Key Verse for Children: *[The expert in the law] answered:
"'Love the Lord your God with all your heart and with all
your soul and with all your strength and with all your mind';
and, 'Love your neighbor as yourself.'" Luke 10:27.*

Lesson Aim

To show the love of Christ by having compassion on
the needy.

Lesson Setting

Time: A.D. *29*
Place: *Perea, east of the Jordan River*

Lesson Outline

The Good Samaritan

I. The Question about Eternal Life: Luke 10:25-28
   A. *The Legal Expert's Question: vs. 25*
   B. *The Answer Found in the Mosaic Law: vss. 26-28*
II. The Parable of the Good Samaritan:
   Luke 10:29-37
   A. *The Question about Neighborliness: vs. 29*
   B. *The Insensitivity of a Priest and a Levite: vss. 30-32*
   C. *The Compassion of a Samaritan: vss. 33-35*
   D. *The Point of the Parable: vss. 36-37*

Introduction for Adults

Topic: *Being a Neighbor*

Booker T. Washington, the noted African-American educator, was taking a walk with a Caucasian friend when a pedestrian roughly elbowed Washington into the gutter. His friend was furious and asked him, "How can you tolerate such an insult?" Washington replied, "I defy any man to make me hate him."

This is what true Christian faith does—it defies all the bitterness and hatred in the world. It also sweeps aside all the barriers that separate people. Because Jesus makes a difference in our social relationships, Christians can build bridges of love.

Jesus' parable of the good Samaritan forces us to look deep inside ourselves. How easy it is for us to say we love God, but then do nothing for our neighbors. Also, how hard it is for us to cast aside our own desires for the sake of helping those in great need.

Introduction for Youths

Topic: *Who's My Neighbor?*

The expert in the Mosaic law who questioned Jesus was experienced in creating diversion, and, sadly, many people today follow his tactics. They find it relatively easy to talk about spirituality. But they find it difficult to stick to the main point, namely, their need for Jesus to save them from their hypocrisy and self-righteousness.

It's a huge step for us to confess that we aren't good enough to merit eternal life. Perhaps that's why some people talk about the sins of others without ever facing the reality of their own transgressions. They have no desire to repent of their sins and be saved. They also have no interest in having compassion on the needy.

From the parable of the good Samaritan we learn three principles about loving our neighbor. First, lack of love is often easy to justify, even though it is never right. Second, our neighbor is anyone of any race, creed, or social background who is in need. Third, love means acting to meet the person's need.

Concepts for Children

Topic: *Jesus Taught about a Good Neighbor*

1. An expert in the Bible asked Jesus about inheriting eternal life.
2. The expert talked about the most important commands in the Bible.
3. The expert wanted Jesus to explain what it meant to be a neighbor.
4. Jesus told a story to show how the least respected of three people took time to help someone in need.
5. As Jesus' followers, we should reach out to people in need.
6. By doing this we show Jesus' love to others.

The Lesson Commentary

I. THE QUESTION ABOUT ETERNAL LIFE: LUKE 10:25-28

A. The Legal Expert's Question: vs. 25

On one occasion an expert in the law stood up to test Jesus. "Teacher," he asked, "what must I do to inherit eternal life?"

One day an expert in the Jewish law (a scribe) asked Jesus a question to test Him (Luke 10:25). In Jesus' day, scribes were members of a learned class who studied the Mosaic law and served as copyists, scholars, and teachers. At first all the priests in Israel were responsible for the study and communication of this legal code. But this function eventually passed to the scribes. Their official interpretation of the meaning of the law eventually became more important than the law itself.

Before A.D. 70, large numbers of priests in Jerusalem served as scribes. Because they were not paid for their services, they had to earn a livelihood in another way. Though some of the scribes were Sadducees, the bulk of them came from the ordinary priestly ranks (such as merchants, carpenters, flax combers, and tentmakers).

One striking difference between Jesus and the scribes of His day was the difference between their tendency to make many laws out of a few and His gift for making few laws out of many. They had identified a law for every Hebrew letter (613 of them) in the Ten Commandments. Generally, they emphasized laws about external behavior, such as maintaining cleanness and keeping the Sabbath.

Jesus, by contrast, summarized the entire law very briefly—love God (Matt. 22:37). Jesus knew that the Father did not give the law to burden people with endless rules, but so that they would love Him. Obedience should be an outgrowth of love for God.

The scribe who questioned Jesus asked, "What must I do to inherit eternal life?" (Luke 10:25). The legal expert's question reflected the popular Jewish approach to finding favor with God. Most Jews thought one had to earn God's favor by good works. They couldn't fathom that eternal life is God's free and immediate gift to those who come to Him in repentance and faith (Rom. 6:23; Eph. 2:8-9).

B. The Answer Found in the Mosaic Law: vss. 26-28

"What is written in the Law?" he replied. "How do you read it?" He answered: "'Love the Lord your God with all your heart and with all your soul and with all your strength and with all your mind'; and, 'Love your neighbor as yourself.'" "You have answered correctly," Jesus replied. "Do this and you will live."

No doubt the scribe wanted to discredit Jesus by outwitting Him in public debate. But Jesus turned the tables on the legalist. Instead of saying something that might sound like a contradiction of the law, Jesus asked the scribe to use the law to answer his own question (Luke 10:26). We can imagine Jesus pointing to the phylactery (a small square leather box or case) on the scribe's forearm or forehead, in which was written the compendium of the law.

The scribe quoted two Old Testament passages. The first was Deuteronomy 6:5, which emphasizes love for God (Luke 10:27). Together "heart," "soul," "strength," and "mind" are a way of saying "entire being." Every part of us should be involved in our devotion to God.

The scribe next quoted Leviticus 19:18, which says we are to love our neighbors as ourselves. The idea is that we need to work out our love for God in daily life. A supreme love for God will always find expression in unselfish love for others.

We must always use the two principles of a supreme love for God and an unselfish love for others to test the priorities by which we order our daily lives. If we fail these tests, then our life, and even our religion, will bring little fulfillment.

Jesus approved of the scribe's response and urged him to put his insight into action (Luke 10:28). Then Jesus said, "Do this and you will live." This is the promise of the law (Lev. 18:5). But since no sinner can obey perfectly (Jas. 2:10), the impossible demands of the law are meant to drive us to seek divine mercy (Gal. 3:23-24). The scribe should have responded with a confession of his own guilt. Instead, he arrogantly tried to justify himself.

The problem, then, was not with the law's commands; rather, it was with the scribe's inability to keep them. Similarly, our total failure to heed God's laws makes it impossible for us to merit eternal life. Because of our indwelling sin nature, we are powerless to live in a perfectly virtuous manner. Accepting this fact drives us to Jesus for forgiveness, eternal life, and an upright standing in God's presence. We cannot partake of Christ's saving grace until we are convinced of our inability to earn eternal life by our own efforts.

II. THE PARABLE OF THE GOOD SAMARITAN: LUKE 10:29-37

A. The Question about True Neighborliness: vs. 29

But he wanted to justify himself, so he asked Jesus, "And who is my neighbor?"

The scribe felt uncomfortable with his own answer. Perhaps he knew that his behavior didn't measure up to the standard he had quoted. Thus he raised a technicality, hoping to justify his failure. He would be glad to love his neighbor, he implied, if only Jesus would tell him who his neighbor was (Luke 10:29).

In Jesus' day, the widespread opinion among scribes and Pharisees was that one's neighbors only included the upright. Supposedly the wicked were to be hated because they were enemies of God. The religious leaders defined the wicked as sinners (such as tax collectors and prostitutes), Gentiles, and especially Samaritans. Psalm 139:21-22 was used to legitimatize this view.

It's true that a love for righteousness will lead to a hatred of evil. However, this does not make it right to be hostile and malicious toward sinners. The upright should abhor the corrupt lifestyle of the lost but never harbor a vindictive loathing of them as human beings. Instead, the godly should display a brokenhearted grieving over the sinful condition of the lost. Such is undergirded by a genuine concern for the eternal condition of the lost (Matt. 5:44-48; Luke 6:27-36).

Tragically, the scribes and Pharisees had made a virtue out of being antagonistic toward the sinful. The result was a renunciation of Leviticus 19:18, the command to love one's neighbor. The parable Jesus told shattered the legalistic notion of hating one's enemies.

B. The Insensitivity of a Priest and a Levite: vss. 30-32

In reply Jesus said: "A man was going down from Jerusalem to Jericho, when he fell into the hands of robbers. They stripped him of his clothes, beat him and went away, leaving him half dead. A priest happened to be going down the same road, and when he saw the man, he passed by on the other side. So too, a Levite, when he came to the place and saw him, passed by on the other side.

Jesus responded with a story about a man who traveled from Jerusalem to Jericho. Jesus' listeners would immediately recall that notorious stretch of road. In less than 20 miles it descended nearly 3,600 feet. It had plenty of hazardous twists and turns and steep inclines, with rocks and caves lining the way. The road's conditions gave robbers ample opportunity to prey upon travelers.

That's what happened to the traveler in Jesus' story. Some men beat him, robbed him, and left him lying by the side of the road (Luke 10:30). But the wounded man was not alone for long. Three travelers passed by in turn: a priest, a Levite, and a Samaritan.

Many priests and Levites lived in Jericho. So perhaps we should imagine the priest returning home to Jericho after serving at the temple in Jerusalem. When he came along, he saw the victim, beaten and bloody. Now he was faced with a decision: to help or not to help. Sadly, the priest chose not to help (vs. 31). Whatever reasoning he used in making his decision was inadequate to justify shirking his duty to show mercy to a hurting person (Mic. 6:8).

Next, a Levite came along. He was a member of a group that was responsible for maintaining the temple and its furniture and utensils. Like the priest, he too may have been coming from (or going to) the temple on religious business. And he, too, choose not to help the injured traveler (Luke 10:32). Likewise, the Levite was guilty of being unmerciful.

The priest and the Levite saw no connection between their temple worship and the needs of the beaten traveler. Though the religious leaders affirmed their love for God, they denied by their actions the importance of loving their fellow human beings. Such hypocrisy was abhorrent to God.

C. The Compassion of the Samaritan: vss. 33-35

But a Samaritan, as he traveled, came where the man was; and when he saw him, he took pity on him. He went to him and bandaged his wounds, pouring on oil and wine. Then he put the man on his own donkey, took him to an inn and took care of him. The next day he took out two silver coins and gave them to the innkeeper. 'Look after him,' he said, 'and when I return, I will reimburse you for any extra expense you may have.'"

A Samaritan was the third person to come upon the injured man. Samaritans were Jews who had intermarried with people from other nations following the deportation of much of the Israelite population by the Assyrians 750 years before Christ (2 Kings 17:24-41). Over the following centuries, racial prejudice and a history of animosity fueled an intense rivalry between Jews and Samaritans.

The Jews bitterly hated the Samaritans, for the Jews prided themselves on their supposedly "pure" ancestry. Additionally, Jews despised Samaritans for their hybrid religion. Samaritans accepted the Torah (the five books of Moses), but inserted some of their own interpretations. And they worshiped on Mount Gerizim rather than on Mount Zion in Jerusalem (John 4:20).

Given this climate of animosity, the Samaritan in Jesus' parable could have rationalized failing to assist the injured man more easily than the priest and Levite did. But the Samaritan did not do that. Instead, feeling deep pity, he decided to help the stranger (Luke 10:33).

The Samaritan was thorough in the assistance he gave. He began by administering first aid. He bandaged the man's wounds, pouring on oil (which acted as a salve) and wine (which acted as an antiseptic). Then the Samaritan turned his donkey into a makeshift ambulance. He transported the man to an inn (vs. 34). Finally, the Samaritan arranged to pay the man's expenses. Since one denarius was equal to a laborer's daily pay, the two silver coins (denarii) that the Samaritan paid would probably have lodged the wounded man for several days (vs. 35).

Society has fragmented as people have held each other at arm's length. Consequently, many people today have retreated behind the security and seclusion of their own doors. They don't want others to intrude, and they don't want to get involved with others. But Jesus called us to be neighbors, to interact with others. We cannot be spiritual hermits and adequately love our neighbors. We have to be involved.

D. The Point of the Parable: vss. 36-37

"Which of these three do you think was a neighbor to the man who fell into the hands of robbers?" The expert in the law replied, "The one who had mercy on him." Jesus told him, "Go and do likewise."

At the end of the parable, Jesus asked the scribe which of the three passersby—the priest, the Levite, or the Samaritan—was a neighbor to the robbed man (Luke 10:36). The scribe correctly answered the one who had assisted the man in distress. Jesus told the scribe to act the same way (vs. 37).

The scribe had asked how far he had to go to love others. But Jesus turned the question around. Instead of "Who is my neighbor?" (Luke 10:29), the question became "How can I be a good neighbor?" (vs. 36). The lesson Jesus taught, and the lesson we must live, is that we become good neighbors by showing mercy to everyone we encounter (vs. 37).

Though Jesus' parable takes place in a rural setting, it speaks to a number of urban issues: racial and ethnic divisions, violent crime, and even the struggle of small businesses to collect their debts. The Samaritan—the good neighbor—does not eliminate these problems, but he does act as an agent of mercy to overcome them in small but effective ways. The Samaritan's example challenges us to consider how we can be good neighbors to others, regardless of their racial or ethnic background. Ultimately, God is interested in mercy, not maintaining prejudice.

Discussion Questions

1. Why do you think the legal expert sought to put Jesus to the test?
2. How did Jesus respond to the scribe's challenge?
3. Why did the scribe try to justify his actions?
4. Why do you think the priest and Levite refused to help the injured man in Jesus' parable?
5. What was so unusual about the Samaritan's willingness to help the injured man?
6. What are some ways you can be a neighbor to those around you in need?

Contemporary Application

There is a lawyer's instinct in all of us that seeks careful definitions of our Christian duties. This suggests we suffer from a cold creedalism that can strangle tangible expressions of love.

However, God's command to love all people transcends legal niceties (1 John 4:21). We cannot separate our duties to others from our duties to God. Saying the right words, praying the right prayers, and singing the right hymns cannot make up for a lack of love (1 Cor. 13:1-3).

We have to confess our coldness and our preoccupation with ourselves. And we have to admit how hard it is to find the time and the resources to be good Samaritans to wounded people. Together, we must encourage one another to make our churches places where love springs into action. Otherwise, we may look outwardly holy (like the priest and Levite), but be inwardly full of hypocrisy (like the scribe).

Parables on Prayer

DEVOTIONAL READING

Genesis 32:22-30

DAILY BIBLE READINGS

Monday October 22
Matthew 24:1-8 Signs of the End

Tuesday October 23
Matthew 24:9-18 Those Who Endure Will Be Saved

Wednesday October 24
Matthew 24:36-44 No One Knows the Hour

Thursday October 25
Matthew 24:45-51 The Faithful and Wicked Servants

Friday October 26
Matthew 25:1-13 The Parable of the 10 Bridesmaids

Saturday October 27
Matthew 25:14-30 The Parable of the Talents

Sunday October 28
Matthew 25:31-46 The Parable of the Sheep and the Goats

Scripture

Background Scripture: *Luke 18:1-14*
Scripture Lesson: *Luke 18:1-14*
Key Verse: *Then Jesus told his disciples a parable to show them that they should always pray and not give up.*
Luke 18:1.
Scripture Lesson for Children: *Luke 18:9-14*
Key Verse for Children: *"But the tax collector stood at a distance. He would not even look up to heaven, but beat his breast and said, 'God, have mercy on me, a sinner.'"*
Luke 18:13.

Lesson Aim

To discover the joy of persistence and honesty in prayer.

Lesson Setting

Time: A.D. *29*
Place: *Galilee*

Lesson Outline

Parables on Prayer
  I. Pray Persistently: Luke 18:1-8
     A. *The Widow's Petition: vss. 1-3*
     B. *The Judge's Response: vss. 4-5*
     C. *The Savior's Promise: vss. 6-8*
  II. Pray Honestly: Luke 18:9-14
     A. *The Pharisee's Arrogance: vss. 9-12*
     B. *The Tax Collector's Humility: vs. 13*
     C. *The Savior's Evaluation: vs. 14*

Introduction for Adults

Topic: *Praying Effectively*

"You do believe in prayer, don't you?" the visitor to the church asked. The people in the sanctuary invariably said, "Oh, yes." From there the visitor gently reminded them about the importance of prayer to the Christian life.

Many people say they believe in prayer, but doing it is something else. In John Wayne's version of Davey Crockett fighting at the Alamo, someone asked the great fighter whether he prayed. Crockett stormed off and said tersely, "I don't have time to pray!"

That's vintage Hollywood, of course. Perhaps many of the Alamo's defenders prayed. As the old saying goes, "There are no atheists in foxholes." But we have to confess that many times we get serious about prayer only when we're trapped by some emergency.

Jesus encouraged His followers to pray consistently, not fitfully. This includes being persistent and honest in one's petitions. Prayer is our great privilege, and we are foolish not to use it.

Introduction for Youths

Topic: *No Bragging Allowed*

Prayer for some young people begins with "Now I lay me down to sleep" and ends with the Lord's Prayer. Other youth prefer to leave prayer to the senior saints. Either option is tragic, for it is a privilege to go to God in prayer.

Thankfully there are thousands of teenagers who regularly gather in their youth groups and schools to pray, some of them every day. Their zeal for prayer leaves their elders in the dust. One of the reasons prayer clicks with these teens is that they can be honest with each other and with God. They do not need to use pious language to talk to the Lord.

Teens may not use the right terms all the time, but that's all right, for God looks at their hearts. He is never insulted by their fresh, spontaneous, and conversational prayer. If He finds honesty rather than pretense in their petitions, He is pleased.

Concepts for Children

Topic: *Jesus Taught about Prayer*

1. Jesus told a story about a Pharisee and a tax collector who went to a place of worship (a temple) to pray.
2. The Pharisee thought he was better than others, especially the tax collector.
3. The tax collector, however, simply asked God to forgive his sins.
4. It was the tax collector, not the Pharisee, who was pleasing to God.
5. God is pleased when we put Him and others, rather than ourselves, first.
6. This is the humble way we should be when we pray to God.

The Lesson Commentary

I.   PRAY PERSISTENTLY: LUKE 18:1-8

A. The Widow's Petition: vss. 1-3

Then Jesus told his disciples a parable to show them that they should always pray and not give up. He said: "In a certain town there was a judge who neither feared God nor cared about men. And there was a widow in that town who kept coming to him with the plea, 'Grant me justice against my adversary.'"

As Jesus moved toward Jerusalem and the climax of His ministry, He prepared His disciples for the time when He would no longer be with them. In Luke 17:1-10, He warned about the consequences of enticing believers to sin, taught His followers to forgive those who repent of their wrongdoing, and encouraged the disciples to humbly do their duties.

Verses 11-19 relate how Jesus met 10 lepers and sent them to the priests to be pronounced clean. They were healed as they went, but only one—a Samaritan—returned to thank Jesus and praise God for his healing.

In verses 20-37, Jesus countered the Pharisees' misconception about the Messiah by asserting that the kingdom of God was internal and spiritual. And since He, the King, was in their midst, the Kingdom was (in a sense) already present. Jesus also told His disciples that His Second Coming would occur suddenly, bringing judgment.

In light of the afflictions and hardships of life, and the certainty of approaching judgment, Jesus wanted to encourage His disciples to pray persistently, no matter how dark the circumstances might be (18:1). Praying is talking to God. The act of praying does not change what God has purposed to do. Rather, it is the means by which He accomplishes His will.

Talking to God is not a method of creating a positive mental attitude in ourselves so that we are able to do what we have asked to be done. Instead, prayer creates within us a right attitude with respect to the will of God. Prayer is not so much getting God to do our will as it is demonstrating that we are as concerned as He is that His will be done (Matt. 6:10).

To stress the importance of constant prayer, Jesus told a parable. He noted that in a certain city there was a wicked judge. He did not worship God and he held people in contempt (Luke 18:2). Jesus did not intend this official to represent God but rather to stand in contrast to Him. If such a judge, who didn't care about others, would respond to persistent pleas, how much more would God, who is not only just but also merciful and loving, do so more readily?

Jesus said that a widow lived in the same city. In Bible times widowhood was viewed with reproach by many in society. Thus a widow without legal protection was often vulnerable to neglect or exploitation. If a woman's husband died when her children were adolescents, they were considered orphans. Sadly, it was far too common for greedy and unscrupulous agents to defraud a destitute widow and her children of whatever property they owned.

There were three primary ways a widow could provide for the financial needs of herself and her children. First, she could return to her parents' house; second, she could remarry, especially if she was young or wealthy; and third, she could remain unmarried and obtain some kind of employment. The last prospect was rather bleak, for it was difficult in ancient times for a widow to find suitable work that would meet the economic needs of herself and her family.

The widow in Jesus' parable repeatedly came to the wicked judge. She appealed to him for justice against someone who had harmed her (vs. 3). In other words, the widow wanted to receive fair treatment in a court of law.

B. The Judge's Response: vss. 4-5

"For some time he refused. But finally he said to himself, 'Even though I don't fear God or care about men, yet because this widow keeps bothering me, I will see that she gets justice, so that she won't eventually wear me out with her coming!'"

At first, the hardhearted judge was unmoved by the widow's appeals, but then he relented. He did not change his mind because he saw it as his duty to God and the community. Rather, he did so because the widow's pestering of him would wear him out. He determined that it was better for him to give in to her persistence.

Despite the odds against her, the widow kept going back to the only one who could help her. That is why she illustrates persistence in prayer. She had a specific need and she never stopped pleading her case.

Jesus' disciples could easily make the connection between the helpless widow and themselves. They might have been strongly tempted to give up, for they had neither financial resources nor religious or political power. Only their persistence in prayer would see them through.

C. The Savior's Promise: vss. 6-8

And the Lord said, "Listen to what the unjust judge says. And will not God bring about justice for his chosen ones, who cry out to him day and night? Will he keep putting them off? I tell you, he will see that they get justice, and quickly. However, when the Son of Man comes, will he find faith on the earth?"

Jesus next urged His disciples to learn a lesson from the evil judge in the parable (Luke 18:7). In the end, even this wicked man rendered a just decision. If godless judges (such as this one) responded to constant pressure, how much more will our great and loving God respond to us? Jesus' point is that the Lord will hear the cries of believers (His "chosen ones") for help. He won't put them off; rather, He will give justice to them, especially because they plead with Him day and night.

Jesus was emphatic in stating that God would quickly grant justice. The problem, then, is not with God, but rather with His spiritual children. They often lack the faith and devotion (as seen in perseverance in prayer) that the Lord wants to see (vs. 8). Jesus' comment about finding faith when He returns suggests that, at His Second Coming, the enthusiasm of the faithful will wane because of persecution. Only perseverance (for example, in prayer) will stem such spiritual decline.

Persistence tends to be the most unpopular concept regarding the practice of prayer. Whatever our misgivings about coming before the all-knowing, all-powerful God with the same specific petitions over and over, persistence is scriptural.

God does not become more willing to answer because of our perseverance. Rather, we may become more capable of receiving God's answer to our request. Also, perseverance can clarify in our minds deep-seated desire from fleeting whim. Moreover, talking to God about the deepest desires of our heart can prepare our soul to more fully appreciate the answer He gives to our request.

II. PRAY HONESTLY: LUKE 18:9-14

A. The Pharisee's Arrogance: vss. 9-12

To some who were confident of their own righteousness and looked down on everybody else, Jesus told this parable: "Two men went up to the temple to pray, one a Pharisee and the other a tax collector. The Pharisee stood up and prayed about himself: 'God, I thank you that I am not like other men—robbers, evildoers, adulterers—or even like this tax collector. I fast twice a week and give a tenth of all I get.'"

In Jesus' next parable we find two main characters, a Pharisee and a tax collector, going to the temple to pray (Luke 18:9-10). Regular times of public prayer occurred in conjunction with the morning and evening sacrifices. Of course, worshipers were allowed to go to the temple for private prayer.

In New Testament times, the Pharisees comprised a religious and political party in Palestine. They were known for insisting that the law of God be observed (according to the interpretation of the scribes). Also, the Pharisees were famed for their observance of the laws of tithing, fasting, and ritual purity.

The Pharisees collected and preserved the Talmud and the Mishnah, which were two immense products of oral tradition and Old Testament commentary. By reputation, Pharisees were legalistic and fanatically devoted to rabbinical tradition. Some even refused to eat with non-Pharisees for fear of being contaminated by food not rendered ritually clean.

Tax collectors were agents or contract workers who collected tariffs and tolls in designated areas. In order to make a profit, they would charge several times more than what the Roman government required. The desire for personal gain would invariably lead to the inflation of tolls and customs. Each person involved in the collection process would pocket some of the excess money being charged.

The Jews held their fellow citizens who were tax collectors in disdain because they served as agents of the despised Roman government. Also, everyone could see how the tax collectors became rich at the expense of their own people. Furthermore, Jewish tax collectors were considered ceremonially impure, for they had frequent contact with Gentiles.

It's no wonder, then, that the Pharisee in Jesus' parable showed contempt for the tax collector in the temple. The religious leader, being filled with self-confidence and arrogance, wasted no time in telling God how great he was (especially in contrast to the dishonest tax collector). The legalist noted that he never cheated anyone, wasn't guilty of wickedness, and didn't commit adultery (vs. 11). Instead, the Pharisee fasted twice a week (which was more than what any biblical standard required) and gave God a tenth of his income (vs. 12).

The Pharisee failed to understand that even his human goodness fell far short of God's perfect moral standard (Rom. 3:23). It was only by renouncing his own righteousness and receiving by faith the righteousness Christ offered freely and unconditionally that the Pharisee could enjoy God's favor and forgiveness.

B. The Tax Collector's Humility: vs. 13

"But the tax collector stood at a distance. He would not even look up to heaven, but beat his breast and said, 'God, have mercy on me, a sinner.'"

Unlike the proud Pharisee, the tax collector stood some distance away and did not even dare lift his eyes to heaven as he prayed. And, in abject sorrow for his sin, the tax collector repeatedly beat his chest. The only thing he could think of doing was to ask God for mercy, even though he was a sinner (Luke 18:13).

It's helpful to note that the Greek verb rendered "be merciful" literally means "to be propitiated." In other words, the tax collector was asking God to turn away from His wrath for the man's sins. The Father, in love, could do this because of the atoning sacrifice that His Son, Jesus Christ, would make on the cross. Because Jesus is the sacrifice for our sin, God's wrath is appeased and the punishment for our transgressions has been satisfied (Rom. 3:24-26; 1 John 2:2).

C. The Savior's Evaluation: vs. 14

"I tell you that this man, rather than the other, went home justified before God. For everyone who exalts himself will be humbled, and he who humbles himself will be exalted."

Jesus declared that when the two men went home, it was the tax collector, not the Pharisee, whom God justified (Luke 18:14). By this Jesus meant that the Lord had declared the tax collector to be forgiven and in a right standing before Him. From this we see that humility and repentance, not arrogance and self-righteousness, please God. The latter causes a person to despise others and prevents him or her from coming to God.

Jesus explained that if we put ourselves above others, God will use the circumstances of life to bring us down. In contrast, if we humble ourselves, God will honor us. The path, then, to true identity is not building ourselves up and tearing other people down. Instead, it is being honest about ourselves and becoming as humble as Christ.

There is no risk in admitting our sins to God, for He already knows about them. And when we come to Him in repentance and faith, we experience His forgiveness and restoration. Conversely, if we try to build ourselves up by looking down on others who are less fortunate or gifted than us, we will reap loneliness and resentment from others and disdain from God.

Discussion Questions

1. How did the wicked judge initially respond to the widow's request?
2. How did the official respond after the widow persisted in making her request to him?
3. How does this parable apply to us as believers?
4. In what ways did the Pharisee and the tax collector contrast with each other? What similar need did they have?
5. Why did the tax collector, rather than the Pharisee, leave the temple justified?
6. Why is it always best for us to approach God with humility rather than arrogance?

Contemporary Application

The joy of prayer is that it can be both spontaneous and scripted. We can blurt out to God whatever is on our minds, and we can join others in prayer during our worship services. The foremost concern is to talk to God, regardless of the circumstances.

Because Jesus is the Son of God (Mark 1:1), He regularly prayed to His Father, sometimes throughout the night (Luke 6:12). When Jesus prayed, He sought to glorify God (John 17:1-5). In His prayers, Christ did not use meaningless repetition, but rather made every word count (Matt. 6:7). His communion with God was characterized by great fervency (Luke 22:44) and intense emotion (Heb. 5:7). Jesus asked the Father to strengthen the faith of His followers (Luke 22:31-32), to provide for their daily needs (Matt. 6:11), to forgive their sins (Luke 11:4), and to preserve them in the faith (John 17:11).

Prayer includes much more than asking for things, though the Bible encourages us to bring our needs and desires to God. Prayer includes intercession for others and thanksgiving. Paul wrote that thanksgiving is to be a regular part of our prayer life (1 Thess. 5:18). Thanksgiving is an aspect of praise in which we express gratitude to God. It should spring from an appreciative heart, though it is required of all believers, regardless of their initial attitude.

We can thank God for His work of salvation and sanctification, for answering our prayers, and for leading us in the path of righteousness (Phil. 1:3-5; Col. 1:3-5). We can also express gratitude to God for His goodness and unending mercy, and for leading us to spiritual victory in Christ (Ps. 107:1; 1 Cor. 15:57).

The New Testament reveals that Christians have a great High Priest—Jesus Christ—whom they can run to in their time of need (Heb. 4:14-16). Jesus is not austere, aloof, or fear-inducing. Rather, He can sympathize with our weaknesses because He became one of us and experienced life—with its joys and sorrows, highs and lows—just as we do (yet without sinning). Instead of turning away from transgressors, Christ invites such people to God's throne of grace to receive mercy and help in their time of need.

The Sheep and the Goats

Scripture

Background Scripture: *Matthew 25:31-46*

Scripture Lesson: *Matthew 25:31-45*

Key Verse: *"The King will reply, 'I tell you the truth, whatever you did for one of the least of these brothers of mine, you did for me.'"* Matthew 25:40.

Scripture Lesson for Children: *Matthew 25:14-29*

Key Verse for Children: *"His master replied, 'Well done, good and faithful servant! You have been faithful with a few things; I will put you in charge of many things. Come and share your master's happiness!'"* Matthew 25:23.

Lesson Aim

To recognize the value of ministering to people in need and thereby glorify Christ.

Lesson Setting

Time: *A.D. 30*

Place: *Mount of Olives outside Jerusalem*

Lesson Outline

The Sheep and the Goats

I. The Sheep and the Goats: Matthew 25:31-33
   A. *The Coming Judge: vs. 31*
   B. *The Determination: vss. 32-33*
II. Those on Christ's Right: Matthew 25:34-40
   A. *The Promise of the Kingdom: vs. 34*
   B. *The Deeds of the Blessed: vss. 35-36*
   C. *The Questions Asked by the Blessed: vss. 37-39*
   D. *The Response Given by the Lord: vs. 40*
III. Those on Christ's Left: Matthew 25:41-45
   A. *The Pronouncement of Judgment: vs. 41*
   B. *The Failures of the Condemned: vss. 42-43*
   C. *The Questions Asked by the Condemned: vs. 44*
   D. *The Response Given by the Lord: vs. 45*

Introduction for Adults

Topic: *Serving Christ by Serving Others*

Several years ago when King Abdullah succeeded his father King Hussein on the throne of Jordan, he decided to discover the needs of his people. He assumed several roles in disguise, such as taxi driver, money changer, and so on. The people he worked with had no idea they were serving their king.

We recognize something similar taking place in Jesus' parable of the sheep and the goats. The sheep had no idea they helped Jesus, and the goats had no idea they refused to come to His aid. How many times do we make the same mistake? We simply do not recognize that by helping needy people, we are ministering to our Lord and King.

Introduction for Youths

Topic: *On the Other Hand . . .*

A group of Christian college students decided to find out what it was like to be homeless. They spent several weekends living among the homeless in Chicago by sleeping out at night on cardboard pallets and scrounging for their food.

This incident reminds us that young people generally have a keen sense of helping others. They organize food drives, and walk, run, and swim for charity. They go overseas to build houses, drill wells, and teach people to read.

Jesus said these sorts of activities really count with Him. The idea is that by investing our lives in others, we invest in Him. Conversely, by refusing to help others in need, we also refuse to minister to our Savior.

Concepts for Children

Topic: *Jesus Taught about Using Talents*

1. Jesus told the story of a man who went on a long journey.
2. The man left his property in the care of his servants.
3. Two of the master's servants doubled their share of his property, but one servant hid his share of the property.
4. When the master returned, he thanked the first two servants and gave them more property to manage.
5. The master, however, was unhappy with the third servant and gave his share of the property to the first servant.
6. Jesus is pleased when we wisely use what He gives us.

The Lesson Commentary

I. THE SHEEP AND THE GOATS: MATTHEW 25:31-33

A. The Coming Judge: vs. 31

"When the Son of Man comes in his glory, and all the angels with him, he will sit on his throne in heavenly glory."

Matthew 24:1—25:46 is the last of the five discourses in the first Synoptic Gospel. Because Jesus was sitting on the Mount of Olives when He taught this material to His disciples, it has been called the Olivet Discourse. It contains some of the most noteworthy prophetic passages in all of Scripture.

In 24:1-14, Jesus revealed the signs of His return. He then talked about perilous times (vss. 15-28) and the glory associated with His Second Coming (vss. 29-31). In the parable of the fig tree (vss. 32-35), Jesus said that as the buds of a fig tree tell that summer is near, so will signs tell that Christ's return is imminent. Then in verses 36-44, Jesus said that only the Father knew the time of His return. The coming of the Son of Man will be so sudden that the wicked and the righteous will be separated instantaneously.

Following the parable of the wise and wicked servants (vss. 45-51), Jesus told three more parables related to His return: the parable of the 10 virgins (25:1-13), the parable of the talents (vss. 14-30), and the parable of the sheep and the goats (vss. 31-46). All of these stories have to do with being ready for Christ's return by being faithful to Him.

Each of these parables, however, has a slightly different slant. In the parable of the 10 virgins, Christ called His disciples to exercise foresight and wisdom as they prepared themselves for His return. In the parable of the talents, Jesus stressed that His followers were to be wise stewards of all He had entrusted to their case. And in the parable of the sheep and the goats, Jesus revealed that the righteous will be rewarded for their concern and hospitality, while the wicked will be punished for their indifference.

In the final parable that Jesus delivered on the Mount of Olives, He provided a few details about what His return will be like. First, Jesus will come in "glory" (vs. 31), or divine splendor, no longer simply appearing as an ordinary man. Second, He will bring with Him "all the angels," who will no doubt serve as His assistants. Third, Jesus will "sit on his throne in heavenly glory," meaning He will rule in splendor.

B. The Determination: vss. 32-33

"All the nations will be gathered before him, and he will separate the people one from another as a shepherd separates the sheep from the goats. He will put the sheep on his right and the goats on his left."

Once Jesus is seated on His throne, all the nations will be gathered in His presence. He will then separate them as a shepherd separates sheep from goats (Matt. 25:32). In other words, the purpose of the judgment will be to separate the righteous from the wicked. Only God can do that with perfect justice.

Shepherding was a prominent occupation in ancient Palestine. Shepherds had to make sure that their master's flock was provided for and protected. Shepherds would lead their animals to good pasturelands and ample supplies of water. They would find adequate shelter for their flocks and assist any crippled or exhausted animals. If necessary, shepherds would risk their own lives to ensure the safety of the flock.

Jesus compared the separation of humans to the way a shepherd would separate sheep from goats. In ancient Palestine sheep and goats often grazed together during the day. When night came, however, they were herded into separate folds. That was because the goats, unlike the sheep, could not easily endure the cooler night air and thus had to be grouped to keep warm.

The point of the comparison lies in the fact that sheep and goats were separated at the end of the day. As the shepherd of judgment, Jesus will put the "sheep" on His right and the "goats" on His left (vs. 33).

There are two primary ways of understanding Jesus' parable. Some say the "nations" (vs. 32) refer to all peoples, while others claim they refer to Gentiles only. One group thinks the judgment occurs at the conclusion of history; in contrast, the second group says it takes place when Jesus comes to set up a kingdom on earth. For those in the first group, the judgment determines who goes to heaven and who goes to hell. Oppositely, those in the second group say the judgment concerns who enters Jesus' earthly kingdom and who doesn't.

II. THOSE ON CHRIST'S RIGHT: MATTHEW 25:34-40

A. The Promise of the Kingdom: vs. 34

"Then the King will say to those on his right, 'Come, you who are blessed by my Father; take your inheritance, the kingdom prepared for you since the creation of the world.'"

The remainder of Jesus' parable describes what He will do with the sheep (or the righteous) and the goats (or the wicked) once He has them separated. First He commented on the sheep (Matt. 25:34-40) and then the goats (vss. 41-45).

While seated on His throne, Jesus will reign as King and judge as King. He will address those on His right side as "blessed by my Father" (vs. 34). They will be favored by God in the blessing they will receive as an inheritance from Him, namely, the kingdom of heaven. Jesus described this Kingdom as having been "prepared for you since the creation of the world." All along it has been a part of God's plan to bless the righteous with His kingdom. Upon Christ's return, it will be time for the plan's fulfillment.

The kingdom of God embraces all who walk in fellowship with God and do His will. It is governed by God's laws, which are summed up in our duty to love God supremely and love others as ourselves. And this Kingdom, which was announced by the prophets and introduced by Jesus, will one day displace all the kingdoms of this world, following the return of Christ.

How can formerly sinful people share in the divine Kingdom? It's because they have trusted in God's Son, whom He sent to earth to die for humanity's transgressions (John 3:16). The believers' place in God's kingdom is assured because they are forgiven in Christ (Eph. 1:7). And their hope of salvation is sure because it rests on the work of Christ (1 Pet. 1:3-5).

B. The Deeds of the Blessed: vss. 35-36

"For I was hungry and you gave me something to eat, I was thirsty and you gave me something to drink, I was a stranger and you invited me in, I needed clothes and you clothed me, I was sick and you looked after me, I was in prison and you came to visit me.'"

Jesus said the righteous will inherit the Kingdom because of how they have treated Him. They will have met His needs for food, drink, shelter, clothing, nursing, and visitation (Matt. 25:35-36). These are things that anyone at any time in any society can understand, for they are the common concerns of life everywhere.

Thus, the test of faith that stands Christ's inspection will be how we performed deeds of mercy, love, and kindness. After all, this is what Jesus did for people while He was here on earth. And His righteous sheep follow His example. They show that their faith is practical and touches the lives of hurting people. Clearly, then, valid Christian faith is more than saying the right prayers or singing the right hymns. It includes standing alongside people in the harshest circumstances.

C. The Questions Asked by the Blessed: vss. 37-39

"Then the righteous will answer him, 'Lord, when did we see you hungry and feed you, or thirsty and give you something to drink? When did we see you a stranger and invite you in, or needing clothes and clothe you? When did we see you sick or in prison and go to visit you?'"

Jesus called His sheep "the righteous" (Matt. 25:37). They were upright because of their faith in Christ, and their lives were marked by righteous living because they cared for people in need.

The righteous ask a series of good questions in verses 37-39. In their spot, we too might wonder when we ever had an opportunity to do such things for Jesus. Here we see that Jesus wants us to show His love to others. Even the simplest act of kindness to the seemingly most insignificant person meets with God's approval and will be rewarded.

D. The Response Given by the Lord: vs. 40

"The King will reply, 'I tell you the truth, whatever you did for one of the least of these brothers of mine, you did for me.'"

Jesus said that the deeds the righteous had done "for one of the least of these brothers of mine" (Matt. 25:40) were done for Him. In other words, service done for Jesus' needy brothers and sisters is the same as service done for Him. This is an astounding truth, for it radically transforms our motivation for performing deeds of mercy.

There has been much discussion about the identity of the "brothers." Some have said they are the Jews; others say they are all Christians; still others say they are suffering people everywhere. Such a debate is much like the lawyer's earlier question to Jesus, "And who is my neighbor?" (Luke 10:29).

The point of Jesus' parable is not the *who*, but rather the *what*; in other words, the importance of serving where service is needed. The focus of this story about the sheep and the goats is that we should love every person and serve anyone we can. Such compassion and kindness glorifies God by reflecting our love for Him.

III. THOSE ON CHRIST'S LEFT: MATTHEW 25:41-45

A. The Pronouncement of Judgment: vs. 41

"Then he will say to those on his left, 'Depart from me, you who are cursed, into the eternal fire prepared for the devil and his angels.'"

Jesus next focused on the goats. Instead of being invited to come, like the ones on the right (the place of honor in ancient times), the ones on the left (the place of dishonor) will be told to depart. Instead of being blessed by the Father, these people will be cursed. Instead of inheriting the Kingdom prepared for the righteous, these people will be consigned to the eternal fire (hell) prepared for Satan and demons (Matt. 25:41).

B. The Failures of the Condemned: vss. 42-43

"For I was hungry and you gave me nothing to eat, I was thirsty and you gave me nothing to drink, I was a stranger and you did not invite me in, I needed clothes and you did not clothe me, I was sick and in prison and you did not look after me.'"

Just as the righteous will inherit the Kingdom for meeting Jesus' needs, the wicked will be consigned to hell for not meeting His needs. They will have been presented with the same opportunities to give Him food and drink and the rest, but they will have chosen not to do so (Matt. 25:42-43).

For those who spurn Christ, all that remains is for the Lord to condemn them. It will be a terrifying scene as He issues a verdict of guilty against the unsaved.

C. The Questions Asked by the Condemned: vs. 44

"They also will answer, 'Lord, when did we see you hungry or thirsty or a stranger or needing clothes or sick or in prison, and did not help you?'"

The wicked will be just as mystified as the righteous about when they had the opportunities that Jesus mentioned. They will ask when they chose not to help the Lord (Matt. 25:44). They didn't realize that the basis for judgment will be whether they showed love to others, whom God has created in His image (1 John 3:14-18).

D. The Response Given by the Lord: vs. 45

"He will reply, 'I tell you the truth, whatever you did not do for one of the least of these, you did not do for me.'"

Christ's solemn reply will be that refusing to help others in need is the same as refusing to help Him (Matt. 24:45). Verse 46 concludes both the story of the sheep and the story of the goats. The wicked and righteous have radically different futures. The first group is eternally condemned, while the second group is eternally blessed. Jesus' judgments will be beyond appeal.

Discussion Questions

1. What will be the first thing Jesus does after sitting on His glorious throne?
2. What will be the destiny of those on Jesus' right?
3. What explanation did Jesus offer for this outcome?
4. What will be the destiny of those on Jesus' left? Why will this be so?
5. Which of our neighbors needs the touch of God's love through our hands?

Contemporary Application

As Jesus approached His crucifixion, He never wavered from judgment. He told His people to get ready, to keep watching, to keep working, and to take care of one another when they were hungry, sick, imprisoned, and so on. In fact, He pictured a grand finale of judgment when He will separate everyone, some to His kingdom and some to eternal fire.

We should not misinterpret the parable of the sheep and the goats to mean that one's eternal state is based upon good works. The New Testament is clear that faith in Christ (or its absence) determines our eternal destiny. Nevertheless, we can take away from this parable the ideas that Jesus rewards service done to Him, that real faith is expressed in works, and that He counts service done to His people as the same as service done to Him.

And what acts of service are they that receive the reward of the Kingdom? Included are simple things any of us can do—offering a meal to a hungry person and giving a cup of water to a thirsty person. Let's get busy! And let's get ready for Jesus to come!

There are 40 million children living on the streets of Latin America and over 1.5 million children on the streets of Manila in the Philippines. A lost generation to their countries. Lost to Christ.

Cross-cultural books that teach about God and his love for children are most effective and are used as a means of evangelizing and discipling children in the care of street children ministries. Cook Communications Ministries International *has literature that can mean the difference between utter hopelessness or a life full of meaning.*

To learn more about the global ministry projects of Cook Communications Ministries International, you can visit their web site at www.ccmi.org or call 1-800-323-7543.

Rewards and Responsibilities

DEVOTIONAL READING

Psalm 24

DAILY BIBLE READINGS

Monday November 5
Galatians 3:19-29 The Law in Perspective

Tuesday November 6
Luke 11:37-52 Burdensome Laws Are Barriers to Faith

Wednesday November 7
Luke 12:1-7 Hypocrisy Doesn't Work

Thursday November 8
Matthew 5:21-26 Murder, Anger, or Reconciliation

Friday November 9
Matthew 5:27-37 Lust: Adultery in the Heart

Saturday November 10
Matthew 5:38-48 Be Perfect

Sunday November 11
Matthew 5:17-20 Fulfilling, Not Abolishing, the Law

Scripture

Background Scripture: *Matthew 5:1-16*
Scripture Lesson: *Matthew 5:1-16*
Key Verse: *In the same way, let your light shine before men, that they may see your good deeds and praise your Father in heaven.* Matthew 5:16.

Lesson Aim

To recognize the value of growing in godly character.

Lesson Setting

Time: A.D. *28*
Place: *Galilee*

Lesson Outline

Rewards and Responsibilities

I. The Sermon's Setting: Matthew 5:1-2
II. The Sermon's Blessings: Matthew 5:3-12
 A. *For the Poor in Spirit: vs. 3*
 B. *For the Mournful: vs. 4*
 C. *For the Meek: vs. 5*
 D. *For the Spiritually Hungry: vs. 6*
 E. *For the Merciful: vs. 7*
 F. *For the Pure in Heart: vs. 8*
 G. *For the Peacemakers: vs. 9*
 H. *For the Persecuted: vss. 10-12*
III. The Sermon's Challenges: Matthew 5:13-16
 A. *To Be Salt: vs. 13*
 B. *To Be Light: vss. 14-16*

Introduction for Adults

Topic: *Finding Supreme Happiness*

With the proliferation of legalized gambling, more and more people think they can find happiness by winning lots of money. Players envision paying off their debts and buying a new home, car, or boat. They also dream of traveling to distant lands and enjoying idyllic vacations.

Occasionally, we read stories about the troubles that have plagued overnight millionaires. This should not surprise us, for as Christians we know that money cannot buy happiness. Perhaps that's why Jesus, in His Sermon on the Mount, did not pronounce His blessings on the materially rich.

While we acknowledge the perils of money, we find it hard *not* to define our lives in terms of how much we have. It should come as no surprise, then, that we need the Sermon on the Mount for our eternal wellness. In it Jesus strikes at the heart of our desires and values. By taking His spiritual medicine, we will make our souls vibrant and strong.

Introduction for Youths

Topic: *The Good Life!*

For many youth in the West, the good life means wearing the right clothes, using the right words, having the right friends, and driving the right car. This is pure, crass materialism, and it is of no eternal value.

Jesus called His followers to be salt and light in the midst of such selfishness and greed. Interestingly, in His Sermon on the Mount, He did not tell the disciples to start by preaching to the proud, rich, and self-sufficient. Rather, He told His followers to be humble, meek, and peaceful. They were to seek God and bravely endure persecution.

Those character qualities will make a difference in Christian youth. Of course, they might be ridiculed by their peers for choosing to be upright. Nevertheless, Jesus promised the deepest fulfillment in life when saved teens stand for His values and reject those of the world.

Concepts for Children

Topic: *Jesus Preached about Responsibilities*

1. Jesus' disciples gathered around Him, and He taught them.
2. Jesus brings us joy when we try to live for Him.
3. Jesus watches over us even when others are mean to us.
4. Jesus will give us the wisdom and courage to do what is right.
5. Jesus wants us to share His love and goodness with others.

The Lesson Commentary

I. THE SERMON'S SETTING: MATTHEW 5:1-2

Now when he saw the crowds, he went up on a mountainside and sat down. His disciples came to him, and he began to teach them, saying: . . .

Jesus announced that God's kingdom was drawing near (Matt. 4:17). What attitudes and actions were appropriate for a citizen of God's kingdom? Christ answered this question in what is known as the Sermon on the Mount (chaps. 5—7). Although Jesus' primary audience would have been His disciples, there was a larger crowd of people who listened to Him teach (7:28).

There are two views regarding when and where the Sermon on the Mount was preached. One group asserts that it is a compilation of various teachings that were given on different occasions in several places. A second group believes the sermon was delivered at one time early in Jesus' ministry and in one location (for example, on the side of a mountain near Capernaum).

Portions of the Sermon on the Mount are similar to Jesus' Sermon on the Plain (Luke 6:20-49). Some experts think these passages represent two different messages given on separate occasions, while others think the two passages represent the same message. According to the second view, Luke presented an abbreviated version of the longer sermon recorded in Matthew.

The "crowds" of Matthew 5:1 who came to hear Jesus' sermon are presumably the same as the "large crowds" of 4:25 who followed Jesus. They came from at least a 100-mile radius of the territory to listen to Jesus teach (5:2). God's supreme Old Testament revelation—the law—was given by Moses, accompanied by thunder and lightning, from Mount Sinai. One greater than Moses gave this sermon also from a mountain region probably near the Sea of Galilee.

As the Master Teacher, Jesus employed the normal sitting posture of a Jewish rabbi. The ethics that He taught in His sermon contrasted sharply with the legalism of His religious opponents. They were absorbed with external righteousness. Jesus launched His sermon by overthrowing such an approach to life.

II. THE SERMON'S BLESSINGS: MATTHEW 5:3-12

A. For the Poor in Spirit: vs. 3 *humility*

"Blessed are the poor in spirit, for theirs is the kingdom of heaven."

At various times in history, there have been common misconceptions made about the Sermon on the Mount. Some have said it is nothing more than a call to social action, while others regard it simply as a list of things to do to be happy. Still others say the sermon is not applicable for this age, but rather only for the Kingdom age to come. As we read the sermon, we should be careful to put it in its first-century context and let the lessons appearing in it speak for themselves.

For instance, consider Matthew 5:3. In this verse we are immediately struck by the presence of the word "blessed." This refers to the spiritual wellness of believers.

The term conveys the idea of being the privileged recipient of God's favor, and thus enjoying a happier end than the wicked. (Jesus' various declarations of blessedness are commonly called the Beatitudes.)

Jesus pronounced His first blessing on the "poor in spirit," which is a reference to humility. These are believers who have been stripped of their own securities and thus feel deeply their need for God. The Savior's redemption, not their own goodness, is the basis for their citizenship in heaven.

B. For the Mournful: vs. 4

"Blessed are those who mourn, for they will be comforted." [handwritten: Weep because of transgression against God]

Jesus pronounced His second blessing on the mournful, who will receive God's comfort. "Those who mourn" (Matt. 5:4) weep because they know they have transgressed against the Lord. And they cry in confession and repentance, which are a reflection of their humble spirit.

These believers do not look to the world for satisfaction, joy, or comfort. Rather, they find these things in the Savior alone. They come to Jesus in humility and faith, confessing their sins, and He enters their lives and stays there with the sweet assurance of His forgiveness.

C. For the Meek: vs. 5

"Blessed are the meek, for they will inherit the earth." [handwritten: Bear up under provocations, control feelings, refuse to get even; then put others first]

Jesus gave His third blessing to the meek and promised them the earth as an inheritance (Matt. 5:5). Meekness has two aspects. On the one hand, the meek bear up under provocations, control their feelings, and refuse to get even. On the other hand, they are courageous, generous, and courteous. They put others, not themselves, first.

Here we find Jesus explaining the values of the Kingdom. Relationships, possessions, information, prayer, money, and power are a few of the categories He redefined from God's perspective. Jesus showed that following Him involves radical change. For most of us this means undoing the way we've always acted and reconsidering traditional sources of wisdom from our family, friends, and culture. To become like Jesus requires us to do a tough-minded review of our moral values and lifelong goals and dreams.

D. For the Spiritually Hungry: vs. 6 [handwritten: desiring God above all things]

"Blessed are those who hunger and thirst for righteousness, for they will be filled."

Jesus next blessed those who longed for righteousness and promised to fulfill their desires (Matt. 5:6). The attitude is one of desiring God above all things and seeking to be in a right relationship with Him and others. While greed, injustice, and violence consume the unsaved, believers yearn for justice and goodness to be established.

In these first four beatitudes there is a logical progression. First, we admit our spiritual bankruptcy (vs. 3). Seeing ourselves as "poor in spirit" causes us to "mourn" (vs. 4) our condition. Because we grieve over our sorrowful state, we come to a correct notion of ourselves, which is to be humble and meek (vs. 5). Thus, by accepting the appraisal arrived at in verses 3 through 5, we are ready to "hunger and thirst for righteousness" (vs. 6).

E. For the Merciful: vs. 7

"Blessed are the merciful, for they will be shown mercy."

Jesus then blessed the merciful and said they will be treated with mercy (Matt. 5:7). This verse is talking about having a gracious disposition toward others. The merciful are kind, charitable, and ready to sympathize with the sufferings of the afflicted. They long for justice, but are not harsh and cruel. And they seek to be generous to all by showing the love of God without partiality or preconditions.

F. For the Pure in Heart: vs. 8

"Blessed are the pure in heart, for they will see God."

Jesus gave His sixth blessing on the pure in heart and promised that they would see God. The focus here is on being genuine and honest in all one's dealings. Such purity requires spiritual discipline and self-control. It renounces self-love for the love of God.

Sin is the enemy of moral purity, and popular ideas and activities conspire to undo it. Furthermore, the world ridicules and taunts the virtuous for not having fun. But instead of fun, the pure receive the greatest gift of all, namely, a personal encounter with the living God. When we come to know Him through faith in Christ, we are truly fulfilled.

G. For the Peacemakers: vs. 9

"Blessed are the peacemakers, for they will be called sons of God."

In the seventh beatitude, Jesus pronounced a blessing on "the peacemakers" (Matt. 5:9). In saying they "will be called sons of God," Jesus meant they will become spiritual children in God's heavenly family (John 1:12; Eph. 1:5). Peacemakers do not merely stay cool, calm, and collected but also work for peace in their families, schools, churches, businesses, and communities.

Jesus is the ultimate peacemaker, for He destroyed the enmity between sinners and God (2 Cor. 5:18-19; Eph. 2:13-18). Jesus not only brings us peace with God, but also heals our broken relationships.

H. For the Persecuted: vss. 10-12

"Blessed are those who are persecuted because of righteousness, for theirs is the kingdom of heaven. Blessed are you when people insult you, persecute you and falsely say all kinds of evil against you because of me. Rejoice and be glad, because great is your reward in heaven, for in the same way they persecuted the prophets who were before you."

In the final beatitudes, Jesus blessed the persecuted and promised them the kingdom of heaven (Matt. 5:10). He taught that when Christians stand up for truth, righteousness, and goodness, they will be slandered and insulted (vs. 11). Such persecution arises because of taking a stand for righteousness and being known as a follower of Christ.

Jesus gave two reasons His harassed followers could accept their circumstances with an attitude of joy (vs. 12). First, they ought to realize that their eternal reward will exceed their wildest expectations. Second, they can remember that God's enemies also mistreated His prophets.

As followers of Christ, we should not be shocked when we are slandered, physically harmed, or targeted for malicious rumors. Although we feel the intense pain of such injustices, we can persevere by holding to the promise of God's richest blessings.

For instance, Jesus said that heaven belongs to the persecuted. By this He meant they would have a place of distinction in the kingdom of God. In this present world, many believers are harassed and abused by others for the cause of Christ. The world might regard them as nobodies, but God considers them as people of honor who should be given nothing less than unending joy in His presence.

III. THE SERMON'S CHALLENGES: MATTHEW 5:13-16

A. To Be Salt: vs. 13

"You are the salt of the earth. But if the salt loses its saltiness, how can it be made salty again? It is no longer good for anything, except to be thrown out and trampled by men."

Jesus next compared believers to salt (Matt. 5:13). In ancient times, the Jews obtained their salt from the Dead Sea and from mineral deposits they found in the soil. The salinity of the chemical could be lost due to overexposure to the sun and excessively damp conditions. People used salt to season and preserve their food and to bring out its flavor. Ingesting salt also helped people to maintain their electrolytes and prevent dehydration from occurring.

Jesus noted that when salt becomes contaminated with foreign substances, it can lose its distinctive flavor and preservative qualities. When this happened, people would discard such a worthless chemical. Jesus was figuratively referring to the spiritual qualities that should be present in His disciples. In other words, they needed to have a wholesomeness about them that enabled them to be a blessing and a moral preservative in the world.

B. To Be Light: vss. 14-16

"You are the light of the world. A city on a hill cannot be hidden. Neither do people light a lamp and put it under a bowl. Instead they put it on its stand, and it gives light to everyone in the house. In the same way, let your light shine before men, that they may see your good deeds and praise your Father in heaven."

Jesus explained that a city located at the top of a hill cannot escape detection (Matt. 5:14). Likewise, believers who are fully devoted to Jesus could not remain hidden, for the spiritual light of their lives will be visible to everyone. They are to radiate the knowledge and presence of God to people living in spiritual darkness or ignorance.

Christ noted that people in His day did not light a lamp and place it under a wooden basket or clay bowl, which was used to measure ground meal or flour. Rather, they placed the lamp on a stand so that it might radiate its light to every person in the house (vs. 15).

The lamp symbolized the believers' works of righteousness, the light of which shone far into the darkness of the world and gave glory to God. When the unsaved saw the good that believers performed, they were more inclined to praise the "Father in heaven" (vs. 16).

Discussion Questions

1. What do you think it means to be poor in spirit (Matt. 5:3)? How does this contrast with the way the world thinks?
2. What erroneous ideas might people have about meekness (vs. 5)?
3. What would you say it means to be pure in heart (vs. 8)? How is this possible in our age of materialism and vice?
4. Why is it possible to rejoice when we are persecuted?
5. How has your Christian faith given you contentment with life?

Contemporary Application

Jesus began the Sermon on the Mount with the Beatitudes. These blessings list the rewards of poverty of spirit (humility), mournfulness (grieving over sin), meekness (keeping power under control), hunger and thirst after righteousness (spiritual seeking), mercy (being gracious), purity of heart (being forgiven), peacemaking (reconciliation), and persecution (suffering for taking a stand).

Contentment is at the heart of such character qualities. Satisfaction and joy is difficult in our society because so many things tell us we're lacking this or that—a bigger house, a more luxurious car, another television, a thinner figure, a better job, a gorgeous boyfriend or girlfriend, and so on. Yet we know from the teachings of Scripture that God can fill us with contentment despite lacking these things (Phil. 4:11-13).

A godly character is the foundation upon which contentment rests. We know that as Christians, our character should be godly because that's who we are. For instance, if someone asks why we are being peacemakers, our answer should be "It's just my character in Christ." At the same time, we need to cultivate a godly character each day by committing ourselves to being all Christ taught. When we do, we will grow in godly character.

"But I Say to You"

Scripture

Background Scripture: *Matthew 5:17-48*
Scripture Lesson: *Matthew 5:17-20, 38-48*
Key Verse: *"Do not think that I have come to abolish the Law or the Prophets; I have not come to abolish them but to fulfill them."* Matthew 5:17.
Key Verse for Children: *"But I tell you: Love your enemies and pray for those who persecute you, that you may be sons of your Father in heaven."* Matthew 5:44-45.

Lesson Aim

To look for ways to be more loving toward the difficult people in our lives.

Lesson Setting

Time: A.D. 28
Place: *Galilee*

Lesson Outline

"But I Say to You"

   I. A Call to Extreme Righteousness: Matthew 5:17-20
       A. *Affirming the Importance of the Law: vss. 17-19*
       B. *Affirming the Importance of Righteousness: vs. 20*
  II. Responding to Evil: Matthew 5:38-42
       A. *The Sinful Way: vs. 38*
       B. *The Godly Way: vss. 39-42*
  IV. Responding to Our Enemies: Matthew 5:43-48
       A. *The Sinful Way: vs. 43*
       B. *The Godly Way: vss. 44-47*
       C. *The Divine Standard: vs. 48*

Introduction for Adults

Topic: *Fulfilling the Commandments*

Everyone who has gone through military basic training knows what the drill sergeant's idea of "perfection" means. One speck of dust anywhere in the barracks can bring down the wrath of the inspectors. In civilian industry this attitude used to be called "zero defects."

When we consider our lives, we know that we have not reached such a high standard, especially in terms of morality. But that is not an excuse to slack off and settle for second best. Whether it's our character, our maturity, or our compassion for others, we should make every effort to grow in these areas.

The Christian life means growth over a lifetime in obeying the teachings of Scripture. Because we are joined to Jesus by faith, we have the resources we need to be upright in thought and virtuous in conduct. With the Lord's help and the encouragement of His people, we can aim for the goal of being holy in our lives.

Introduction for Youths

Topic: *Love My Enemy?*

Every small group has certain individuals who can be identified as "extra-grace people." They invariably demand extra grace on our part to accommodate their personality. Even in a Christian setting, they require a soft answer and patience. Maybe some people have come to mind as you read this. They are not enemies, just frustrating people who do not return the grace you extend toward them.

Part of the reason we have difficulty responding in love to those who have irritated us is that we don't want to appear like a doormat to others. Thus we become defensive instead of exhibiting the fruit of the Spirit. Neil Anderson answers this issue of defending ourselves in his seminar "Resolving Personal and Spiritual Conflicts." He says, "If you are wrong, you don't have a defense. If you are right, you don't need one!" Isn't it liberating to know that we don't have to respond in kind to extra-grace people?

Concepts for Children

Topic: *Jesus Preached about Loving Others*

1. Jesus told His followers that the rules in the Bible are important to follow.
2. Jesus said that God is pleased when His children obey His commands.
3. Jesus wants His followers to be kind even to mean people.
4. God's children should choose to love, rather than hate, those who are not nice.
5. Prayer is one way Jesus' followers can show concern for their enemies.

The Lesson Commentary

I. A CALL TO EXTREME RIGHTEOUSNESS: MATTHEW 5:17-20

A. Affirming the Importance of the Law: vss. 17-19

"Do not think that I have come to abolish the Law or the Prophets; I have not come to abolish them but to fulfill them. I tell you the truth, until heaven and earth disappear, not the smallest letter, not the least stroke of a pen, will by any means disappear from the Law until everything is accomplished. Anyone who breaks one of the least of these commandments and teaches others to do the same will be called least in the kingdom of heaven, but whoever practices and teaches these commands will be called great in the kingdom of heaven."

God's moral and ceremonial laws were given to help people love God and be compassionate to people. However, throughout Israel's history, these laws had often been misquoted and misapplied. Sadly, by Jesus' time, the religious leaders had turned the laws into a confusing mess of rules.

In the Sermon on the Mount, Jesus talked about a better way to understand God's law. Because of this, some of His antagonists falsely accused Him of trying to set aside the teachings of the Hebrew Scriptures (the Law and the Prophets, as they were commonly referred to in ancient times). Jesus countered by declaring that He did not stand in opposition to the Mosaic law. In fact, He was trying to bring people back to the law's original purpose.

Thus, Jesus did not speak against the law itself, but rather against the abuses and excesses to which it had been subjected. Likewise, His goal was not to set aside, negate, or annul God commands. Rather, Jesus came to fulfill the truth of the Old Testament. All that was written in the law pointed to Him, and everything He did underscored His deep commitment to it (Matt. 5:17).

"The Law" refers to the specific code of rules and regulations that God gave to Moses on Mount Sinai. The law was part of the covenant that set Israel apart as God's people. It governed their worship, their relationship to God, and their social relationships with one another. Though the law was given specifically to Israel, it rests on eternal moral principles that are consistent with God's character. Thus, it is a summary of fundamental and universal moral standards. It expresses the essence of what God requires of people.

When Jesus said "I tell you the truth" (Matt. 5:18), He was making a solemn statement. "The smallest letter" (the Hebrew letter *yodh*) and the "least stroke of a pen" (the slight extension on the Hebrew letter *daleth*) refer to the minutest part of the law. Jesus declared that as long as heaven and earth continued to exist, so would the smallest detail of God's Word until its purpose was achieved.

There were some in the crowds who loved to tell others what to do, even though they failed to live up to the law's commands. Jesus made it clear to these hypocrites that obeying God's laws is more important than just explaining them.

Thus, Jesus condemned those who set aside what they considered the least of the commandments of Scripture and taught others to do the same. Jesus declared that any of His followers who ever committed such an offense would be considered least in the divine Kingdom (vs. 19). In this case, the punishment fit the crime. Conversely, those who obeyed Scripture and taught others to do the same would have an important place in the Kingdom. The contrast between the two options could not be greater.

B. Affirming the Importance of Righteousness: vs. 20

"For I tell you that unless your righteousness surpasses that of the Pharisees and the teachers of the law, you will certainly not enter the kingdom of heaven."

The religious leaders of Israel were exacting and scrupulous in their efforts to follow their laws. It's understandable why many in Jesus' day would see the Pharisees and scribes as icons of virtue. But Jesus declared that even they were not sufficiently good to merit God's approval. In fact, a person's righteousness had to go well beyond that of the Jewish leaders. Unless a person did a better job at being religious, entrance into the kingdom of God would be denied (Matt. 5:20).

We might well ask ourselves how we can be more righteous than people like the Pharisees, who devoted their lives to learning and obeying the law. The answer is that we can have such righteousness through faith in Christ (Phil. 3:9). Moreover, real righteousness surpasses legalistic devotion in that it is not merely external rules-keeping. We can be right with God and enjoy His favor by submitting to Jesus in our heart.

II. RESPONDING TO EVIL: MATTHEW 5:38-42

A. The Sinful Way: vs. 38

"You have heard that it was said, 'Eye for eye, and tooth for tooth.'"

In the rest of Matthew 5, Jesus discussed how His followers were to surpass the religious leaders in righteousness. He dealt with anger (vss. 21-26), lust (vss. 27-30), divorce (vss. 31-32), vows (vss. 33-37), revenge (vss. 38-42), and loving enemies (vss. 43-48).

When Jesus said, "But I tell you" (vss. 22, 28, 32, 34, 39, 44), He was not doing away with the law or adding His own beliefs. Rather, He was clarifying why God instituted the law. For example, the Mosaic law taught a code of retribution known as *lex talionis*, a Latin phrase meaning "the law of the tooth." This is based on the maxim "an eye for an eye, and tooth for tooth" (vs. 38), which the law affirmed (Exod. 21:24; Lev. 24:20; Deut. 19:21). Although in our day this principle seems unnecessarily harsh, it was actually more lenient than the code of retribution practiced by many of Israel's neighbors.

During the Old Testament era, the principle of *lex talionis* helped to deter evil and limit retribution. For instance, if people knew that whatever they did to hurt someone would be done to them, this might make them hesitate before deliberately inflicting injury. Also, if one person put out the eye of another, the victim was not allowed to murder in retaliation. In other words, the punishment had to fit the crime. Such a limitation curbed the custom of blood feuding that was all too common in the ancient world.

This principle of retaliation was never intended to be implemented on a personal level, but appeared in Old Testament passages addressed to civil officials. Sadly, many people eventually reversed its limiting intent to such an extent that by Jesus' day some used it as a guideline for their personal relationships. Those who did so kept track of offenses and looked for an opportunity to retaliate.

B. The Godly Way: vss. 39-42

"But I tell you, Do not resist an evil person. If someone strikes you on the right cheek, turn to him the other also. And if someone wants to sue you and take your tunic, let him have your cloak as well. If someone forces you to go one mile, go with him two miles. Give to the one who asks you, and do not turn away from the one who wants to borrow from you."

Jesus sought to restore the legal standard to its original intent. He thus stated that instead of retaliating, His followers were not to resist at all (Matt. 5:39). Jesus supported this amazing command with four examples taken from the everyday life of believers.

The first example told believers who were slapped on the right cheek to offer the offender the other cheek as well. The mention of the right cheek possibly suggests that Jesus had in mind a backhanded slap, a particularly vicious kind of insult in that culture.

By this example, Jesus was telling His disciples not to seek revenge or retaliate. Rather than try to get even, they were to be loving, kind, and considerate. They were to show compassion to those who hated them, goodwill to those who spoke abusively to them, and patience to those who harassed them. Clearly, only God could enable believers to live in this way.

The second example is set in the court of law. If someone sued Jesus' followers for their tunic, they were to give the "cloak as well" (vs. 40). The tunic was a long undergarment of cotton or linen. The cloak was a heavier outer garment worn as a robe and used as a blanket at night. A person usually had only one cloak, and the law said it could not be taken (Exod. 22:26).

By this example, Jesus was urging His followers to be generous and sympathetic to those in need. If someone asked for food or water, they were to give it readily and willingly. Or if someone asked His disciples for other kinds of help, they were to respond freely and generously. Such responses required an attitude of humility on the part of believers.

The third example was drawn from Israel's experience with the occupying Roman army. Roman soldiers had the authority to seize civilians and force them to carry military equipment the length of one Roman mile. Those who were drafted for such a task did not have the luxury of saying no, but instead had to drop whatever they were doing and comply immediately. Obviously, the tendency would have been to obey only to the limit of the law. Jesus, however, urged His disciples to go two miles (Matt. 5:41).

The fourth example involved a loan. According to the law of Moses, a loan could be made to a fellow Israelite, but no interest could be charged (Exod. 22:25). Jesus' followers, however, were to give without any thought of return (Matt. 5:42).

It's helpful to remember that Jesus spoke in stark contrasts and strong hyper-boles (overstatements for the sake of emphasis) in order to stress that good should prevail over evil, grace over vengeance, and love over hatred. In the midst of this teaching, Jesus challenged His followers to be people of grace and integrity. He thus gave them several examples of ways that He expected them to surpass the religious leaders in virtue.

Although these four examples relate to a variety of situations drawn from human as well as divine law, they all require the believer to forgo certain rights. They also call on the follower of Jesus to go beyond the normal standard. The essential principle behind the commands is that of putting other people first.

III. RESPONDING TO OUR ENEMIES: MATTHEW 5:43-48

A. The Sinful Way: vs. 43

"You have heard that it was said, 'Love your neighbor and hate your enemy.'"

Leviticus 19:18 commanded God's people to love their neighbor. The Pharisees undercut the original intent of this law by asserting that they should love only those who love in return. Some even rationalized away this obligation by defining the concept of "neighbor" narrowly to include only the upright. They also said that Psalms 139:19-22 and 140:9-11 validated their desire to hate their enemies (Matt. 5:43). Clearly, such an attitude contradicted what God had revealed in the law.

B. The Godly Way: vss. 44-47

"But I tell you: Love your enemies and pray for those who persecute you, that you may be sons of your Father in heaven. He causes his sun to rise on the evil and the good, and sends rain on the righteous and the unrighteous. If you love those who love you, what reward will you get? Are not even the tax collectors doing that? And if you greet only your brothers, what are you doing more than others? Do not even pagans do that?"

Jesus commanded His followers to reject the popular misinterpretation of the law and replace it with an accurate understanding. For instance, Jesus urged the disciples to love their enemy as well as their neighbor and pray for anyone who mistreated them (Matt. 5:44). Like their Savior, Christ's disciples were to act in the best interests of those who treated them badly.

Verse 45 reveals that Christian love is to be a reflection of God's own love. The motive Jesus gave for obeying these principles was that His followers would be acting like their Father in heaven, who showered His kindness and blessings on all people regardless of who they were. This was the language of evidence. Believers were to act toward their enemies as the Father in heaven has acted toward us.

According to Jesus, those who love only those who love them follow a standard no higher than that of the tax collectors (vs. 46). These people were widely regarded as extortionists who enriched themselves at the expense of their neighbors. To say that someone was doing no more than a tax collector implied that the person's behavior was unrighteous and self-centered.

Jesus mentioned the custom of greeting one's neighbor because a typical greeting involved the pronouncement of a blessing (vs. 47). Jesus' contemporaries greeted one another with the word *shalom* [shah-LOAM]—a prayer for the bestowal of God's peace upon the recipient.

C. The Divine Standard: vs. 48

"Be perfect, therefore, as your heavenly Father is perfect."

The standard Jesus' followers were to adopt was that of God Himself. As His children, they were to reflect His image. The New Testament term rendered "perfect" (Matt. 5:48) can also be rendered "complete" or "having attained the end or purpose." In other words, Jesus was focusing on moral purity and spiritual maturity, which were demonstrated by the believer's willingness to heed God's commands.

Ultimately, our standard of behavior is the perfect example of Jesus Christ. His life and teaching shows that the call to perfection is a command to love as inclusively and completely as God does. Obviously obedience to such a command requires the transforming work of the Holy Spirit. We cannot love others as Christ does apart from the grace of God.

Discussion Questions

1. What was Jesus' intent with respect to the law?
2. What moral standard of righteousness was needed to enter the divine kingdom?
3. How did Jesus say His followers should respond to those who wronged them?
4. How is it possible for believers to love their enemies?
5. According to Matthew 5:48, in what sense does God want us to be perfect?

Contemporary Application

It's natural for us to feel angry, hurt, and sometimes bitter when others sin against us. The choice to forgive will not automatically cancel out these emotions. What, then, should we do?

First, we can begin by showing love to those who have hurt us, regardless of our feelings. It is possible to act lovingly toward an enemy even while we are struggling with the bitterness or anger we feel. Second, we should acknowledge such emotions to God and ask for His help. There is no need to hide such feelings from God, for He knows the thoughts and intents of our hearts even better than we do.

Third, we should entrust ourselves to the care of God. Jesus' words remind us that God is the only one who can ensure that true justice will be done. As long as our eyes are on the offense of the one who has hurt us, we will be drawn into the vortex of bitterness. But when our focus is on Jesus, we find both an example of forgiveness and the motivation to follow His example.

Concerning Treasures

DEVOTIONAL READING

Philippians 4:4-9

DAILY BIBLE READINGS

Monday November 19
Luke 6:27-36 Love Your Enemies

Tuesday November 20
Luke 6:37-42 Do Not Judge

Wednesday November 21
Luke 13:22-30 Enter through the Narrow Door

Thursday November 22
Romans 13:8-14 Love Fulfills the Law

Friday November 23
Romans 14:1-8 Welcome the Weak

Saturday November 24
Matthew 7:1-12 Ask, Search, and Knock

Sunday November 25
Matthew 7:13-29 Who Will Enter?

Scripture

Background Scripture: *Matthew 6*
Scripture Lesson: *Matthew 6:19-21, 25-34*
Key Verse: *"But seek first his kingdom and his righteousness, and all these things will be given to you as well. Therefore do not worry about tomorrow."* Matthew 6:33-34.
Key Verse for Children: *But seek first his kingdom and his righteousness, and all these things will be given to you as well."* Matthew 6:33.

Lesson Aim

To evaluate our priorities and plan ways to realign them with God's priorities.

Lesson Setting

Time: *A.D. 28*
Place: *Galilee*

Lesson Outline

Concerning Treasures

  I. Two Kinds of Treasure: Matthew 6:19-21
    A. Earthly Treasure: vs. 19
    B. Heavenly Treasure: vs. 20
    C. The Decisive Factor: vs. 21
 II. Two Kinds of Concerns: Matthew 6:25-34
    A. Anxiety about Life: vs. 25
    B. Our Value to God: vs. 26
    C. The Futility of Worry: vs. 27
    D. The Lesson from Nature: vss. 28-30
    E. God's Awareness of Our Needs: vss. 31-32
    F. Kingdom Priorities versus Future Concerns: vss. 33-34

Introduction for Adults

Topic: *Worrying Needlessly*

It's common knowledge that excessive and prolonged worrying is not good for our health. We also know that worrying can rob us of peace and contentment. It should come as no surprise, then, that Jesus told us not to worry. He saw it as an exercise in futility. How then can we stop worrying?

Many books and sermons on tape give us good practical advice. The simplest answer, of course, is to focus our attention on the Lord. When we start the day with praise and thanks to God as well as meditation on His Word, we are in good shape to deal with the problem of worrying.

It also helps to have some good friends. These would not be people who dream up more stuff for us to worry about, but rather those who are good listeners and who can draw us back to our resources in Christ. Occasionally, we all need encouragement to let go of our worries and give them to the Lord.

Introduction for Youths

Topic: *Hidden Treasures*

In his book *Come Before Winter*, Charles R. Swindoll writes, "I don't have many temptations to worship evil things. It's the good things that plague me. It isn't as difficult for me to reject something that is innately bad or wrong as it is to keep those good and wholesome things off the throne."

Although many teens try to meet the demands of living, they seem to pile up like unfolded laundry. Since each day has only 24 hours, Christian young people need to be selective. Meanwhile, their use of the time and energy that God gives them indicates where their priorities lie. Jesus' teaching in this week's lesson Scripture will help young people to understand how they can spend their time and energy in ways that have eternal value.

Concepts for Children

Topic: *Jesus Preached about God's Care*

1. Jesus said that it is much better to store up our treasures in heaven.
2. Jesus urged us not to worry about food, drink, or clothing, because life is much more than these things.
3. Jesus said that God will provide for us, especially because we are more valuable than birds or flowers.
4. Jesus urged us to put God's desire and work first in our lives.
5. God is like a loving parent who will provide for us at all times.

The Lesson Commentary

I. TWO KINDS OF TREASURE: MATTHEW 6:19-21

A. Earthly Treasure: vs. 19

"Do not store up for yourselves treasures on earth, where moth and rust destroy, and where thieves break in and steal."

The second half of Jesus' Sermon on the Mount begins with three don'ts and a do. First, He said, "Don't store up earthly treasures, don't worry about your life, and don't judge others" (Matt. 6:19—7:6). Then He said, "Do ask what you want of God" (7:7-12). The sermon comes to its conclusion with advice to stay away from false teaching and embrace Jesus' teaching (vss. 13-27).

In our age of consumerism and materialism, the first don't is terribly important for us to hear. Consider, for example, one bumper sticker's definition of success: "Those who have the most toys when they die, wins!" Jesus, however, taught that we should not measure life's value in terms of possessions that can be destroyed or stolen. After all, He indicated, fine clothes can be eaten by moths, metal jewelry and utensils can rust, and money and valuables can be stolen (6:19).

The wealthy religious professionals of Jesus' day apparently endorsed the notion that material riches were a sign of God's blessing. Consequently, Jesus' listeners who were poor might have asked, "Since we are poor, where do we stand with God?" Jesus, however, did not directly address that question, for His teaching about riches was quite different from that of the scribes and Pharisees.

We should note that in this discussion Jesus was not saying that money is inherently evil, or even that being rich is necessarily immoral. Rather, He was concerned about greed, which is the desire to acquire greater wealth no matter what. He was urging His followers to live contentedly with whatever they had, for they had chosen what is eternal and lasting.

B. Heavenly Treasure: vs. 20

"But store up for yourselves treasures in heaven, where moth and rust do not destroy, and where thieves do not break in and steal."

Scripture teaches that heaven is the dwelling place of God and the abode of His sanctuary (Ps. 102:19; Isa. 63:15). As God's dwelling place, heaven is not a cosmic shelter where the Lord isolates Himself from the earth. Rather, it is the divine workplace, where He sends blessings to His people and punishment on His enemies (Deut. 26:15; Ps. 11:4-7). A time is coming when what's above will no longer exist as we know it. As God once spread the heavenly tent, so He will wrap up the heavens like a scroll (Isa. 34:4). Then a new heaven and new earth will appear (65:17; 66:22).

Instead of hoarding, Jesus' followers were to invest their lives in accumulating heavenly riches (Matt. 6:20). Perhaps Jesus was referring to rewards from God for such things as serving others in love and forgiving those who have inflicted harm. In heaven there is no loss; the treasures stockpiled there are safe.

Storing treasures in heaven is not limited to giving money to a local church or other Christian ministry. It is also accomplished by all kinds of acts of obedience to God. There is a sense in which devoting our lives to God's will and work is like investing in heaven. Of course, we should seek to please God not only in our servicing but also by growing in Christlikeness.

C. The Decisive Factor: vs. 21

"For where your treasure is, there your heart will be also."

With penetrating insight, Jesus declared, "Where your treasure is, there your heart will be also" (Matt. 6:21). By "heart" He did not mean the physical organ in our body. Rather, Jesus spoke metaphorically about the center of mental and spiritual life. In contemporary thinking, the heart is the inner self that thinks, feels, and decides.

Scripture often depicts the heart as the seat of one's true character or personality. One's heart can be pure or evil (Jer. 3:17; Matt. 5:8), earnest or rigid (Exod. 4:21; Col. 3:22), and mature or rebellious (Ps. 101:2; Jer. 5:23). Because people speak and act from the heart, they are to guard it well (Prov. 4:23; Matt. 15:18-19). The most important duty of anyone is to love God with the whole heart (Matt. 22:37).

People who spend their time accumulating earthly possessions have their interests anchored in temporal concerns. Their self-serving interests and greedy desires block their spiritual vision. In contrast, people who spend their time storing up spiritual treasures are focused on eternal matters.

In light of the Lord's teaching, we all should ask ourselves, "Where is my heart?" It would be sad if we realized that our heart was locked up in the vault at our bank downtown. But in that case, it would also be encouraging to realize that it's not too late to change our financial plan, for God can radically change our life priorities (1 Tim. 6:6-19).

II. TWO KINDS OF CONCERNS: MATTHEW 6:25-34

A. Anxiety about Life: vs. 25

"Therefore I tell you, do not worry about your life, what you will eat or drink; or about your body, what you will wear. Is not life more important than food, and the body more important than clothes?"

We can imagine Jesus' listeners on the hillside wondering what would happen to them if they chose to serve God rather than money. Perhaps they also fretted over whether their basic material needs would go unmet if they no longer were zealous to earn money. Jesus' answer, in effect, was not to worry about such things (Matt. 6:25). This is the second of Jesus' three don'ts in the Sermon on the Mount.

Worry, or anxiety, is characterized by such emotions as fear and distress. External circumstances or internal causes can bring it on. When left unchecked, worry can decrease our awareness of things, diminish our ability to cope with life's traumas, and leave us feeling isolated.

Perhaps with this awareness in mind, Jesus told His followers not to fret about maintaining their life by getting food, or about protecting their bodies by getting clothing. Furthermore, the Lord rhetorically asked, "Is not life more important than food, and the body more than clothes?" In other words, by worrying about food and clothing, the people were focusing on insignificant things. Jesus wanted His followers to be focused on what really matters.

B. Our Value to God: vs. 26

"Look at the birds of the air; they do not sow or reap or store away in barns, and yet your heavenly Father feeds them. Are you not much more valuable than they?"

Despite His admonitions, Jesus recognized that His disciples would still be tempted to worry. Thus, He used examples from the natural world to reassure them that God would indeed meet their needs.

Christ likely pointed to some common barn sparrows flying in the sky as He stated that these creatures did not plant or harvest crops, nor stockpile grain in storehouses, and yet the heavenly Father amply supplied their need for food (Matt. 6:26). All about them, the birds could find the insects that they needed to eat—all provided by God. He cared for these little creatures, and so He would certainly provide for the needs of His people, who were of greater value to Him.

C. The Futility of Worry: vs. 27

"Who of you by worrying can add a single hour to his life?"

Some think Matthew 6:27 should be translated as it appears in the NIV, where the emphasis is on time. Others think the phrase "add a single hour to his life" should be rendered "add a single cubit to his height." (A cubit was a unit of measure roughly equal to 18 inches.) In either case, Jesus' point is essentially the same. Worrying is pointless, for it doesn't change anything.

The Bible teaches that because of God's love and unlimited power, we don't have to worry. The implication is that only God can run the world; thus being anxious about things not under our control is senseless. In fact, a preoccupation with ourselves is a form of self-reliance. It's no wonder that when we seek anything other than God as the first priority in our lives, the meeting of our needs is not assured.

D. The Lesson from Nature: vss. 28-30

"And why do you worry about clothes? See how the lilies of the field grow. They do not labor or spin. Yet I tell you that not even Solomon in all his splendor was dressed like one of these. If that is how God clothes the grass of the field, which is here today and tomorrow is thrown into the fire, will he not much more clothe you, O you of little faith?"

Jesus asked His followers why they worried about having clothes to wear. He probably pointed to some lilies growing in the nearby fields as He asked His audience to consider how such delicate flowers grew. These plants did not "labor or spin" (Matt. 6:28) to obtain protective covering; rather, God graciously supplied their glorious color and texture. Solomon the son of David was very wealthy and could afford to dress in the most magnificent clothing available. And yet the lilies carpeting the fields of Palestine were more gloriously dressed than Solomon ever was (vs. 29).

Jesus next directed the attention of His followers to the field of grass surrounding them. The life span of such vegetation was short, and grass was of little value. For instance, people in Bible times would use grass as a cheap and abundant source of fuel to heat their clay ovens. Yet God so decorated these seemingly insignificant plants with beautiful flowers. Jesus asked rhetorically, "Will [the Father] not much more clothe you, O you of little faith?" (vs. 30).

Here Jesus was raising a serious charge. The people lacked faith. This was the first time He mentioned faith in His sermon. He knew that faith is the antidote to being consumed by possessions (vss. 19-23). Faith keeps us from serving money (vs. 24). Faith also protects us from worry (vss. 25-30).

By faith we are compelled to answer *yes* to all the questions Jesus asked. Faith affirms that God will provide our necessities. Faith agrees that we are more valuable than birds and lilies. Faith rises up as a bulwark against worry.

E. God's Awareness of Our Needs: vss. 31-32

"So do not worry, saying, 'What shall we eat?' or 'What shall we drink?' or 'What shall we wear?' For the pagans run after all these things, and your heavenly Father knows that you need them."

Having concluded His nature examples, Jesus returned to directly urging His listeners not to worry. They did not need to wonder about where they would get their food and clothing (Matt. 6:31). To do so was to be like the pagans (vs. 32).

It should come as no surprise that the unsaved are given to excessive worry. Day after day they obsess over where they will obtain the basics of life. Such anxiety indicates their focus is on themselves, not God and other people. In contrast, Jesus' followers can rest in the knowledge that their heavenly Father is aware of and will provide for their needs.

These verses make up one of the most frequently cited passages of Scripture in discussions involving money and work. Sadly, there are some who insist that Jesus was against earning money and that He considered work a distraction from things that really matter. Nothing could be further from the truth. Jesus was condemning worry, not work. He called us to make God the object of our faith, for He is the one who ultimately supplies our needs. There are many ways that God provides for us, but perhaps the most common is through everyday work.

F. Kingdom Priorities versus Future Concerns: vss. 33-34

"But seek first his kingdom and his righteousness, and all these things will be given to you as well. Therefore do not worry about tomorrow, for tomorrow will worry about itself. Each day has enough trouble of its own."

Jesus told His followers to value God's kingdom and righteousness above anything else (Matt. 6:33). In fact, God's kingdom is defined by His righteousness. The latter means that God acts justly and fairly in all His decisions and actions (Dan. 9:14).

God declares as righteous those who acknowledge their sin and put their faith in Christ for forgiveness and eternal life (Mark 2:17; Luke 18:14). In contrast, the unsaved have a false sense of righteousness, for they trust in their moral accomplishments to make others think they are living in accordance with God's holy standard (Matt. 23:28; Luke 18:9).

Thus, rather than assert their own goodness, the life goal of God's people should be to submit to His rule and to call others to do the same. As they do, "all these things" (Matt. 6:33)—meaning food and clothing and other items they need—will be given to them as well.

In light of these truths, Jesus urged His followers not to be filled with distress about what lay ahead. He explained that "tomorrow will worry about itself" (vs. 34). By this Jesus meant that each new day brings with it plenty of anxiety-producing situations, and undue worry about what might happen is pointless. If God's people cannot control the present with its problems, what point is there in being preoccupied with the future? We cannot control our happiness; that is in God's hands.

Discussion Questions

1. Why is it far wiser to store up treasures in heaven rather than on earth?
2. Why is our heart an accurate indicator of what we treasure most?
3. What is worry, and why is it futile?
4. What lessons about trust can we learn by observing nature?
5. What is the difference between worry and proper concern for the future?

Contemporary Application

Before the Israelites entered Canaan, Joshua challenged them to decide whom they would worship (Josh. 24:15). Likewise, every day we choose to serve either God or the world system. Our "little" choices quickly harden, like cement, into habits. Every self-centered decision gives Satan a little more control. However, each time we choose God's will, we make a deposit in our heavenly bank account.

In the financial world investors use money to make more money. In a sense the Spirit is like a broker who is continually reinvesting God's resources in His children's lives. God first invested in us when He sent Christ to buy us back from Satan's kingdom. Now the resulting "dividends" include the fruit of the Spirit (Gal. 5:22-23).

Since everything we have belongs to God, we are stewards, obligated to use our possessions, time, and energy as investments for our Master. Every act of faithful stewardship adds to our spiritual treasure. Where, then, is our heart focused? Do our spiritual lenses need cleaning? Are we using our resources to invest in God's kingdom? Where have we stockpiled our treasures? The answers to these questions indicate that the contents of our character matter more to God than the size of our stock portfolio.

Do Unto Others

Scripture

Background Scripture: *Matthew 7*
Scripture Lesson: *Matthew 7:1-5, 12-20*
Key Verse: *"So in everything, do to others what you would
have them do to you, for this sums up the Law and the
Prophets."* Matthew 7:12.
Scripture Lesson for Children: *Matthew 7:12-20*
Key Verse for Children: *"So in everything, do to others
what you would have them do to you."* Matthew 7:12.

Lesson Aim

To recognize the value of treating others the way we
want them to treat us.

Lesson Setting

Time: A.D. *28*
Place: *Galilee*

Lesson Outline

Do Unto Others

I. The Two Standards: Matthew 7:1-5
    A. *The Admonition against Being Judgmental: vss. 1-2*
    B. *The Admonition to Deal with Ourselves First:
       vss. 3-5*
II. The Two Ways: Matthew 7:12-14
    A. *The Golden Rule: vs. 12*
    B. *The Narrow Gate: vss. 13-14*
III. The Two Fruits: Matthew 7:15-20
    A. *The Warning: vs. 15*
    B. *The Indicators: vss. 16-20*

Introduction for Adults
Topic: *Relating to Others*

Have you ever tried to remove a speck of dirt or a tiny insect from your eye by yourself? It's hard because you can't see well enough to do it. Jesus said that often some things in our lives blur our spiritual vision. Without clear vision, we cannot give help to others, we cannot choose the right moral path, and we cannot discern what is true from what is false.

Jesus made it clear that blurry spiritual vision results from pride, self-righteousness, hypocrisy, and a failure to love others. How important it is, then, to have our spiritual eyes free of obstructions.

Sin clouds our judgment and keeps us from following God's ways. The first step in obtaining clearer spiritual vision is to confess our sin. When we come to Jesus in repentance and faith, we are asking Him to give us clearer vision. The moment we make this our prayer request, our relations with others will improve.

Introduction for Youths
Topic: *Take the High Road*

We sometimes talk about people taking the moral high road, while others take the ethical low road. In a similar vein, Jesus talked about following either the narrow path or the wide thoroughfare. He meant by this that genuine meaning in life is found when we make the right choice to follow Him.

We know, of course, that many young people don't like to be hemmed in by moral restrictions. In fact, some teens want to be free to "do their own thing" (as the saying goes). Many youth, as a result of being flush with a sense of newfound freedom, impulsively make foolish decisions that scar them for the rest of their lives.

If young people are not careful, they might end up following the wide road that leads to destruction. The question is, "Who controls the teens' life, Jesus Christ or self?" On the surface, Jesus might appear to offer a boring existence; however, the life He gives is full and abundant. Thus, teens should not be fooled by the world's spacious and easy road. It leads to ruin.

Concepts for Children
Topic: *Jesus Preached about Doing Good*

1. Jesus told His followers to treat others the way they wanted to be treated.
2. Jesus warned that the easy road of life leads to sadness, while the more difficult road leads to joy.
3. Jesus also warned about people who said they were from God but really were not.
4. Jesus noted that what we say and do shows whether we really love and obey God.
5. God is pleased when we are kind to others and do what we can to help those in need.

The Lesson Commentary

I. THE TWO STANDARDS: MATTHEW 7:1-5

A. The Admonition against Being Judgmental: vss. 1-2

"Do not judge, or you too will be judged. For in the same way you judge others, you will be judged, and with the measure you use, it will be measured to you."

In teaching the principles of the divine kingdom, Jesus touched on several factors that can sour our relations with others. One of our most prevalent ills is a critical spirit. We are prone to be judgmental because it makes us feel superior to those we presume to judge.

Jesus said that those who love Him and His kingdom are marked by the absence of such a critical spirit (Matt. 7:1). Here He was condemning unfair, hypocritical judgment. He was referring to people who magnified the faults of others while excusing their own shortcomings. They were self-appointed experts in evaluating the motives and conducts of others. Sadly, however, they failed to recognize their own bad habits and behavior patterns. It's no wonder Jesus censured them.

Verse 1, of course, does not mean that we countenance sinful, harmful deeds, for we are called to live by God's holy moral standards. He wants us to develop strong spiritual discernment so that we will not be led into sin (Heb. 5:14). There is a proper place, then, to speak up against unrighteousness. The challenge for us is to speak the truth in love and bear one another's burdens at the same time (Gal. 6:2; Eph. 4:15).

Jesus may have been quoting a proverb of His day when He made the statement recorded in Matthew 7:2. If we are guilty of a judgmental spirit, God will be as hard on us as we are on others. In fact, He will use the same standard of evaluation by which we have evaluated others. The only way out of this dilemma is to repent of our sin and leave judging to the Lord, who alone is impartial and upright in His assessments.

B. The Admonition to Deal with Ourselves First: vss. 3-5

"Why do you look at the speck of sawdust in your brother's eye and pay no attention to the plank in your own eye? How can you say to your brother, 'Let me take the speck out of your eye,' when all the time there is a plank in your own eye? You hypocrite, first take the plank out of your own eye, and then you will see clearly to remove the speck from your brother's eye."

Those who are quick to find fault with others often are totally unaware of how hypocritical they are in their evaluations. They insist on setting others straight: "Let me take the speck out of your eye" (Matt. 7:4). But they are oblivious to their own imperfections. They self-righteously assume that they have no faults of their own, even though they may be guilty of the same things for which they condemn others.

To emphasize this point, Jesus made a ludicrous comparison between a speck of sawdust and a plank. The Greek word translated "plank" (vs. 3) refers to the huge branch of a tree or a massive piece of timber. In contrast, the word rendered "speck" refers to a tiny twig or a woodchip from a piece of timber.

Was Jesus speaking literally when He told His followers to "take the plank out of your own eye" (vs. 5)? No, Jesus was using a customary teaching method called hyperbole (that is, intentional exaggeration) to make a point. He frequently spoke in that manner, perhaps to hold His listeners' attention, to touch their imagination, or to show a bit of humor.

Those who are judgmental are quick to spot the tiniest imperfections in others. Yet they are so blinded by their own glaring faults that they cannot possibly see well enough to remove their associate's minor imperfections. The Savior's point is that people tended to exaggerate the flaws of others and overlook their own glaring problems. Jesus' admonition was that the hypocrites get their own lives in order before worrying about the lives of others.

II. The Two Ways: Matthew 7:12-14

A. The Golden Rule: vs. 12

"So in everything, do to others what you would have them do to you, for this sums up the Law and the Prophets."

In Matthew 7:7-11, Jesus taught His disciples to pray when they had legitimate needs. He said that God is like a concerned father who loves his children, and who would provide the good things they requested. Thus, when believers went to the Lord in prayer, they could rest assured that He was right there attentively listening to their petitions and ready to respond to their requests.

Verse 12 is a concluding statement to the whole middle section of the Sermon on the Mount. Back in 5:17-20 we read about Jesus fulfilling the Law and the Prophets, and in 7:12 we read about the Law and Prophets again. All the moral instructions Jesus gave between these two points in His sermon are applications of a simple rule.

That maxim, known as the Golden Rule, is as follows: "Do to others what you would have them do to you." Behind this statement is the realization that we like to be valued and appreciated by others.

Jesus declared that the Golden Rule—when lived out on a consistent basis—fulfilled the Law and the Prophets. For instance, we like to be loved, treated with respect, and forgiven when we do wrong. These things (and more) we should actively be doing to others—loving, respecting, and forgiving them. It's easy to see how this approach to life sums up the Law and Prophets, that is, the entire Old Testament.

Others have noted that the Golden Rule is found in negative form in the ethical teachings of ancient Greeks, Romans, Jews, Hindus, Buddhists, and Confucianists. Among ancient non-Christian thinkers the Golden Rule went something like this: "Do not do to others what you do not want done to you." This formulation is restrictive in nature and premised on the fear of retaliation.

Jesus, however, made the truth a positive obligation, one that was inclusive, not exclusive, in nature. It is based on the generosity, forbearance, and forgiveness of God. Believers were to follow the example of their heavenly Father in the hope that others whom they treated kindly would respond with kindness.

B. The Narrow Gate: vss. 13-14

"Enter through the narrow gate. For wide is the gate and broad is the road that leads to destruction, and many enter through it. But small is the gate and narrow the road that leads to life, and only a few find it."

Jesus gave a graphic picture of two ways of life. One He called the narrow gate and road, and the other He called the wide gate and road (Matt. 7:13-14). The restricted passage leads to life, while the unrestricted passage leads to destruction.

In ancient times city gates were massive wooden doors in a town wall through which traffic passed. Such gates were often reinforced with bronze or iron to provide greater security. They were opened during the day to allow the citizens to come and go, but they were closed at night as a safety measure. And in the event of an attack, the gates were shut and barred to keep out the enemy.

Perhaps while looking at the crowds gathered before Him (vs. 28), Jesus noted that the narrow gate—the one that led to eternal life—was rather small and the road connected with it was constricted. Because of this few people ever found themselves traveling down this path. In other words, a smaller number of people turned to the Savior in faith for eternal life.

Jesus stated that the broad gate—the one that led to destruction—was quite wide and the road connected with it was spacious. It had ample room for the droves of people making their way along its easy, gliding path. The point is that a larger number of people reject the Savior and thus experience eternal separation from Him.

Throughout life people are faced with making decisions concerning whom they will marry, where they will live and work, and what they will buy. More important than any other decision they make is the one concerning eternal life. Will they choose the path of life or the path of ruin? While it might be more popular to choose destruction, picking deliverance through faith in Christ is far wiser.

III. THE TWO FRUITS: MATTHEW 7:15-20

A. The Warning: vs. 15

"Watch out for false prophets. They come to you in sheep's clothing, but inwardly they are ferocious wolves."

False prophets led God's people astray in the Old Testament. They were still around in Jesus' time, and they are also present today (2 Pet. 2:1-3). They masquerade themselves as angels of light and pretend to speak for God (2 Cor. 11:14). But what they do and say reflects the thoughts and actions of Satan (1 Tim. 4:1).

False prophets disguise themselves so cleverly that they look like humble, obedient sheep. But in reality they are ferocious wolves (Matt. 7:15). The Savior warned His followers to beware of those whose words sound religious but who are motivated by money, fame, or power. Believers can detect these frauds because in their teaching they minimize Christ and glorify themselves.

B. The Indicators: vss. 16-20

"By their fruit you will recognize them. Do people pick grapes from thornbushes, or figs from thistles? Likewise every good tree bears good fruit, but a bad tree bears bad fruit. A good tree cannot bear bad fruit, and a bad tree cannot bear good fruit. Every tree that does not bear good fruit is cut down and thrown into the fire. Thus, by their fruit you will recognize them."

Jesus turned in His sermon to the contrast between evil expression and good expression. Drawing comparisons with nature, Jesus taught that people with evil in their hearts naturally say evil things; likewise, people with good in their hearts naturally say good things. Jesus meant for His people to have and to express goodness because of their faith in Him.

Jesus drew a comparison from the fruit industry to make His point about expressing oneself. Orchards and vineyards were common sights in ancient Palestine. The people loved such fruits as figs, grapes, olives, oranges, and pomegranates.

The Savior reminded His hearers that good (healthy) trees never bear bad fruit and bad (unhealthy) trees never bear good fruit. Similarly, thornbushes don't bear figs and briers don't bear grapes. These things are impossible because they would be contrary to the laws of nature. Similar laws govern morality. Good people express themselves in good ways and evil people express themselves in evil ways (Matt. 7:16-18).

Ancient farming practices form the backdrop for Jesus' comment in verse 19. There were times when certain plants or trees failed to yield any fruit due to diseases, locust attacks, and other pests, such as mice, worms, fruit bats, and weeds. These plants or trees were not allowed to remain in the soil. Farmers eventually uprooted or chopped down and burned the ones that yielded worthless fruit. The same thing could be said of the spiritual realm.

Jesus again emphasized that religious charlatans could be recognized by the fruits they produced. Genuine believers produced spiritual fruit that was acceptable, while imposters produced spiritual fruit that was unacceptable (vs. 20). The Savior's teaching in this passage gives us at least two practical truths. First, God must change people's hearts before they can become truly good individuals. Second, speech and other behaviors are indicators of the state of a person's heart.

Discussion Questions

1. What kind of judgment was Jesus condemning?
2. What did Jesus say summed up the Law and the Prophets?
3. What characterizes the narrow gate and the broad gate?
4. What was Jesus' intent in mentioning healthy trees and sickly trees?
5. Why is it important for us to be able to recognize spiritual frauds?
6. What do the words coming from our mouths indicate about what's in our hearts?

Contemporary Application

Matthew 7:12 is perhaps the point around which this week's lesson revolves. Jesus said we should treat others as they want us to treat them. It's not very difficult to refrain from harming others, but it's much more difficult to take the initiative in doing something good for them. This verse advocates showing kindness and mercy perhaps because it reflects the goodness and love that God shows to us every day.

Consider how such an attitude can transform the way we relate to others. We will be far less inclined to be judgmental toward them. Instead, we will focus on examining our own motives and conduct. By evaluating ourselves first, we will be more inclined to lovingly forgive and help our family, neighbors, and co-workers.

Having a kind and merciful heart means that we will want to choose the path that leads to life, rather than the road that leads to destruction. We affirm that believing in Jesus is the only way to heaven, for He alone died for our sins and enables us to be justified in God's sight. The Christian life, of course, is more than making a profession of faith. It also involves what we say and how we act.

It's no wonder, then, that Jesus urged us to consider the beliefs and behavior of people. For example, do they teach false doctrine or God's Word? Also, are they characterized by moral purity or impurity? Moreover do they exalt themselves or the Lord? Answering these questions can help us examine the motives of self-proclaimed religious teachers, the direction of their lives, and the outcome of their actions.

This does not mean we should have witch-hunts that lead to throwing out Sunday school teachers, pastors, and other Christian workers who are less than perfect. After all, every one of us is subject to sin. It therefore behooves us to show the same mercy to others that we expect for ourselves. This last point nicely captures the thought behind the Golden Rule—"So in everything, do to others what you would have them do to you, for this sums up the Law and the Prophets."

Light for All People

The Servant's Mission

DEVOTIONAL READING

Isaiah 49:8-13

DAILY BIBLE READINGS

Monday December 3
Isaiah 1:1-9 God's Children Have Rebelled

Tuesday December 4
Isaiah 1:10-20 Do Justice, Not Empty Rituals

Wednesday December 5
Isaiah 2:1-5 An Age of Peace

Thursday December 6
Isaiah 12 Give Thanks to the Lord

Friday December 7
Isaiah 14:1-8 Compassion for God's People

Saturday December 8
Isaiah 11:1-9 The Branch from David's Line

Sunday December 9
Isaiah 11:10-16 The Remnant's Second Chance

Scripture

Background Scripture: *Isaiah 49:1-7*

Scripture Lesson: *Isaiah 49:1-6*

Key Verse: *[The LORD] says: "It is too small a thing for you to be my servant to restore the tribes of Jacob and bring back those of Israel I have kept. I will also make you a light for the Gentiles, that you may bring my salvation to the ends of the earth."* Isaiah 49:6.

Scripture Lesson for Children: *Isaiah 49:6; Luke 1:26-38*

Key Verse for Children: *The angel answered, "The Holy Spirit will come upon you, and the power of the Most High will overshadow you. So the holy one to be born will be called the Son of God."* Luke 1:35.

Lesson Aim

To explore ways to share the Gospel with people from other national and cultural groups.

Lesson Setting

Time: *740–700 B.C.*

Place: *Judah*

Lesson Outline

The Servant's Mission

    I. A Vessel for God's Glory: Isaiah 49:1-4

        A. The Servant's Call: vs. 1

        B. The Servant's Preparation: vs. 2

        C. The Servant's Purpose: vs. 3

        D. The Servant's Trust in God: vs. 4

    II. An Instrument of Blessing: Isaiah 49:5-6

        A. To the Tribes of Jacob: vs. 5

        B. To the Gentiles: vs. 6

Introduction for Adults

Topic: *The Gift of Light*

Depending on what we are doing, light can be either a help or a hindrance. We need good light to repair our glasses and remove a splinter. But we prefer darkness when we are trying to hide something.

In spiritual and moral terms, the world is shrouded in darkness because people have rejected the Lord. Thankfully, the world is not as dark as it could possibly be, for God restrains evil. Nevertheless, conflicts arise in our lives and in society that often are a battle between light and darkness.

As we approach this Christmas season, many of us will celebrate it using different kinds of lights. This is because they somehow sparkle and lift up our spirits. But until we allow the light of Jesus to shine in our hearts, the inner chambers of our soul will remain in darkness.

Introduction for Youths

Topic: *Mission Possible!*

Every play in a football game is a mission for success. On the chalkboard everyone blocks his opponent and we score a touchdown. But in the real game the touchdown mission succeeds far less frequently because people keep getting in the way. Our blockers don't connect, our runners get tackled, and our quarterback gets sacked.

Long ago God used Isaiah the prophet to reveal His game plan (so to speak) for us. Seven hundred years before Jesus was born, the Lord declared what Jesus would be like and what He would do for us. The fulfillment of this prophecy is one of the strongest building blocks of our faith.

God's eternal plan has been to make redemption possible through faith in Christ. And the Lord wants us, as His spiritual children, not only to believe in Jesus but also to share the message of salvation with those who have never heard it. This is possible, not in our strength, but rather in the grace and power of God.

Concepts for Children

Topic: *God's Promise to Mary*

1. God's desire is to bring salvation to all people.
2. An angel from God told Mary she would have a son, whom she would name Jesus.
3. This child would be great, and His rule would have no end.
4. The angel said this child would be called the Son of God.
5. Mary wanted to do whatever God said.
6. God is pleased when we obey Him, too.

The Lesson Commentary

I. A Vessel for God's Glory: Isaiah 49:1-4

A. The Servant's Call: vs. 1

Listen to me, you islands; hear this, you distant nations: Before I was born the LORD called me; from my birth he has made mention of my name.

This is the first of nine lessons from Isaiah's prophecy. Five lessons center on God's sending the Messiah to bring justice, righteousness, and peace, and four lessons focus on God's deliverance and His response to those who turn to Him in repentance and faith.

Isaiah's name means "The LORD saves." From Isaiah 1:1 we learn that he ministered in and around Jerusalem as a prophet to Judah during the reigns of four Judean kings (from 740–681 B.C.): Uzziah, Jotham, Ahaz, and Hezekiah. Isaiah prophesied during the period of the divided kingdom and condemned the empty ritualism and idolatry of his day.

Isaiah foresaw that Sennacherib's effort to take Jerusalem would fail. The prophet also predicted that the Lord would heal Hezekiah's critical illness. Isaiah foresaw the coming Babylonian captivity of Judah because of the nation's departure from the Lord. And long before Cyrus, king of Persia, appeared on the scene, Isaiah named him as Judah's deliverer from Babylonian captivity.

Isaiah made prophecies about the Messiah. In fact, the centerpiece of Isaiah's prophecies is his depiction of the Messiah as the slain lamb of God (chap. 53). Isaiah also spoke much about the grace of God toward Israel.

Whereas the first part of Isaiah (chaps. 1—35) focuses on God's judgment on Israel by Assyria, the second part (chaps. 40—66) concerns the remnant's return from exile in Babylon in the remote future. Chapters 36—39 form a historical bridge between these two sections. This passage records the fulfillment of Isaiah's predictions that the Lord would judge Judah by bringing the Assyrian army to the gates of Jerusalem and then would judge the invaders by destroying them there.

In Isaiah 42:1-9, the prophet spoke about a coming Servant, namely, the Messiah. This Servant of the Lord would bring justice and salvation to the people. In 42:10—48:22, we find prophecies on various subjects. Condemnation on the people's sin is one subject. The promise of liberation from exile is another. But perhaps the most common subject in these chapters is the contrast between the powerless idols of Babylon and the all-powerful God of Israel. This part of the book ends with a call to leave Babylon.

This week's lesson Scripture is the second of the four "Servant Songs." Here we find Isaiah proclaiming a glorious future because of the ministry of the Lord's Servant.

Some consider the Servant to represent Israel as a collective, namely, an ideal Israel that is fully submissive to the will of God. Others say the Servant represents a corporate personality of sorts, where an individual (like a king or father figure) represents Israel as a nation.

Despite the possible attractiveness of these views, the one with the most merit is that the Servant represents a historical individual who acts as a representative of God's people. This person is more than just an obedient follower of God. The Lord called and empowered Him to carry out a unique mission, one that fulfilled God's eternal purposes in a significant way. Thus, the Servant of God is the Messiah. He would deliver the people of God—not only from their enemies but also from their sinful condition.

Isaiah 49:1 reveals that before the Servant, the Messiah, was born, God had chosen Him to bring the light of the Gospel (namely, the message of salvation) to the world. Clearly, the Servant's mission was not a self-created one, but rather a uniquely God-crafted assignment. His work would affect far-off lands, referred to as "islands" and "distant nations." The language of the verse suggests that God would be with His Servant in whatever He did. Because of God's blessing on the Servant, He was assured of unqualified success in His mission.

God always intended the Gospel to be for all people, whether Jews or Gentiles. This is reflected in God's promise to Abraham that through him all nations would be blessed (Gen. 18:18). This pledge came true in Christ. He now calls the church to shine His light on those who are in darkness so that they might hear the truth and be saved.

B. The Servant's Preparation: vs. 2

He made my mouth like a sharpened sword, in the shadow of his hand he hid me; he made me into a polished arrow and concealed me in his quiver.

God not only called His Servant, but also completely and perfectly provided Him with spiritual equipment for His ministry. Using graphic metaphors, the Servant described each part of His preparation.

The penetrating character of the Servant's message is compared to "a sharpened sword" (Isa. 49:2) and "a polished arrow." The imagery is that the Servant's ministry would be powerful and true. In fact, His messages would be so powerful that they would cut through every defense. By speaking the words of God, the Servant would accomplish the purpose for which God had called Him. Also, in declaring the message of God to people, the Servant would bring honor and delight to the Lord.

The sword of the Servant was hidden in His hand and His arrow was concealed in His quiver. This suggests that the Servant would be revealed for action at just the right time. In fact, His coming would be timed according to the plan of God, who loves all nations. This last point reminds us that Jesus was under His Father's continual care. The Lord's Servant did not trust His own strength, but rather in God to meet His needs. Even when Jesus hung on the cross, He was doing the Father's will.

C. The Servant's Purpose: vs. 3

He said to me, "You are my servant, Israel, in whom I will display my splendor."

Originally, God made the nation of Israel holy and set apart from the Gentile cultures, which were filled with idolatry and immorality. And unlike their neighbors, the Israelites were strongly monotheistic. In other words, they worshiped the one true God, and no one else. This distinction was supposed to serve as a magnet to draw the other nations to God. Tragically, however, things didn't turn out that way.

Whereas God intended His people to be a light to the nations, Gentiles became despised among the Israelites. And in the struggle to remain pure from the false religions of their neighbors, the ancient Israelites became elitist and racist. After the Israelites drifted from Yahweh, He ironically used the Gentile nations to discipline His people and bring them back to Him.

The naming of the Servant as Israel does not undercut the view that Jesus is the Servant. God ordained a servant role for Israel, but the nation largely failed at it. So Jesus came as the ideal "Israel" and perfectly fulfilled the role of the Servant. Thus, shortly before His death He could declare to God, "I have brought you glory on earth by completing the work you gave me to do" (John 17:4). The reference to "Israel" (Isa. 49:3), then, is not to the nation as it was but as it should have been.

Though national Israel fell far short of doing what God originally intended, the Messiah perfectly accomplished the Lord's redemptive plan. When people saw the Servant, they witnessed God's "splendor" (Isa. 49:3). Jesus was so "full of grace and truth" (John 1:14) that those who walked with Him could say, "We have seen his glory, the glory of the One and Only, who came from the Father."

Hebrews 1:3 says that Jesus radiates the glory of God and bears the impress of His nature. As the Servant of the Lord, Jesus also maintains the existence of the universe and bears it along to its God-ordained conclusion. Christ truly is the perfect revelation of the Father's will and glory!

D. The Servant's Trust in God: vs. 4

But I said, "I have labored to no purpose; I have spent my strength in vain and for nothing. Yet what is due me is in the LORD'S hand, and my reward is with my God."

Isaiah 49:4 reveals that the Servant felt as if He had "labored to no purpose." The text gives the impression that the Servant was completely worn out from toiling so hard. Despite all His efforts, it seemed as if His time had been wasted and His strength had been spent for nothing.

Though conflict seems to lurk beneath the Servant's words in verse 4, God would widen, not narrow, His mission. No longer would the message of hope be limited to the Jews. God would also give His Servant as a "light for the Gentiles" (vs. 6). In this way, the Jewish rejection of the divine message would lead to the inclusion of both Jews and Gentiles into the restorative purposes of God. Through His Servant, the Messiah, God would proclaim "salvation to the ends of the earth."

Perhaps this is why, even in the midst of disappointment, the Servant could express faith and hope. He knew that He had been serving the Lord, not people, and that He would leave His work in God's hands. The Servant announced He could do this because He trusted God to be just and to give Him the reward He desired for all His strenuous labor (vs. 4).

II. AN INSTRUMENT OF BLESSING: ISAIAH 49:5-6

A. To the Tribes of Jacob: vs. 5

And now the LORD says—he who formed me in the womb to be his servant to bring Jacob back to him and gather Israel to himself, for I am honored in the eyes of the LORD and my God has been my strength—

Isaiah 49:5 echoes verse 1 by noting that, even before the incarnation of the Servant (the Messiah), the Lord had chosen Him for His divine mission. It was God's intent for His Servant to bring the people of Israel back to Him in repentance and faith. This mission was necessary because the nation had wandered away from God. Israel had committed spiritual adultery by consorting with pagan idols. The nation's gross disobedience was the reason for God's righteous judgment.

Thankfully, God did not stop loving His people. He sent His Servant to restore the relationship that the Lord had wanted when He first called Israel out of bondage in Egypt. God's love and mercy were so great that He sent His Son as His emissary to offer forgiveness, salvation, and restoration.

Like a shepherd rounding up a dispersed flock, the Servant was to call back these exiles, not merely from Babylon, but also from sin and rebellion. While sin divides and disperses, God's Servant unites. This is why He would be honored in God's sight and would be empowered by Him. The Servant had determined He would faithfully serve God, especially in reuniting Israel with the Lord. With God as His strength, the Servant was certain to succeed in His mission.

B. To the Gentiles: vs. 6

He says: "It is too small a thing for you to be my servant to restore the tribes of Jacob and bring back those of Israel I have kept. I will also make you a light for the Gentiles, that you may bring my salvation to the ends of the earth."

The goal of the Servant was to bring salvation and restoration to Israel for the fulfillment of the covenant promises God made to His people. The Servant's mission, though, was not limited to Israel. The Lord wanted Him to be a "light for the Gentiles" (Isa. 49:6). Here "light" is parallel in thought to "salvation" and refers to the work of the Messiah to make redemption available to all humankind.

Israel's mission had always been to bring the nations to God (19:24; 42:6). The Servant fulfills the call of Abraham and the nation of Israel to be a blessing to the nations (Gen. 12:1-3; Exod. 19:5-6). After Jesus' death and resurrection, the Great Commission of global evangelism is carried on by His disciples (Matt. 28:18-20; Acts 13:47; 26:23).

Discussion Questions

1. Why is it significant that God called the Servant from His birth?
2. Why did the Servant compare His mouth to a sharp sword?
3. How should the Israelites have fulfilled their role as God's servants?
4. Why is the Servant glorious in the Lord's eyes?
5. How does the example of the Servant encourage you about the burdens you may have to bear?

Contemporary Application

The world's peoples need God just as much as they ever did. They hunger for forgiveness and salvation. Meanwhile, we as God's people have the only true bread of life. We know the Gospel of salvation through faith in Christ, and as servants of the Lord, we need to share it with those who have never heard it.

God cares about people in other cultures, and so does the Servant of the Lord. Indeed, God is the rightful ruler over every nation and culture, and the Servant is the supreme King. All peoples of the earth will one day bow before Jesus and acknowledge His lordship.

The wonderful truth about crossing cultural barriers to share the Gospel is that it benefits everybody. First, it glorifies God by announcing the salvation He has provided. Second, it benefits the hearers, for it gives them the opportunity to receive forgiveness and eternal life. Third, it benefits us because it draws us closer to God and gives us new and special relationships in Christ. Finally, it immensely aids us in seeing that our customs aren't the only proper ones. We begin to understand the beauty in God's creation of variety.

Three considerations, then, fire our desire to share Christ across national and cultural lines: (1) that God's glory may be declared in every part of the world; (2) that sinners may acknowledge Him and come to salvation in Christ; and (3) that we may fulfill the purpose for which God redeemed us by His grace.

The Peaceful Kingdom

DEVOTIONAL READING

Isaiah 12

DAILY BIBLE READINGS

Monday December 10
Isaiah 45:18-25 Turn to God and Be Saved

Tuesday December 11
Isaiah 44:1-8 God Promises Better Days

Wednesday December 12
Isaiah 44:9-20 The Folly of Idols

Thursday December 13
Isaiah 44:21-28 The God Who Redeems

Friday December 14
Isaiah 40:1-17 God Will Restore Jerusalem

Saturday December 15
Isaiah 40:18-24 Human-Made Idols versus Almighty God

Sunday December 16
Isaiah 40:25-31 The Everlasting, Creator God

Scripture

Background Scripture: *Isaiah 11:1-9*
Scripture Lesson: *Isaiah 11:1-9*
Key Verse: *The wolf will live with the lamb, the leopard will lie down with the goat, the calf and the lion and the yearling together; and a little child will lead them.* Isaiah 11:6.
Scripture Lesson for Children: *Isaiah 11:2-4; Matthew 1:18-25*
Key Verse for Children: *But after he had considered this, an angel of the Lord appeared to him in a dream and said, "Joseph son of David, do not be afraid to take Mary home as your wife, because what is conceived in her is from the Holy Spirit. She will give birth to a son, and you are to give him the name of Jesus, because he will save his people from their sins."* Matthew 1:20-21.

Lesson Aim

To discover ways to promote peace and righteousness in the world.

Lesson Setting

Time: *740–700 B.C.*
Place: *Judah*

Lesson Outline

The Peaceful Kingdom

  I. A Righteous, Peaceful Root: Isaiah 11:1-3a
      A. *The Messiah's Ancestry: vs. 1*
      B. *The Messiah's Empowering: vs. 2*
      C. *The Messiah's Delight: vs. 3a*
  II. A Righteous, Peaceful Reign: Isaiah 11:3b-9
      A. *Justice and Righteousness: vss. 3b-5*
      B. *Peace in the Animal Kingdom: vss. 6-8*
      C. *Worldwide Knowledge of the Lord: vs. 9*

Introduction for Adults

Topic: *The Gift of Peace*

Christmas will soon be here, and no doubt your students have recently heard many songs about the Messiah bringing peace on earth. Indeed, peace is a major theme when we celebrate the birth of Jesus, whom Scripture calls the Prince of Peace (Isa. 9:6).

Although Jesus suggested that His peace will often bring turmoil even among family members (Luke 14:26), He also asks us to be at peace with all men and women. Christmastime, however, can be a season of incredible tension, with rushed schedules, parties, programs, shopping, and crowds. The peace brought by the birth of Christ can easily be lost during the holiday season.

Nevertheless, adults are actually more desirous to bring peace into relationships through forgiveness than most would think. A recent Gallup poll showed that 48 percent of adults would like to "try to forgive" and 8 percent would like to "try to get even." By six to one, adults would rather seek peace than revenge!

Introduction for Youths

Topic: *Peace at Last!*

The old tree in the yard showed signs of wear and tear. It was a clump birch with three strong trunks. One by one they fell to drought and disease. Then one day a tiny sprout emerged from the stump. Each year it grew taller and taller. Today it stands eight feet tall, and two new shoots have sprung up as well!

Sometimes life's experiences cut us deeply. We are wounded by disappointments, losses, and precarious escapades. We are left feeling damaged physically, emotionally, and spiritually. Our lives look like stumps, not beautiful trees.

Thankfully, God does not quit on us. He revealed through Isaiah that one day the seemingly dead stump of Israel would produce a righteous Branch that would rule the world with peace and justice. God operates similarly in our lives, for He is the God of fresh starts and new shoots. He is the source of peace, for He gives rest, healing, and hope to His wounded people. When we are discouraged, we can turn to our Lord and Redeemer for strength to continue.

Concepts for Children

Topic: *God's Promise to Joseph*

1. The Spirit of God would be on the Messiah (or Savior).
2. When Joseph found out that Mary was going to have a child, at first he decided not to marry her.
3. An angel told Joseph to take Mary as his wife, for the son she was carrying was sent by God.
4. Joseph was to name the child Jesus, for He would rescue His people from their sins.
5. Just as Joseph and Mary trusted in and obeyed God, so can we.

109

The Lesson Commentary

I. A RIGHTEOUS, PEACEFUL ROOT: ISAIAH 11:1-3A

A. The Messiah's Ancestry: vs. 1

A shoot will come up from the stump of Jesse; from his roots a Branch will bear fruit.

Isaiah lived in chaotic times. In fact, many thought that nothing but a few dried-up stumps and roots would be left of the once glorious tree that represented the kingdom of David and Solomon. Enemies of Israel seemed to be on the verge of cutting down the main part of the tree.

To the untrained eye, the situation looked bleak. But Isaiah declared that a day was coming when the stump would flourish again. The Lord promised that a new branch would sprout from the old root of Jesse's family line (Isa. 11:1). This tender shoot would be none other than the Messiah. One day He would rule the earth with an iron scepter (Ps. 2:9; Rev. 19:15), rescue the righteous, condemn the wicked (Rev. 20:11-15), end all war (21:1-4), and break down the barriers that divide people from one another and from God Himself (Eph. 2:14-22).

Isaiah 11:1 says that a shoot will spring up from the "stump of Jesse." Scripture reveals that Jesse was the father of King David and an ancestor of Jesus (1 Sam. 16:1; Matt. 1:5-6). Jesse, whose name possibly means "man" or "manly," belonged to the tribe of Judah and lived in Bethlehem (1 Sam. 16:18). He was the son of Obed and the grandson of Boaz and Ruth (Ruth 4:17). Jesse had eight sons—Eliab, Abinadab, Shimea (Shammah), Nethanel, Raddai, Ozem, Elihu, and David—and two daughters, Zeruiah and Abigail (1 Chron. 2:13-16; 27:18).

B. The Messiah's Empowering: vs. 2

The Spirit of the LORD will rest on him—the Spirit of wisdom and of understanding, the Spirit of counsel and of power, the Spirit of knowledge and of the fear of the LORD—

The Holy Spirit would be the basis for the Messiah's effectiveness (Isa. 11:2). In fact, the sixfold naming of God's Spirit indicates that He would empower the Messiah fully and perfectly and enable Him to carry out His royal tasks. The Spirit would give the Branch understanding, wisdom, and insight. Because of the work of the Spirit in the Messiah's life, He would know the Lord intimately and honor Him in all that He did. And the greatest joy of the Branch would be to obey the Lord.

"Wisdom" is the ability to grasp the essence and purpose of an issue and to find the best way to achieve it. "Understanding" is the ability to discern circumstances and relationships. "Counsel" is the means by which proper decisions are made. "Power" is the ability to execute decisions. The "knowledge" of the Lord is being aware of His will and His ways. It comes from a loving, trusting relationship with God. Because such knowledge is more a matter of the heart than the mind, it produces the "fear of the LORD." This is the desire to revere and obey God.

A review of the New Testament indicates that Isaiah 11:2 is fulfilled in Christ. Jesus was conceived by the Holy Spirit (Matt. 1:20). After Jesus' baptism, the Spirit came down on Him like a dove (3:16). The Spirit then led Jesus into the desert, where Satan tempted Him (Luke 4:1).

During Jesus' public ministry, He taught with the Spirit's wisdom and power (Matt. 12:18; Luke 4:18). Jesus drove out demons by the Spirit's power (Matt. 12:28) and lived totally under the Spirit's control (Luke 4:14; Acts 10:38). Clearly, the Spirit's presence and grace marked Christ's life, work, and teachings.

C. The Messiah's Delight: vs. 3a

And he will delight in the fear of the LORD.

According to Isaiah 11:3, the Messiah would be totally submitted to the will of God. His submission was not grudging, but rather willing and cheerful. More than anything else, Jesus delighted in pleasing God (John 4:34; 5:30; 6:38; 14:31).

II. A RIGHTEOUS, PEACEFUL REIGN: ISAIAH 11:3B-9

A. Justice and Righteousness: vss. 3b-5

He will not judge by what he sees with his eyes, or decide by what he hears with his ears; but with righteousness he will judge the needy, with justice he will give decisions for the poor of the earth. He will strike the earth with the rod of his mouth; with the breath of his lips he will slay the wicked. Righteousness will be his belt and faithfulness the sash around his waist.

The Davidic kings of the Old Testament era were characterized by injustice and oppression (Isa. 3:14-15; 10:2). For example, they took bribes from the wicked rich and harshly treated the godly poor. In contrast, the Branch, sprung from Jesse's roots, would conduct a righteous, peaceful reign based on immediate and unerring reverence for the Lord and His will.

This statement is based on Isaiah 11:3b-5, which tells us that the Messiah would rule with perfect integrity. In contrast with the rulers of Isaiah's day, equity and virtue would characterize the Messiah. He would not judge merely by external appearances. Indeed, some clever trial witness would never fool Him with false evidence. The Messiah would judge with perfect justice because He Himself is perfect in every way.

The Messiah would make it His personal business to protect the rights of the poor and the defenseless. This protection is in sharp contrast to the wicked leaders of Judah, who dealt unjustly with the poor (1:23).

The Messiah would effectively deal with the wicked. In Scripture, God's spoken word is always powerful and active (55:10-11). As 11:4 says, the Messiah's word of judgment against the wicked would also be powerful and active. Indeed, the wicked would die at His command.

Some see this truth as a contradiction to the statement often made by Christians that the God of Scripture is characterized by love. It's helpful to remember that, while God displays anger, it is quite different from the irritation human beings often display. When people get angry, they tend to spew their rage on others in vindictive, self-centered ways. This might help them to vent their pent-up emotions, but it does nothing to promote justice, kindness, and peace.

In contrast, the anger of God is based on His just and righteous character. When the Lord judges nations and individuals, it's not intended to soothe upset feelings. Rather, the hand of God's discipline reflects His goal of bringing about justice for wrongs that people have committed. Because God is holy, He cannot allow evil and wickedness to prevail.

In contrast to the wicked, the Messiah would be perfectly righteous. In ancient times, people tied up their loose garments with a belt before engaging in vigorous action. The belt or sash worn by the Messiah would be one of righteousness and fruitfulness (vs. 5). These two virtues would characterize all His activities.

When people vent their rage, it often leads to more violence, suffering, and bitterness. In contrast, when the Messiah displays His anger, it leads to peace and equity. This is because He seeks to eliminate unrighteousness and replace it with true justice. Scripture reveals that, in the divine Kingdom, a golden age of peace and faithfulness will prevail.

Thus, from what we have said, it's clear that the Messiah's character is incomparable. No one has ever fit this description except Jesus. He alone is the epitome of righteousness and faithfulness. He was sinless and completely obedient to His Father's will. And He continues to be faithful and righteous to all who come to Him in faith.

B. Peace in the Animal Kingdom: vss. 6-8

The wolf will live with the lamb, the leopard will lie down with the goat, the calf and the lion and the yearling together; and a little child will lead them. The cow will feed with the bear, their young will lie down together, and the lion will eat straw like the ox. The infant will play near the hole of the cobra, and the young child put his hand into the viper's nest.

These verses comprise one of the most memorable parts of Isaiah's prophecy. It's no wonder they have been the subject of countless paintings, for the magnificence of their vision stretches our faith, hope, and imagination.

Isaiah depicted this golden age as a time of unparalleled tranquility. It's hard to imagine wolves resting with lambs, leopards lying down with young goats, and calves and lions eating together peacefully. Even more amazing is the idea of cows and bears sharing the same pasture, and lions and oxen eating straw. But that's the way things will be during the Messiah's righteous, peaceful reign (Isa. 11:6-7).

The reign of Messiah will make the world a perfectly safe place for the most vulnerable of children. Isaiah described nursing children playing by the hole of a cobra, and weaned children placing their hands in a nest of deadly snakes (vs. 8). In each case, no harm would come to these little ones. This reflects the peace and protection they would enjoy in the golden age.

Down through the centuries, Christians have interpreted these verses with varying degrees of literalness. Some who take this passage less literally say this prophecy depicts what happens in the environment now when Christ reigns. Others say these verses poetically represent the harmony that exists imperfectly in the church and perfectly in heaven.

Some who understand this passage more literally say these verses are yet to be fulfilled quite concretely in an earthly messianic kingdom. Others (who don't go as far as this) say there really will come a time when aggression and hostility will be absent from people and animals on the earth after Christ's return.

C. Worldwide Knowledge of the Lord: vs. 9

They will neither harm nor destroy on all my holy mountain, for the earth will be full of the knowledge of the LORD as the waters cover the sea.

To sum up his description of tranquility, Isaiah said that animals "will neither harm nor destroy on all [God's] holy mountain" (Isa. 11:9). God's holy mountain is also known as Mount Zion.

Zion is first mentioned in 2 Samuel 5:7 as a Jebusite fortress on a hill. After being captured by King David, this fortress was called the City of David. Here David brought the ark of the covenant, thereby making the hill a sacred site (6:10-12). In the Old Testament, Zion is also called God's "holy hill" (Ps. 2:6), "the city of God" (46:4), God's "resting place" (132:14), "the holy city" (Isa. 48:2), and "the beautiful holy mountain" (Dan. 11:45). Eventually, Zion came to stand for the whole city of Jerusalem. In early Christian thought, Zion also represented "the heavenly Jerusalem, the city of the living God" (Heb. 12:22).

Perhaps most stunning of all was Isaiah's prophecy of a world filled with the knowledge of the Lord. This does not refer to mere intellectual knowledge. It includes the idea of living according to God's Word (Jer. 31:34).

Because God's Word will be obeyed everywhere, there will be no place for harm and destruction. The preeminence of war in human relations will be removed forever. The tragic outcomes of battles (especially in terms of death and desolation) will never again tarnish the world.

Discussion Questions

1. Why do you think Isaiah introduced the Messiah as a new shoot sprouting from the roots of an old stump?
2. Why, in your opinion, would the Spirit of God enhance the characteristics of the Messiah listed in Isaiah 11:2?
3. How would the judgment of the Messiah lead to righteousness and peace?
4. How would the reign of the Messiah affect the world of nature?
5. How does seeking to follow the Lord help us also to pursue righteousness and faithfulness in our lives?

Contemporary Application

God sent His Son into the world to bring His peace to it. The consummation of His kingdom awaits a future glorious time, but presently He reigns in the hearts and lives of every man, woman, and child who yield themselves to Him as Lord. Righteousness is one quality that will emerge and stand out in the lives of yielded believers.

Practicing righteousness is not the same as a cold, routine performance of religious duties. It means the believer chooses to act in a kind and just manner toward others. Such conduct is based on the perfect and unchanging standard of God's Word. It is made possible through the saving work of Christ and the indwelling presence of the Spirit.

How righteous are we? We answer that question by using the Word of God to help us evaluate our relationships with everyone around us. Our ability to be a peacemaker in our family depends on what kind of husband, wife, parent, or grandparent we are. Our ability to be a peacemaker with our friends depends on the loyalty and integrity of our friendships. Our peacemaking in our neighborhood can only grow out of true neighborliness. The righteousness of our working relationships limits or enhances our peacemaking on the job.

Jesus set the example for us all. He loved God with all His heart and His neighbor as Himself. That is the starting point for all righteousness and the beginning place for all peacemaking.

We have a wonderful opportunity this Christmas to be peacemakers among those who are feeling stressed and fatigued from all the demands they face from family, friends, and co-workers. When God is in control of the believer's life, he or she will grow in the likeness of Christ and be a catalyst for His peace.

Comfort for God's People

DEVOTIONAL READING

Isaiah 40:25-31

DAILY BIBLE READINGS

Monday December 17
Isaiah 6:1-5 A True Worship Experience

Tuesday December 18
Isaiah 6:6-13 Isaiah Answers God's Call

Wednesday December 19
Isaiah 7:10-17 The Lord's Special Sign

Thursday December 20
Isaiah 9:1-7 To You a Child Is Born

Friday December 21
Luke 1:26-38 The Lord Is with Mary

Saturday December 22
Luke 1:41-55 Mary's Soul Magnifies the Lord

Sunday December 23
Luke 2:1-7 The Birth of Jesus

Scripture

Background Scripture: *Isaiah 40:1-11*

Scripture Lesson: *Isaiah 40:1-5, 8-11*

Key Verse: *"The grass withers and the flowers fall, but the word of our God stands forever."* Isaiah 40:8.

Scripture Lesson for Children: *Luke 1:5-8, 11-13, 18-20, 57, 67, 76*

Key Verse for Children: *But the angel said to him: "Do not be afraid, Zechariah; your prayer has been heard. Your wife Elizabeth will bear you a son, and you are to give him the name John."* Luke 1:13.

Lesson Aim

To thank God for ways He has provided consolation during difficult times.

Lesson Setting

Time: *740–700 B.C.*

Place: *Judah*

Lesson Outline

Comfort for God's People

I. Comfort for Jerusalem: Isaiah 40:1-2
    A. *Consolation Offered: vs. 1*
    B. *Ending the Captivity: vs. 2*

II. Preparation for God's Coming: Isaiah 40:3-5, 8
    A. *The Glory of the Lord: vss. 3-5*
    B. *The Enduring Quality of God's Word: vs. 8*

III. Judah's Message of Peace: Isaiah 40:9-11
    A. *The Lord's Presence: vs. 9*
    B. *The Lord's Might: vs. 10*
    C. *The Lord's Care: vs. 11*

Introduction for Adults

Topic: *The Gift of Comfort*

Different things represent comfort to different people. Some perceive a soft chair, an expensive car, warm temperatures, stretchy clothes, or a large bank account as something that can make them comfortable. Others think they would be comfortable if they had good health, no pressure, or no money problems. Nevertheless, adults are rarely satisfied with the comfort that surrounds them. There is always something about which they can complain.

Our level of comfort has much to do with what we have experienced. That's why adults need to understand that God's comfort may not come in ways that they want. However, that does not mean God is trying to make their life miserable.

Adults tend to be comfortable when they receive the things they want. That's why it is difficult for them to thank God for difficult times. It is even more difficult for them to see the ways God seeks to comfort them, for He may choose to console them in ways that they don't expect. His approach, though, is always best.

Introduction for Youths

Topic: *Better Days Ahead!*

What do you do with a broken-down car that needs repairs and paint? You see beyond the wreck and envision a sparkling new paint job and a motor that purrs sweetly. You give that car all the sweat you can muster because you have great plans for it and yourself.

Perhaps if we were writing Isaiah's sermons today, rather than comparing God to a tender shepherd, we would compare Him to a sensitive, careful, hardworking, and loving mechanic. That's because we bestow the same kind of love on our cars that shepherds do on their sheep.

The main point is that God can bring about restoration and healing in the lives of youth, especially if they submit to His will. He has wonderful plans for them that they can't even imagine. Metaphorically speaking, God can take their dings and dents, and all the misfirings of their cylinders, and make a beautiful automobile out of their lives. Through faith in His Son they can make a fresh start.

Concepts for Children

Topic: *God's Promise to Zechariah*

1. A priest named Zechariah and his wife Elizabeth obeyed God.
2. This couple had no children and were growing old.
3. When Zechariah was serving at the altar in the temple, an angel appeared to him.
4. The angel said that Elizabeth would have a son named John.
5. John would prepare the way for Jesus.
6. It is better to trust in God than doubt Him.

The Lesson Commentary

I. COMFORT FOR JERUSALEM: ISAIAH 40:1-2

A. Consolation Offered: vs. 1

Comfort, comfort my people, says your God.

Isaiah 36—39 is a historical interlude between the first and second parts of the book. Much of the information in these chapters is contained in a similar form in 2 Kings 18:13—20:19. The compiler of 2 Kings may have used Isaiah as one of his sources, or perhaps both authors drew on another source.

Chapters 36 and 37 of Isaiah are easy to understand simply by reading them. They describe events leading up to and including the lifting of the Assyrian siege against Jerusalem in 701 B.C. Chapter 38 recounts Hezekiah's illness and healing, while chapter 39 details his lapse of judgment in welcoming the envoys from Babylon.

Between the circumstances of chapter 39 and those of chapter 40 lie a century and a half or more. During this period, God's people continued to decay spiritually and—as promised by God—were taken as captives to Babylon. Isaiah wrote chapters 40—66 as though the exile had already begun and was, in fact, nearly at an end.

Not all the people of Judah were taken to Babylon. Some of the poorest in the land were left behind (2 Kings 25:8-12). The old Judean aristocracy, however, did not escape exile. Previously they had commanded positions of power, status, and wealth in Jerusalem. But in Babylon, life was filled with sorrow and humiliation.

For the Judeans left behind in their native land, the initial situation seemed just as dismal. The deaths caused by the Babylonian invasion, the deportation of the aristocracy, and the destruction of the temple wiped out all the institutions that had held Judean society together.

Thus, both the Jews in Babylon and Judea needed hope and consolation. The promise of a brighter future could be found only in the faithfulness of God. Such comfort is offered in Isaiah 40. Without ignoring the sins of the past or minimizing the conditions of the exile to come, the prophet described a future when God's people would experience the Lord's faithfulness when He restored them to their land.

Thus, whereas chapters 1—39 primarily contain messages of judgment, chapters 40—66 focus mainly on the deliverance and restoration of God's people. The first 11 verses of chapter 40 appear to describe God's telling Isaiah what to declare to His people. First and foremost, the prophet was to speak words of consolation (vs. 1). The Hebrew word rendered "comfort" is repeated twice to underscore that there would be an end of punishment and the coming of a new day of freedom.

B. Ending the Captivity: vs. 2

Speak tenderly to Jerusalem, and proclaim to her that her hard service has been completed, that her sin has been paid for, that she has received from the LORD's hand double for all her sins.

117

The Lord directed Isaiah to speak "tenderly" (Isa. 40:2) to "Jerusalem" (namely, the people of Judah) like a mother speaking to her children. This was not the time for the people to hear harsh words of censure and condemnation. Now, speaking prophetically, Isaiah was to tell the people that their "hard service," or exile, was soon to be over.

The people had endured the judgment God had given them for their sins. In fact, the exiles had "received from the Lord's hand double for all her sins." This does not mean that the people were over-punished but rather that they had been fully punished in the exile—as much as they deserved. Isaiah's promise of the Lord's comfort would bring renewed hope and assurance into the hearts of the Jews, whom God would not leave in a strange land.

In this verse we find both God's holiness and grace at work. Because of continuous idolatry in Judah and Jerusalem, God would exercise His holy, righteous judgment and send His people into exile. The Babylonian captivity was not just the sad outcome of war; more importantly, it was directed by God's hand.

The Lord, however, refused to abandon His people. Once they had endured enough suffering, He declared that He would release them from their captivity. With the ending of their exile, the faithful remnant could start fresh with God in the land of promise. This was the message of comfort and hope the people needed to hear.

II. PREPARATION FOR GOD'S COMING: ISAIAH 40:3-8

A. The Glory of the Lord: vss. 3-5

A voice of one calling: "In the desert prepare the way for the LORD; make straight in the wilderness a highway for our God. Every valley shall be raised up, every mountain and hill made low; the rough ground shall become level, the rugged places a plain. And the glory of the LORD will be revealed, and all mankind together will see it. For the mouth of the LORD has spoken."

In Isaiah 40:3-5, a procession is described. First we are told of a voice calling. (It's not clear whether this is the voice of God, an angel, or Isaiah.) The voice was "in the desert," namely, land of a dry and desolate nature, and made up mostly of rock and sand. The wilderness is often used in the Bible as a symbol of life without direction.

The people of God were told to prepare for the Lord's coming. In ancient times a herald was often sent ahead of a royal procession to make sure the path was sufficiently smooth. All obstacles were cleared off the road and the general direction of the route was straightened to make travel easier for the visiting monarch.

Isaiah used hyperbole (purposeful exaggerations) to describe the leveling and smoothing process. He said, for example, valleys would be filled in and mountains would be flattened so that the path would be even. Certainly, creating a road for the arrival of a king in ancient times periodically required extensive construction and reconstruction.

This passage has both an immediate and a distant application. In the immediate context, Isaiah commanded that a path be cleared for the Lord to lead a procession of His people from Babylon to Jerusalem. But, as Luke 3:4-6 makes clear (by quoting Isaiah 40:3-5), the prophet's declaration also applies to the ministry of John the Baptist. Luke 3:3 reveals that John (the son of an elderly couple named Zechariah and Elizabeth) was traveling through the rural areas of the Jordan River Valley and urging people to repent and be baptized.

John was helping the people of his day get ready for Jesus. Within a short time after John began his ministry, Jesus would begin His ministry. The people needed to know that God was sending them the Messiah and that they would receive either salvation or judgment from His hands. John attuned the people to their spiritual need and built up an expectancy for the Savior, who could meet their need.

Isaiah said that in Judah's deliverance the glory of the Lord would appear for all to see (Isa. 40:5). All the nations would know that God had rescued His people from exile, and this deliverance would bring great glory to Him. The faithful remnant could derive much consolation from the knowledge that God stood behind His promises of deliverance and restoration.

B. The Enduring Quality of God's Word: vs. 8

"The grass withers and the flowers fall, but the word of our God stands forever."

In Isaiah 40:6-8, the frailty of humankind is contrasted with the eternalness of God and His Word. From the Lord's perspective (whom Daniel 7:9 calls the "Ancient of Days"), humans are as temporal as grass and live no longer than flowers. It's humbling to realize that at God's command not only flowers and grass but also people disappear (Isa. 40:6).

"The breath of the LORD" (vs. 7) pictures God's wrath on the wicked as the summer wind that blows on the grass and dries it up. Like plants that wither when the weather gets hot, people weaken and die because of their physical nature. In contrast, what God has said will never change (vs. 8).

Some think the withering of the grass and the fading of the flower depicted in verse 8 is an indirect reference to the sirocco or khamsin. This wind comes from the deserts east and south of Israel, bringing scorching heat and whirling dust (Jer. 4:11). It is a fitting picture of the breath of the Lord's judgment (Isa. 40:24).

Although the plans and purposes of powerful nations such as Assyria and Babylon would ultimately fail, those of the Lord would prevail and endure. This is because His word is eternal and brings to pass His will.

The exiles of Judah would need this reminder, because as they waited for the promised deliverance, they might begin to lose hope of being rescued. The faithful remnant could be confident that the Lord really would deliver them as He promised. In the same way, we need to remember that God's promises to us do not depend on frail human ability, as human promises do, but rather on His never-ending power.

III. JUDAH'S MESSAGE OF PEACE: ISAIAH 40:9-11

A. The Lord's Presence: vs. 9

You who bring good tidings to Zion, go up on a high mountain. You who bring good tidings to Jerusalem, lift up your voice with a shout, lift it up, do not be afraid; say to the towns of Judah, "Here is your God!"

In view of God's enduring promises, the Lord's messenger (probably Isaiah) was instructed to go up on a high mountain and fearlessly proclaim "good tidings" (Isa. 40:9) to the exiles. The messenger was to present God to the people. This is because the Lord Himself would deliver them from exile and lead them back to their land.

This passage also applies to Jesus Christ. During His time on earth, He personally came to Jerusalem to set His people free from sin (Matt. 21:5). He will one day come again to reward the upright and judge the wicked (Isa. 62:11; Rev. 22:12). In the meantime believers are commanded by the Lord to proclaim the good news of salvation to all the world (Acts 1:8).

B. The Lord's Might: vs. 10

See, the Sovereign LORD comes with power, and his arm rules for him. See, his reward is with him, and his recompense accompanies him.

Isaiah 40:10 reveals that the Lord would come "with power." The idea is that God would display His power and sovereignty in unmistakable ways. No earthly power would be able to prevent Him from freeing His people. He would both defeat the enemies of Judah and deliver His people from sin and death. In fact, He would bring His reward—His delivered people—with Him as He came.

C. The Lord's Care: vs. 11

He tends his flock like a shepherd: He gathers the lambs in his arms and carries them close to his heart; he gently leads those that have young.

In Isaiah 40:11, the Lord is portrayed as a tender shepherd who cares for His "lambs"—the returning exiles. He not only would carry them in His arms (by holding them close to His heart), but also gently lead the mother sheep with their young. In other words, God would guide His people out of captivity and back to their own land.

In Bible times shepherds performed numerous duties. In addition to finding adequate shelter for sheep, shepherds also had to lead them to good pasturelands and ample supplies of water. Knowing that their flocks were easy prey, shepherds spent part of their time warding off attacks from savage animals. If necessary, shepherds were willing to risk their own lives to ensure the safety of the flock.

The New Testament pictures Jesus as the Good Shepherd (John 10:1-18). As our Shepherd, Jesus cares for us, protects us, leads us, and fellowships with us. We, His sheep, have the responsibility to follow where He leads.

Discussion Questions

1. How do you think the Judahites who personally heard Isaiah responded to his prophecy of God's comfort?

2. What similarities and differences do you see between the Lord's coming to redeem the Israelites and Christ's coming to save people?

3. Why did Isaiah describe humans in the presence of God as being like grass and flowers?

4. What reasons did the people of God have for being sure that the Lord's promise to deliver them from captivity would really come true?

5. How do you understand the concept of God as a shepherd who brings comfort to us?

Contemporary Application

In Isaiah's prophecy he underscored the promise of God to deliver His people in their times of need. God's compassion and care for them undergirded His commitment to fulfill His pledge.

The Lord is also able to help us in our times of need, and His unfailing love is the basis for this promise. The mystery of God's love is that it accepts and meets us at the point of our deepest need. When we trust God's promises, we experience His comfort and blessings in our lives.

It would be incorrect to think that when God comforts us, all our troubles go away. Being comforted may mean we receive strength to endure our trials and hope to face a potentially troubled future. The greater the difficulty we face, the more God reaches out to us in love to comfort us. Even in the darkest moments of our lives He is always present to give us strength and hope to endure.

God has never failed in His promise to comfort us. We should not only acknowledge this truth but also thank the Lord for the ways He has comforted us during difficult times in the past. Unlike flowers, which are a temporary delight in our eyes, God's love and care are everlasting. Let us express our gratitude to God for being like a shepherd in His care for us, especially when life is rough.

The Prince of Peace

DEVOTIONAL READING

Luke 2:8-20

DAILY BIBLE READINGS

Monday December 24
Luke 2:8-14 The Good News of Great Joy

Tuesday December 25
Luke 2:15-20 All Who Heard Were Amazed

Wednesday December 26
Luke 2:25-35 A Light for Revelation to the Gentiles

Thursday December 27
Isaiah 42:1-17 The Servant of the Lord

Friday December 28
Isaiah 42:18-25 Israel's Blindness

Saturday December 29
Isaiah 43:1-7 God Has Called You by Name

Sunday December 30
Isaiah 43:8-13 The Lord Is the Only Savior

Scripture

Background Scripture: *Isaiah 9:1-7; Luke 2:1-20*

Scripture Lesson: *Isaiah 9:2-7*

Key Verse: *For to us a child is born, to us a son is given, and the government will be on his shoulders. And he will be called Wonderful Counselor, Mighty God, Everlasting Father, Prince of Peace.* Isaiah 9:6.

Scripture Lesson for Children: *Luke 2:4-19*

Lesson Aim

To rejoice because the promised Messiah has come.

Lesson Setting

Time: *740–700 B.C.*

Place: *Judah*

Lesson Outline

The Prince of Peace

   I. God's Light: Isaiah 9:2-3
      A. *The Coming Dawn: vs. 2*
      B. *The Coming Joy: vs. 3*
  II. God's Judgment: Isaiah 9:4-5
      A. *The Oppressor's Yoke: vs. 4*
      B. *The Warrior's Garments: vs. 5*
 III. Messiah's Reign: Isaiah 9:6-7
      A. *The Messiah's Names: vs. 6*
      B. *The Messiah's Justice: vs. 7*

Introduction for Adults

Topic: *The Gift of Wholeness*

Not all the gifts we receive really make a difference. Some of the stuff we get at Christmas is easily disposable, and some of it we don't even want. Sometimes when we are asked what we want for Christmas, we feel hard-pressed to think about what we really need.

What a wonderful opportunity, then, for Christmas to be a time when we can give gifts that will change people's lives! For example, we can give the gift of forgiveness in which we pledge to get over past hurts and grudges. We can also give the gift of reconciliation to our families, and the gift of peace and healing for people suffering emotionally and physically.

Most of all, by proclaiming the Gospel, we can share the gift of peace through faith in Christ. And why shouldn't we do this, for He came to make people whole. What He has to offer really counts—both now and in eternity.

Introduction for Youths

Topic: *Birth of New Hope!*

Gary Smalley cites four things that many youth perceive as the basis for their hope but that are ultimately undependable. *People* can bring us hope. Unfortunately, though, we can't control them. *Places* can bring us hope. But the fact is, we get bored with them. *Possessions* can offer us hope. Yet we never seem to get enough. A *position of prominence* can bring us hope. Sadly, though, we never seem to be able to climb high enough.

W. P. Keller in his book *Salt for Society* discusses several potent yet simple ways adolescent Christians can bring new hope to others: (1) They supply encouragement. (2) They bring optimism. Even in the midst of a decadent society, they have hope. (3) They give comfort. They share the Spirit of God's joy to replace the spirit of a heavy heart. (4) They love by giving their time. (5) They are friends, injecting humor without sarcasm or ridicule. (6) They exercise empathy by seeing themselves in other people's shoes.

Concepts for Children

Topic: *God Sent Jesus*

1. Joseph and Mary, who were expecting a child, went from Nazareth to Bethlehem to be listed.
2. While they were there, Mary gave birth to Jesus.
3. Angels told some shepherds the good news of Jesus' birth.
4. The shepherds quickly went to see Mary, Joseph, and the baby.
5. The shepherds then told others what they had seen and heard.
6. We can thank God for the gift of His Son.

The Lesson Commentary
I. GOD'S LIGHT: ISAIAH 9:2-3

A. The Coming Dawn: vs. 2

The people walking in darkness have seen a great light; on those living in the land of the shadow of death a light has dawned.

In Isaiah's prophecy, chapter 9 stands at a pivotal turning point. King Ahaz had stubbornly refused to seek God's help and protection. Instead, he had turned to the Assyrians. However, in God's plan Assyria would become His "razor" of judgment (7:20). Isaiah predicted terrible times ahead. People would starve and curse God (8:21). Distress, darkness, and gloom would overcome them (8:22).

Isaiah envisioned this blanket of darkness descending upon the land of Zebulun and Naphtali. (Zebulun and Naphtali correspond to the Assyrian province of Galilee.) God, however, did not intend His people to experience anguish and gloom forever. In fact, He promised to one day honor them and make their land great. He would fulfill His word by bringing a great light of deliverance and hope to His people (9:1).

We learn from verse 2 how God would directly address the need of His people. He would replace their dark and gloomy existence with "great light." Additionally, the Lord would bring renewal (which is implied by the light dawning or shining) on all who live in the land. The result will be a complete reversal of the people's deplorable condition.

In this verse, as in other parts of Scripture, darkness and light are used in symbolic ways. For instance, darkness is used to represent human ignorance of God's will, especially as such ignorance is manifested in sin. In contrast, light has been associated with the presence, truth, and redemptive activity of God.

The origin of light rests with God, and He is the very essence of light. This indicates that He is the ultimate source of all knowing and understanding. Conversely, darkness rests with Satan, and he is the very essence of darkness. This implies that he is the ultimate source of all ignorance, superstition, and oppression.

Notice that the prophecy in Isaiah 9:2 uses a tense that indicates past action: "The people walking in darkness *have seen* a great light; . . . a light *has dawned*" (emphasis added). It reads as if what is described has already taken place. This is a common feature of Hebrew prophecy, indicating absolute certainty that a prophecy will come to pass. (The prophecies of verses 3 to 7 also use a past tense.)

A diamond always sparkles more brightly when set against a dark velvet backdrop. Even so, the "light" announced in 9:2 blazes more brilliantly against the backdrop of 8:18-22. The prophecies of chapters 9—12 may have applied in a limited degree to King Hezekiah or to another king of Judah. But they apply in the fullest sense to Jesus, the Messiah. He would bring a great light of deliverance and hope to His people.

The Messiah would offer salvation to both Jews and Gentiles (42:6; 49:6). As we know from biblical history, the people of Israel had to wait over 700 years before Jesus, "the light of the world" (John 8:12), shone in splendor upon them.

B. The Coming Joy: vs. 3

You have enlarged the nation and increased their joy; they rejoice before you as people rejoice at the harvest, as men rejoice when dividing the plunder.

The coming of the Messiah would have concrete results. For example, instead of decreasing the nation by judgment so that only a remnant was left, the Messiah's coming would bless the nation so that it would enlarge (Isa. 9:3). The future Assyrian oppression of Israel would leave its citizens feeling humiliated and diminished as a people. But Isaiah's prophecy pointed to a future day when the peace and prosperity of God would prevail.

Isaiah's exuberance about the Messiah's coming joy led the prophet to compare the event to the satisfaction farmers have at harvesttime or the delight soldiers experience when dividing the plunder of a conquered foe. This joy of God's people is in marked contrast to the gloom mentioned in verse 1.

Isaiah likely was overwhelmed by the broad vision of the future—with all its various judgments and blessings—that he was permitted to glimpse. He may have been moved to awe-filled silence, reverence, and worship. God's deliverance should also inspire praise and worship in us. Likewise, such should spring from enlarged hearts that are focused on God.

II. GOD'S JUDGMENT: ISAIAH 9:4-5

A. The Oppressor's Yoke: vs. 4

For as in the day of Midian's defeat, you have shattered the yoke that burdens them, the bar across their shoulders, the rod of their oppressor.

One reason for the great joy mentioned in Isaiah 9:3 is that the Messiah would lift the people's burdens from their shoulders (vs. 4). They bore a heavy yoke. (This was a wooden frame that was placed on the necks of animals to hold them together while they worked.) The people also carried a massive bar across their shoulders and were beaten with a rod by the enemy.

Isaiah thought about the time when the Israelites were delivered from Midianite oppression. Genesis 25:2 and 4 say that the Midianites were descendants of Abraham and Keturah. Tragically, the Midianites usually were foes rather than friends of the Hebrew people. (The land of Midian was located principally in northwest Arabia, although the Midianites roamed throughout portions of northern Sinai, the Negev, and the southern Transjordan region.)

Though the Midianites once had a powerful army, God used Gideon and 300 Israelite soldiers to overwhelm their foe (Judg. 7:19-23). Similarly, the Messiah would release His people from their burden by shattering the power of their oppressors. This prophecy had a more immediate fulfillment in Jerusalem's miraculous deliverance from an Assyrian siege in 701 B.C. (Isa. 37:36-37).

B. The Warrior's Garments: vs. 5

Every warrior's boot used in battle and every garment rolled in blood will be destined for burning, will be fuel for the fire.

In ancient times nations such as Assyria often used bloodstained uniforms from past battles as a deliberate scare tactic to frighten enemies in an upcoming battle. Perhaps Isaiah had this background information in mind when he declared that in the day of peace, uniforms would never again be bloodstained by war. Likewise, battle gear would no longer be issued (Isa. 9:5).

The idea is that the clothing of war would be rendered obsolete at the Messiah's coming. There would be no more need for such clothing, since Jesus' reign would be characterized by perfect peace. From this information we see that the Lord's triumph over the enemy would be complete and His redemption of His people would be absolute.

III. MESSIAH'S REIGN: ISAIAH 9:6-7

A. The Messiah's Names: vs. 6

For to us a child is born, to us a son is given, and the government will be on his shoulders. And he will be called Wonderful Counselor, Mighty God, Everlasting Father, Prince of Peace.

Isaiah gave many reasons for joy and celebration—the oppressor's yoke would be broken, battle gear would be destroyed, and God would redeem His people. Isaiah's prophecy took an abrupt turn with the announcement of the birth of someone who would one day be the King of kings.

Isaiah envisioned this birth as having been already accomplished: "A child is born . . . a son is given" (Isa. 9:6). In other words, God's promises would be fulfilled no matter how far-fetched they might seem. The prophecy pointed to Christ's incarnation. He was born in the normal human way as a baby in Bethlehem.

Isaiah next noted that Israel's Redeemer would carry the government "on his shoulders." This may be a reference to the royal robe worn by ancient kings. Such robes hung on the shoulders and represented authority to rule.

Down through the years, Israel had suffered through the reigns of many wicked, apostate kings. The coming Messiah, however, would rule uprightly for the good of God's people. The Savior would be God's just and faithful King.

Isaiah gave the Messiah four names or descriptions. As the "Wonderful Counselor," He brings the words of life to His people. Humanity undoubtedly would be less besieged by psychological problems if it seriously acknowledged Christ as a wonderful counselor.

The Messiah also is "the Mighty God." The image in verse 6 is that of a valiant and stout fighter who is without equal. The emphasis is on the Messiah's ability to defend the cause of His people and protect their interests. With Him on their side, no foe would overcome them or threaten their existence.

Christ furthermore is the "Everlasting Father." The word "Father" refers to the

Messiah's role as an ideal king. His rule is eternal and filled with compassion. When He reigns on the throne of David, the Messiah will provide for and watch over His people. Not one of their temporal and eternal needs will be overlooked or neglected by Him.

The Messiah moreover is the "Prince of Peace." This indicates more than the absence of war. The Messiah will bring peace in the fullest sense of the word—peace between God and people as well as between person and person. Also, during Jesus' reign, spiritual healing and wholeness will prevail throughout society.

When we look at these majestic, descriptive titles, we conclude that no human emperor has ever come close to living up to them. Many rulers and kingdoms have come and gone, but none of them has achieved what Isaiah prophesied. The fulfillment will only come when Jesus returns. Celebrating His birth at Christmas means we can look to the future with confidence.

B. The Messiah's Justice: vs. 7

Of the increase of his government and peace there will be no end. He will reign on David's throne and over his kingdom, establishing and upholding it with justice and righteousness from that time on and forever. The zeal of the LORD Almighty will accomplish this.

The child mentioned in Isaiah 9:6 "will reign on David's throne" (vs. 7). This is an important prophecy in light of the New Testament's numerous references to David, many of which actually pertain to his greatest descendant, Jesus Christ.

God promised David a kingdom that would have no end (1 Chron. 17:10-14). This could not have referred to the kingdom of David's son Solomon and his other short-term successors, for the Israelite kingdom divided (1 Kings 12:19). Also, both resulting kingdoms eventually came to an end (2 Kings 17:18; 2 Chron. 36:17-21).

Nevertheless, the line of David continued and eventually culminated in the birth of Jesus (Matt. 1:1). Luke 1:32 says, "the Lord God will give him the throne of his father David." In fact, the Messiah will "reign over the house of Jacob forever; his kingdom will never end" (vs. 33). Thus, we see that in Jesus the divine promise to David was and is fulfilled.

We learn from Isaiah 9:7 that the reign of the Messiah will be characterized by peace. His government will be ever expanding and never ending. Fairness and justice will be the hallmarks of His rule, and His passionate commitment for His people will guarantee that all the divine promises to them will be fulfilled.

Isaiah 9:7 mentions "the zeal of the LORD Almighty." This phrase depicts God as a jealous lover who refuses to desert His people. His zeal is filled with devotion and single-minded allegiance, and this is the reason why His promise to the Israelites concerning the Davidic kingdom would be fulfilled (37:32; 42:13).

Discussion Questions

1. What great light would the people walking in darkness see?
2. What symbols of rejoicing are found in Isaiah 9:3 and 5? What modern symbols

or mental associations might you make with joy in your life?

3. Why do you think Isaiah mentioned the burning of clothes rather than weapons in verse 5?

4. What do you think Isaiah meant when he said the child would have "the government" (vs. 6) on His shoulders?

5. How do the descriptive titles of the Messiah in verse 6 relate to the event that we call Christmas?

Contemporary Application

"Rejoice greatly," sings one line of Handel's *Messiah*. Why rejoice? Because "light has come into the world" (John 3:19). People who walk in darkness can see a great light (Isa. 9:2).

In Charles Dickens's *Great Expectations*, an eccentric old woman named Miss Havisham has spent most of her time in a dark room—since the day of her scheduled wedding when her fiancé jilted her. At the end of the book, a young man named Pip throws open the curtains that have kept the room shrouded for years in darkness. Light rushes in. All is exposed by the light.

Light flooded into our world when Christ came (John 1:5, 9). By His presence He dispelled the darkness of superstition and ignorance. Through His ministry of teaching and healing He shone the light of God's truth and purity for the whole world to see.

Do we have any reason for rejoicing because Christ has come and will one day return to reign? Indeed, we have! We no longer blindly stumble in darkness. Instead, the Savior has made us aware of God's love for and goodness toward us. We are also assured that, in the day when Christ returns to reign, He will bring peace, righteousness, and unparalleled blessing to all who have trusted in Him. Because of these wonderful truths, we can rejoice!

Justice for the Nations

DEVOTIONAL READING

Isaiah 43:1-7

DAILY BIBLE READINGS

Monday December 31
Luke 4:14-21 Jesus' Messianic Mission

Tuesday January 1
Isaiah 60:1-9 God's People Will Prosper

Wednesday January 2
Isaiah 60:10-14 The Nation's Gates Will Stay Open

Thursday January 3
Isaiah 60:15-22 God Will Be Your Light

Friday January 4
Isaiah 61:1-7 Anointed to Bring Good News

Saturday January 5
Isaiah 61:8-11 Righteousness Before All Nations

Sunday January 6
Matthew 2:1-12 Worshipers from Afar

Scripture

Background Scripture: *Isaiah 42:1-9*
Scripture Lesson: *Isaiah 42:1-9*
Key Verse: *"Here is my servant, whom I uphold, my chosen one in whom I delight; I will put my Spirit on him and he will bring justice to the nations."* Isaiah 42:1.
Scripture Lesson for Children: *Matthew 2:1-12*
Key Verse for Children: *On coming to the house, they saw the child with his mother Mary, and they bowed down and worshiped Him. Then they opened their treasures and presented him with gifts of gold and of incense and of myrrh.* Matthew 2:11.

Lesson Aim

To understand that God strengthens and enables believers to fulfill His plans for them.

Lesson Setting

Time: *740–700 B.C.*
Place: *Judah*

Lesson Outline

Justice for the Nations

   I. The Servant's Mission: Isaiah 42:1-4
      A. *To Bring Justice: vs. 1*
      B. *To Bring Peace and Healing: vss. 2-3*
      C. *To Establish Truth and Righteousness: vs. 4*
  II. The Servant's Call: Isaiah 42:5-7
      A. *God the Creator: vs. 5*
      B. *God's Care of His Servant: vs. 6*
      C. *God's Intention for His Servant: vs. 7*
 III. The Character of God: Isaiah 42:8-9
      A. *The Integrity of God: vs. 8*
      B. *The Certainty of God's Promises: vs. 9*

Introduction for Adults

Topic: *The Gift of Justice*

W. P. Keller states that "there is an unfortunate tendency among some Christians to withdraw from society. There lurks the inclination to retreat into sheltered secluded situations." This resistance to involve ourselves in ministry can grow out of an attitude of apathy or futility.

It should come as no surprise, then, that saved adults typically feel that what they do or can do to serve the Lord is unimportant. Supposedly, since they aren't leaders or doing something that radically impacts the culture in which they live, their ministry or possible ministry isn't important. They may wonder, "What difference does my ministry make in the big picture?"

Bill Bennett, however, writes that in our effort to impact our culture and society, what really matters is "what we do in our daily lives—not the big statements that we broadcast to the world at large, but the small messages we send through our families and our neighborhoods and our communities."

This week's lesson assures us that God seeks to sustain us in the ministry to which He has called us. God will never call us where His grace will not sustain us.

Introduction for Youths

Topic: *Justice Rules!*

Imagine this scenario. You purchase a ticket to fly from the closest international airport in your area to London, England. After checking in your luggage and boarding the plane, you find your assigned seat and get comfortable for the long flight.

Soon after taking off, however, you notice that the plane does not seem to be heading in any specific direction. Puzzled by it, you ask a flight attendant if anything is wrong. She responds, "Oh, don't worry. The pilot decided to scrap the planned itinerary. We're just flying around the area for a while before landing. Relax and enjoy the ride."

Most teens would protest over the pilot's decision. Just as they would want the plane to be flying to a specific destination, so God wants their lives to be filled with direction and purpose. The theme of purposeful living is a prominent one in this week's Scripture passage. We will learn that God wants saved adolescents to pursue their ministries with gentleness and fairness.

Concepts for Children

Topic: *Wise Men Visited Jesus*

1. When Jesus was born, wise men came to worship Him.
2. An evil king named Herod wanted to harm Jesus.
3. Thankfully, the Wise Men did not go along with Herod's plan.
4. These visitors gave Jesus valuable gifts and worshiped Him.
5. God is pleased when we offer thanks and praise to Jesus.

The Lesson Commentary

I. THE SERVANT'S MISSION: ISAIAH 42:1-4

A. To Bring Justice: vs. 1

"Here is my servant, whom I uphold, my chosen one in whom I delight; I will put my Spirit on him and he will bring justice to the nations."

Chapters 40 and 41 of Isaiah—leading up to this week's study passage—are filled with majestic themes and memorable verses rich with prophecy. It all could have seemed overwhelming to God's people. These passages reassured them that, regardless of a currently turbulent political atmosphere and the terrible afflictions to come, their nation was firmly in the Lord's hands.

The worship of idols plagued the Israelites for many years. In 41:21-29, God declared that all pagan deities were lifeless and powerless. He made it clear that He alone controlled the destiny of His people and that of the entire world. Then in 42:1, God directed His people to focus their attention on His true Servant.

Apparently, some aspects of the Servant's ministry (described in vss. 1-9) relate to delivering the exiles from Babylon; other aspects relate to Christ's earthly ministry; still other aspects may relate to His work in the end times. Clearly, the main focus here is on the Messiah. He is the standard toward which every one of God's servants is to strive.

Isaiah 42:1 discloses that God would choose and strengthen the Servant to do His will. Also, the Holy Spirit would indwell the Lord's Servant in full measure. Moreover, unlike earthly kings who were unjust, the Servant would bring justice to the nations and establish a righteous world order.

Isaiah 42:1-4 is quoted in Matthew 12:18-21 with reference to Christ. The immediate context of that passage indicates the religious leaders were questioning Jesus' authority. The Savior responded by declaring that He was Lord of the Sabbath. In fact, He backed up His claim by healing a man with a shriveled hand on the Sabbath (vss. 1-13). He also continued to heal the sick, though He warned the people not to say who He was (vss. 14-17).

The typical first-century expectations of the Messiah included political agendas, military campaigns, and great fanfare (John 6:14-15). Matthew 12:18-21 quotes Isaiah 42:1-4 to stress that the Messiah was not this type of king. Instead, He would be a quiet, gentle ruler who would bring justice to the nations. And as God's chosen Servant, the Messiah would be noted for His encouragement and truth, not violence and trickery (John 18:33-37).

B. To Bring Peace and Healing: vss. 2-3

"He will not shout or cry out, or raise his voice in the streets. A bruised reed he will not break, and a smoldering wick he will not snuff out. In faithfulness he will bring forth justice."

Isaiah 42:1-4 points to specific characteristics of God's Servant. We have already noted several of these in our look at verse 1. In verse 2 we learn that, unlike many pompous rulers, the Servant would have a quiet and unassuming ministry. And rather than call attention to Himself with a loud voice or flashy rhetoric, He would patiently and humbly point people to God.

This Servant would also be characterized by gentleness in His dealings with people. Two metaphors in verse 3a illustrate this. The Servant would be careful not to break a "bruised reed," and He would be mindful not to snuff out a "smoldering wick." In other words, He would deal very gently with the weak, and would mend lives, not break them.

Many of us, at one time or another, feel as though our lives are in need of mending. Also, sometimes circumstances become too burdensome and they break us. How wonderful that we can bring all our needs to Christ, the divine Servant, who heals our wounds and carries all our burdens!

In verse 3b we discover that God's Servant would remain loyal and undeterred in establishing "justice" on the earth. Regardless of how difficult this task might be, the Messiah would succeed in His noble endeavor. He would continue to work until His task was completed.

C. To Establish Truth and Righteousness: vs. 4

"He will not falter or be discouraged till he establishes justice on earth. In his law the islands will put their hope."

Isaiah 42:3 says that the Servant's overarching goal was to bring full justice to all who have been wronged. In verse 4 we discover that the Servant would not give up in pursuing this goal. He would untiringly work to establish justice on the earth. The Servant's desire would be for God's truth and righteousness to prevail throughout the world.

There have been periods throughout human history when nations and their governments were characterized, at least in some way, by justice. But for the most part human rulers (even those of Judah) have fallen short of being consistently fair and upright in their statements, goals, and actions. And sadly, the wicked rich oftentimes have been permitted to exploit the poor and oppress the disadvantaged (1:10-17; 5:7).

Isaiah envisioned a future day when the Messiah would permanently end all forms of injustice and iniquity. As 42:1 reveals, He would "bring justice to the nations." This righteous world order will know no bounds (vs. 4). In that longed for day, the Messiah's government will be ever expanding, peaceful, and unending (9:7). He will judge the poor "with righteousness" (11:4) and make decisions on behalf of the afflicted "with justice."

II. THE SERVANT'S CALL: ISAIAH 42:5-7

A. God the Creator: vs. 5

This is what God the LORD says—he who created the heavens and stretched them out, who spread out the earth and all that comes out of it, who gives breath to its people, and life to those who walk on it.

Previously God was presenting His Servant. Now the Lord speaks directly to His Servant and reveals what He would enable the Servant to do.

It's helpful to note that Isaiah 42:5 contains the prophet's identification of the one who would be speaking to the Servant. The speaker is none other than the supreme Lord of Israel and the world. He created and sustains the heavens, the earth, and all the plant life on the globe. He gave breath and a living spirit to all the people of the earth.

When Isaiah prophesied, the Israelites were living in a period of great uncertainty. Isaiah wanted them to know that God's promises regarding His Servant would surely come to pass by stressing that the Lord had created everything in the universe. Surely He who was so powerful and great would be able to fulfill His redemptive plans for His people through His Servant.

This verse is a clear affirmation of God as the Creator of the universe. Genesis 1:1—2:3, of course, is the main place in Scripture where we find a detailed account of God's creation activity. At first, the earth was "formless and empty" (1:1). But then over a period of time, God brought order and fullness to the world.

B. God's Care of His Servant: vs. 6

"I, the LORD, have called you in righteousness; I will take hold of your hand. I will keep you and will make you to be a covenant for the people and a light for the Gentiles."

The Lord declared that He had called the Servant to demonstrate His righteousness (Isa. 42:6). From this we see that it was the Lord who chose and commissioned His Servant to fulfill a noble mission. God, of course, was entirely just in picking this course of action. He alone would sustain and protect His Servant in all phases of His ministry.

Verse 6 reveals that the Lord would appoint the Messiah as a "covenant for the people." To better understand what this verse is saying, it is helpful to note what covenants were in Bible times. They represented a binding pact, treaty, alliance, or agreement between two parties. Human covenants were either between equals or between a superior and an inferior. Divine covenants, however, were always the second type.

The covenant is a central, unifying theme in Scripture. In fact, God's covenants with individuals and the nation of Israel find ultimate fulfillment in the new covenant of Jesus Christ (Jer. 31:31-34). In this unconditional pledge, the Lord promised forgiveness of sins and an intimate knowledge of Him.

As a "covenant for the people" (Isa. 42:6), the Servant would fulfill every salvation promise that God made to Israel. God's Servant would also be a light (a source of truth and deliverance) to Gentile believers. Thus, the scope of God's revelation would widen from the Jews to the Gentiles through the Messiah.

Israel had originally been commissioned to be a light to the nations, but had failed in that mission. Here we learn that what Israel had failed to accomplish, the divine Servant would succeed in doing.

C. God's Intention for His Servant: vs. 7

To open eyes that are blind, to free captives from prison and to release from the dungeon those who sit in darkness.

A key aspect of the Servant's ministry would be to "open the eyes that are blind" (Isa. 42:7) and to "free captives from the prison." This verse apparently has both a literal and a spiritual meaning. God would certainly heal the exiles physically and set them free from Babylon's prisons. But the Servant would also open spiritually blind eyes, set spiritually bound captives free, and release people from the dungeon of sin and spiritual darkness.

This sounds very much like the ministry recorded in the New Testament. Note, for example, the incident that occurred when John the Baptist was in prison. He sent some of his followers to ask Jesus if He was the Messiah (Matt. 11:2-3). Jesus, in turn, affirmed His identity to them by declaring "the blind receive sight, the lame walk, those who have leprosy are cured, the deaf hear, the dead are raised, and the good news is preached to the poor" (vs. 5).

Jesus' constant presence gives us the strength we need to live out His will for us despite our circumstances. Because of His strength, we need not wrestle with frustration, anger, or fear. We have God's power working through us; we need only surrender to His gentle, just Spirit.

III. THE CHARACTER OF GOD: ISAIAH 42:8-9

A. The Integrity of God: vs. 8

"I am the LORD; that is my name! I will not give my glory to another or my praise to idols."

Isaiah 42:8 makes it clear that the Lord would not share His glory with any graven images. He alone was the source of the prophecies concerning His Servant. These declarations did not come from the false gods of evil nations. Thus, they would not receive the praise that belonged only to God.

B. The Certainty of God's Promises: vs. 9

"See, the former things have taken place, and new things I declare; before they spring into being I announce them to you."

God affirmed that earlier predictions had come to pass for His people. In the same way, new prophecies—such as those about the Servant—would come to pass as well. God declared in advance that these things would happen: "Before they spring into being I announce them to you" (Isa. 42:9).

Unlike the idols that Israel worshiped, the Lord was able to declare what He had planned to do in advance and then bring them to pass. The liberating work of His Servant was like a seed that had been planted in the earth. This seed would one day sprout above the ground and bring new life to God's people according to His will.

Discussion Questions

1. What characteristics of God's Servant are described in Isaiah 42:1-4?
2. In what ways would the Servant bring justice to the Gentiles?
3. Why did Isaiah make a point that the Lord is the Creator?
4. Why did God stress His identity as the Lord?
5. What things do people give more glory and pride to than to God? How do you feel about this?

Contemporary Application

In Isaiah's prophecy he underscored the promise of God to deliver His people in their times of need. God's compassion and care for them undergirded His commitment to fulfill His pledge.

The Lord is able to help us in our times of need as well, and God's unfailing love is the basis for this promise. The mystery of God's love is that the Lord accepts and meets us at the point of our deepest need. When we trust God's promises, we experience His comfort and blessings in our lives.

We also know that the Lord is eternal and unchanging, and is as mighty today as He was in the day of Creation. He does not grow weak with the passing of time, and He is not tired from having to sustain the universe. Because of these truths, we can trust the Lord to bring about His plan and purpose for us. We can rest assured that He will strengthen us to do His will.

It would be wrong to think that when God strengthens us, all our troubles go away. Instead, the Lord enables us to endure our trials and face a potentially troubled future. The greater the difficulty we face, the more God reaches out to us in love to uphold and comfort us.

God has never failed in His promise to strengthen us in our difficult times. We should not only acknowledge this truth but also thank the Lord for the ways He has enabled us to do His will in the past. Unlike flowers, which are a temporary delight in our eyes, God's love and care are everlasting. Let us express our gratitude to God for being like a shepherd in His care for us, especially when life is rough.

Good News for All Nations

DEVOTIONAL READING

Isaiah 60:17-22

DAILY BIBLE READINGS

Monday January 7
*Psalm 34:1-10 When We
Seek Him, the Lord Answers*

Tuesday January 8
*Psalm 63:1-8 The Soul That
Thirsts for God*

Wednesday January 9
*Psalm 105:1-7 Seek the
Lord's Strength*

Thursday January 10
*Isaiah 54:4-8 The Holy One
Redeems You*

Friday January 11
*Isaiah 54:9-17 The Heritage
of the Lord's Servants*

Saturday January 12
*Isaiah 55:1-5 Accept the
Lord's Free Offer*

Sunday January 13
*Isaiah 55:6-13 Return to the
Lord*

Scripture

Background Scripture: *Isaiah 60—61*
Scripture Lesson: *Isaiah 60:1-3; 61:1-4*
Key Verse: *"Arise, shine, for your light has come, and the
glory of the LORD rises upon you."* Isaiah 60:1.
Scripture Lesson for Children: *Isaiah 61:1-2;
Luke 4:16-22*
Key Verse for Children: *"The Spirit of the Lord is on me,
because he has anointed me to preach good news to the poor."*
Luke 4:18.

Lesson Aim

To proclaim God's message of hope and restoration to
those who are hurting.

Lesson Setting

Time: *740–700 B.C.*
Place: *Judah*

Lesson Outline

Good News for All Nations

   I. The Glory of Zion: Isaiah 60:1-3
      A. *The Command to Shine: vss. 1-2*
      B. *The Splendor of Zion: vs. 3*
   II. The Ministry of the Messiah: Isaiah 61:1-4
      A. *A Ministry of Healing and Freedom: vs. 1*
      B. *A Ministry of Justice and Hope: vss. 2-3*
      C. *A Ministry of Restoration: vs. 4*

Introduction for Adults

Topic: *A Time for Building*

One of the great tasks in business, education, and the military is building morale. Astute leaders know that nothing drags down productivity like low morale. In fact, it takes only a few malcontents to stir up trouble.

The same principle holds true in the life of the church. Morale sags for many reasons and soon we are robbed of the joy of our faith. We start to think like unsaved people, not like God's redeemed children.

That's when we need morale builders like our Scripture lesson for this week. Isaiah's stirring words remind us that we serve a powerful, wise, and loving God who will one day defeat all our foes. He has the ability to lift us out of our morass. When this happens, our enthusiasm for Jesus will begin to spread throughout the entire body of Christ.

Introduction for Youths

Topic: *A Light in the Night*

Tell your teens that the church is planning a Colorado ski trip, and you'll have excitement in the air. But pass around a clipboard for them to sign up to go downtown next Thursday night to witness, and you'll have many of them nervously passing the clipboard. Something in their human nature doesn't want them to impose their faith in Christ on others.

Nevertheless, this week's lesson focuses on God's call for saved teens (and all believers) to proclaim His message of hope and restoration to the lost. Sharing Christ with those who think they don't need the Gospel can be frustrating, but also it feels scary. That is why adolescents need to look away from their own insecurities and focus on the needs of others.

A friend of mine—the son of an evangelist—shared with me a truth he had learned long ago. He noted that the first fundamental of sharing Christ with others is to make nonbelievers aware of their need for God. But in order to do that, Christians must be concerned about their need for God. Let your students know that the Lord wants to use them to bring His message of hope to the lost.

Concepts for Children

Topic: *Listen to Good News*

1. Isaiah said that God would send the Savior to tell others a wonderful message.
2. In a place of worship, Jesus read some Bible verses to the people.
3. Jesus said that God had sent Him to bring the good news of salvation.
4. The people spoke well of what Jesus had said.
5. God wants us to let others know about the good news of salvation.

The Lesson Commentary

I. THE GLORY OF ZION: ISAIAH 60:1-3

A. The Command to Shine: vss. 1-2

"Arise, shine, for your light has come, and the glory of the LORD rises upon you. See, darkness covers the earth and thick darkness is over the peoples, but the LORD rises upon you and his glory appears over you."

In Isaiah 59:20, we learn that the Lord would come as Redeemer to a repentant remnant of His people. (This probably refers initially to God's protection of the returned exiles, but ultimately to Jesus Christ.) Then, in verse 21, the Lord promised to establish an everlasting covenant with those whom He redeemed. His Spirit and His words would remain with them and their descendants forever. (This pledge seems to refer, mainly, to the new covenant established by Jesus.)

In Isaiah 60:1, God is the speaker, and He addressed Zion (or Jerusalem) personified as a woman lying down in defeat and darkness. The Lord had judged His sinful and idolatrous people by allowing them to be attacked and defeated by their enemies (for instance, the Assyrians and Babylonians). The holy city would be able to shine because a light would beam upon it. This light was the redeeming glory of the Lord.

When the Israelites journeyed through the wilderness, the glory of God was evident in the pillar of cloud (Exod. 14:19-20). Isaiah 60:1 announced a new manifestation of the Lord's glory. His splendor would be like a source of great light shining its rays down on Jerusalem. God's glory would transform the holy city and bring it His salvation, prosperity, and joy.

In verse 2, we learn that darkness as black as night would cover all the nations of the earth. Darkness in Scripture usually symbolizes chaos and disorder, whereas light brings meaning and order to the world. In the Bible darkness is often associated with God's judgment. For instance, Jesus described the outer darkness as a place of punishment for unrepentant humans and rebellious angels (Matt. 8:12).

In Scripture darkness is often given ethical qualities. Evil people prefer the darkness so that their deeds will not be exposed (John 3:19-20). Wickedness is often described as the "dark ways" (Prov. 2:13). One cannot hide from God, however, even in the dark. Of course, darkness can never separate us from the love of God (Rom. 8:38-39).

It is evident that the impenetrable darkness of Isaiah 60:2 symbolizes sin, wickedness, ignorance, suffering, and destruction. Despite this, the Lord promised to shine His glory upon Zion. This reminds us of John 1:5, which says that Christ, the Light, shines in the darkness and can never be extinguished by it.

As we consider these promises, it is natural for us to long for their fulfillment. Nevertheless, we must wait patiently for God to bring about what He has pledged. We can rest assured that He is in control of all life's events and that He weaves together all our lives into His plan.

B. The Splendor of Zion: vs. 3

"Nations will come to your light, and kings to the brightness of your dawn."

Isaiah 60:3 reveals that, as the light of God's glory shines upon Zion, the Gentiles would see His splendor radiating from the holy city. Consequently, they would "come to your light." The light would draw people from all nations to it, and not just common folks, but even people of high rank, such as princes and kings.

God was not saying that Zion's light would save Gentiles. Rather, He was announcing that the splendor radiating from the holy city would be like a beacon that projects from a lighthouse. Zion's light would guide people to the Lord, who had the power to save them and transform their lives.

This truth reminds us of Isaiah 2:1-5, a passage in which Isaiah described a time of righteousness, justice, and peace. In that future day of blessing, the mountain of the Lord's temple will be the highest of all, and every nation will throng to it. Many people—both Gentiles and Jews—will want to worship the Lord in His sanctuary.

In the remaining verses of Isaiah 60, we learn that Israel will be blessed with unimaginable wealth. God, the Holy One, will be honored to bring these things to pass. That future day will be a time of abundance, recognition, and rejoicing for the people of God. The glory of Lord will illumine His people and they will remain devoted to Him.

II. THE MINISTRY OF THE MESSIAH: ISAIAH 61:1-4

A. A Ministry of Healing and Freedom: vs. 1

The Spirit of the Sovereign LORD is on me, because the LORD has anointed me to preach good news to the poor. He has sent me to bind up the brokenhearted, to proclaim freedom for the captives and release from darkness for the prisoners.

Isaiah 61 begins with the description of a ministry that belonged in a limited sense to Isaiah but belongs fully to the Messiah. The people of Judah who first received Isaiah's message had not yet gone into Babylonian captivity, and so they would not have comprehended the full implications of his prophecy. Through captivity the people of Judah would later become poor and brokenhearted as prisoners of Babylon. After the fall of Babylon, they would be set free from bondage and would return to their ancestral lands.

The Lord called Isaiah to minister to needy people, and the Spirit of almighty God empowered Isaiah for his important task (Isa. 61:1). The prophet realized that he was "a man of unclean lips" (6:5) and that he lived "among a people of unclean lips." Isaiah was able to minister as a prophet of God because the Lord had taken away his guilt and atoned for his sin (vs. 7).

God not only commissioned Isaiah to declare messages of judgment but also of hope. For instance, he would announce the good news of release from captivity (61:1). Isaiah's preaching would encourage the poor and bandage the wounds of the brokenhearted. He would tell the captives that God would set them free and declare to the prisoners that the Lord would release them from their exile.

At times it's tempting to doubt God's ability to bring restoration and comfort. The Lord wants us to reassure those who are grieving that He genuinely is concerned for them and deeply loves them. They need to know that God is always present and will never let them down.

B.   A Ministry of Justice and Hope: vss. 2-3

To proclaim the year of the LORD's favor and the day of vengeance of our God, to comfort all who mourn, and provide for those who grieve in Zion—to bestow on them a crown of beauty instead of ashes, the oil of gladness instead of mourning, and a garment of praise instead of a spirit of despair. They will be called oaks of righteousness, a planting of the LORD for the display of his splendor.

Many scholars think the Year of Jubilee is the background for the prophecy recorded in Isaiah 61:2. Every 50 years in ancient Israel property was supposed to be returned to its original owners (Lev. 25:10, 13), and those who sold themselves into slavery to pay off debts were to be freed (vss. 39, 54).

Isaiah was to proclaim the year of the Lord's favor, the time when His redemptive blessings would be lavished on His people. As the exiled Jews left Babylon, their land and liberty would be restored to them. As the light of God's freedom shone on them, they also would be delivered from their spiritual and moral bondage.

Isaiah was also to declare the time of punishment for God's enemies (61:2). The Lord was not only the Savior of His people but also the judge of the wicked. They would not remain guiltless for their crimes against the Jews.

At the beginning of Jesus' public ministry, He quoted the first part of this passage (up through the first line of Isa. 61:2; see Luke 4:16-21). Christ did not quote any further because the time of vengeance would not occur until His second coming. Even more than Isaiah, Jesus was anointed to minister to the needy. The blessings of Isaiah 61 are, in part, blessings given through the Messiah.

God wanted Isaiah to comfort all who mourned (vs. 3). Perhaps they grieved over their sin and over the destruction of their holy city. Isaiah's ministry to the afflicted inhabitants of Jerusalem involved three exchanges. First, instead of the ashes that people would place on their heads to show their desolation, Isaiah would give them a headdress, or ornamental turban, of beauty. Second, instead of mourning, he would give them oil, which Jews would anoint themselves with on happy occasions. Third, instead of the "spirit of despair," or sorrow, he would give them the "garment of praise."

As a result of all the blessings God would give His people (in part through Isaiah and ultimately and fully through the Messiah), they would be "oaks of righteousness." They would be righteous people firmly planted in the land, showing off God's splendor.

Our churches and neighborhoods are full of the hidden wounded. God wants us to tell them that we stand by them and will help them whenever they are ready to share their pain with us. We might sometimes feel inadequate reaching out to others this way. We can remind ourselves that God will give us the strength to comfort hurting people with His restorative message. We can rest assured that no problem is too big and no difficulty is too hard for God to resolve.

C. A Ministry of Restoration: vs. 4

They will rebuild the ancient ruins and restore the places long devastated; they will renew the ruined cities that have been devastated for generations.

After the Babylonians removed the Jews living in Judah, the invaders completely destroyed Jerusalem. Isaiah 61:4 indicates that God's people would rebuild the holy city after they returned from their exile in Babylon. The Jews would also restore the sites that had been devastated for so long and repair the cities of Judah that had been demolished by the enemy. In a future day, God's people would no longer be the objects of His wrath. Instead, they would be the recipients of His richest blessings.

This passage reveals that God greatly cares for His people and that He is ready and willing to rescue them from their plight. We learn that He is unlimited in power, upright in His ways, and faithful to His word. He shows His compassion and grace by redeeming all who trust and obey Him, and He shows His holiness and righteousness by punishing all who reject Him and His commands.

No doubt all of us can recall times in our lives when we were filled with sorrow, struggling with grief, or experiencing great personal loss. God can rebuild our lives by replacing our sorrow with joy, comforting us in our time of grief, or enabling us to courageously face and overcome our losses. We know from experience that the Lord loves us, keeps us from falling, and gives us the strength to endure.

Discussion Questions

1. Why do you think God commanded Zion (Jerusalem) to arise and let its light shine?
2. In what way would the nations of the world come to see the light of Zion?
3. What kinds of needy people are talked about in Isaiah 61:1-4? How would God meet their needs?
4. In your opinion, what does this passage say about the character of God?
5. What might be some tactful ways to comfort a hurting person who is doubting God's goodness?

Contemporary Application

What good is proclaiming God's message of hope to someone struggling with cancer? Or whose parent or spouse has just died? Or who has discovered they don't have enough retirement money to get by? How dare we minimize their pain with pie-in-the-sky talk about God's promises!

While we pray and consider ways of communicating God's greatness, we can have confidence that describing God's care and faithfulness will be a source of encouragement to others. Presenting God's plans for the future is a time-tested antidote to despair. Not only did Old Testament prophets do this, but in the Book of Revelation the apostle John also comforted a persecuted New Testament church with descriptions of coming glory. When we offer hope and comfort by speaking about the realities of God, we speak the truth. We are offering facts about the future, not just guesses and wishes no one has any reason to believe.

For those experiencing death or the desertion of those they love, life can seem empty and dark. Their life is full of bad news, gloomy news, even desperate news. Christians are called to bring good news to them. For instance, a prison inmate gets bad news from a lawyer that there's no possibility for an appeal. This inmate needs good news from Christians presented in a sensitive way. In situations such as this, believers become God's messengers of hope and reassurance.

We can also comfort people who are hurting by sending them a card with a cheerful message, giving them a warm hug, taking them out to lunch, offering to pray with them, or volunteering to do a devotional study of Scripture with them. At times they might just want someone to listen who will not try to minimize their pain or act as if it isn't really there. In these simple and tactful ways, we can comfort a hurting person with God's message of hope and restoration.

Seek the Lord

DEVOTIONAL READING

Psalm 85:4-9

DAILY BIBLE READINGS

Monday January 14
John 4:19-26 Worship in Spirit and in Truth

Tuesday January 15
Malachi 1:6-14 Worship with Honor

Wednesday January 16
Amos 5:18-24 Worship in Righteousness

Thursday January 17
Isaiah 56:1-5 A Heritage for Those without Heirs

Friday January 18
Isaiah 56:6-8 Foreigners Can Share the True Sabbath

Saturday January 19
Isaiah 57:14-21 Not Too Late to Repent

Sunday January 20
Isaiah 58:3-14 What the Lord Truly Honors

Scripture

Background Scripture: *Isaiah 55*
Scripture Lesson: *Isaiah 55:1-3, 5-9*
Key Verse: *Seek the LORD while he may be found; call on him while he is near.* Isaiah 55:6.
Scripture Lesson for Children: *Isaiah 55:6-7; Matthew 4:18-25*
Key Verse for Children: *At once they left their nets and followed him.* Matthew 4:20.

Lesson Aim

To recognize the importance of turning to the Lord in faith for meaning and satisfaction in life.

Lesson Setting

Time: *740–700 B.C.*
Place: *Judah*

Lesson Outline

Seek the Lord

  I. The Invitation to an Abundant Life: Isaiah 55:1-2
     A. Satisfaction for a Thirsty Soul: vs. 1
     B. Satisfaction for a Hungry Soul: vs. 2
  II. The Exhortation to Respond: Isaiah 55:3, 5-7
     A. An Everlasting Covenant: vs. 3
     B. A Revived Interest in the Lord: vs. 5
     C. A Renewed Desire to Seek the Lord: vss. 6-7
  III. The Uniqueness of God's Ways: Isaiah 55:8-9

Introduction for Adults
Topic: *Seek the Lord*

The unbeliever turned to his Christian friend and challenged him to explain the apparent unfairness of God's judgments. The Christian made no attempt to justify God's ways, though he knew that God was eminently fair. He simply said to his friend, "How many people do you know who are genuinely seeking God?"

It's so easy to throw "bricks" at God without admitting that many people want no part of Him. They prefer to ignore Him and to flout His laws. They also prefer to blame Him, rather than accept responsibility for not seeking Him.

The Bible makes clear in many ways that God welcomes all those who want to know Him. And Isaiah's invitation is one of the most brilliant explanations of how God yearns for people to come to Him. Best of all, the prophet made it clear that anyone can come without any special credentials. God welcomes the spiritually needy, not people who think they don't need Him.

Introduction for Youths
Topic: *Something for Nothing*

The order placed on the company's web site was simple enough, but when the package arrived it did not contain what the customer had wanted. Of course, the company quickly sent the correct order, and to make up for its error, the company gave the customer a $10 gift certificate. In this case the customer got something for nothing. However, in most situations we have to work hard for what we get.

When God spoke to His disobedient people He offered them something for nothing. The prophet Isaiah compared God's offer to a free shopping spree at the mall. He also likened God's invitation to a rich banquet. What was the catch? The people had to come to the Lord in repentance and faith.

Sadly, many youth refuse to turn to the Lord. In fact, they want nothing to do with God. Thankfully, there are some adolescents who want what the Lord has to offer. Through faith in His Son they find sublime delights and eternal satisfaction.

Concepts for Children
Topic: *Follow God's Call*

1. Isaiah invited people to seek God and His forgiveness.
2. Jesus called people to become His disciples and to help with His work.
3. Peter, Andrew, James, and John quickly answered Jesus' call.
4. Great crowds followed Jesus wherever He went to teach and heal people.
5. God is pleased when we decide to follow Jesus.

The Lesson Commentary

I. THE INVITATION TO AN ABUNDANT LIFE: ISAIAH 55:1-2

A. Satisfaction for a Thirsty Soul: vs. 1

"Come, all you who are thirsty, come to the waters; and you who have no money, come, buy and eat! Come, buy wine and milk without money and without cost."

When Isaiah began his ministry in 740 B.C., the northern kingdom of Israel was near collapse due to political, spiritual, and military deterioration. Things were going from bad to worse. In 723 B.C., the weakened northern kingdom finally fell to the Assyrian Empire, which had been expanding steadily for the past century and a half.

The southern kingdom of Judah was heading for a similar end. In fact, under the leadership of wicked King Ahaz, Judah was ripe for a fall. The nation had become corrupt socially, politically, and religiously. It was during this time that Isaiah delivered his messages to the people of Judah.

Isaiah called Judah to repent of idolatry and moral degeneracy. But then, failing to turn the nation Godward, Isaiah informed the people of Judah that their rebellion would lead to captivity at the hands of the Babylonians. Isaiah also predicted that, following the captivity, God would restore His people. God's foretelling all this in advance (through Isaiah) was intended to convey His sovereignty in contrast to the powerlessness of false gods.

Isaiah 54 describes the splendor of Judah at the time of the exiles' return. In verses 1-3, Judah's fruitfulness and expansion to come are contrasted with its barrenness during the Exile. In verses 4-10, exiled Judah is pictured as a wife separated from her faithful husband (the Lord), but who eventually will be restored to Him. The restored nation is then compared to a city of righteousness and security (vss. 11-17).

As chapter 55 begins, we find God calling His people to move from the comfort and relative prosperity of Babylon to half-ruined Jerusalem. Although the Jews were forcibly relocated to Babylon, eventually they grew accustomed to their new life. On the whole, the Babylonians treated them leniently, even allowing them to buy property and conduct business.

When Cyrus the Persian took over Babylon in 539 B.C. and instituted policies of religious toleration, the Jews were faced with a decision—to go back to Judah or to stay in Babylon. Many of the Jews decided to stay. Most had been born in Babylon and knew about Judah only through stories told by the older generation. Also, according to the first-century A.D. historian Josephus, many Jews decided to remain in Babylon because they were "not willing to leave their possessions."

In verses 1-5, we hear God calling out to the exiles as if He were a street vendor selling food and water. (A common sound in cities of the ancient Near East was a street vendor calling out enticements to potential customers.) The idea is that returning to Judah would prove more spiritually satisfying than staying in Babylon.

Life for the exiles in Babylon may not always have been good, but it was at least secure and familiar. A return to Judah would involve unknown hardships and hazards. So God promised spiritual benefits if the exiles would take the risk of returning.

As a street vendor, God had many products to sell, including water, wine, and milk (representing spiritual benefits). He urged people to buy His goods, but to buy them "without money and without cost" (vs. 1). That would be like a store owner in our day putting up a SALE sign and giving away all his stock for nothing! It's a marvelous picture of God's free and abundant grace.

B. Satisfaction for a Hungry Soul: vs. 2

"Why spend money on what is not bread, and your labor on what does not satisfy? Listen, listen to me, and eat what is good, and your soul will delight in the richest of fare."

God tried to persuade His potential customers to stay away from His competitors. He warned them that, if the people didn't buy what He was selling, they would be spending their money without getting what they needed and would be laboring without satisfaction. In other words, if they stayed in Babylon, their lives would be spiritually unproductive. But on the other hand, if they listened to Him and took His spiritual food, their souls would thrive on "the richest of fare" (Isa. 55:2).

Jesus said, "I have come that [My followers] may have life, and have it to the full" (John 10:10). But just as the exiles could not enjoy God's rich fare without leaving Babylon, so people today cannot enjoy the abundant life Christ spoke of without turning from sin to Him in faith.

II. THE EXHORTATION TO RESPOND: ISAIAH 55:3, 5-7

A. An Everlasting Covenant: vs. 3

"Give ear and come to me; hear me, that your soul may live. I will make an everlasting covenant with you, my faithful love promised to David."

Again in Isaiah 55:3 we find an exhortation for God's people to come to Him with ears wide open. They were told to heed His commands so that their "soul may live." By obeying the Lord, the people would receive the benefits of the everlasting covenant God made with David (2 Sam. 7:11-13).

In that covenant, God promised David that his line would continue forever, culminating in the coming of the Messiah. The Lord also pledged to give a permanent homeland to the Israelites, to eliminate the threat from pagan nations, and to make them victorious over their foes. Sadly, Israel did not fulfill its part of the agreement to obey God and shun idolatry. Nevertheless, the Lord was ready to renew His covenant again, for He is a forgiving God.

This should come as no surprise. After all, the Lord is characterized by "faithful love" (Isa. 55:3). God had not forsaken His people. He would keep His word to them.

B. A Revived Interest in the Lord: vs. 5

"Surely you will summon nations you know not, and nations that do not know you will hasten to you, because of the LORD your God, the Holy One of Israel, for he has endowed you with splendor."

Through Isaiah, God declared, "See, I have made him a witness to the peoples, a leader and commander of the peoples" (Isa. 55:4). The "him" is David, who would be represented by one of his descendants. But since the Davidic royalty was not restored when the exiles returned to Judah, this prophecy must point to another of David's descendants—the Messiah. Jesus, the Messiah, would fulfill the Davidic covenant promising a glorious leader from the line of David.

God also promised that a time would come when Israel would issue a command to the nations and they would come running to obey (vs. 5). The people of foreign nations would flock to God's people because they would be attracted by the splendor with which God would endow His people. Since this gathering of the nations did not happen in restored Judah, this prophecy too must apply to the messianic age.

The ultimate fulfillment of this prophecy rests with God. After all, He alone is "the Holy One of Israel." Only He could make His people glorious. He was to be their source of trust and the foundation of their faith.

C. A Renewed Desire to Seek the Lord: vss. 6-7

Seek the LORD while he may be found; call on him while he is near. Let the wicked forsake his way and the evil man his thoughts. Let him turn to the LORD, and he will have mercy on him, and to our God, for he will freely pardon.

A non-response on the part of the exiles was not an option. If they refused God's invitation to return to their homeland, they would not spiritually prosper. The people were also not to delay their response indefinitely. They were to seek the Lord while the opportunity to do so continued to exist. The context, of course, is returning to Judah from exile. The people were also to call on God for help "while he is near" (Isa. 55:6). The idea is that only the Lord could enable them to succeed in such a venture.

The spiritual blessings that God offers us in Christ must be appropriated by faith. Like the people of Old Testament times, we must come to the Lord, heed His commands, seek His favor, and respond to His summons. His salvation is freely offered, but we must eagerly receive it in order for our souls to be nourished. If we don't nourish our bodies with physical food, we will starve. Similarly, if we fail to feed our souls with the nourishment that God offers in Christ, we will spiritually starve.

It was imperative for the exiles to heed God's invitation to return to their homeland. That's why the Lord urged them to turn from their wicked deeds and banish from their minds any thought of doing wrong (vs. 7). If they turned to the Lord in repentance and faith, they would experience His mercy, not His wrath. They would encounter His abundant pardon, not His terrifying judgment.

From this we see that God's blessings can be enjoyed only by those who have turned to the Lord. In the case of the exiles, they were exhorted not to delay in seeking Him. This would involve calling on God, turning from idolatry and immorality, and looking to God for forgiveness.

There are times when God seems far removed from us. In reality it is we who have moved away from Him, not He from us. For instance, we erect barriers of sin between ourselves and the Lord. Rather than allow ourselves to wallow in this predicament, it is better to abandon our sinful ways and confess them to God. If we seek the Lord with humility, He will pardon and cleanse us (1 John 1:9).

Our salvation depends totally on God's mercy. We can do nothing to save ourselves except to turn to Him in repentance and faith. Because we have sinned against God by disobeying His commands, we must have His pardon. Otherwise, we are forever condemned. Thus we should seek God now, while we can, before it is too late.

III. THE UNIQUENESS OF GOD'S WAYS: ISAIAH 55:8-9

"For my thoughts are not your thoughts, neither are your ways my ways," declares the LORD. "As the heavens are higher than the earth, so are my ways higher than your ways and my thoughts than your thoughts."

It can be disagreeable to be told that we need to abandon our wicked ways and turn to the Lord for forgiveness (Isa. 55:6-7). Perhaps this is why God was careful to assure the Jewish exiles of their need for repentance by pointing out His own superiority over them.

God's thoughts and ways are different from those of humankind (vs. 8). And His thoughts and ways are higher than those of humankind, in fact "as the heavens are higher than the earth" (vs. 9). By trusting that the Lord knew best, the exiles could muster up the courage to return to Judah.

In light of this, the Jewish people would have been foolish to contradict God and act as if they knew what was best for them. Similarly, we are foolish to try to make God's plans and purposes conform to ours. After all, His knowledge and wisdom far exceed our own. It is thus far wiser for us to strive to fit into His plans.

Discussion Questions

1. What were the exiles being urged to do in Isaiah 55:1? Why would this have been difficult for them to carry out?
2. According to verse 2, what was the key to the spiritual prosperity of God's people?
3. What was the "everlasting covenant" (vs. 3) that God made with David and his descendants?
4. When would people of foreign nations flock to God's people (vs. 5)?
5. Why did Isaiah warn the exiles not to delay in seeking the Lord?
6. Why is it best for us to conform our plans and purposes to the will of God?

Contemporary Application

No thinking person can deny that something about the world, including humanity's part in it, is seriously wrong. The big differences of opinion are about what is wrong, how it got that way, and what the solution is.

Isaiah's answers to all three questions are remarkably direct and simple. Sin is what is wrong; the cause was—and still is—humanity's turning away from God to their own way; and the only solution is trusting in Christ for salvation and forgiveness.

In *The Healing of Persons,* Dr. Paul Tournier describes an incident involving a Christian doctor who had heard from an old friend suffering from Parkinson's disease. The man wrote a note in which he told the doctor, "Come only if you have some new remedy. I've had enough of doctors who say they cannot cure me."

The doctor decided to accept the challenge. After arriving at his friend's home and greeting him, the doctor said, "I brought you a new remedy—Jesus Christ!" The doctor was not being trite or superficial in his words. Rather, he was filled with deep and genuine fervor as he shared with his friend how Christ had transformed his life.

As the doctor talked, his friend gradually started to soften in his attitude. It took several more visits before the man began to show a remarkable change in the way he thought and spoke. Because of his decision to trust in Christ for salvation, he became less irritable and more pleasant. People began noticing the dramatic changes and drew strength from his joyful demeanor.

John Bunyan, author of *Pilgrim's Progress,* imagined Christ coming after him "with a pardon in His hand." When Jesus' pardon comes to us, how will we respond? All people need to seek God's forgiveness for their sins by receiving the awesome pardon the Lord offers through faith in Christ. This is the message we need to embrace by faith and declare to the lost around us.

True Worship

Scripture

Background Scripture: *Isaiah 58*

Scripture Lesson: *Isaiah 58:3-9*

Key Verse: *"Is not this the kind of fasting I have chosen: to loose the chains of injustice and untie the cords of the yoke, to set the oppressed free and break every yoke?"* Isaiah 58:6.

Scripture Lesson for Children: *Isaiah 58:6-7; Matthew 25:34-40*

Key Verse for Children: *"The King will reply, 'I tell you the truth, whatever you did for one of the least of these brothers of mine, you did for me.'"* Matthew 25:40.

Lesson Aim

To commit to worshiping God with a pure heart and sincere motives.

Lesson Setting

Time: *740–700 B.C.*

Place: *Judah*

Lesson Outline

True Worship

   I. Hypocritical Fasting: Isaiah 58:3-5

      A. Insincere Acts: vs. 3a

      B. Inhumane Treatment of Others: vss. 3b-4

      C. Empty Religious Ritual: vs. 5

  II. Genuine Fasting: Isaiah 58:6-9

      A. Practice Justice: vs. 6

      B. Provide for the Poor: vs. 7

      C. Assurance of Divine Favor: vss. 8-9

Introduction for Adults

Topic: *True Worship*

Jesus said, "I am the way and the truth and the life. No one comes to the Father except through me" (John 14:6). In other words, Jesus was declaring Himself to be the only legitimate means of access to the Father. Thus when believers talk about true worship, at the core of their thinking is faith in Christ.

Of course, worship can take a wide variety of forms. Sadly, much of it is idolatrous in nature. People are eager to placate their false gods in the hope of finding some sort of salvation. This kind of worship rests on the assumption that if one does enough, prays enough, or sacrifices enough, the deity will be pleased.

The Christian faith rests on an entirely different foundation. In fact, the Bible teaches that no one can ever do enough to earn salvation. For believers, true worship is the acknowledgment that God has done everything necessary through His Son. Thus, those who truly worship God hammock themselves upon Jesus as their Savior. It should come as no surprise that God will not settle for anything less.

Introduction for Youths

Topic: *Get It Right*

Many young people are turned off to the Gospel because they see adults pretending to be holy (for instance, by going to church) while at the same time transgressing God's commands. A prophet such as Isaiah might have said, "What good is your church attendance when you keep on fighting and quarreling?" (see Isa. 58:4).

Adolescents are skilled at spotting phonies. And they lose respect for adults who preach one thing but do the opposite. That concern was the heart of Isaiah's indictment of Israel. The people mourned in public shows of fasting and humility while they gouged their poor neighbors.

The Gospel demands that a believer's worship matches his or her life (Jas. 1:27). If adults fail to match their creed with their conduct, their worship is vain and they will drive young people from the church.

Concepts for Children

Topic: *Worship God by Helping Others*

1. Some people thought that by not eating for a time, they would please God. But He was more concerned with the way they treated others.
2. Jesus talked about those who will be welcomed in God's kingdom.
3. The King will welcome those who gave Him food, drink, and clothing when He was in need.
4. Jesus said that by caring for the least regarded person in God's family, believers were actually caring for Him.
5. We show our love for Jesus by reaching out in love to those in need.

151

The Lesson Commentary

I. HYPOCRITICAL FASTING: ISAIAH 58:3-5

A. Insincere Acts: vs. 3a

"'Why have we fasted,' they say, 'and you have not seen it? Why have we humbled ourselves, and you have not noticed?'"

Isaiah ministered both in times of calamity and in times of prosperity. For instance, under the rule of Uzziah, Judah prospered economically, politically, and militarily. This state of prosperity, however, ended up producing a spiritual malaise. This, in turn, paved the way for greed, injustice, spiritual insensitivity, and dead formalism in worship.

As we will discover in this week's Scripture passage, Isaiah had to speak fearlessly, for he knew that he could easily be opposed or misunderstood. He had to speak clearly and memorably, for he did not have sophisticated communication technology. But above all, he had to speak with unwavering conviction, for there were others who claimed to be prophets of God but were in effect spreading disinformation from the enemy—Satan.

God did use Isaiah to denounce the evil and unjust practices of His people. To do so effectively, though, the prophet had to live uprightly himself. God demanded justice and uprightness from His people. That's why Isaiah not only preached this message but also lived it.

In Isaiah 58, we hear the Lord's message to His people about true service to God. It consists not in merely following certain rituals but in doing good and leading holy lives. This message seems to have been directed primarily to Jews who would be reading it during the postexilic period. The problem is that after returning to Judah, the people were fasting improperly and breaking the Sabbath law.

Fasting may be defined as abstaining from eating for a limited period of time. Throughout history, believers have fasted for a variety of reasons: to express grief (1 Sam. 31:13), to petition God (2 Sam. 12:15-23), to humble oneself before God (1 Kings 21:27-29), to seek God's help (2 Chron. 20:1-4), to confess sins (Neh. 9:1-2), and to prepare oneself spiritually (Matt. 4:1-2).

Fasting is difficult, requiring self-discipline and sacrifice. It gives believers the opportunity to devote more time to spiritual pursuits. It says to God, in effect, "This concern I seek from You is more important to me even than eating." When we fast quietly and sincerely, God endows our work in the Kingdom with spiritual power.

Sadly, the people of Judah were fasting for the wrong reasons. We find them portrayed in Isaiah 58:2 and 3a as voicing concern over God's apparent lack of response to their fasting. After all, the people gave every appearance of diligently seeking God and His will, just as if they were an obedient nation.

The people abstained from eating food, perhaps on annual fast days or on special onetime occasions. They also adopted at these times traditional signs of humility, such as bowing their heads and lying on sackcloth and ashes. Yet God apparently paid no attention to their fasting, for He had not given them what they wanted. They wondered why this was so.

It is helpful to note that Old Testament law commanded only one annual fast, which was held on the tenth day of the seventh month—the Day of Atonement (Lev. 16:29-31). But according to later writings, Jews during and after the Exile observed additional fasts on the anniversaries of calamities that had befallen Jerusalem: the burning of the temple (tenth day of the fifth month), the murder of Gedaliah (second day of the seventh month), the beginning of the siege of Jerusalem (tenth day of the tenth month), and the fall of Jerusalem (ninth day of the fourth month).

B. Inhumane Treatment of Others: vss. 3b-4

"Yet on the day of your fasting, you do as you please and exploit all your workers. Your fasting ends in quarreling and strife, and in striking each other with wicked fists. You cannot fast as you do today and expect your voice to be heard on high."

True worship changes conduct, while phony worship leaves people free to go on breaking God's laws. This explains why, when God's people fasted, they kept on oppressing their workers (Isa. 58:3). This was a common practice in Israel, especially by wealthy landowners. By various unscrupulous means they kept their workers in virtual poverty and debt.

The Lord (through Isaiah) asked the people what good their fasting accomplished when they continually fought and quarreled. Such abstaining from food would never get them anywhere with God, for it did not originate from a sincere faith. Also, it was not reflected in the humane treatment of the poor and disadvantaged.

Just being at the Jerusalem temple and following the religious rituals accomplished nothing. The people would have been better off staying at home. In fact, Isaiah concluded that the Lord would not respond to the prayers of the quarrelers. Prayer should be a vital part of worship, but it is meaningless if our hearts are full of animosity and bitterness.

C. Empty Religious Ritual: vs. 5

"Is this the kind of fast I have chosen, only a day for a man to humble himself? Is it only for bowing one's head like a reed and for lying on sackcloth and ashes? Is that what you call a fast, a day acceptable to the LORD?"

Outwardly, the people of God appeared to be humble, devoted, and pious. They apparently put on a remarkable show at their fasts. As a sign of penance, they bowed their heads like a blade of grass in the wind. And, as a sign of anguish and mourning, they dressed in sackcloth and covered themselves with ashes.

The Lord, however, was not impressed, for He saw right through the hypocrisy of His people. He knew their hearts were far from Him, even though they performed the prescribed rituals at the temple. Because of their evil ways, God would not accept their fast.

Here we see that all religious acts, no matter how showy, are invalidated when the life of the worshiper is marred by selfishness, exploitation, strife, and violence. These sins prove that the hearts of the performers are not genuinely prepared to obey God. It's no wonder that He is not impressed by such activities.

II. GENUINE FASTING: ISAIAH 58:6-9

A. Practice Justice: vs. 6

"Is not this the kind of fasting I have chosen: to loose the chains of injustice and untie the cords of the yoke, to set the oppressed free and break every yoke?"

God did more than condemn the people for their hypocritical fasts. He also explained some of the acts that would indicate genuine fasting (Isa. 58:6). The people were to free those who had been wrongly imprisoned, rather than keep them in their deplorable state of confinement. Also, rather than oppress those who worked for them, the wealthy were to treat the poor (as well as all people) with fairness and pay them what they had earned.

Clearly, the people of Isaiah's day had missed the point when it came to fasting. God didn't want their pious acts when they had unforgiven sin in their hearts and they continued their immoral lifestyle. They may have had correct worship and doctrine. But they should have also had genuine compassion for the oppressed, the poor, and the helpless.

We are reminded here of Micah 6:8, where the Lord clarified what He wanted from those who truly worshiped Him. All along He required His people "to act justly and to love mercy and to walk humbly with your God." These three requirements are ones that Christian adults today ought to strive to fulfill. God still expects His people to treat others with Christlike love and to live a life of devotion to Him.

B. Provide for the Poor: vs. 7

"Is it not to share your food with the hungry and to provide the poor wanderer with shelter—when you see the naked, to clothe him, and not to turn away from your own flesh and blood?"

To underscore the true nature of justice, Isaiah told the people to feed the hungry and provide clothing and shelter for the poor (Isa. 58:7). Apparently the well-to-do in Israel ignored the poor among them. Isaiah chastised the rich for turning away their fellow citizens.

The laws of Moses carefully prescribed how Israel was supposed to take care of the poor in the land (Deut. 15:1-11). For instance, those who enjoyed good harvests were supposed to share with those in need. Sadly, these laws had been ignored for the most part, and many disadvantaged Israelites suffered accordingly.

The most likely candidates for poverty were widows, orphans, and landless aliens. The Mosaic law made provision for them (24:19-22), but they were often victimized by greedy people, especially moneylenders. The yoke of oppression came by usury,

154

and debtors often were thrown off their farms.

Such injustices are why spokespersons for God (such as Isaiah) continually cried out against the wicked rich in Israel. The prophets declared that true worship meant obeying God's laws, including the care of the poor. "Spend yourselves in behalf of the hungry and satisfy the needs of the oppressed," Isaiah declared (Isa. 58:10). Otherwise, the people's worship was a pious fraud.

C. Assurance of Divine Favor: vss. 8-9

"Then your light will break forth like the dawn, and your healing will quickly appear; then your right-eousness will go before you, and the glory of the LORD will be your rear guard. Then you will call, and the LORD will answer; you will cry for help, and he will say: Here am I."

It was not too late for the people who were fasting improperly. They could yet change their ways. And if they did, God was prepared to bless them richly.

One group of promises of divine blessings is contained in Isaiah 58:8 and 9. If the people practiced true fasting—that is, helped the needy—then "light" (spiritual blessing) would break forth and "healing" (spiritual restoration) would quickly appear. Not only that, but righteousness would go before the people and the glory of the Lord would follow them. This description reflects the experience of the Israelites of the Exodus, which was a time of great blessing.

Although God did not answer the people's prayers when they fasted improperly (vs. 4), their obedience would open the way for Him to answer them and declare, "Here am I" (vs. 9). He would be there for them.

If our prayer life seems dry or unproductive, maybe the problem does not lie with our prayers. Perhaps disobeying God is the source of the problem. The Lord does not stop loving us and caring for us when we sin, but we cannot expect to receive what we ask for if we are harboring unconfessed sin.

We know from the New Testament that we cannot be saved apart from faith in Jesus Christ. However, our faith lacks sincerity if we refuse to reach out to others in need. We have seen from this week's lesson that the Lord wants our fasting (and other religious activities we might perform) to go beyond our own personal growth to include acts of generosity, kindness, and fairness. This truly is pleasing to the Lord.

Discussion Questions

1. From the perspective of Scripture, what is involved in fasting? What should be the worshiper's intent?
2. What complaint did the people of Judah make to God (Isa. 58:3)?
3. Why was the Lord displeased with the fasting of His people?
4. What were some of the sinful activities the people were guilty of committing?
5. What kind of fasting did the Lord desire from His people? How did He want them to treat the poor and disadvantaged?
6. In what way are we worshiping God by giving to the needy?

Contemporary Application

The indictments against God's people are all too familiar. Rather than love the Lord and those He created, we busy ourselves in a flurry of religious activities. The solution is exactly as Isaiah concluded: God's salvation, and participating in His new covenant. As Isaiah 59:21 so aptly sums up, only God's Spirit and His Word in our lives can bring about uprightness. And only God Himself could fulfill justice and bring us salvation.

That alone is how we can be righteous and practice righteousness. Anything else must amount to hypocrisy, as the pathetic examples of worship that Isaiah saw happening around him illustrated. God doesn't want our symbolic sacrifices. Rather, He wants our lives given to Him in living worship. And He must dwell within us in order for that to happen.

Certainly those of us who have been saved and have God dwelling within us know that there are times when we still live in less than worshipful ways. But God assures His people in Isaiah's age and in ours today that confession and repentance before God is all that it takes to return to relationship with Him. Christ has made us righteous, so we must live as the transformed, upright creatures that we are.

Best of all, Christians have God's Spirit, who will live in us and through us. God will use His wonderful riches in Christ to supply us with everything we need in order to be upright—such as ministering to those in need, and promoting the just treatment of others.

God's New Creation

DEVOTIONAL READING

Revelation 21:1-7

DAILY BIBLE READINGS

Monday January 28
*Deuteronomy 10:12-22 You
Were Strangers in Egypt*

Tuesday January 29
*Deuteronomy 26:1-15 Tithes
for Aliens, Orphans, and
Widows*

Wednesday January 30
*Jeremiah 7:1-8 Act Justly
and Do Not Oppress Others*

Thursday January 31
*Jeremiah 22:1-9 Do Not
Wrong Widows and Aliens*

Friday February 1
*Deuteronomy 24:14-21
Provide for Widows and
Aliens*

Saturday February 2
*Ruth 1:1-14 Three Widows
in Moab*

Sunday February 3
*Ruth 1:15-22 Your God Will
Be My God*

Scripture

Background Scripture: *Isaiah 65:17-25*
Scripture Lesson: *Isaiah 65:17-24*
Key Verse: *"Behold, I will create new heavens and a new
earth. The former things will not be remembered, nor will they
come to mind."* Isaiah 65:17.
Scripture Lesson for Children: *Isaiah 65:24; Matthew
6:7-15*
Key Verse for Children: *"Before they call I will answer;
while they are still speaking I will hear."* Isaiah 65:24.

Lesson Aim

To recognize the importance of committing ourselves
to the Lord's cause for now and forever.

Lesson Setting

Time: *740–700 B.C.*
Place: *Judah*

Lesson Outline

God's New Creation

   I. The Transformation of Creation: Isaiah 65:17-19
       A. *The Promise of New Heavens and a New
          Earth: vs. 17*
       B. *The Command to Rejoice: vs. 18*
       C. *The Elimination of Sorrow: vs. 19*
   II. The Transformation of Life: Isaiah 65:20-24
       A. *The Promise of Longevity: vs. 20*
       B. *The Promise of Fruitfulness and Blessing: vss. 21-23*
       C. *The Promise of Answered Prayer: vs. 24*

Introduction for Adults

Topic: *A New Creation*

When a flood ripped through his town, an elderly man looked at his ruined home and exclaimed, "This was all I had. Now it's gone!" For many people life is limited to their possessions. They have no life beyond their homes, furniture, and cars.

As Christians, we believe there is more to life than mere possessions, but it's hard to define what we mean. Paul got it right when he noted that, through faith in Christ, we become "a new creation" (2 Cor. 5:17). "The old has gone, the new has come!"

This truth explains why we look at everything in life from a new perspective. It's also what Isaiah urged God's people to do. Through the prophet, God gave His promise to create new heavens and a new earth, and a new Jerusalem. In fact, those in new Jerusalem would have long life, profitable work, answers to their prayers, and peace.

Introduction for Youths

Topic: *Perfect World*

A radical change takes place when adolescents trust in Christ. They experience new life. This means the Spirit graciously replaces their fallen human nature with a new one. Their relationship with God is restored, obedience to and dependence on the Lord supplant their rebelliousness and unbelief, and their hatred is exchanged for unconditional love.

For some youth the idea of being given new life sounds bizarre. For others, the advantages of being born again appear too good to be true. Finally, there are individuals who feel smugly comfortable in their life of sin and do not want to change.

The world might scoff at the idea of receiving new life in Christ. However, saved teens know from God's Word that it is a reality. They also need to know that inner renewal cannot be purchased with money or earned by doing good deeds. The lost must put their faith in Christ in order to experience the new birth.

Concepts for Children

Topic: *Pray to God*

1. The prophet Isaiah said that God hears and answers our prayers.
2. Jesus told His followers not to use a lot of fancy words when they prayed, for God already knew their needs.
3. Jesus taught His followers how to pray by giving them a model prayer.
4. Jesus said that by forgiving others, we show God how much we value His forgiveness of us.
5. Jesus is pleased when we spend time in prayer and ask God for help in loving others.

The Lesson Commentary

I. THE TRANSFORMATION OF CREATION: ISAIAH 65:17-19

A. The Promise of New Heavens and a New Earth: vs. 17

"Behold, I will create new heavens and a new earth. The former things will not be remembered, nor will they come to mind."

A glorious future awaits God's people. In fact, the final group of chapters in Isaiah begins with a call for Zion to awaken to its God-given glory. This brilliant light, the promise of salvation, will draw many nations out of their darkness—out of former desolation with which Zion herself had been all too familiar (60:15-22).

Chapter 61 begins with the description of a ministry that, while in a limited sense belonged to Isaiah, belongs fully to the Messiah, who will usher in the future glory of Zion. In that light, the next chapter describes the commitment of Isaiah and others to continue interceding for Zion until God restores it.

God's response is recorded in chapter 63, in which He reminds the prophet of the coming judgment of the wicked. Then Isaiah recited God's goodness in the past, imploring Him to act similarly on behalf of His people. Chapters 65 and 66 contain the Lord's reply to Isaiah's prayer. God would act, bringing judgment on the wicked, but salvation for the righteous.

Isaiah's final prophecies probably applied in part to the exiles returned from Babylon. But his language clearly goes beyond any fulfillment in ancient history. For instance, notice that earlier, while prophesying about end-time judgments, Isaiah had said, "The heavens will vanish like smoke, the earth will wear out like a garment" (51:6). Now the prophet recorded God's declaration that in place of the old heavens and earth He would create "new heavens and a new earth" (65:17).

We are reminded of Revelation 21:1, where the apostle John declared that he saw "a new heaven and a new earth." These are total replacements for their old counterparts, which God had destroyed. He evidently did this to eliminate any corrupting presence or influence of sin (2 Pet. 3:7, 10-13). But John was not thinking merely of a world free of sin and hardness of heart. More importantly, the apostle's vision was of a creation new in all its qualities.

So glorious would the new creation be that God said "the former things will not be remembered, nor will they come to mind" (Isa. 65:17). Those former things, such as weeping and crying, would give way to new things, including gladness, rejoicing, and delight.

B. The Command to Rejoice: vs. 18

"But be glad and rejoice forever in what I will create, for I will create Jerusalem to be a delight and its people a joy."

The Lord commanded His people to "be glad and rejoice forever" (Isa. 65:18). They were to express joy over what God would create. He pledged to create the new Jerusalem as a place of happiness, and the people inhabiting her would be a source of joy for the community of the redeemed.

We find parallel thoughts in Revelation 21:2, which makes mention of "the Holy City, the new Jerusalem," which God sent down out of heaven. The Lord magnificently adorned the new Jerusalem (the bride) for her husband (the groom). The implication here is that the city surpassed the beauty of everything else God had made.

It remains unclear to Bible scholars and students whether this is to be taken as a literal city where God's people dwell for all eternity or a symbol of the redeemed community in heaven. In either case, Scripture clearly reveals that a new world is coming, and it will be glorious beyond imagination.

C. The Elimination of Sorrow: vs. 19

"I will rejoice over Jerusalem and take delight in my people; the sound of weeping and of crying will be heard in it no more."

God, too, would find joy in the new creation. He would "rejoice over Jerusalem, and take delight in [His] people" (Isa. 65:19). What a contrast with God's previous dismay over His chosen nation! In the holy city, no one would ever again hear "the sound of weeping and of crying."

In the New Testament, John revealed that in the eternal state God will permanently dwell, or tabernacle, among the redeemed of all ages. They will be His people, and He will be their God. Also, five scourges of human existence will not exist in the eternal state—tears, death, sorrow, crying, and pain. The new order of things will eliminate all these forms of sadness (Rev. 21:3-4).

The apostle Peter, too, mentioned that Christians await with expectancy the new heavens and new earth of the end times (2 Pet. 3:13). He also wrote, "So then, dear friends, since you are looking forward to this, make every effort to be found spotless, blameless and at peace with [the Lord]" (vs. 14). Down through the centuries, the hope for new heavens and a new earth should be a purifying factor in our lives.

II. The Transformation of Life: Isaiah 65:20-24

A. The Promise of Longevity: vs. 20

"Never again will there be in it an infant who lives but a few days, or an old man who does not live out his years; he who dies at a hundred will be thought a mere youth; he who fails to reach a hundred will be considered accursed."

In Isaiah 65:20-25, the prophet described what the new creation would be like for God's people. Expositors differ over whether these verses refer to the heavenly state (the metaphorical view) or to a future period in which Christ will rule on earth (the literal view).

Regardless of whether one takes the passage metaphorically or literally, they contain four promises of blessing. Those who would live in the newly created Jerusalem (1) would have long lives, (2) would not labor in vain, (3) would be speedily answered by God when they pray, and (4) would live in an environment without hostility. Seen together, these blessings seem to indicate that the effects of the Fall would be reversed in the new heavens and new earth and new Jerusalem.

The first blessing is *longevity* (vs. 20). The Old Testament reports that lives stretching to hundreds of years was the rule in early human history. Similarly, in the new creation, infant mortality would drop to zero; all would live to adulthood. Moreover, a tombstone recording a life span of 100 years would not be remarkable for denoting a long life, as in our day, but for denoting a short life.

B. The Promise of Fruitfulness and Blessing: vss. 21-23

"They will build houses and dwell in them; they will plant vineyards and eat their fruit. No longer will they build houses and others live in them, or plant and others eat. For as the days of a tree, so will be the days of my people; my chosen ones will long enjoy the works of their hands. They will not toil in vain or bear children doomed to misfortune; for they will be a people blessed by the LORD, they and their descendants with them."

The second blessing in the new creation is *profitable toil* (Isa. 65:21-23). The people of Isaiah's time lived and died with the vagaries of agricultural life. Droughts and pestilence caused great damage. The pagans prayed to fertility and weather gods and goddesses. But God's people were supposed to trust Him to supply all their needs.

After the Fall, God's curse on humanity included the declaration that labor to earn food would be difficult (Gen. 3:17-19). In the new creation people would continue to work, but they would have no worries about not receiving the fruits of their labor. Others (perhaps unscrupulous rich people or invaders) would never take what they have earned with their own hands. Generation after generation, the people of God would be blessed.

Isaiah related these truths in terms that could be understood. For instance, God's people would live in the houses they built and eat the fruit of their vineyards (Isa. 65:21). The Lord would prevent invaders from taking these from them. In fact, God would enable His people to live a long life and enjoy the "works of their hands" (vs. 22).

The labor of the redeemed community would not be in vain, and their children would not be "doomed to misfortune" (vs. 23). After all, the Lord would bless them and their children with safety, health, and prosperity. Such blessings would be both physical and spiritual in nature.

C. The Promise of Answered Prayer: vs. 24

"Before they call I will answer; while they are still speaking I will hear."

The third blessing in the new creation is *answered prayer* (Isa. 65:24). In the Garden of Eden, Adam and Eve enjoyed the immediate presence and conversation of the Lord. Similarly, while people in the new creation are praying, even before they make the request, God would answer them. This describes a close fellowship between God and people.

Such is echoed in Revelation 22:3-4. The apostle John noted that in the new creation the Father and the Son will be seated on their thrones, and the redeemed will worship and serve them continually. God will establish unbroken communion with His people, and He will claim them as His own.

(4) Of noteworthy mention is the fourth blessing in the new creation, namely, *peace* (Isa. 65:25). The Fall introduced hostility into the world, and murder was committed by the next generation. But in the new creation even the animals will stop preying on one another. Perfect harmony will reign.

We see this expectation for wellness and wholeness repeated in the New Testament. God promised to give water from the life-giving fountain to everyone who was thirsty (Rev. 21:6). This pledge is a vivid reminder of the refreshment and satisfaction believers will enjoy in heaven. In the eternal state, God will satisfy the yearnings of the soul. This assurance is grounded in the Lord's own nature. Those who overcome in this life will receive an eternal inheritance and an eternal relationship. They will be the eternal children of the eternal God (vs. 7).

In the new Jerusalem, God will be worshiped face-to-face. The city will be a cosmopolitan place, where redeemed humanity in all its cultural diversity will live together in peace. God will vindicate the faith of the redeemed by not permitting anything immoral or wicked to enter the holy city (vss. 22-27).

In previous chapters of Isaiah, the prophet had foretold both the demise of Judah and the exile of the nation's inhabitants to Babylon. But he also foresaw their return to Judah. Beyond that, Isaiah saw the glorious future awaiting all the redeemed, namely, intimacy and unbroken communion with the Lord. It's no wonder the apostle Paul declared, "I consider that our present sufferings are not worth comparing with the glory that will be revealed in us" (Rom. 8:18).

At present we see the world as it is—physically decaying and spiritually infected with sin. But Christians do not need to be pessimistic, for they have hope for future glory. They look forward to the new heavens and new earth that God has promised, and they wait for God's new order that will free the world of sin, sickness, and evil.

Discussion Questions

1. What do you think will happen to this present creation when God brings the new heavens and new earth into existence?
2. What sort of emotions will prevail among the inhabitants of the new Jerusalem?
3. How will the lives of the redeemed be different in the future time of glory?
4. What are some of the blessings associated with the newly created Jerusalem?
5. How can the hope for new heavens and a new earth become a purifying factor in our lives as Christians?

Contemporary Application

As believers, eternal life does not begin when we die and go to heaven. It starts here and now. God wants us to enjoy to the fullest extent the new vistas of joy, satisfaction, and fruitfulness that the presence of His indwelling Holy Spirit makes possible.

Once we've put our faith in Christ, we are immediately forgiven and redeemed. So we have God's power within us to bring about an amazing transformation in our character and conduct. And that's just a foretaste of the glorious future that awaits us in the eternal state.

It's because God has so richly blessed us that we naturally desire to commit ourselves to His cause, both in the present and in the future. We enthusiastically renounce sin and urge others to join us. It's a choice for life, not death. That's why we proclaim the Gospel and implore the lost to accept its message.

Most of all, we give glory to God for the wonderful things He has in store for His spiritual children. That in essence is Isaiah's message: the meaning of life and the purpose for which we were created is to glorify God and to exist in His glory. So let us choose life!

Ruth Chose Naomi's God

DEVOTIONAL READING

Psalm 8

DAILY BIBLE READINGS

Monday February 4
Ruth 2:1-7 Gleaning in the Right Field

Tuesday February 5
Ruth 2:8-13 A Safe Place to Glean

Wednesday February 6
Ruth 2:14-23 A Generous Kinsman

Thursday February 7
Ruth 3:1-6 An Obedient Daughter-in-Law

Friday February 8
Ruth 3:7-18 Ruth Is a Worthy Woman

Saturday February 9
Ruth 4:1-12 Boaz Marries Ruth, the Moabite

Sunday February 10
Ruth 4:13-22 Ruth's Son, the Grandfather of David

Scripture

Background Scripture: *Ruth 1*
Scripture Lesson: *Ruth 1:1-8, 16-17*
Key Verse: *But Ruth replied, "Don't urge me to leave you or to turn back from you. Where you go I will go, and where you stay I will stay. Your people will be my people and your God my God." Ruth 1:16.*

Lesson Aim

To value loyalty and demonstrate it in one's own relationships.

Lesson Setting

Time: *1375–1050 B.C.*
Place: *Judah and Moab*

Lesson Outline

Ruth Chose Naomi's God

  I. The Predicament: Ruth 1:1-5
     A. *Famine: vss. 1-2*
     B. *Death: vss. 3-5*
  II. The Plan: Ruth 1:6-8
 III. The Pledge: Ruth 1:16-17
     A. *Ruth's Faith: vs. 16*
     B. *Ruth's Love: vs. 17*

Introduction for Adults

Topic: *Remaining Loyal*

According to the dictionary, loyalty has an object. You cannot simply be loyal; you have to be loyal to something or someone. This week's lesson challenges us to remain loyal in our relationships. Certainly Ruth is a wonderful example of loyalty in her relationship with Naomi.

But what causes disloyalty among adults? Each of us struggles with a different set of weaknesses. Some adults struggle with sexual immorality, and it is difficult for them to be faithful to their spouse. Other adults harbor deep anger toward a family member or friend who has hurt them in some way. Still other adults can't seem to help but break the trust of a loved one by relating confidences to others.

Honesty, forgiveness, unselfishness, and loyalty are God-honoring character traits. As we study Ruth's loyalty to Naomi, we will be encouraged to examine our own relationships. Perhaps we will be prompted to reshape our loyalties so that our life will be more pleasing to the Lord.

Introduction for Youths

Topic: *Lifetime Commitment*

Adolescents soon learn that short-term loyalties, like fireworks, blaze intently for a brief time and then vanish. They also come to discover that constant loyalty glows like a light bulb pointing the way through a dark tunnel. This week's lesson makes clear that, as Orpah's loyalty faded, she returned home. But Ruth's commitment was permanent.

Jesus' last earthly promise to His disciples in Matthew 28:20 was "And surely I am with you always." Christian love is not commitment by convenience, which disappears when life becomes difficult. Real love says, "I'll be there for you when times are tough for you." Saved teens need Christian fellowship, especially in hard places. The Lord did not intend that any of them should go it alone.

Concepts for Children

Topic: *Ruth Was Loyal to Naomi*

1. During the time of the judges, Elimelech, his wife Naomi, and their two sons moved to Moab to escape a food shortage.
2. Elimelech and his two sons died, leaving Naomi, Orpah, and Ruth widows.
3. Naomi decided to return to Judah, where there was food, and her daughters-in-law planned to go with her.
4. Naomi urged her daughters-in-law to return to their mothers' homes.
5. Orpah returned; but Ruth pledged to stay with Naomi, join her people, and worship her God.
6. God is pleased when we decide to love and obey Him.

The Lesson Commentary

I. THE PREDICAMENT: RUTH 1:1-5

A. Famine: vss. 1-2

In the days when the judges ruled, there was a famine in the land, and a man from Bethlehem in Judah, together with his wife and two sons, went to live for a while in the country of Moab. The man's name was Elimelech, his wife's name Naomi, and the names of his two sons were Mahlon and Kilion. They were Ephrathites from Bethlehem, Judah. And they went to Moab and lived there.

Most Old Testament history studies God's collective relationship with Israel. The short narrative of Ruth, however, presents God's dealings with one family. By remaining loyal to Naomi despite the dangers and the pain, Ruth participated in God's larger purpose to bless all nations, for Ruth—a non-Israelite—became the ancestor of King David and of the Messiah.

Ruth 1:1 places the account in the period when the judges ruled Israel, or about 1375–1050 B.C. Furthermore, it appears that Ruth was the great-grandmother of David, who was born about 1040 B.C. Most likely, therefore, Ruth and the other characters in the account lived sometime in the 1100s B.C.

Ruth's quiet, intimate account contrasts sharply with the chaotic times in which she lived. In "the days when the judges ruled" (Ruth 1:1), "everyone did as he saw fit" (Judg. 21:25). Against this gloomy panorama of tribal jealousy and civil war, the commitment of Ruth and Naomi to God and to each other sparkle like emeralds.

It's common today for families to up and move to a new community because of job or economic circumstances. In Ruth 1:1, we learn that a family from Bethlehem in Judah did the same. Although the name of their hometown, Bethlehem, means "House of Bread," there was a famine in the area that made survival tough. Just as hunger had forced Jacob's sons to seek food in Egypt (Gen. 42:1-2), starvation drove Elimelech and Naomi from Bethlehem to Moab.

Moab was an area across the Salt Sea (Dead Sea) from Bethlehem. Moab's territory stretched from the south of the sea to its middle, and the edge of the Syrian desert formed the kingdom's eastern boundary. The entire .territory measured only 60 miles north to south and 20 miles east to west, while several ravines divided it. Through the middle of Moab from north to south ran "The King's Highway," a route of strategic military and commercial importance.

Moab was a well-organized kingdom. The Moabites' buildings were well constructed and their cities well fortified. Meanwhile, their lands could be used for farming and ranching. Wheat and barley grew especially well in this region. Also, part of the area in the hills above the Salt Sea was fertile, and obviously it was untouched by the famine that forced Naomi's family out of the territory of Judah.

Moving their family to this alien land must have been a difficult decision. Elimelech and Naomi knew that their reception might not be a friendly one because of ancient hatred between the Moabites and the Israelites (Judg. 3:12-14). This animosity stretched back to the time of Balaam, a prophet who was hired by the frightened king of Moab to curse the Israelite people who were approaching his country from Egypt (Num. 22:1-8). Overruled by God, however, Balaam's curses became blessings for God's people (23:19-20).

B. Death: vss. 3-5

Now Elimelech, Naomi's husband, died, and she was left with her two sons. They married Moabite women, one named Orpah and the other Ruth. After they had lived there about ten years, both Mahlon and Kilion also died, and Naomi was left without her two sons and her husband.

Sometime after Elimelech and Naomi's arrival in Moab, tragedy struck. Elimelech's death left Naomi dependent on her sons (Ruth 1:3). Apparently Mahlon and Kilion liked Moab well enough to marry and settle down (vs. 4). These marriages would have been frowned upon by orthodox Israelites, for whom Moab long represented temptation to immorality. For instance, during the Israelites' wandering in the wilderness, their men had been easily seduced by Moabite women (Num. 25:1-5).

During the third and second millennia B.C., the religion of the Moabites was similar to that of their neighbors the Canaanites. Over time, the two peoples' religious practices became distinct. Chemosh was the Moabites' national god, and they became known as "the people of Chemosh." This idol was believed to be a god of war who led his people to victory.

Ten years after Naomi's family had moved to Moab, tragedy struck again. The names of Naomi's sons indicate they were physically weak (perhaps from birth). Mahlon means "weak" or "sick," and Kilion means "failing" or "annihilation." Ruth and Orpah were probably widowed soon after their weddings (Ruth 1:5).

After Mahlon and Kilion died, all three women were left without support. In ancient patriarchal societies, women depended on male relatives for protection and care. Sadly, widows were usually ignored and destitute. Jewish law commanded the nearest relative of the dead husband to care for the widow (Deut. 25:5-10), but Naomi had no other family in Moab.

II. THE PLAN: RUTH 1:6-8

When she heard in Moab that the LORD had come to the aid of his people by providing food for them, Naomi and her daughters-in-law prepared to return home from there. With her two daughters-in-law she left the place where she had been living and set out on the road that would take them back to the land of Judah. Then Naomi said to her two daughters-in-law, "Go back, each of you, to your mother's home. May the LORD show kindness to you, as you have shown to your dead and to me.

Eventually word came from Bethlehem that the famine had ended (Ruth 1:6). Naomi made the courageous decision to return home. The women had to cross about 50 miles of barren desert. The risks of this journey were great: heat exhaustion, starvation, and attacks by beasts or bandits. However, for Naomi, death on the road would be no worse than destitution and loneliness in a foreign land.

Naomi's daughters-in-law were determined to go with her, a decision that underscored how much they appreciated her (vs. 7). Soon, however, Naomi told the women to go back to their families, find husbands, and start life over. Despite her need for their support, the older woman unselfishly set her daughters-in-law free.

Naomi could not provide husbands for these two women, and she cared too much for them to let them live as widows, especially since they had been good to her sons and herself. Perhaps Naomi also wanted to protect Ruth and Orpah from abusive discrimination, which they might face in Bethlehem (vs. 8).

Naomi softened the blow of her directive by giving Orpah and Ruth a double blessing. In the first part of the blessing, Naomi wished the Lord's kindness on them. And in the process of doing so, she expressed her appreciation for the kindness the young women had shown to her sons and to herself. In the second part of the blessing, Naomi wished her daughters-in-law rest in a new husband's home (vs. 9). In this case "rest" meant ceasing from toil and trouble and experiencing life-long protection and blessing from the Lord.

We can see from Naomi's double blessing that she did not hesitate to speak about Yahweh, the Israelites' God, in the presence of her Moabite daughters-in-law. Indeed, Naomi's words show that she believed He was the one who had the power to bless them.

Naomi kissed Orpah and Ruth to show her love for them. At this the young women wept. Through the tears, however, both declared their intention to continue with Naomi (vs. 10). Clearly, Naomi's love for them had evidently made a powerful impact on them.

III. THE PLEDGE: RUTH 1:16-17

A. Ruth's Faith: vs. 16

But Ruth replied, "Don't urge me to leave you or to turn back from you. Where you go I will go, and where you stay I will stay. Your people will be my people and your God my God."

Despite the initial pledges made by Ruth and Orpah, Naomi repeated her command for them to return home (Ruth 1:11). Israelite tradition formed the backdrop of her reasoning. In ancient times, it was usually considered a man's duty to marry his brother's widow so as to see that she was taken care of (Deut. 25:5-10). This was called levirate marriage.

Naomi, however, had no more sons to marry Ruth and Orpah. Also, Naomi did not expect to marry and have more sons, and even if she did bear sons, it would take too long for them to reach marriageable age (Ruth 1:12-13). Thus, if the young women traveled to Judah with her, Naomi wouldn't be able to give them more of her sons to marry.

This second attempt to turn the young women back somewhat worked. After some more tears and more kissing, Orpah headed home (vs. 14). This decision to return to Moab is not a reproach on her character; rather, she was showing a practical concern for herself. Also, her tearful parting from Naomi indicates a fondness for the older woman.

While Orpah made a commonsense decision, Ruth chose to place Naomi's needs first. Ruth's clinging to Naomi indicated a love stronger than formal regard. Self-centered choosing wants to know, "What's in it for me?" Loyalty like Ruth's asks, "What can I do for you?"

In her pledge of loyalty, Ruth made four choices (vs. 16). First, she decided to leave the comforts of home to travel across the desert. Second, she would live where Naomi lived, even in poverty. Third, Ruth would identify herself with Naomi's people, even though she knew they might reject her. Ruth's most significant commitment—the fourth one—was to Yahweh, the God of Israel: "your God [will be] my God."

Loyalty like Ruth's doesn't mushroom in moments of crisis; rather, it develops through long association. Ruth had probably already been a source of strength to Naomi after Elimelech died. By sharing their grief, the two women had learned to trust each other.

B. Ruth's Love: vs. 17

"Where you die I will die, and there I will be buried. May the LORD deal with me, be it ever so severely, if anything but death separates you and me."

Ruth had probably never read the Scripture or heard a biblical sermon. Her knowledge of Israel's God had come from observing Naomi. The older woman's witness, even in times of great suffering, had shaped the younger woman's faith. Living up close and personal, family members know whether our actions match our testimony. Would our example convince someone to follow the Lord?

Ruth's pledge in the name of Israel's God may be paraphrased, "May a severe judgment fall on me if I am not true to this vow" (Ruth 1:17). Naomi not only realized that Ruth was determined to follow her no matter what perils lay ahead, but also Naomi saw that Ruth had a deep faith in the God of Israel. Thus Naomi no longer tried to persuade her daughter-in-law to remain in Moab (vs. 18). Ruth's loyalty must have filled Naomi's heart with joy as they began the long trek together.

God calls us to love our family members unconditionally. Though we may not always get along, family ties are not easily broken.

Discussion Questions

1. Putting yourself in Elimelech and Naomi's place, describe your conflicting feelings as you decide to take your family to Moab.
2. What fears would Ruth and Orpah have felt after their husbands died?
3. How did Naomi show both courage and sensitivity by telling Ruth and Orpah to return to their families?
4. If you were one of Naomi's daughters-in-law, how would you have felt about going to Bethlehem?
5. What does Ruth's pledge to Naomi reveal about Ruth's character?
6. How does Christ's love motivate us to be loyal to other believers?

Contemporary Application

Christ gave up His heavenly "rights" so as to be our Savior (Phil. 2:6-8). And He showed His disciples how to love when He took the lowest servant role and washed their feet. The Master then instructed them to serve as He had ministered to them (John 13:14). This is the reason why Christian loyalty puts others first (Phil. 2:3-4).

Loyalty in Christ means choosing to act for the good of another. Such loyalty, of course, always costs time and energy. For instance, helping someone else often destroys our well-planned schedules. We know that God's most effective servants are those ready and willing to help others in need.

The world's brand of loyalty often says, "I'll scratch your back if you'll scratch mine." Christian loyalty means giving without expecting anything in return. Consider Ruth. Her trip with Naomi meant great personal sacrifice and also having to endure a difficulty journey. Ruth's life affirms the truth that sacrificial service is the route to genuine contentment. A simple formula for such loyalty spells JOY: *J*esus first, *O*thers second, *Y*ourself last.

God's Blessing for Ruth

DEVOTIONAL READING

Psalm 126

DAILY BIBLE READINGS

Monday February 11
*Acts 8:26-40 Good News for
the Ethiopian Eunuch*

Tuesday February 12
*Acts 10:1-16 God Makes
Things Clean*

Wednesday February 13
*Acts 10:19-33 Peter Greets
Cornelius*

Thursday February 14
*Acts 10:34-48 God Shows
No Partiality*

Friday February 15
*Jonah 1:1-6 Jonah Flees from
God's Call*

Saturday February 16
*Jonah 1:7-17 Jonah Is
Thrown Overboard and the
Sea Calms*

Sunday February 17
*Jonah 2 Jonah Prays from
the Fish's Belly*

Scripture

Background Scripture: *Ruth 2—4*
Scripture Lesson: *Ruth 2:1, 8-12; 4:13-17*
Key Verse: *"May the LORD repay you for what you have done.
May you be richly rewarded by the LORD, the God of Israel,
under whose wings you have come to take refuge."* Ruth 2:12.
Key Verse for Children: *Be kind and compassionate to one
another, forgiving each other, just as in Christ God forgave
you.* Ephesians 4:32

Lesson Aim

To treat others kindly and respectfully, regardless of
their gender, race, or economic status.

Lesson Setting

Time: *1220–1050 B.C.*
Place: *Bethlehem*

Lesson Outline

God's Blessing for Ruth

   I. The Kindness of Boaz toward Ruth:
      Ruth 2:1, 8-12
      A. *The Introduction of Boaz: vs. 1*
      B. *The Instructions Given by Boaz: vss. 8-9*
      C. *The Commitment of Ruth to Naomi: vss. 10-12*
  II. The Descendants of Boaz: Ruth 4:13-17
      A. *The Birth of Ruth's Son: vs. 13*
      B. *The Well Wishes of the Local Women: vss. 14-15*
      C. *The Extended Family Tree: vss. 16-17*

Introduction for Adults

Topic: *Showing Kindness*

Kindness is easily pushed aside in a culture that persists in looking out for number one. With our focus on satisfying our own needs comes an appalling lack of interest in and concern for others. Many social tragedies could be averted if we spent more time developing habits of kindness and less time on seeking self-fulfillment.

"I'm too busy" is one of the most frequent excuses for not giving time to people in need. This is sad, for in many cases people are starving for companionship and encouragement. Elderly people are easily forgotten, and young people complain that their parents do not care about them.

The Book of Ruth shows that one person can make a difference. Boaz did not allow his concern for profits to overshadow the needs of a foreign widow. He not only gave her food to eat, but also tried to meet her deeper needs—all at considerable expense to himself. He sets the example for showing kindness to others.

Introduction for Youths

Topic: *Faithfulness Rewarded*

Homeless, hungry refugees often fill our television screens. We watch them clamor and fight for food and clothing being thrown from trucks. Ruth, a refugee of sorts from Moab, found shelter in Bethlehem.

What kept Ruth going? It was her faith in God and courage to remain devoted to His people. Ruth had no earthly prospects and was reduced to foraging for food. Yet she did not quit, for she knew that trusting and obeying the Lord was her highest goal.

Many adolescents can relate to the struggles Ruth experienced—losing a loved one, moving to a strange place, struggling to make ends meet, and so on. Saved teens also know that peers who do not share their faith in Christ sometimes treat them like outcasts. They should be encouraged to remain loyal to their Christian faith and heritage. They can do so knowing that the Lord will be with them every step of the way.

Concepts for Children

Topic: *Boaz Was Kind*

1. Ruth followed her mother-in-law, Naomi, back to Bethlehem from Moab.
2. Ruth had to pick through the leftover grain in the fields to find food.
3. Boaz took care of Ruth and eventually married her.
4. Ruth's life shows us the value of courage and faith in God.
5. Boaz is an example of how to be kind to people in need.
6. God wants us to be kind to those who are hurting.

The Lesson Commentary

I. THE KINDNESS OF BOAZ TOWARD RUTH: RUTH 2:1, 8-12

A. The Introduction of Boaz: vs. 1

Now Naomi had a relative on her husband's side, from the clan of Elimelech, a man of standing, whose name was Boaz.

Eventually Naomi and Ruth completed the journey to Bethlehem. Their arrival caused quite a stir among Naomi's former neighbors (Ruth 1:19). Apparently life had taken its toll on Naomi. Ten years in a foreign culture, the loss of a husband and sons, hard work and long journeys—all this must have affected Naomi's appearance. It certainly had affected her attitude.

"Naomi" means "pleasant," but she told the other local women to call her "Mara," which means "bitter" (vs. 20). This play on words reflected the pain of Naomi's circumstances. She had left in a time of famine and had returned in a time of plenty. Ironically, though, she considered herself to have been full before (because she had a family) and empty now (because her husband and sons were gone; vs. 21).

Although Naomi felt her life was bitter and full of loss, little did she know that blessing was right around the corner. This is the way with many sufferers. From where they stand in time, they can't see the great blessings that God is ready to give them if they'll wait just a little longer.

At this point in the drama we are introduced to the third major character: Boaz. He was a wealthy and honorable aristocrat of Bethlehem from the tribe of Judah. He was also a relative of Elimelech and owned fields outside the town. Although Naomi had sought to send her daughters-in-law back to their homes because she didn't have any more sons for them, Boaz would prove to be a relative who would protect Ruth and Naomi.

B. The Instructions Given by Boaz: vss. 8-9

So Boaz said to Ruth, "My daughter, listen to me. Don't go and glean in another field and don't go away from here. Stay here with my servant girls. Watch the field where the men are harvesting, and follow along after the girls. I have told the men not to touch you. And whenever you are thirsty, go and get a drink from the water jars the men have filled."

Ruth and Naomi were poor, defenseless widows, and depended on the kindness of friends, relatives, and even strangers for their daily sustenance. Soon help came in the form of harvesttime.

As the fields were picked of their grain, it was the custom that the needy were allowed to trail behind the hired workers and pick up any scraps of grain they could glean. It was also the law that a field could not be picked all the way to its borders, allowing an additional grain supply for gleaners (Lev. 19:9; 23:22).

Of course, it was not in the financial interest of farmers to permit gleaning. Thus, when Ruth offered to go into the fields and glean, she hoped to find some who would look favorably upon her and allow her to do work in their fields (Ruth 2:2). With Naomi's permission, Ruth went out to glean in a field belonging to Boaz, though at this time Ruth did not know who he was (vs. 3).

As Ruth was gleaning that morning, Boaz himself arrived. He greeted the workers with a blessing and received theirs in return (vs. 4). Clearly, Boaz was a godly man and well liked by his employees. When Boaz inquired about Ruth, the foreman identified her and also mentioned her request to be allowed to glean. The foreman also noted that Ruth had only taken one short rest in a makeshift hut of branches (vss. 5-7).

As Ruth gleaned behind the harvesters, Boaz paid her special attention. Having learned about her devotion to her mother-in-law, he urged her to glean only in his fields, where he could guarantee her safety. It was not unusual for gleaners to move from field to field, searching for food wherever they might find it. But Boaz told Ruth not to follow that practice. He emphasized his message by telling Ruth to join with his servant girls (vs. 8).

At harvest men and women both played important roles due to the urgency of getting the produce completed on time. For instance, the men might cut down the crops, while the women were responsible for tying them in bundles. Because of the close working relationship, it apparently was common for the male workers to harass the women who followed behind. Gleaners—usually poor people with no social standing—would be particularly easy targets. But Boaz arranged for Ruth to follow closely behind the workers, and he informed the men that they were not to bother her (vs. 9).

Boaz also arranged for Ruth to quench her thirst after hot hours in the fields. By being able to drink from what the men had drawn (likely carried from a well some distance away), she would save herself the laborious, time-consuming process of having to stop and fetch water herself.

C. The Commitment of Ruth to Naomi: vss. 10-12

At this, she bowed down with her face to the ground. She exclaimed, "Why have I found such favor in your eyes that you notice me—a foreigner?" Boaz replied, "I've been told all about what you have done for your mother-in-law since the death of your husband—how you left your father and mother and your homeland and came to live with a people you did not know before. May the LORD repay you for what you have done. May you be richly rewarded by the LORD, the God of Israel, under whose wings you have come to take refuge."

When met with the unusual kindness of Boaz, Ruth fell on her face, the sign of extreme humility and gratitude. Boaz had done more than the social laws of conduct had required and Ruth responded accordingly, thanking him in a profound way. Yet even as she demonstrated her gratitude, she wondered what she had done to merit Boaz's actions. After all, she was a foreigner, not one of his own people (Ruth 2:10).

The reason for Boaz's actions was simple. He was impressed with Ruth's kindness and devotion, especially the sacrifice she had made to leave her land and people to remain with her mother-in-law. Boaz knew that no law or custom obliged her to do so; she had already fulfilled her duties as a daughter-in-law. Still, she had chosen to be loyal and devoted to Naomi (vs. 11).

Boaz clearly hoped to reward Ruth in a small way for her sacrifices by making her gleaning successful and safe. But in giving Ruth a blessing, Boaz expressed his wish that the Lord—the true source of blessing—would reward her richly. By saying that Ruth had come under the wings of Israel's God, like a little bird snuggling under its mother's wings, Boaz may simply have been referring to the fact that Ruth was now living in the territory of God's people. But the statement may also indicate that Boaz believed Ruth had a personal faith in the Lord (vs. 12).

Ruth humbly responded with her own wish that Boaz would continue to look upon her favorably. Ruth also expressed her thanks to him (vs. 13). Later, after sharing a meal of bread and wine vinegar with Ruth, Boaz instructed his men to make her work easier by leaving behind some stalks of good grain as they worked the fields (vss. 14-16).

II. THE DESCENDANTS OF BOAZ: RUTH 4:13-17

A. The Birth of Ruth's Son: vs. 13

So Boaz took Ruth and she became his wife. Then he went to her, and the LORD enabled her to conceive, and she gave birth to a son.

When Ruth returned home to Naomi, Naomi learned at last just whose field her daughter-in-law had been gleaning. Naomi arranged for the two to have a second meeting. This time Boaz was so taken with Ruth that he arranged to buy Elimelech's remaining property from Naomi and thus, according to the laws of that time, "inherit" the responsibility of marrying the widow Ruth.

Here we find Boaz acting as a kinsman-redeemer. In ancient times such a person was a kind of family vindicator. If a relative's life had been taken, the related redeemer could bring about vindication for the victim (Num. 5:8). Also, if the family had been forced to forfeit property, the kinsman-redeemer had the right to redeem it before the Year of Jubilee (Lev. 25:10-17). Moreover, according to marriage customs, a brother-in-law (or another close male relative) should marry his brother's widow in order to provide family heirs. This was the cultural custom behind the Book of Ruth.

Having removed the one obstacle to marriage by negotiating with the nearer relative, Boaz went ahead and wed Ruth and began to have relations with her. In the providence of God, Ruth became pregnant and gave birth to a son (4:13). The Bible often speaks of God's determining birth or barrenness.

B. The Well Wishes of the Local Women: vss. 14-15

The women said to Naomi: "Praise be to the LORD, who this day has not left you without a kinsman-redeemer. May he become famous throughout Israel! He will renew your life and sustain you in your old age. For your daughter-in-law, who loves you and who is better to you than seven sons, has given him birth."

Although Boaz and Ruth were the newborn child's biological parents, the honor for the birth belonged to Naomi, who had at last been given the heir she had been denied through the deaths of her two sons. And so the women of the town celebrated her good fortune. She had not been left barren. Instead, they hoped that this newborn would become famous in Israel—a hope that would come true in the lineage that produced the great King David and, later, Jesus (Ruth 4:14).

The local women prayed that the newborn would restore Naomi's youth and care for her in her old age. The women then offered a tribute to Ruth, stating that she was better to Naomi than seven sons (vs. 15). In ancient times, a successful family was one with many sons; in some Hebrew settings a family with seven sons was considered ideal. For one woman in that culture to be regarded as better than seven sons was a monumental compliment.

C. The Extended Family Tree: vss. 16-17

Then Naomi took the child, laid him in her lap and cared for him. The women living there said, "Naomi has a son." And they named him Obed. He was the father of Jesse, the father of David.

Naomi next took the newborn on her lap. In this way, she symbolically adopted the child as her own (Ruth 4:16). While this may strike modern readers as odd, it was the fulfillment of dreams that Naomi had believed were dead forever.

The local women seem to have been involved in naming the child, though that wasn't a common practice. They gave the boy the name Obed, which means "servant" (vs. 17). They hoped he would be a faithful servant of the Lord. It was a fitting name for a child who would become the grandfather of King David.

The book ends with a genealogy stretching from Perez to David. The genealogy helps readers see that God remains in control, even though the events of our lives may seem chaotic or hopeless. Who could have imagined that the Lord would bring together a loyal young Moabite woman and a faithful older Israelite man to become ancestors of the great King David—and of the greater King Jesus? If God can do that, He can also bring about resolutions to our difficult problems and add new blessings to our lives.

Discussion Questions

1. What does the statement Boaz made in Ruth 2:8 and 9 say about his character?
2. Why was Boaz impressed with Ruth?
3. How did Boaz's words and actions confirm Ruth's faith in God?
4. How might Boaz's marriage to Ruth be seen as an act of kindness?
5. How did Boaz's kindness toward Ruth become a blessing to Naomi as well?
6. What opportunities do you have to act kindly toward others, especially those in great need? How might you do so?

Contemporary Application

Of the various themes that can be traced in the Book of Ruth, the idea that God is close at hand seems to be one of the most significant. Though He is hidden in terms of His being, the movements of events and characters flowed under His constant supervision. He controlled famine and harvest, chose the destiny of individuals, took the lead in bringing people together, and even guided in conception.

The active involvement of people in remaining faithful and doing what is right is also important in the book. Each of the characters had a role to play in discovering and working out the plan of God. Along the way they learned that the paths of God are not always smooth, but may involve poverty, hard work, complications, and grief.

Yet in this account, loyalty is rewarded. Making a personal sacrifice to maintain the values and laws of God resulted in the activity of God on the faithful's behalf. And faith in the face of tragedy, minimal as that faith might have been in its wrestling match with human emotions, resulted in the tender redemption of God. Last, the strength and experience of a godly man led a path through the harassment of rough laborers and the red tape of legal counsel to redeem the lives of two struggling people. His loving act sustained a lineage that includes not only King David but also Jesus Christ.

Jonah Rejects God's Call

DEVOTIONAL READING

Psalm 40:1-8

DAILY BIBLE READINGS

Monday February 18
Acts 15:1-11 The Gentiles Hear the Good News

Tuesday February 19
Acts 15:12-21 God's Wonders Seen among the Gentiles

Wednesday February 20
Acts 15:22-35 No Further Burdens on the Gentiles

Thursday February 21
Jonah 3:1-5 Nineveh Believes and Repents

Friday February 22
Jonah 3:6-10 God Decides Not to Destroy Nineveh

Saturday February 23
Jonah 4:1-5 Jonah Is Displeased at God's Mercy

Sunday February 24
Jonah 4:6-11 God's Concern for the People of Nineveh

Scripture

Background Scripture: *Jonah 1—2; Nahum 3*
Scripture Lesson: *Jonah 1:1-4, 11-17; 2:1, 10*
Key Verse: *But Jonah ran away from the LORD and headed for Tarshish. He went down to Joppa, where he found a ship bound for that port. After paying the fare, he went aboard and sailed for Tarshish to flee from the LORD.* Jonah 1:3.
Key Verse for Children: *"But I gave them this command: Obey me, and I will be your God and you will be my people. Walk in all the ways I command you, that it may go well with you."* Jeremiah 7:23.

Lesson Aim

To repent of rebellious attitudes or actions in our relationship with God.

Lesson Setting

Time: *785–775 B.C.*
Place: *Israel; the Mediterranean Sea*

Lesson Outline

Jonah Rejects God's Call

   I. God's Call: Jonah 1:1-4
      A. *The Assignment: vss. 1-2*
      B. *The Refusal: vs. 3*
      C. *The Storm: vs. 4*
  II. Jonah's Plight: Jonah 1:11-17
      A. *The Confession of Jonah: vss. 11-12*
      B. *The Plea of the Sailors: vss. 13-16*
      C. *The Confinement of Jonah: vs. 17*
 III. Jonah's Rescue: Jonah 2:1, 10
      A. *Jonah's Prayer: vs. 1*
      B. *Jonah's Deliverance: vs. 10*

Introduction for Adults
Topic: *Running from God*

"Where can I go from your Spirit? Where can I flee from your presence?" (Ps. 139:7), David asked the Lord. David knew from his pleasant and unpleasant experiences that it was useless to try to escape from God. Thus, David took God's universal presence as a comfort and blessing, not as a threat.

Yet, when we sense the Spirit convicting us about something sinful in our lives, we are tempted to think that we know better than God does about how to make constructive changes. Also, Satan plants fear, doubt, and mistrust in our hearts. He comes up with reasons why it would be better to disobey the Lord. Before long, our emotions take control, and we cannot think clearly about the facts. Self-will intrudes and clouds our minds.

Therefore, we must constantly remind ourselves that God loves us. He does not withhold eternally good things from us. Thus, we can fully trust the Lord to take care of us, especially when we obey Him. Clearly, then, trying to avoid God makes no sense and the temptation to do so should be resisted.

Introduction for Youths
Topic: *Are You Listening?*

Perhaps you are familiar with the scene. A parent walks into an adolescent's bedroom and asks him or her to turn down the music being played. But the teen can't hear the request because the music is being played too loudly.

Even more frustrating than this is the situation in which young people do not heed God. They have allowed their minds to be pumped so full of the world's images and messages that God's truth is never given the slightest bit of attention. Sadly, the Lord is pushed aside for the allurement of temporal distractions.

The remedy to this problem is for youth to redirect their attention back to God. This isn't necessarily difficult, though at first it might be challenging. But once it is done, a wonderful opportunity exists for real change and lasting spiritual growth. The transformation that can occur is quite profound!

Concepts for Children
Topic: *God Called Jonah*

1. God directed Jonah to tell His message to the people of Nineveh, but Jonah said no.
2. After Jonah got on a ship, God caused a great storm to pound it.
3. The sailors were afraid, and the captain asked Jonah to pray for help.
4. When the sailors threw Jonah overboard, the storm ended.
5. A large fish swallowed Jonah, and when he prayed to God for help, the fish spewed up Jonah onto dry land.
6. God wants us to obey Him even when we don't feel like doing so.

The Lesson Commentary

I. GOD'S CALL: JONAH 1:1-4

A. The Assignment: vss. 1-2

The word of the LORD came to Jonah son of Amittai: "Go to the great city of Nineveh and preach against it, because its wickedness has come up before me."

Unlike the other Minor Prophets, the Book of Jonah is not a collection of prophecies. Instead, it is an account of a period in the prophet's life. The book falls into two distinct parts. The first section shows us Jonah's attempt to escape God's call to preach in the Assyrian city of Nineveh. The second part portrays Jonah's reluctant obedience to that command.

In 1:1, we learn that the Lord spoke His word to Jonah the son of Amittai. Virtually nothing is known about Amittai. Second Kings 14:25 notes that Jonah was a prophet from Gath Hepher, a town in the territory of the tribe of Zebulun (Josh. 19:13) and located about three miles northeast of Nazareth.

That same verse in 2 Kings indicates that Jonah had foretold Jeroboam II's restoration of the territory of Israel from the entrance of Hamath (a city in central Syria) to the Dead Sea. Since Jeroboam II reigned from 793–753 B.C., Jonah's life and ministry most likely occurred during the early eighth century B.C.

The Book of Jonah records another episode in the prophet's life—the time when God commanded him to declare an important message of judgment to foreigners (1:2). The Lord directed Jonah to get up and go to the great city of Nineveh, the main urban center of the powerful Assyrian Empire. The city was located on the Tigris River about 550 miles northeast of Gath Hepher, the hometown of Jonah. Nineveh was heavily fortified and a great hub for commerce and trade.

Jonah was to denounce Nineveh for its many crimes. The Lord said that the wicked practices of the city's inhabitants were so great that it was as if they reached to the heights of heaven. God was fully aware of the atrocities taking place in Nineveh and He was prepared to punish the people for their transgressions.

B. The Refusal: vs. 3

But Jonah ran away from the LORD and headed for Tarshish. He went down to Joppa, where he found a ship bound for that port. After paying the fare, he went aboard and sailed for Tarshish to flee from the LORD.

From the latter part of the account recorded in the Book of Jonah, we gather that God conditioned His judgment on the response of the Ninevites. If they reacted favorably to Jonah's message, the Lord would withhold His judgment. But if they reacted unfavorably, He would visit them with calamity.

As far as we know from the Bible, Jonah was the only true prophet who disobeyed a direct commission from God to prophesy. Jonah "ran away from the LORD" (1:3), for he disliked the possibility of the Ninevites repenting and experiencing the mercy of God. Although Assyria's power was temporarily on the wane in Jonah's day, Assyria remained guilty of cruelly oppressing Israel and other neighboring states. Jonah's nationalism and his righteous indignation made it difficult for him to accept God's willingness to show mercy to the Ninevites. This helps us to understand Jonah's reluctance to go to Nineveh.

The prophet would have preferred to see the enemy destroyed rather than delivered. That's why Jonah tried to run away from the Lord's presence by going to Tarshish. The prophet's efforts, of course, were in vain because God is present everywhere (Ps. 139:7-12).

Tarshish was a Mediterranean seaport that some have identified with ancient Tartessus, a Phoenician colony located in southwest Spain. Others have identified Tarshish with Tarsus in Cilicia, Carthage in North Africa, and Sardinia (an Italian island south of Corsica). Regardless of which of these locations is correct, it is clear that Jonah intended to flee in the opposite direction from the one ordered by God.

For this purpose Jonah first went to Joppa, a small port city on the Mediterranean coast about 35 miles northwest of Jerusalem. When the prophet found a ship that was sailing to Tarshish, he paid the passenger fare and boarded the vessel. Jonah erroneously thought that by being on this vessel he could flee from God and His call.

Few of us will take to the sea to escape from God. Yet there are many other ways we may try to run away from Him and His demands on our lives. We may become absorbed in our work or our leisure activities. We may turn to artificial stimulants and depressants. We may even use the bustle and noise of church activities to drown out the still, small voice of God. But all such attempts are as futile as Jonah's flight would turn out to be. God is always waiting for us to do His will, and it would be better for us to submit to Him sooner rather than later.

C. The Storm: vs. 4

Then the LORD sent a great wind on the sea, and such a violent storm arose that the ship threatened to break up.

The Lord would not sit idly by and allow His prophet to avoid doing what He had commanded. God hurled a wind of tremendous force on the sea, making the waters hazardous. The storm became so intense that the waves pounding against the ship threatened to break it apart.

The Bible does not tell us what kind of ship Jonah boarded in Joppa. It may, however, have been one of the "ships of Tarshish" that are frequently mentioned in the Old Testament (Ps. 48:7). Reports indicate that these were large merchant vessels capable of transporting heavy cargoes. Ships of that era were powered by double banks of oars and rowed by 20 to 30 sailors. During violent storms, the sailors would tie ropes around the hull to prevent the ship from falling apart—a practice called frapping. However, it didn't help the sailors on Jonah's ship, for the storm was too violent.

II. JONAH'S PLIGHT: JONAH 1:11-17

A. The Confession of Jonah: vss. 11-12

The sea was getting rougher and rougher. So they asked him, "What should we do to you to make the sea calm down for us?" "Pick me up and throw me into the sea," he replied, "and it will become calm. I know that it is my fault that this great storm has come upon you."

Regardless of what the mariners did, they could not improve their situation. They eventually discovered that Jonah was the cause of their problems. Upon being questioned by the mariners, he revealed that he was a Hebrew and that he worshiped Yahweh, the God of heaven. Jonah also told them that he was trying to flee by sea from the presence of the Lord (Jonah 1:5-10). The prophet's decision seemed especially futile in light of his identification of God as the Creator of the sea and dry land.

Jonah's statement terrified the mariners. Perhaps with alarmed voices, they asked the prophet why he was trying to flee from the presence of the Lord. Jonah evidently did not offer a convincing or reassuring explanation for his actions. Even worse, he seemed to be hardened to the fact that his willful defiance of God's command had endangered the lives of the pagan sailors.

The situation grew desperate, as the waves of the sea became increasingly rough. Having run out of options of their own, the mariners asked Jonah what he thought they should do to him to make the sea calm once again (vs. 11). The prophet said that if they picked him up and hurled him into the raging sea, it would return to a tranquil state (vs. 12).

Although Jonah knew his disobedience was the reason for the fierce storm, apparently he was unrepentant. Perhaps he felt that justice would be served only if he died. Jonah may have been depressed and looked forward to a quick end. Clearly, he seemed to prefer death over the option of preaching to the Ninevites.

B. The Plea of the Sailors: vss. 13-16

Instead, the men did their best to row back to land. But they could not, for the sea grew even wilder than before. Then they cried to the LORD, "O LORD, please do not let us die for taking this man's life. Do not hold us accountable for killing an innocent man, for you, O LORD, have done as you pleased." Then they took Jonah and threw him overboard, and the raging sea grew calm. At this the men greatly feared the LORD, and they offered a sacrifice to the LORD and made vows to him.

The pagan sailors initially did not like the idea of throwing Jonah into the sea, probably because they feared the wrath of God. The mariners exhausted all their efforts to row their vessel back to land. Despite their noble attempt, however, their efforts proved futile. They did not have the ability to counter the effects of the sea, which grew increasingly turbulent (Jonah 1:13).

In desperation the mariners cried out to the Lord. They earnestly begged Him not to end their lives for drowning His prophet. Although they were about to throw Jonah into the stormy sea, they pleaded with God not to charge them with the guilt for killing an innocent man. (In this situation, the prophet was anything but innocent.) The mariners acknowledged that the Lord, whom Jonah represented, had done as He had pleased in bringing about the catastrophic situation (vs. 14).

Clearly, the mariners respected God's power and feared His wrath. They did not want to do anything to displease Him. Jonah, on the other hand, was defiant toward God. The prophet evidently did not expect mercy from God, believing that He just wanted to drown him. Jonah showed no desire to pray to God—for forgiveness or rescue or anything.

When the sailors picked up Jonah and threw him overboard into the sea, it grew calm (vs. 15). Upon seeing this, the mariners stood in awe of the Lord. They offered a sacrifice to Him and made vows to worship and serve Him (vs. 16). Possibly this happened later, once the ship had landed and the men had made their way to an Israelite town, if not to the Jerusalem temple itself.

C. The Confinement of Jonah: vs. 17

But the LORD provided a great fish to swallow Jonah, and Jonah was inside the fish three days and three nights.

After being thrown into the sea, Jonah could easily have drowned. But the Lord did not allow this to happen. Instead, He graciously provided a great fish to swallow His prophet (Jonah 1:17). Without fanfare, this verse records the extraordinary occurrence of Jonah's lodging inside a large sea creature (we don't know what kind) for three days and nights.

The fish saved Jonah from drowning. Contrary to what the sailors thought, God's intention had never been to destroy Jonah. He wanted to preserve Jonah and to teach him obedience. God likewise may permit hard times to enter our lives, but He hopes that we will respond by looking to Him. When we recognize our sins and repent, God will surely show us mercies—in this life and in the life to come.

III. JONAH'S RESCUE: JONAH 2:1, 10

A. Jonah's Prayer: vs. 1

From inside the fish Jonah prayed to the LORD his God.

From inside the great fish, Jonah prayed to the Lord (Jonah 2:1). In this prayer Jonah remembered what had gone on in his mind while he was sinking into the water. In his most dangerous predicament, Jonah cried to the Lord for help. And God had favorably responded to his request, graciously sparing his life. This had renewed Jonah's faith and determination to serve the Lord (vss. 2-9).

When we are swamped with troubles of our own making, we do well to remember Jonah's spiritual turnabout while underwater. If there is rebellion within us, it is not too late to turn to the Lord. And because God is all-powerful, salvation in some unexpected form may come—even at the last minute.

B. Jonah's Deliverance: vs. 10

And the LORD commanded the fish, and it vomited Jonah onto dry land.

Jonah had repented of his rebellious attitudes and actions and determined in his heart to do what God had commanded. The prophet was now ready to be sent on his way to Nineveh to proclaim a message of judgment. The Lord therefore commanded the fish to release Jonah. The animal, in turn, cast the prophet onto dry land (Jonah 2:10).

Discussion Questions

1. Why would God want one of His people to proclaim His judgment against a pagan people? What does this say about God?
2. What mistakes did Jonah make when he took off for Tarshish?
3. How do the actions of the pagan sailors contrast with those of Jonah?
4. Why do you think God chose the means of rescue for Jonah that He did?
5. What can happen if we allow a rebellious attitude to persist?

Contemporary Application

There is no middle ground with respect to God's commands. He wants us to be fully committed to doing His will. He cannot bless any rebellious attitudes or actions in our relationship with Him.

That is why we should repent of thoughts and deeds that are in opposition to the will of the Lord (1 John 1:9). Repentance involves being sorry for doing something wrong and choosing not to do it again. The truly repentant believer rejects attitudes and actions that are insubordinate and adopts those that are in harmony with God's commands (2 Cor. 7:8-12).

Repenting is never easy or enjoyable. This is because we are saying *no* to our sinful desires and tendencies and saying *yes* to God and the teachings of His Word. We are choosing to die to our unwholesome urges and submitting as the will of the Lord replaces them. We are putting to death our old sinful ways and allowing the life of the Spirit to be present in all we do (Rom. 6:1-14).

We will never regret repenting of our rebellious attitudes and actions. Our joy in serving the Lord will be renewed and our ability to witness effectively for Him will be enhanced. We will be better able to relate to others in a godly manner and we will be more sensitive to the leading of the Spirit. Repentance can also be a major factor in our becoming more Christlike and mature.

God's Mercy to Nineveh

Scripture

Background Scripture: *Jonah 3–4*
Scripture Lesson: *Jonah 3:1-5, 10; 4:1-5, 11*
Key Verse: *He prayed to the LORD, "O LORD, is this not what
I said when I was still at home? That is why I was so quick to
flee to Tarshish. I knew that you are a gracious and compassionate God, slow to anger and abounding in love, a God who
relents from sending calamity."* Jonah 4:2.

Lesson Aim

To become more compassionate and forgiving.

Lesson Setting

Time: *785–775 B.C.*
Place: *Nineveh*

Lesson Outline

God's Mercy to Nineveh
    I. Preaching God's Judgment: Jonah 3:1-5, 10
        A. *God's Command: vss. 1-2*
        B. *Jonah's Preaching: vss. 3-4*
        C. *Nineveh's Repentance and God's Mercy: vss. 5, 10*
    II. Pouting over God's Decision: Jonah 4:1-5, 11
        A. *Jonah's Displeasure: vs. 1*
        B. *Jonah's Request: vss. 2-3*
        C. *God's Question: vs. 4*
        D. *Jonah's Brooding and God's Response: vss. 5, 11*

Introduction for Adults

Topic: *Showing Mercy*

The Book of Jonah leaves us hanging. We don't know if Jonah ever got to the point of being glad that God was merciful to the people of Nineveh. But there is one fact we do know. God expects us—Christian adults living in a new millennium—to be merciful as He is merciful.

Because of our sinful nature, we, like Jonah, find it hard to be merciful to those who have hurt us. But unlike Jonah, we know Christ and have the Holy Spirit dwelling within us. Therefore, we *can* be compassionate and forgiving.

Even if people have been hard on us, that does not mean it is right for us to hate them or unlovingly condemn them. We should not set preconditions on showing God's compassion to other people. If we are truly Christlike, we will display the love of God to other people in an unconditional and unselfish manner, regardless of how they have treated us.

Introduction for Youths

Topic: *It's Not Fair!*

This week's lesson emphasizes two of God's characteristics that saved teens are to exhibit in their lives—compassion and forgiveness. Sadly, these were absent from Jonah's life. He censured God for choosing not to destroy the Ninevites. And Jonah was upset that God would forgive a people who were terribly evil. God chose to show compassion, and Jonah couldn't handle it.

Many young people are like Jonah. It's far easier to want revenge than to forgive. It's human nature to want misfortune to fall on their enemies rather than show compassion. In fact, youth sometimes work at staying angry with people or even become upset when God doesn't punish the wicked.

The key is for teens to stop focusing on the harm or injustice that's been done to them. If they can set that aside for a moment, they will be better able to see that the one who has hurt them is a hurting person too. With the Spirit's help, saved youth can do what they could never do on their own, namely, to show compassion and forgiveness to the unlovable.

Concepts for Children

Topic: *God Forgave the People of Nineveh*

1. God again directed Jonah to tell His message to the people of Nineveh.
2. After entering the city, Jonah told the people what God was going to do.
3. The people believed the message and were sorry for their sins.
4. Jonah became angry that God would not punish the people of Nineveh.
5. God told Jonah that the lives of people and animals were of concern to Him.
6. God wants us to be loving and forgiving to others, regardless of how they have treated us.

The Lesson Commentary

I. PREACHING GOD'S JUDGMENT: JONAH 3:1-5, 10

A. God's Command: vss. 1-2

Then the word of the LORD came to Jonah a second time: "Go to the great city of Nineveh and proclaim to it the message I give you."

Last week's lesson focused on Jonah's disobedience of God's command for him to deliver a warning of judgment against the people of Nineveh. But in this week's lesson Scripture we see that the Lord, in His superabundant love, gave the prophet another opportunity to serve Him. God revealed His will to Jonah a second time by telling him to travel to the great city of Nineveh to proclaim to its inhabitants a somber message of judgment (Jonah 1:1-2).

This major city of Assyria underwent it's greatest expansion during the reign of King Sennacherib [sin-ACK-uh-rib]. He constructed many buildings and parks and reestablished the walls, gates, and water supply system. His palace became famous in the annals of history. The libraries of Nineveh were also noteworthy. They held thousands of tablets containing business accounts, letters, royal records, historical documents, legends, and myths.

The fall of Nineveh, predicted by the prophets Nahum and Zephaniah, occurred in August of 612 B.C. to the combined forces of the Babylonians, Medes, and Scythians. This was several decades after Jonah's appearance there. After the siege, the city was allowed to crumble to ruins.

B. Jonah's Preaching: vss. 3-4

Jonah obeyed the word of the LORD and went to Nineveh. Now Nineveh was a very important city—a visit required three days. On the first day, Jonah started into the city. He proclaimed: "Forty more days and Nineveh will be overturned."

Unlike before, this time Jonah did not hesitate to heed the command of God. Instead of running away, he went at once to Nineveh. This reminds us that God often gives His wayward people a second chance. If we repent after going astray, we will find that He is yet calling out to us. He wants us to obey Him with a willing heart and with gratitude for His patient love.

It probably took Jonah at least a month to make the journey from Israel to Nineveh. Jonah would have followed the well-traveled trade routes along the Fertile Crescent—an area stretching north of Israel and then east and south into Mesopotamia. Of course, the book focuses not on the journey but on what happened once Jonah got to Nineveh.

A visit to this chief city of the Assyrian Empire "required three days" (Jonah 3:3). Some understand the reference to mean that it would have taken three days just to cross from one end of Nineveh to the other. An ancient Near Eastern city such as Nineveh might technically have included both the metropolis itself and its surrounding territories. Therefore, it may have taken Jonah three days to traverse the city proper and its outlying districts.

There are two ways of understanding verse 4. On the one hand, Jonah might have walked for an entire day through Nineveh before he began to proclaim God's message of doom. On the other hand, the prophet might have declared the somber warning throughout the first day's journey.

Imagine Jonah venturing through various small streets and markets as he announced God's judgment. What a stir he must have caused! In 40 days the great city of Nineveh would be destroyed!

C. Nineveh's Repentance and God's Mercy: vss. 5, 10

The Ninevites believed God. They declared a fast, and all of them, from the greatest to the least, put on sackcloth. . . . When God saw what they did and how they turned from their evil ways, he had compassion and did not bring upon them the destruction he had threatened.

The inhabitants took to heart what Jonah had declared. They not only believed the prophet's message of judgment but also proclaimed a citywide fast. They put on sackcloth to display their grief and anguish over what Jonah had pronounced against them. (Sackcloth was a coarse material woven from the hair of goats or camels.) All the people of the city wore the rough material, from the most important inhabitants to the least important inhabitants (Jonah 3:5).

There is some uncertainty about the nature of the Ninevites' repentance. Some think the people were genuinely converted to faith in Yahweh, while others think their remorse was superficial and temporary. In any case, the immediate response of the Ninevites to Jonah's preaching seemed genuine (vss. 6-9).

The repentance of the Ninevites might be easier to understand when we take into account factors that may have affected their frame of mind in the mid-eighth century B.C.—the probable time when Jonah appeared in their midst. Political threats to Assyria's stability may have made the Ninevites uneasy about their future. Riots and rebellions cropped up around the Assyrian Empire between 772 B.C. and 758 B.C. The kingdom of Urartu took land and major cities away from the Assyrians between 760 B.C. and 750 B.C.

There also occurred natural events that would certainly have been viewed as signs of God's displeasure. A violent earthquake shook the region sometime between 772 B.C. and 755 B.C. Famine left many hungry in the years 765 B.C. to 759 B.C. And a total eclipse of the sun occurred on June 15, 763 B.C. Prepared by this combination of disasters and evil omens, the people of Nineveh could easily have been quick to believe a foreign prophet warning that God would overrun their city in 40 days.

Of course, the grace of God working in the lives of the Ninevites was the ultimate cause of their repentant response. From a human perspective, they should have reacted stubbornly to Jonah's message of judgment. However, the Lord enabled the inhabitants of the city to see the error of their ways and to embrace the truth Jonah proclaimed.

Because the people had repented, God, in turn, "did not bring upon them the destruction he had threatened" (vs. 10). This means (in our terms) that He reversed His previous decision to overturn Nineveh. In canceling His threatened punishment, God was not being arbitrary or inconsistent. His warning of judgment on the Ninevites had been conditional and tentative, for He had planned from the beginning to anchor His response to the reaction of the Ninevites. Since they responded favorably to God, He treated them favorably. Ultimately, it was not God who changed His mind, but the people of Nineveh who changed.

The word for "repentance" used in the Book of Jonah literally means "to turn." Repentance implies that we have been moving in the wrong direction. When we turn back to God, we do so with mind, heart, and body.

II. Pouting over God's Decision: Jonah 4:1-5, 11

A. Jonah's Displeasure: vs. 1

But Jonah was greatly displeased and became angry.

When Jonah learned that the Lord would not destroy Nineveh, he became extremely unhappy and upset (Jonah 4:1). He was displeased over the fact that God would be merciful to the enemies of Israel. So strong was his nationalistic feeling that he would have preferred to see the Assyrians destroyed even after they had turned from their sins.

B. Jonah's Request: vss. 2-3

He prayed to the LORD, "O LORD, is this not what I said when I was still at home? That is why I was so quick to flee to Tarshish. I knew that you are a gracious and compassionate God, slow to anger and abounding in love, a God who relents from sending calamity. Now, O LORD, take away my life, for it is better for me to die than to live."

Jonah complained to the Lord that his worst fears had been realized. The prophet noted that when he had been in Israel, he had anticipated that the Ninevites might repent and that God would spare them from being judged. To forestall such an event, Jonah had tried to flee to Tarshish and avoid God's call (Jonah 4:2).

Jonah wanted God to be gracious and merciful to His people—the Israelites—in keeping with His character. The prophet, however, did not want Him to be that way with the wicked, pagan Ninevites—Israel's enemies. Jonah would have applauded the Lord for being slow to anger, abundant in unfailing love, and always ready to relent from inflicting punishment on the Israelites when they repented of their sins. But the prophet wanted God to treat the Ninevites in an entirely different manner.

In a rebellious pout, Jonah asked the Lord to take his life (vs. 3). He evidently thought it would be better for him to die than to live and see the Lord spare Israel's oppressors. What a pathetic attitude Jonah displayed! He operated according to a double standard. He had been glad when God had mercifully saved him from drowning, but he was incensed that now God was being merciful to Gentiles. God was more compassionate than was His prophet.

Hebrews 12:15 warns that bitterness defiles. Jonah is an example of that principle in action. His hatred of the Assyrians was so great that it eventually displaced his appreciation for God. By rejecting God's attributes of grace and forgiveness, Jonah was rejecting God Himself.

C. God's Question: vs. 4

But the LORD replied, "Have you any right to be angry?"

Rather than granting Jonah's request, God asked him a question (Jonah 4:4). This was His way of getting His despondent prophet to think about the implications of his attitude and actions. God asked whether it was right for Jonah to be angry. Was his deep grief a proper response? Clearly, the answer was no.

Jonah should have accepted the fact that whatever God does is right. Furthermore, Jonah should have had the same forgiving attitude toward the Ninevites that God had. When we are angry, it is a good idea to ask God's question of ourselves: Do I have a right to be angry? Then we should answer honestly.

D. Jonah's Brooding and God's Response: vss. 5, 11

Jonah went out and sat down at a place east of the city. There he made himself a shelter, sat in its shade and waited to see what would happen to the city. . . . "But Nineveh has more than a hundred and twenty thousand people who cannot tell their right hand from their left, and many cattle as well. Should I not be concerned about that great city?"

Jonah did not reply to God's question. Instead, he tried to avoid the issue by leaving Nineveh and finding a place east of the city to sit down. At that spot he made a crude shelter, reclined in the shade it provided, and waited to see what God would do to Nineveh and its inhabitants (Jonah 4:5). In a sense, Jonah was challenging God to destroy the Ninevites.

Verses 6-10 reveal that God caused a plant (evidently a gourd plant with large leaves) to quickly grow up over Jonah. The plant brought the prophet much joy because it provided additional shade for his head and relief from the misery of the heat. At dawn the next day, the Lord caused a worm to attack and destroy the plant. Jonah responded with petulant anger, which revealed that he cared more for a single plant than he did for hundreds of people. The Lord indicated to His sulking prophet that his priorities were misplaced. He pitied the loss of a plant for which he had not labored, but refused to show the same concern for the inhabitants of Nineveh.

God's point in doing this was for Jonah to see that if it was legitimate for him to pity a single plant, why should he be angry with God for showing compassion and forgiveness to the repentant Ninevites? In addition to the numerous livestock dwelling in the great metropolis, well over 120,000 persons were living in the city. They needed to hear the truth about God, especially concerning His displeasure with their wicked ways (vs. 11).

From a moral standpoint, the Ninevites could not discern their right hand from their left. In His unfailing love, the Lord mercifully reached out to the Ninevites with a message of warning and hope. Through Jonah's message they were spared from otherwise certain destruction. Jonah should have been thankful, not vexed, over the fact that God had used him to save the Ninevites from wickedness and destruction.

The tension raised by God's final question to Jonah is never resolved. In fact, we are not told whether the prophet learned the lesson God had taken such pains to teach. Clearly, Jonah stands as a warning to succeeding generations of the dangers created by despising God's blessings.

Discussion Questions

1. If you had been in Jonah's sandals, how would you have delivered the message of God's judgment against the Ninevites?
2. Why do you think the Ninevites heeded the words of an Israelite prophet?
3. What did Jonah reveal about himself when he became angry with the Lord?
4. Why was Jonah wrong for pouting?
5. Why is it so hard for us to be as compassionate and forgiving to others as God has been to us?

Contemporary Application

Imagine the most terrible crime someone could possibly commit against you. How would you feel after being so cruelly treated? How readily would you be willing to extend forgiveness if that person eventually came and asked to be pardoned for the hurt he or she had inflicted?

It would be extremely difficult for most of us to be compassionate and forgiving to someone who has severely mistreated us. The sinful response would be to lash out in anger, hold a grudge, or seek to get even. The godly response would be to forgive the person who has been abusive or destructive in his or her behavior. Although this is rarely easy to do, it is the only response that meets with God's approval and will be blessed by Him.

First John 4:7 urges believers to love one another because love comes from God. By striving to show the Lord's compassion to others, we reveal that we are His children and truly know Him. Conversely, when we do not love as the Lord does, we show that we do not know God, who is characterized by pure and unbounded compassion for others, as we should (vs. 8). According to verse 11, believers should seek to be as loving to others as God has been to them.

By imitating our compassionate and forgiving God, we can bring comfort to the needy. We can help them see the love of God as it works through us. We can even inspire others to begin showing compassion and forgiveness. In a cold world, a little love can produce some unexpected and much-needed warmth.

The Power of the Gospel

God's Righteousness Revealed

DEVOTIONAL READING

Psalm 34:1-8

DAILY BIBLE READINGS

Monday March 4
  Ephesians 1:3-14 God's Grace Is Freely Bestowed

Tuesday March 5
  Ephesians 1:15-23 Called to Hope

Wednesday March 6
  Ephesians 2:1-10 Saved by Grace

Thursday March 7
  Ephesians 2:11-22 We Are No Longer Strangers and Aliens

Friday March 8
  Romans 2:17—3:8 God Is True

Saturday March 9
  Romans 3:9-20 The Law Brings Knowledge of Sin

Sunday March 10
  Romans 3:21-31 Justified by God's Grace

Scripture

Background Scripture: *Romans 1*
Scripture Lesson: *Romans 1:1-13, 16-17*
Key Verse: *I am not ashamed of the gospel, because it is the power of God for the salvation of everyone who believes: first for the Jew, then for the Gentile. For in the gospel a righteousness from God is revealed, a righteousness that is by faith from first to last.* Romans 1:16-17.
Scripture Lesson for Children: *John 12:12-19*
Key Verse for Children: *"Hosanna! Blessed is he who comes in the name of the Lord!"* John 12:13.

Lesson Aim

To realize the importance of the Gospel and to communicate it clearly to others.

Lesson Setting

Time: A.D. *57*
Place: *From Corinth to the church in Rome*

Lesson Outline

God's Righteousness Revealed
  I. Paul's Identity and Calling: Romans 1:1-7
      A. *Set Apart for the Gospel: vss. 1-4*
      B. *Called to the Gentiles: vss. 5-6*
      C. *Called to the Romans: vs. 7*
  II. Paul's Desire: Romans 1:8-13
      A. *Paul's Prayer: vss. 8-10*
      B. *Paul's Purposes: vss. 11-13*
  III. Paul's Confidence: Romans 1:16-17
      A. *In the Gospel's Power: vs. 16*
      B. *In God's Righteousness: vs. 17*

Introduction for Adults

Topic: *Getting Right with God*

Paul declared that the good news about Christ did not embarrass him, for the Gospel represented the power of God at work in saving everyone who believes (Rom. 1:16). Sadly, we find many people in our culture who reject the importance of getting right with God by embracing the Gospel. It's true that, according to the polls, a lot of people claim to be "religious." Nevertheless, many in the West take little account of God. Perhaps there is little fear of facing a holy God because the idea of sin has virtually been abolished.

The Gospel, which Paul proclaimed, won't make the evening news on television. It won't even make newspaper headlines. It's thus the responsibility of believers to carry the Good News far and wide so that all may hear it and have the opportunity to be saved. Perhaps God in His grace might use our proclamation of the Gospel to prompt some who hear it to get right with Him.

Introduction for Youths

Topic: *Power Source*

A man bought two batteries, took them home, and inserted them into his tape recorder. Surprisingly, nothing happened. He then returned the batteries to the store and received two new ones. However, he eventually discovered that his problem was not with the batteries but rather with the way he had inserted them.

The same sort of thing happens when we carve out our own plans for pleasing God. We trick ourselves into thinking that, regardless of what we do, God is pleased most of the time. This reasoning reflects the mind-set of a college student who said that God would accept him because he did what was right 99 percent of the time. This is flawed thinking, for as James 2:10 says, the person who keeps all of the laws except one is as guilty as the person who has broken all of God's laws.

Who, then, has the power to obey God? Apart from Christ, no one has this ability. But the good news is that through faith in Him we not only are declared righteous but also receive power to obey God. With Jesus at our side, we can live in a way that genuinely pleases God.

Concepts for Children

Topic: *Jesus Entered Jerusalem*

1. A large crowd of people got palm branches and went out to meet Jesus.
2. The people shouted praises to Jesus.
3. At that time Jesus' followers didn't understand what was happening.
4. Many people wanted to see Jesus because He had raised Lazarus from the dead.
5. The good news about Jesus should fill us with joy.
6. We should praise Jesus for His goodness and mercy.

The Lesson Commentary

I. PAUL'S IDENTITY AND CALLING: ROMANS 1:1-7

A. Set Apart for the Gospel: vss. 1-4

Paul, a servant of Christ Jesus, called to be an apostle and set apart for the gospel of God—the gospel he promised beforehand through his prophets in the Holy Scriptures regarding his Son, who as to his human nature was a descendant of David, and who through the Spirit of holiness was declared with power to be the Son of God by his resurrection from the dead: Jesus Christ our Lord.

"All roads lead to Rome." This common proverb seemed almost true during Paul's lifetime. This booming metropolis was connected to other parts of the ancient world by an intricate system of highways. Its communications system was unsurpassed at the time. During the first century A.D., Rome was at the hub of trade and commerce. Because of its location and prestige, Rome was a strategic city for the spread of the Gospel, which is the focus of this quarter's lessons.

It's not surprising that we begin our study with the Book of Romans, for it presents a comprehensive and systematic doctrine of salvation in Christ. This letter has singularly fired great people of the faith, such as Augustine, Martin Luther, John Bunyan, and John Wesley. Romans is Paul's theological masterpiece.

Paul called himself a servant, or slave, of Jesus Christ (Rom. 1:1). In other words, Paul belonged to and obeyed the Savior. As a bondslave of the Lord, Paul had been bought with a price and then set free so that he could serve Jesus in love for the rest of his life.

Paul said he was a "called" apostle. In other words, he did not enter his ministry as the result of personal choice; rather, he had received a divine summons, which put him into that position. Paul traced his appointment to a divine decision in the counsel of eternity. God had marked Paul off for the work of proclaiming the Gospel even before he was born (Gal. 1:15).

The Good News that Paul heralded had its origin in the Hebrew Scriptures and had been the subject of the prophets' interest (Rom. 1:2). In fact, the message of truth had even been proclaimed to Abraham (Gal. 3:8). Thus the truth Paul heralded was not something novel or deviant, but rather grounded in the revelation of the Old Testament.

The person of the Gospel is God's Son, "Jesus Christ our Lord" (Rom. 1:4). The message emphasizes Jesus' real humanity; according to the flesh—that is, His human nature in its entirety—He descended from King David through Mary (vs. 3). The Gospel also stresses Christ's absolute deity. He is the eternal Son in union with the Father (vs. 4).

The good news includes the fact that Jesus' resurrection from the dead transferred Him from His condition of humiliation to a new phase of lordship and glory. His entrance into post-resurrection glory was perfectly compatible with the essential sinlessness of His humanity and the direct result of the Holy Spirit's limitless power.

B. Called to the Gentiles: vss. 5-6

Through him and for his name's sake, we received grace and apostleship to call people from among all the Gentiles to the obedience that comes from faith. And you also are among those who are called to belong to Jesus Christ.

> Paul attributed his ability to carry out the functions of his apostolic office to the grace of God (Rom. 1:5). In fact, Paul's apostleship was God's gracious gift to him. The purpose for which the Lord saved and called Paul was that he might bring the Gentiles to obedience through faith in Christ.
>
> The good news that Paul proclaimed announces that God's kingdom is at hand and that forgiveness is available through faith in Christ. It is the duty of everyone who hears the truth to obey its first demand—trust in Christ. The moment we believe in Him, we are obeying the Gospel. Oppositely, to reject the Good News is to disobey it.
>
> Paul's readers had already heard and believed the Good News (vs. 6). And by their obedient faith they had joined God's family. They thus belonged to Jesus Christ, and He was their Savior and Lord.

C. Called to the Romans: vs. 7

To all in Rome who are loved by God and called to be saints: Grace and peace to you from God our Father and from the Lord Jesus Christ.

> God had commissioned Paul to carry Jesus' name "before the Gentiles" (Acts 9:15). This included the people in Rome. As the apostle wrote to the Roman believers, he called them "saints" (Rom. 1:7). By this Paul meant God's holy people. Like other Christians, they had renounced their sin and devoted their lives in service to the Lord.
>
> Paul's standard greeting of grace and peace is included in the letter he wrote to the Romans. Through their faith in Christ, they became the recipients of the Father's unmerited favor and unending peace. Ephesians 2:7 reminds us that God has shown "the incomparable riches of his grace, expressed in his kindness to us in Christ Jesus." Such is a magnificent display of the Lord's great love for us (vs. 4).

II. PAUL'S DESIRE: ROMANS 1:8-13

A. Paul's Prayer: vss. 8-10

First, I thank my God through Jesus Christ for all of you, because your faith is being reported all over the world. God, whom I serve with my whole heart in preaching the gospel of his Son, is my witness how constantly I remember you in my prayers at all times; and I pray that now at last by God's will the way may be opened for me to come to you.

> As in other letters Paul wrote, this one to the believers in Rome contained his expression of gratitude for them. He was especially thankful that their faith in God was becoming known "all over the world" (Rom. 1:8). Rome was the center of the empire and the inhabited world. Thus whatever happened in the capital city

became known throughout the realm. The testimony of the church in Rome was so strong that in A.D. 49 Claudius the emperor expelled all the Jews because of the influence of someone named "Chrestus," which most likely is a reference to Christ (Acts 18:2).

Paul's concern for the Roman Christians was not an abstraction. Instead, it was real and concrete. The apostle related that God knew how often Paul had prayed for his fellow believers in the capital. This wasn't an occasional occurrence. Rather, Paul lifted them up in prayer "constantly" (Rom. 1:9). And this wasn't an idle claim, for the apostle called on God as his witness, the same God whom he served with his whole heart in the proclamation of the Gospel.

Paul had wanted to visit Rome numerous times, but up until then had not been able to do so (vs. 13). During those intervening years, the apostle had done his evangelistic preaching and church planting in Greece and Asia Minor. Now he saw his way clear to make a possible visit to the capital of the empire. Paul thus asked that God would give him a prosperous journey to Rome (vs. 10). Paul, of course, knew that God would decide how and when his prayer request would be fulfilled. Later on the Lord did open the way for Paul to visit Rome, but as a prisoner.

B. Paul's Purposes: vss. 11-13

I long to see you so that I may impart to you some spiritual gift to make you strong—that is, that you and I may be mutually encouraged by each other's faith. I do not want you to be unaware, brothers, that I planned many times to come to you (but have been prevented from doing so until now) in order that I might have a harvest among you, just as I have had among the other Gentiles.

Paul noted two compelling reasons to visit Rome. First, he wanted to work with the Roman Christians in seeing a vast multitude of new converts to the faith. Second, the apostle wanted to partner with his fellow believers in Rome in seeing the church spiritually strengthened (Rom. 1:11).

Paul saw himself as a strengthener and encourager of others. And these were the spiritual gifts he wanted to utilize in Rome. Paul's building plan was people, not structures. He sensed he could encourage other Christians by his biblical teaching and godly example.

It's important to note that Paul didn't want his relationship with the Roman Christians to be one-sided. In other words, the apostle wanted both to minister to them and be ministered to by them (vs. 12). And that's why Paul sought mutual encouragement from them. This fits his description of how spiritual gifts are to be used in the church (Eph. 4:11-13).

Paul anticipated a bountiful spiritual "harvest" (Rom. 1:13) of Gentile converts resulting from his ministry with the other believers in Rome. By the end of the apostle's third missionary journey, he had traveled through Syria, Galatia, Macedonia, and Achaia. He now sensed that the time had come to redirect his ministry efforts to the eastern part of the empire.

III. Paul's Confidence: Romans 1:16-17

A. In the Gospel's Power: vs. 16

I am not ashamed of the gospel, because it is the power of God for the salvation of everyone who believes: first for the Jew, then for the Gentile.

Paul's ambition to herald the Gospel in Rome arose from his sense of indebtedness to all people (Rom. 1:14). He was under assignment to preach to the civilized and the uncivilized, to the cultured and the uncultured. Paul felt it was his duty to reach all regardless of their race, social status, or mental ability. The capital was the great prize to be won, and Paul anticipated his visit with eagerness. He was ready to go (vs. 15).

Paul had no reason to be ashamed of the Gospel he proclaimed. To be sure, it had no special appeal to the intellectuals. And the Good News could not boast of a great antiquity in that city, like the pagan religions of Rome. Nevertheless, the preaching of the Gospel unleashed the power of God (vs. 16). When the Lord exercised His power through the heralding of the Good News, He delivered the lost from eternal ruin. God rescued people from the tyranny of the devil, the mastery of the sin-principle, and the state of spiritual death.

Salvation is the experience of all who trust in Christ. In fact, salvation never occurs apart from faith. Salvation covers everything God does for us in Christ. God forgives our sins and grants us eternal life. We face the prospect of enjoying His presence forever.

Salvation is the possession equally of Jews and Gentiles. Neither has any priority on the claims of the Gospel. Of course, since Jews were the heirs of the promises of Abraham and the people from whom the Messiah came, it was appropriate that the Gospel should have been preached first to them. Paul followed this order on several occasions. In general, the Jews rejected the message of salvation through a crucified Messiah, and Paul then turned to the Gentiles.

B. In God's Righteousness: vs. 17

For in the gospel a righteousness from God is revealed, a righteousness that is by faith from first to last, just as it is written: "The righteous will live by faith."

Paul noted that the Gospel message included God's gift of righteousness by faith. The Good News revealed a God of righteousness, holiness, and justice who both judged people righteously and then declared them righteous by means of their faith in Christ (Rom. 1:17).

In this verse Paul was not talking about a divine attribute, namely, God's justice. Rather, the apostle was referring to a righteousness of which the Lord is the author and which provides an answer to the sinful condition of people. The Gospel explains how unrighteous people can receive an upright standing before a holy God. People must appropriate this righteousness by faith. It is the experience of all who trust in Christ.

A right standing with God comes by faith and appeals to faith—"from first to last." "The righteous will live by faith" is a quotation from Habakkuk 2:4. Paul took pains to connect the Gospel of Jesus Christ to the Old Testament. The prophet Habakkuk's words confirm Paul's point that righteousness comes through faith.

Discussion Questions

1. How had Christ and His Gospel radically changed Paul's life?
2. Why do you think Paul made the preaching of the Gospel such an important part of his ministry?
3. Why did Paul stress both the true humanity and absolute deity of Christ?
4. Why did Paul call on God as his witness concerning his claim regarding his prayers for the Romans?
5. Under what circumstances might some believers today be ashamed of the Gospel?
6. What would you say to someone who remarks, "I think the Gospel of Christ is ridiculous"?

Contemporary Application

Powerful ideas have spawned a chain of events that have affected the world. For instance, some historians say that the American Revolution was one of those episodes that left a permanent imprint on the history of humankind. In our time we could point to political and economic ideas that have impacted humankind both positively and negatively. In the end, though, none of these philosophies can match the Gospel of Christ, for none of them deals with our basic need to find forgiveness and righteousness from God.

Paul knew a lot about religion in his time, and he debated with some of the best Greek and Jewish minds of his day. The apostle never flinched when it came to staking out the claim that the Gospel was God's power to change people and give them eternal life. Paul made it clear that he was not just offering a new idea. In fact, he preached a person, Jesus of Nazareth, whom the authorities had executed and whom God had raised from the dead. Only this message can offer the lost eternal hope and peace. When they believe in Jesus, God declares them righteous.

The truth is that Jesus Christ, God's anointed Son, is alive and in heaven. We thus need not make any apologies for believing in Him. Rather, like Paul, we should be eager to tell the Good News with confidence.

Gift of Grace

DEVOTIONAL READING
  Psalm 33:13-22

DAILY BIBLE READINGS
  Monday March 11
    *Genesis 15:1-6 Descendants
    as Numerous as the Stars*
  Tuesday March 12
    *Genesis 15:12-21 A Promise
    to Abraham and His
    Descendants*
  Wednesday March 13
    *Acts 13:13-25 God Chose
    Our Ancestors*
  Thursday March 14
    *Acts 13:26-41 God Fulfilled
    His Promises by Raising
    Jesus*
  Friday March 15
    *2 Timothy 3:10-17 Continue
    Your Heritage*
  Saturday March 16
    *Romans 4:1-12 Abraham's
    Faith Was Reckoned as
    Righteousness*
  Sunday March 17
    *Romans 4:13-25 We Are
    Heirs through Faith*

Scripture

Background Scripture: *Romans 3*
Scripture Lesson: *Romans 3:1-4, 19-31*
Key Verse: *For all have sinned and fall short of the glory of God, and are justified freely by his grace through the redemption that came by Christ Jesus.* Romans 3:23-24.
Scripture Lesson for Children: *Luke 22:7-16, 19-20*
Key Verse for Children: *And he {Jesus} took bread, gave thanks and broke it, and gave it to them. . . . In the same way, after the supper he took the cup.* Luke 22:19-20.

Lesson Aim

To thank God for the gift of righteousness by faith alone.

Lesson Setting

Time: *A.D. 57*
Place: *From Corinth to the church in Rome*

Lesson Outline

Gift of Grace

  I. Jewish Advantages: Romans 3:1-4
    A. *The Revelation of God: vss. 1-2*
    B. *The Faithfulness of God: vss. 3-4*
  II. Forgiveness through Christ: Romans 3:19-31
    A. *The Purpose of the Law: vss. 19-20*
    B. *The Way to Be Saved: vss. 21-23*
    C. *The Basis for Justification: vss. 24-26*
    D. *The Elimination of Pride: vss. 27-28*
    E. *The Impartial Love of God: vss. 29-31*

Introduction for Adults

Topic: *Admitting Need*

Grandpa tried to help his grandson put together a new toy. "I know how to do this," the boy said, rejecting his grandfather's assistance. Perhaps initially we might think such a attitude represents childish pride. But then it's sobering to realize that this way of thinking is evident in many of us as adults.

"I don't need your help" means we feel self-sufficient. When we have such an attitude, it's humiliating to admit that we need help. Perhaps this is the greatest stumbling block that keeps many people from coming to faith in Christ. After all, who wants to admit sin and guilt? And who wants to say that God's judgment is fair and well deserved?

The Gospel cuts to the heart of the issue—our stubborn pride and willful independence from God. Until we understand and accept the consequences of our sins, we will not be prepared to come to Him on His terms. It's only when we admit our need that we will be ready to receive His gift of salvation through faith in Christ.

Introduction for Youths

Topic: *Equal Justice for All*

Children grow up expecting each other to play fairly. Perhaps that's why arguments and fights erupt when someone cheats. And even as they get older, adolescents expect justice to be built into the social system under which they live.

How interesting it is, then, when Christians declare that God is just and punishes rule breakers. "That isn't fair," some teens might say. Where did they get their ideas of justice? And how does it mesh with the truth of the Gospel?

When we accept God's justice, we become the recipients of His love and grace. We are saying to God that we come to Him on His terms, not ours. We admit that we have no excuses for our sin and no solution to our dilemma. We also acknowledge that He alone is able to forgive us because Jesus died for us. Now that's good news worth sharing!

Concepts for Children

Topic: *Jesus Ate with His Disciples*

1. When the day of Passover arrived, Jesus made preparations to eat a special meal with His followers.
2. At the proper time Jesus and His followers took their places at the table.
3. Jesus said that He was eager to eat this meal with His followers.
4. Jesus said that the bread and cup were to remind His followers of His death on the cross.
5. Jesus suffered for us so that we might enjoy His love and presence in our lives.
6. Jesus wants us to share the good news of His love with others.

The Lesson Commentary

I. JEWISH ADVANTAGES: ROMANS 3:1-4

A. The Revelation of God: vss. 1-2

What advantage, then, is there in being a Jew, or what value is there in circumcision? Much in every way! First of all, they have been entrusted with the very words of God.

From Romans 1 we learned that Paul described the power of the Gospel in terms of God declaring believing sinners righteous. From 1:18 to 3:20 the apostle discussed why all people need God's righteousness. Because of sin, every human being stands condemned before the Lord, who is holy.

Paul advanced his argument by first expounding the failure of the Gentiles to worship and obey God (1:18-32). Then the apostle focused on the fairness of God's judgment of humankind (2:1-16). Paul followed this discussion with a description of the failure of the Jews to live up to God's perfect moral standard (2:17—3:8). The apostle concluded that the entire world is guilty of disobeying the Lord (3:9-20).

Paul anticipated how the Jews would react to his explanation in 2:25-29. They were likely to reply in this way: "If being a true Jew depends on the inward condition of the heart rather than on racial and ritual distinctions, what advantage then is it to be a Jew? How is a Jew better off to have circumcision when, in the final analysis, circumcision does not really count?" (3:1).

Paul declared that there was a decided advantage in being a Jew. The principal benefit was that God had made the Jews the special custodians of His written revelation to humanity (vs. 2). Jewish birth gave them a unique exposure to God's Word. The oracles of God promised the Jews a permanent redemption through the Messiah, preserved them from the grosser immoralities of pagans, and prepared them for receiving the Gospel.

B. The Faithfulness of God: vss. 3-4

What if some did not have faith? Will their lack of faith nullify God's faithfulness? Not at all! Let God be true, and every man a liar. As it is written: "So that you may be proved right when you speak and prevail when you judge."

The spiritual benefits God had bestowed on the Jewish people were undeniable. But with such privileges came great responsibilities. Sadly, many Jews were not faithful in their responsibility. Indeed, they failed to live up to God's holy standards.

The fact that the Jews were the recipients of God's Word raised the important issue of faith in God's Word (Rom. 3:3). More specifically, Paul addressed the issue as to whether the lack of faith on the part of the Jews nullified God's faithfulness. The apostle immediately answered, "Not at all!" (vs. 4). God is always portrayed in Scripture as being utterly faithful to His Word (Deut. 7:9; 1 Cor. 1:9; Heb. 10:23). Paul expanded upon this theme of God's faithfulness in the face of Israel's unfaithfulness in Romans 9 through 11.

Paul made a puzzling statement when he declared, "Let God be true, and every man a liar" (Rom. 3:4). The apostle was emphasizing God's faithfulness in the face of the Jews' unfaithfulness. In other words, in light of God's spotless integrity, all people do appear as liars.

In support of Paul's argument, he quoted from Psalm 51:4. From this we learn that God's judgment against sin displays His faithfulness to His righteous character. God's faithfulness means He will never ignore sin, and when He judges, His judgment is perfect.

God's faithfulness is both comforting and challenging for us as Christians. It is a comfort to know that God will always fulfill the promises He has made. It is a challenge in that we can count on God's discipline when we sin.

II. FORGIVENESS THROUGH CHRIST: ROMANS 3:19-31

A. The Purpose of the Law: vss. 19-20

Now we know that whatever the law says, it says to those who are under the law, so that every mouth may be silenced and the whole world held accountable to God. Therefore no one will be declared righteous in his sight by observing the law; rather, through the law we become conscious of sin.

Throughout the first three chapters of Romans, Paul argued that at the bar of divine justice three witnesses testified against humanity. The creation pressed charges against the pagan for having rejected the light of nature. The conscience accused the moralist for having broken the moral law that God has written on the tablet of the human heart. And Scripture witnessed against the Jew for having violated the law of Moses. As 3:5-18 makes clear, the evidence was undeniable and condemning.

Paul affirmed that the pronouncements of the law are for all those who are "under the law" (vs. 19). His readers were under the law in the sense that they were obligated to obey it. They were answerable to the law because of their accountability to God Himself.

The purpose of the law was to silence every mouth and hold the entire world accountable to God. The law effectively and inarguably points to God's righteous and holy standards, and points to our utter inability to measure up to it. No one is in a position to argue sin away or make excuses, for the law invalidates all rationalizations.

Paul closed this section by pointing out that the law was never provided as a means of attaining righteousness or of being pronounced righteous before God (vs. 20). Rather, the law was given to make people aware of their sin. It is through the law that human beings become conscious of sin and see their need for a solution to the problem. In this light the law is an instrument of condemnation, not justification. The law, written on the hearts of all, shines the spotlight on our need for redemption. Admitting this is a crucial step toward being saved.

B. The Way to Be Saved: vss. 21-23

But now a righteousness from God, apart from law, has been made known, to which the Law and the Prophets testify. This righteousness from God comes through faith in Jesus Christ to all who believe. There is no difference, for all have sinned and fall short of the glory of God.

Paul had said that no one can be declared righteous by observing the law (Rom. 3:20). Since the law cannot save, but only shine the spotlight on sin, God's provision for salvation must be made "apart from law" (vs. 21), that is, "through faith in Jesus Christ" (vs. 22).

Righteousness apart from the law was previously revealed in "the Law and the Prophets" (vs. 21)—namely, the Old Testament. The word "Law" here refers to the first five books in the Old Testament, while "Prophets" refers to the other Old Testament books. The means of receiving this righteousness is by trusting in Christ (vs. 22). It is not something that can be worked for or earned. Whether Jew or Gentile, faith is the sole requirement. Faith is not considered a work, but rather a response of the broken heart to the saving work of God.

Paul said that, no matter who we are or what we have done, we are all saved in the same way. This is because all human beings—both Jew and Gentile—are sinners before God (vs. 23). Even the Jewish people could not be exempted from God's condemnation, for they were as guilty as the Gentiles.

Paul had in mind two aspects of sin: overt transgression and failure to do what is right. We are all guilty on both counts. Regardless of what we do—no matter how noble it might be—we still fall short of God's glorious standard.

The term for "fall short" is a single word in the Greek and is in the present tense to indicate continuing action. The tragedy is that human beings perpetually fall short of God's glory. The word rendered "glory" refers not just to God's magnificent presence but also to the outward display of His attributes, including His goodness, righteousness, and holiness. Our sin has separated us from God and excludes us from enjoying these displays of His glory.

C. The Basis for Justification: vss. 24-26

And are justified freely by his grace through the redemption that came by Christ Jesus. God presented him as a sacrifice of atonement, through faith in his blood. He did this to demonstrate his justice, because in his forbearance he had left the sins committed beforehand unpunished—he did it to demonstrate his justice at the present time, so as to be just and the one who justifies those who have faith in Jesus.

Against the dark backdrop of our sin and guilt, Paul painted a brilliant picture of God's grace. God not only is just and holy but also kind, loving, and gracious. Without these there would be no hope for any of us.

We are justified (or declared righteous by God) "freely" (Rom. 3:24). Because of God's grace, there is no charge. In fact, nothing we can do will ever earn God's righteousness. When we think we can do enough good to satisfy God's holiness, we insult His grace.

Paul used the Greek word translated "redemption" to describe what God has done for us in Christ. This word pictures God rescuing us out of the slave market of sin. In a sense, He has purchased our freedom out of the riches of His incomparable grace.

The person and work of the Christ is the overwhelming proof of God's grace. Because God's justice demanded a sacrifice for our sins, Jesus died on the cross. He took the punishment of our sins and satisfied God's anger against us. When we believe that Jesus shed His blood and sacrificed His life for us, God declares us to be righteous (vs. 25).

In God's "forbearance" (literally, "holding back"), He had suspended the full punishment for sins before Jesus' death. Such sins had been symbolically atoned for in the animal sacrifices of the temple. These sacrifices, however, were merely the shadow of Christ's saving work on the cross.

Paul noted that, because of what Jesus had done, God was entirely fair to not punish those who had sinned in former times. Likewise, the Lord was entirely just in this "present time" (vs. 26) to declare believing sinners to be right in His sight. Sinners cannot hurtle the legal barrier, but Christ can and did for them as their representative. Consequently, God can legitimately welcome and pardon them when they trust in Christ.

D. The Elimination of Pride: vss. 27-28

Where, then, is boasting? It is excluded. On what principle? On that of observing the law? No, but on that of faith. For we maintain that a man is justified by faith apart from observing the law.

Paul next asked some hard-hitting questions. First, "Where, then, is boasting?" (Rom. 3:27). He declared that boasting was "excluded" (or, "completely shut out"). Since human beings are justified by grace through faith, no works can be involved. Hence, no one can boast, for salvation is a free gift (Eph. 2:8-9).

This prompted a second question: "On what principle [is boasting excluded]? On that of observing the law?" (Rom. 3:27). Paul answered, "No" (or, "Not at all"). As the apostle stated earlier, God did not give the law to provide justification but rather to show people their state of sin and their need to be reconciled with God. Justification (or being "declared righteous") is available only through faith, "apart from observing the law" (vs. 28).

E. The Impartial Love of God: vss. 29-31

Is God the God of Jews only? Is he not the God of Gentiles too? Yes, of Gentiles too, since there is only one God, who will justify the circumcised by faith and the uncircumcised through that same faith. Do we, then, nullify the law by this faith? Not at all! Rather, we uphold the law.

Apparently some thought God was the exclusive property of Jews. Paul countered by noting that Gentiles do not have one God and the Jews another (Rom. 3:29). Likewise, faith is not a national possession. God does not save Gentiles on the basis of a different principle from that by which He saves Jews. One God justifies both

Jews and Gentiles by faith (vs. 30).

Paul then noted that God declares righteous those who come to Christ by faith. They thereby receive a perfect standing of uprightness before the Lord. Their new status in God's sight fulfills all the demands that any divine moral code could have ever required of them (vs. 31).

Discussion Questions

1. What spiritual advantages did Paul say there were to being a Jew?
2. How has God proven Himself to be just in His treatment of the Jews, despite the unfaithfulness of some to Him?
3. Why would God go to so much trouble to forgive those who have rebelled against Him?
4. What role does the law serve in bringing us to Christ?
5. Why do you think anyone would spurn God's gracious offer of salvation through faith in Christ?

Contemporary Application

If God were only just, humanity would not have a prayer. Our situation is clear: we have sinned before a holy God. The only just response from God is death. At the same time, if God were solely loving, we would all be swept up to His bosom without a glance at the sinfulness of our hearts.

Neither happens, however, because God is neither exclusively just nor exclusively loving; He's all both. He loves us and wants us to join Him in His eternal kingdom. But He first had to establish a way for our sin to be annulled. That was what He accomplished through Jesus Christ.

In a metaphorical sense, God has sent us an invitation marked RSVP (*Répondez s'il vous plaît*)—French for "Please reply." Although our Lord waits patiently for our favorable response, He has set a limit on how long He will wait. At some point He must say, "Enough!" and the doors of heaven will swing shut. Before it's too late, we must say *yes* to His invitation and join His great banquet.

Heirs of the Promise

DEVOTIONAL READING

Psalm 32:6-11

DAILY BIBLE READINGS

Monday March 18
Psalm 32:1-5 Happy Are Those Who Are Forgiven

Tuesday March 19
1 Corinthians 15:1-11 By the Grace of God

Wednesday March 20
1 Corinthians 15:20-28 Made Alive in Christ

Thursday March 21
Romans 5:1-11 Justified by Faith

Friday March 22
Romans 5:12-21 The Free Gift of Righteousness

Saturday March 23
Zechariah 9:9-13 Your King Arrives on a Donkey

Sunday March 24
Matthew 21:1-11 Hosannas for the Son of David

Scripture

Background Scripture: *Romans 4*
Scripture Lesson: *Romans 4:2-3, 13-25*
Key Verse: *What does the Scripture say? "Abraham believed God, and it was credited to him as righteousness."* Romans 4:3.
Scripture Lesson for Children: *John 18:1-5, 12*
Key Verse for Children: *Then the detachment of soldiers . . . and the Jewish officials arrested Jesus.* John 18:12.

Lesson Aim

To recognize that true righteousness is received by faith.

Lesson Setting

Time: *A.D. 57*
Place: *From Corinth to the church in Rome*

Lesson Outline

Heirs of the Promise

  I. Abraham's Justification—Not by Works: Romans 4:2-3
 II. Abraham's Justification—Not by the Law: Romans 4:13-17a
III. Abraham's Justification—By Faith: Romans 4:17b-22
 IV. Abraham's Faith and Ours: Romans 4:23-25

Introduction for Adults

Topic: *Following an Example of Faith*

The young mother's husband died after a long illness. A year later she and her two children decided to hold a "Heaven Party" to focus on their loved one's perfect place of residence. More than 60 friends came to play games, talk about what heaven might be like, and to eat and sing together. Their faith encouraged many people.

The power of faith remains undiminished from Abraham's time to ours. Such faith compels us to hold strongly to Jesus, "the author and perfecter of our faith" (Heb. 12:2). When we consider Abraham's testimony, we see how he struggled when God's promise of a son through the patriarch's wife, Sarah, seemed humanly impossible to fulfill. But Abraham's faith in God kept him going. The same principle held true for the young widow and her children mentioned above.

We can help fellow believers in their struggles by being an example of faith. And we can bear testimony to those who were role models of faith to us. Such faith has the potential to make a profound difference!

Introduction for Youths

Topic: *A Treasure from the Past*

The toughest words for parents to handle are, "But you promised!" Children find it hard to understand why their parents break their pledges. And as youth grow older, they might sometimes wonder whether God keeps His promises. These doubts, in turn, can undermine their confidence in the Lord.

Abraham struggled with feelings like that. As he grew older and older, his longing to have a son through Sarah, his wife, seemed as if it would never happen. After all, he and his wife were elderly, and she had been barren for many years.

Despite all this, Abraham's faith in God and His ability to keep His word never faltered. That's why the patriarch's faith is worth considering. His trust in the Lord shines brightly against the dark background of unbelief. And Abraham's faith stands out against all who would try to merit salvation. Abraham, our spiritual father, truly represents what it means to live by faith.

Concepts for Children

Topic: *Jesus Was Arrested*

1. After Jesus prayed, He went with His followers to a garden across the Kidron Valley.
2. Judas, who was about to betray Jesus, brought soldiers and police to arrest the Savior.
3. Jesus, who knew what was going to happen, said that He was the person for whom they were looking.
4. The soldiers and police then arrested Jesus and tied Him up.
5. We can thank God that Jesus was willing to suffer so much for us.

The Lesson Commentary

I. Abraham's Justification—Not by Works: Romans 4:2-3

If, in fact, Abraham was justified by works, he had something to boast about—but not before God. What does the Scripture say? "Abraham believed God, and it was credited to him as righteousness."

Paul built his case for faith-righteousness on Abraham and David—two of the most respected figures in the Old Testament. Abraham would be particularly important as an example, for the Jews thought they had a privileged relationship with God by virtue of their physical relationship with Abraham as his descendants. Paul knew that if he could show that Abraham was justified by faith and not by works, then their false presumptions would fall like a house of cards.

Paul began by asking, "What then shall we say?" (Rom. 4:1). His concern was to address what Abraham discovered on the issue of justification by faith. Abraham, of course, was the ancestor of the Jews and the central person in their history. Did he become justified on the basis of obedience to some moral code?

The Jews of Paul's day believed that Abraham had so much righteousness in terms of good works that he had a surplus of merit. This merit was allegedly available to Abraham's descendants. Many Jews also believed that Abraham was a perfect example of a person justified by works. Paul fully agreed that Abraham was an upright person and that, as such, he had something to boast about before people— but not before God (vs. 2).

To underscore his point, Paul appealed to Genesis 15:6, which he quoted in Romans 4:3, "Abraham believed God, and it was credited to him as righteousness." Because Abraham believed the divine promise concerning a son, God credited (or "imputed") righteousness to the patriarch's account. (The Greek word for "credited" was an ancient accounting term.) Hence, Abraham's life was a perfect illustration of Paul's point, namely, that righteousness comes through faith and not through obedience to the law of Moses. Abraham, therefore, is the spiritual ancestor of all who believe (Gal. 3:7).

It's the perennial temptation to imagine we have to earn God's approval. We tend to think, "If only I try a little harder, He'll accept me because of my goodness." But in reality, there has always been only one way to feel the smile of God's favor upon us. That way is by putting our faith in Jesus Christ.

The experience of David illustrates the same truth from a different angle. Sinful David had to come to God by faith. His works could not earn him the Lord's favor, for his deeds were tainted by sin (Rom. 4:6). Those whom God blessed have not merited His good pleasure; rather, He graciously declares them to be righteous in His sight. On the basis of His unmerited favor, God cancels the debt of sin. Consequently, they are no longer guilty in His sight and are not under His wrath (vss. 7-8).

The Jews might ask what relationship circumcision had to the justification of Abraham. Paul declared that the patriarch was justified at least 14 years before he submitted to the rite of circumcision (vss. 9-10). Thus, circumcision had nothing at all to do with Abraham's right-standing before the Lord. Circumcision was the visible guarantee that the patriarch would become the father of many spiritual descendants among the Gentiles as well as the Jews. All who exercise the same kind of faith that Abraham displayed will participate in the spiritual blessings that God promised to the patriarch (vss. 11-12).

II. ABRAHAM'S JUSTIFICATION—NOT BY THE LAW: ROMANS 4:13-17A

It was not through law that Abraham and his offspring received the promise that he would be heir of the world, but through the righteousness that comes by faith. For if those who live by law are heirs, faith has no value and the promise is worthless, because law brings wrath. And where there is no law there is no transgression. Therefore, the promise comes by faith, so that it may be by grace and may be guaranteed to all Abraham's offspring—not only to those who are of the law but also to those who are of the faith of Abraham. He is the father of us all. As it is written: "I have made you a father of many nations."

Paul noted that it was not through the law that Abraham received the promise that "he would be heir of the world" (Rom. 4:13). In point of fact, God's promise to the patriarch—contained in the Abrahamic covenant in Genesis 12:1-3—occurred several centuries before God gave the law through Moses (Gal. 3:17).

The Lord promised Abraham that he would have many descendants, and that through his seed the peoples of the earth would be blessed (Gen. 12:3). This is probably what Paul was referring to in saying that Abraham "would be heir of the world" (Rom. 4:13). This incredible promise was given several hundred years prior to the giving of the law.

Paul next pointed out that if the Jews could become Abraham's heirs by simply keeping the law, then "faith has no value" (vs. 14, or "has been made empty"). In such a situation the divine promise is made invalid. To assert that God's blessing goes to the law keepers also amounts to saying that His promises to those who have faith (which would include Abraham and David) are meaningless and useless.

As Paul stressed in verse 15, when we try to keep the law, we always end up being under God's wrath. Keeping the law in order to gain God's favor (and salvation) only produces spiritual arrogance, for the purpose of the law was to reveal sin, not to bring justification.

Paul affirmed that where there is no law, there is no transgression. If people don't know right from wrong, then in one sense they cannot be held accountable for their actions. Of course, as Paul pointed out in 2:14-15, even those who do not have the Mosaic law have God's moral law written on their hearts. Thus all people intuitively know right from wrong, and therefore all are responsible and are without excuse for disobeying God.

Paul declared that all of Abraham's offspring—both the Jews ("those who are of the law," 4:16) and believing Gentiles ("those who are of the faith of Abraham")—receive the promise of righteousness (or justification) by faith and according to

God's grace. If it were received by keeping the works of the law, then no one could receive it, for all are guilty of breaking the law.

Paul added the significant point that God's promise of salvation is extended to all who believe, whether Jews and Gentiles. Through faith in Christ, all can receive God's righteousness and call Abraham their spiritual ancestor. It's no wonder that God called the patriarch "a father of many nations" (Gen. 17:5; Rom. 4:17).

III. ABRAHAM'S JUSTIFICATION—BY FAITH: ROMANS 4:17B-22

He is our father in the sight of God, in whom he believed—the God who gives life to the dead and calls things that are not as though they were. Against all hope, Abraham in hope believed and so became the father of many nations, just as it had been said to him, "So shall your offspring be." Without weakening in his faith, he faced the fact that his body was as good as dead—since he was about a hundred years old—and that Sarah's womb was also dead. Yet he did not waver through unbelief regarding the promise of God, but was strengthened in his faith and gave glory to God, being fully persuaded that God had power to do what he had promised. This is why "it was credited to him as righteousness."

Our faith in God is the one factor that relates us all (whether Jew or Gentile) to Abraham, for the patriarch himself was one who had faith in God. Indeed, Abraham believed in the God "who gives life to the dead and calls things that are not as though they were" (Rom. 4:17). Paul was referring here to the birth of Isaac to Abraham and Sarah, both of whom were so old that, from a physical standpoint, it was impossible for them to have children (Gen. 18:11). But because of God's miraculous work, they gave birth to Isaac in their old age. We must not forget that God has the miraculous power to create out of nothing, to make possible what seems impossible—even our salvation.

While from a human perspective there was no hope that Abraham and Sarah could give birth to a child, Abraham still believed in God and His ability to fulfill His promise (Rom. 4:18). In so doing, Abraham became the spiritual ancestor of many people, as God had promised in Genesis 15:5.

If Abraham walked merely by sight and not by faith, things would have seemed bleak. After all, his body was "as good as dead" (Rom. 4:19), meaning that he was advanced in age—about 100 years old. To make matters worse, Sarah's womb was infertile. Even in earlier years, she had been unable to conceive a child (Gen. 16:1-2; 18:11). But now that she was 90 years old, there was virtually no likelihood (at least from outward appearances) that she would be able to give birth to a child. Despite this, Abraham's faith remained steadfast.

Romans 4:19 says Abraham "faced the fact" of his aged body and his elderly wife. Faith in God does not involve a refusal to deal with reality. Likewise, it doesn't involve an ignorance of the true state of affairs around us. Rather, faith looks beyond earthly realities to the God who can supernaturally change things.

The testimony of Abraham is that he never wavered in believing the promise of God. In fact, the patriarch's faith grew stronger, and in that "gave glory to God" (vs. 20). Despite the apparent odds against him, Abraham was absolutely convinced that the Lord was able to do anything He promised—including the birth of a son through Sarah (vs. 21). Because of Abraham's faith, God declared him to be righteous (vs. 22).

God is glorified when we trust in His promises. Our assurance that God will keep His word gives us strength to face our problems. With the kind of faith that Abraham had at our side, we will be less doubtful about the Lord and His intentions. We will be more at ease with ourselves and our circumstances

IV. ABRAHAM'S FAITH AND OURS: ROMANS 4:23-25

The words "it was credited to him" were written not for him alone, but also for us, to whom God will credit righteousness—for us who believe in him who raised Jesus our Lord from the dead. He was delivered over to death for our sins and was raised to life for our justification.

The historical facts in Abraham's case are not isolated and irrelevant data. Rather, they have consequences for believers today. For instance, Paul noted that the wonderful truth of God declaring Abraham to be righteous wasn't just for his benefit (Rom. 4:23). What was true for the patriarch thousands of years ago remains applicable for believers today (vs. 24).

We have the assurance of Scripture that when we believe in the Lord, He will "credit righteousness" to us. This is the same God who not only enabled Sarah to conceive and bear a son in her old age but also brought Jesus our Lord back "from the dead." Perhaps at first His crucifixion seemed like a needless tragedy. But in the Father's eternal plan He allowed His Son to die on the cross because of our sins. And then God raised Jesus from the dead so that we could be made right with Him (vs. 25).

It's helpful to note that, throughout the history of the church, Jesus' "sacrifice of atonement" (3:25) has been understood in different ways: 1) Jesus' death paid a ransom to Satan for souls held captive in the devil's domain; 2) Jesus' death reversed the effects of sin begun by Adam; 3) Jesus' death was the supreme act of victory that won the release of people held in bondage; 4) Jesus mysteriously took on sinful human nature while on the cross and triumphed over it; 5) Jesus' death provided an example of obedience for all Christians to follow; 6) Jesus' death softens the hearts of people so that they will repent; 7) God rewarded Jesus for His obedience, and Jesus passed this reward (salvation) along to believing people; and 8) Jesus died in the place of sinful people and paid the penalty of their sin.

Regardless of which view is preferred, it is nonetheless clear that we can enjoy fellowship with God thanks to the work of Christ. We give Him our sins, and He forgives us and makes us right with the Lord (2 Cor. 5:21). What incredible good news this is!

Discussion Questions

1. What was the basis for God declaring Abraham to be righteous?
2. In addition to Abraham and David, can you think of any other Old Testament characters who were justified by faith?

3. What was the basis of God's promise to Abraham that he would be "heir of the world" (Rom. 4:13)?
4. What prevented Abraham from doubting God's promise?
5. How can the example of Abraham encourage us in our times of doubt?
6. How is it possible for our faith to grow in the face of seeming impossibilities?

Contemporary Application

How do we develop an abiding faith in the Lord? We must take God at His word and apply the teachings of Scripture to our lives. As we step out in faith and obey God, He demonstrates His reliability to us time after time. Our faith in God increases as we live for Him and serve Him in new and different ways. The more we trust Him, the more assured we become that He'll uphold us regardless of the circumstances.

We might continue to struggle with doubts even after we're seasoned in our faith. Instead of allowing uncertainty to control us, we should examine it in the light of what Scripture teaches. The truth of God's Word can calm us when we're feeling anxious about something.

Our faith in God can also be strengthened by reflecting on our past experiences and those of other believers (for instance, Abraham). God's faithfulness to us and others in the past can encourage us when we're going through difficult times. When we consistently trust in the Lord, we become increasingly convinced that He knows what's best for us. We also become more willing to wait for His timing when it comes to enjoying the blessings of faith. Some of these come in this life, but most are received in eternity.

Christ Died for Us

DEVOTIONAL READING
Psalm 32:1-5

DAILY BIBLE READINGS
Monday March 25
   Romans 6:1-14 Alive to God in Christ

Tuesday March 26
   Romans 6:15-23 The Gift of Eternal Life through Christ

Wednesday March 27
   Romans 7:4-13 Sin Brings Death

Thursday March 28
   Romans 7:14-25 Thanks Be to God for Rescuing Me

Friday March 29
   John 20:1-9 The Stone Removed from the Tomb

Saturday March 30
   John 20:10-18 Mary Sees the Lord

Sunday March 31
   John 20:19-23 Jesus Stood among Them

Scripture
Background Scripture: *Romans 5*
Scripture Lesson: *Romans 5:1-11, 18-21*
Key Verse: *Therefore, since we have been justified through faith, we have peace with God through our Lord Jesus Christ.* Romans 5:1.
Scripture Lesson for Children: *John 19:13-19, 25-30*
Key Verse for Children: *"It is finished."* John 19:30.

Lesson Aim
To praise God for the love and peace He makes available through faith in Christ.

Lesson Setting
Time: *A.D. 57*
Place: *From Corinth to the church in Rome*

Lesson Outline
Christ Died for Us
   I. A New Relationship with God: Romans 5:1-11
      A. *Partaking of God's Grace: vss. 1-2*
      B. *Rejoicing in Life's Trials: vss. 3-5*
      C. *Reflecting on God's Love: vss. 6-8*
      D. *Accepting God's Reconciliation: vss. 9-11*
   II. Justification for All Who Believe: Romans 5:18-21
      A. *Righteousness through Christ: vss. 18-19*
      B. *Grace through Christ: vss. 20-21*

Introduction for Adults

Topic: *Reaping the Benefits*

The first rule of advertising is to describe the benefits of the goods being sold. This is based on the awareness that, before making a purchase, people want to know how their life will be better for using certain products and services. Perhaps that's why, when we watch those 30-second dramas being enacted on television commercials, we're told that using the right item will make us successful.

We know, of course, that such promises are inflated. This is far different than God's pledges to us. For instance, the Lord has promised that when we trust in Christ, we reap the eternal benefits of divine righteousness and grace. We don't have to make any purchases or perform a noble deed. In fact, there is nothing we can do on our own to enjoy the riches of God's love. We must simply put our faith in Jesus for salvation and forgiveness.

Introduction for Youths

Topic: *A Powerful Kind of Love*

Once in a while we read about someone stepping forward to pay another person's debt or fine. But nowadays we never hear about people volunteering to take the placed of a convicted criminal on death row.

During World War II, however, a Polish priest offered to take the place of a man the Germans had decided to execute. The Germans took his offer and shot him instead. He died in the condemned man's place as his substitute. Now that was a powerful kind of love!

God's love for us is even more profound. When we were utterly helpless to save ourselves, God sent His Son to rescue us from our plight. And even though we were guilty of rebelling against God, He still allowed Jesus to die in our place on the cross, so great is God's love for us (Rom. 5:6-8). Such love should fill us with joy and love for others.

Concepts for Children

Topic: *Jesus Died*

1. When a ruler named Pilate brought Jesus outside at about noon, the crowd of people shouted that they wanted to see Jesus crucified.
2. Jesus was taken to a place named Golgotha, where He was crucified with two other people.
3. Jesus' mother and some of Jesus' followers were standing near the cross.
4. God allowed Jesus to die on the cross so that we might be saved.
5. It was God's deep love for us that moved Him to send His Son.
6. Because of what Jesus did for us, our sins can be forgiven when we put our faith in Him.

The Lesson Commentary

I. A NEW RELATIONSHIP WITH GOD: ROMANS 5:1-11

A. Partaking of God's Grace: vss. 1-2

Therefore, since we have been justified through faith, we have peace with God through our Lord Jesus Christ, through whom we have gained access by faith into this grace in which we now stand. And we rejoice in the hope of the glory of God.

In Romans 3:21—4:25, Paul defined what it meant to be justified. Then in chapter 5, he focused on the benefits of justification. For Paul, justification was not only an event that put believers in a right position with God. Being declared righteous also had practical, lifelong implications for Christians.

1) First among these benefits is the peace we have with God through Jesus Christ (vs. 1). Because of sin, we were separated from God and faced eternal condemnation (1:18—3:20). But because of Christ, not only do we avoid receiving the wrath we deserve, we also enjoy a state of peace with God. We deserve fury and instead receive grace.

Paul was not talking about peace as simply a restful feeling. More importantly, he was talking about a state of harmony between the believer and God. All this is possible because of what Jesus did on the cross (Eph. 2:14). Formerly we were God's enemies; now we are His friends (Col. 1:21-22).

2) A second benefit that results from justification is direct access to God (Rom. 5:2). Formerly we were prevented from coming into the presence of God because of sin. Now we have full and unrestricted access. The Greek word translated "access" means the "privilege of approach." This is now available through faith in Jesus Christ.

3) A third key blessing we enjoy is "this grace in which we now stand." Because believers have been justified—that is, declared righteous—they live in the sphere of God's grace. And it is here that they enjoy every spiritual blessing in Christ. The gift of grace gives them the hope of experiencing God's glory—the glory from which they previously fell short (3:23). Grace may be viewed as a foot in the door of God's glory, which will one day swing wide open and grant believers unhindered access to the immediate presence of God.

As Paul reflected on these themes, he called his readers to rejoice in the hope of sharing God's glory (5:2). This wasn't wishful thinking but rather a firm assurance based on the unchanging promises of God. Believers look with confidence to all that the Lord has in store for them in Christ.

Why should we rejoice? We do so because we are acquitted of our sins and counted as righteous before God by means of our faith. We also rejoice because we have peace with God. Whereas once we were fearful, now we are joyful. Though we were previously doubtful, we now are certain about our future in union with Christ. We look to the time when we will enter into the fullness of God's majesty and splendor, rid forever of the stain and stigma of sin.

B. Rejoicing in Life's Trials: vss. 3-5

Not only so, but we also rejoice in our sufferings, because we know that suffering produces perseverance; perseverance, character; and character, hope. And hope does not disappoint us, because God has poured out his love into our hearts by the Holy Spirit, whom he has given us.

It would be incorrect to assume that peace with God brings peaceful circumstances in the course of daily living. All of us go through times of suffering when our circumstances may seem anything but peaceful. Therefore, in Romans 5:3-5 Paul turned his attention to the believer's attitude toward suffering.

Notice that Paul said we were to rejoice "in" our sufferings, not "because of" them (vs. 3). This is an important distinction. Paul was not telling us that we should be joyful since things go wrong in our lives; rather, he was telling us that we can be joyful in the midst of troubling situations.

The word rendered "sufferings" could also be translated "afflictions," "distresses," or "pressures." These are broad words that encompass all kinds of things that can go wrong. Some people have financial pressures; some have health afflictions; some have job-related distresses; others struggle with broken relationships. Whatever the difficult situation, Paul said, we can have joy in the midst of it. In Christ we have the power to choose how we will respond to our circumstances, no matter how burdensome they are.

Notice the steady progression in verses 3 and 4: suffering produces perseverance (or steadfast endurance); perseverance strengthens our character; and character leads to hope. Believers can have a joyful attitude in the midst of suffering for they know that enduring such trials is not meaningless. The pain God allows them to experience can bear Christlike fruit, namely, perseverance, character, and hope.

Paul affirmed that hope does not disappoint us, for God has lavished us with His love (vs. 5). The verb translated "poured out" speaks of the inexhaustible supply of God's compassion given to believers through the Spirit. He is the agent who expresses God's love in and through the hearts of believers. Such love enhances our hope because it does not hinge on circumstances. Even when life throws us a punch, God's love continues to flow through our hearts.

False offers of hope arise from many quarters, but the only lasting assurance comes when we discover and trust in God's love. Human feelings tend to vacillate from hot to cold, but God's compassion endures and touches us where and when we need it. We no longer need to paper over life's problems, for we can face them realistically in the light of God's love.

C. Reflecting on God's Love: vss. 6-8

You see, at just the right time, when we were still powerless, Christ died for the ungodly. Very rarely will anyone die for a righteous man, though for a good man someone might possibly dare to die. But God demonstrates his own love for us in this: While we were still sinners, Christ died for us.

To illustrate the love of God he had just described, Paul stated that "at just the right time, when we were still powerless, Christ died for the ungodly" (Rom. 5:6). For centuries the Mosaic law had been in operation—provoking and exposing sin, and showing people their need to be reconciled with God. But now the time had come for the Messiah to be born, at just the right time in God's eternal plan of redemption (Gal. 4:4).

Christ came when we were "powerless" (Rom. 5:6). The original word means "weak," "without strength," "feeble," and "sickly." In the present context, it points to those who are weak in terms of their ability to create any righteousness for themselves. Though they couldn't, God did by having Jesus take our place on the cross and dying on our behalf.

What an amazing thing Jesus did for us! People rarely give up their lives for others. Occasionally we might find someone who is willing to die for a good person (vs. 7), but we were neither upright nor good—not in the sense that God reflects these qualities. The profound truth is that Christ died for sinners—even while we were alienated from the Lord (vs. 8).

The contrast is stark between the one who laid down His life and those for whom He died. Such an act of devotion can only be motivated by boundless love. And indeed, this love was demonstrated when Christ laid down His life on our behalf. Jesus' death on the cross illustrates the relentless and amazing pursuit of God for us.

D. Accepting God's Reconciliation: vss. 9-11

Since we have now been justified by his blood, how much more shall we be saved from God's wrath through him! For if, when we were God's enemies, we were reconciled to him through the death of his Son, how much more, having been reconciled, shall we be saved through his life! Not only is this so, but we also rejoice in God through our Lord Jesus Christ, through whom we have now received reconciliation.

The good news is that the sacrifice of Christ enables us to be made right in God's sight (Rom. 5:9). This being the case, Jesus will certainly rescue us "from God's wrath." "Wrath" in this verse refers to God's final judgment of humankind (1 Thess. 1:10). Since we are forgiven in Christ, the Lord will not subject us to His eternal condemnation of the wicked (John 5:24).

Paul reasoned that if we, as God's enemies, were restored to friendship with Him through Jesus' death, we will certainly be delivered from eternal punishment because of the Savior's life. "Reconciliation" (Rom. 5:10) refers to removal of the ill-will that previously stood between us and God. At one time we were God's enemies because of our disobedience. But because of Jesus' death, we have been restored in our relationship with God.

Paul's point, then, is that since God no longer looks on us as His enemies, the basis of our salvation is complete. Furthermore, Jesus ministers to us "through his life." This refers to His post-resurrection life. In what ways does Jesus presently meet our spiritual needs? As our great High Priest, Christ makes intercession for us from heaven (Heb. 7:25). He prays for us continuously (1 John 2:1).

Our being reconciled to the Father through the Son is not just a biblical truth we affirm. It is also a present reality that fills us with joy. After all, we who were once God's enemies are now His friends (Rom. 5:11). And as the Lord's ambassadors, we should share this wonderful news with others.

II. JUSTIFICATION FOR ALL WHO BELIEVE: ROMANS 5:18-21

A. Righteousness through Christ: vss. 18-19

Consequently, just as the result of one trespass was condemnation for all men, so also the result of one act of righteousness was justification that brings life for all men. For just as through the disobedience of the one man the many were made sinners, so also through the obedience of the one man the many will be made righteous.

Paul noted that when Adam sinned, his offense brought the entire world under the reign of death, and humanity became enslaved to sin (Rom. 5:12). In contrast, all who receive God's wonderful and gracious gift of righteousness experience new life in Christ and triumph over sin (vs. 17). It's true that Adam's one sin brought condemnation to the entire human race. Nevertheless, Jesus' "one act of right-eousness" (vs. 18, namely, His death on the cross) makes all believers right in God's sight and gives them eternal life.

The meaning of the phrase "brings life for all men" is debated. Some think Paul was teaching that all human beings in the end will be saved—a view known as universalism. But such a view would contradict Paul's teaching that all human beings are lost because of sin (2:12). The truth is that only those who trust in Christ are declared righteous, while those who reject Him remain lost in their sins.

The joy of the Gospel is that Jesus enables us to trade judgment for forgiveness. Paul explained that, because of Adam's single act of disobedience, the entire human race was plunged into sin. In contrast, Jesus' work on the cross enables all who believe to "be made righteous" (5:19).

B. Grace through Christ: vss. 20-21

The law was added so that the trespass might increase. But where sin increased, grace increased all the more, so that, just as sin reigned in death, so also grace might reign through righteousness to bring eternal life through Jesus Christ our Lord.

Paul's Jewish readers might have wondered where the Mosaic law fit into the discussion. The apostle noted that God added the law so that the people could be more aware of how sinful they are. But instead of turning from their evil ways, people sinned more and more. The entire human race would have surely perished had it not been for the abundant kindness that God provided in Christ (Rom. 5:20).

Throughout history sin has ruled over all people and brought them to death. But the good news is that the grace of God rules. His kindness in Christ gives us a right standing in His presence and forgiveness of sins (vs. 21). Clearly, the grace of God is more than a doctrine. It is a life principle that affects us on a daily basis. Paul assured us that, because we have trusted in Christ, we will live eternally in Him.

Discussion Questions

1. What is the basis for our access into God's heavenly presence?
2. How is it possible to rejoice in sufferings?
3. Why would the Father allow His Son to die for the ungodly?
4. What is the basis for our reconciliation with God?
5. What would our lives be like if God had not made the effort to reconcile us to Himself?

Contemporary Application

When sin entered the world, it seemed as if all was lost. But that was not the end of the story. To match the terrible consequences of sin, God intervened with His powerful, sustaining grace. Grace prevailed in the person of Christ. Grace prevailed on the cross. Grace prevailed in the empty tomb. And God's grace still prevails today in the life of believers.

When we receive the truth of the Gospel, we have multiple reasons to rejoice. For instance, we have peace, hope, and the certainty of enjoying God's wonderful presence. We also receive the overflowing power of God's love. We furthermore are reconciled to God. And because of Jesus' work on the cross, God declares us righteous and makes us fit for heaven.

What a relief it is to know that we have been transferred from the domain of sin and death to the kingdom of God's beloved Son! We are now free to obey—out of love, not necessity, and through God's power, not our own. Even if we occasionally stumble, Jesus will catch us and hold us in His loving arms.

New Life in Christ

Scripture

Background Scripture: *John 20:1-18; Romans 6*
Scripture Lesson: *John 20:1, 11-17; Romans 6:3-8*
Key Verse: *We were therefore buried with him through bap-
tism into death in order that, just as Christ was raised from
the dead through the glory of the Father, we too may live a new
life.* Romans 6:4.
Scripture Lesson for Children: *John 20:1, 11-18*
Key Verse for Children: *"I have seen the Lord!"* John 20:18.

Lesson Aim

To understand that identification with Christ brings
freedom from both the penalty and the power of sin.

Lesson Setting (John 20)

Time: A.D. *30*
Place: *Jerusalem*

Lesson Setting (Romans 6)

Time: A.D. *57*
Place: *From Corinth to the church in Rome*

Lesson Outline

New Life in Christ
  I. Mary at the Tomb: John 20:1
  II. Mary in the Garden: John 20:11-17
      A. *Mary's Sorrow: vss. 11-13*
      B. *Mary's Recognition of Jesus: vss. 14-16*
      C. *Jesus' Commands: vs. 17*
  III. United in Christ's Death and Resurrection:
      Romans 6:3-5
      A. *United in Jesus' Death: vss. 3-4*
      B. *United in Jesus' Resurrection: vs. 5*
  IV. Crucified with Christ: Romans 6:6-8
      A. *Freed from Sin: vss. 6-7*
      B. *Alive with Christ: vs. 8*

Introduction for Adults

Topic: *Experiencing New Life*

One of the common testimonies of people whose heart ailments have been treated with bypass surgery is that they have found new life. Instead of feeling weak, tired, and short of breath, they now have energy to do things they could not do before.

Christ's resurrection does the same sort of thing for us in the spiritual realm. At one time we were "dead in . . . transgressions and sins" (Eph. 2:1). But when we trusted in Jesus for salvation, we passed from death to life (vs. 5). This is possible because we have been identified with Christ's death, burial, and resurrection (Rom. 6:1-4).

If we think of our old, sinful life as dead and buried, we have a powerful motive to resist sin. We now have the option of consciously choosing to treat the temptations and desires of the old nature as if they were dead. Such is possible because of the wonderful new life we have in Jesus.

Introduction for Youths

Topic: *Power for Real Life*

One day a teenager returned to his job after having been to a Christian summer camp. While away he had made a commitment to God that he would quit a certain habit that he knew was not good for him. After his return, his peers saw the difference in his behavior, and he became afraid that they would ridicule him. But when the teenager explained his conversion experience, one of his friends simply said, "More power to you!"

It's easy for us to think of power in terms of athletes with large muscles or automobiles with big engines. In the spiritual realm, however, it is something quite different. It's the ability to say *no* to sin and *yes* to God and His will. The reason is clear. The divine kingdom is not "a matter of eating and drinking, but of righteousness, peace and joy in the Holy Spirit" (Rom. 14:17). This is the wonderful message of Easter!

Concepts for Children

Topic: *Jesus Arose*

1. Mary Magdalene came to Jesus' tomb and wept.
2. Mary saw that the stone had been removed and that two angels were sitting where Jesus' body had lain.
3. While Mary was talking with the angels, Jesus appeared, but Mary did not recognize Him.
4. When Mary asked where Jesus' body had been taken, Jesus spoke her name and she knew who He was.
5. Just as Mary told Jesus' followers what she had seen and heard, so too we can tell our friends about the Savior.

The Lesson Commentary

I.   MARY AT THE TOMB: JOHN 20:1

Early on the first day of the week, while it was still dark, Mary Magdalene went to the tomb and saw that the stone had been removed from the entrance.

Mary Magdalene was one of the women who stood near the cross upon which Jesus was executed (John 19:25). And early Sunday morning, while it was still dark, Mary was the first disciple to come to the tomb where Jesus' body had been placed (20:1). Mark informs us that Mary came to Jesus' tomb after the Sabbath to pour spices over His body, a cultural expression of love for the dead person (Mark 16:1).

Such devotion on Mary's part was not unusual. After all, Jesus had exorcised seven demons from her (Luke 8:2). As an early follower of Jesus, Mary proved to be an energetic and caring woman. She not only traveled with Jesus, but also contributed to the needs of the group.

When Mary came to the tomb, she saw that "the stone had been removed from the entrance" (John 20:1). She then ran and found Peter and John, and told them that Jesus' body had been stolen from the tomb. When the two disciples got to the tomb, they discovered that Jesus' body was indeed gone. But upon examining the evidence further, they came to the stunning realization that the Savior had risen from the dead (vss. 2-10).

II.   MARY IN THE GARDEN: JOHN 20:11-17

A.   Mary's Sorrow: vss. 11-13

But Mary stood outside the tomb crying. As she wept, she bent over to look into the tomb and saw two angels in white, seated where Jesus' body had been, one at the head and the other at the foot. They asked her, "Woman, why are you crying?" "They have taken my Lord away," she said, "and I don't know where they have put him."

Mary evidently had returned to the tomb with Peter and John. At this point Mary had not yet figured out that Jesus had risen from the dead. Mary still thought bandits had stolen Jesus' body, and this possibility so traumatized Mary that she "stood outside the tomb crying" (John 20:11). At some point Mary decided to look in the tomb, and when she did, she saw two white-robed angels sitting at the head and foot of the place where the body of Jesus had been lying (vs. 12).

Even while Mary was reexamining the tomb, she had continued to weep. This prompted the angels to ask her, "Woman, why are you crying?" (vs. 13). Mary explained that she was grieved over the fact that Jesus' body had somehow been stolen. She still as yet did not realize that her Lord had risen from the dead.

B.   Mary's Recognition of Jesus: vss. 14-16

At this, she turned around and saw Jesus standing there, but she did not realize that it was Jesus. "Woman," he said, "why are you crying? Who is it you are looking for?" Thinking he was the gardener, she said, "Sir, if you have carried him away, tell me where you have put him, and I will get him."

Jesus said to her, "Mary." She turned toward him and cried out in Aramaic, "Rabboni!" (which means Teacher).

When Mary glanced over her shoulder, she saw someone standing behind her. Though she didn't realize it, the person was Jesus (John 20:14). The Savior, with undeniable compassion, asked Mary why she was weeping and whom she was trying to find (vs. 15).

Mary, while still in a state of shock, mistakenly thought that Jesus was the local gardener. The reason for Mary's inability to recognize Jesus is uncertain. Perhaps it's because her tears blurred her eyes, or possibly the memories of Jesus' bruised and battered body were still etched in Mary's mind. Another option is that the Lord supernaturally prevented Mary from recognizing Him until He chose for her to do so.

In any case, it took a direct statement from Jesus to Mary to get her to see that she was talking to the Savior (vs. 16). On that first Easter morning tears, defeat, and despair had clouded Mary's heart and mind. She was loving and brave, but she needed a special word from Jesus to grasp the reality of His resurrection.

Suddenly Mary's sorrow was turned to joy, and she exclaimed, "Rabboni!" Mary had spoken in Aramaic, which was the language the people of Palestine commonly spoke in Jesus' day. The apostle John explained to his readers that "Rabboni" meant "Teacher."

C. Jesus' Commands: vs. 17

Jesus said, "Do not hold on to me, for I have not yet returned to the Father. Go instead to my brothers and tell them, 'I am returning to my Father and your Father, to my God and your God.'"

Excitedly, Mary tried to hold Jesus, but He stopped her (John 20:17). It wasn't that Jesus forbade Mary to touch Him at all; rather, the phrase "Do not hold on to me" conveys the idea of "don't cling to me." Mary wanted to cling to the Lord she thought she had lost, but He had an ascension for Himself and an assignment for her. Mary was to return to the disciples with the great news of Jesus' victory over death. Mary couldn't have run fast enough to them.

For centuries skeptics have considered the Gospel writers' resurrection accounts as myth or legend. In this regard, it is significant that after Jesus' resurrection He first appeared to Mary Magdalene and then assigned to her the responsibility of informing His disciples of His return to the Father. In ancient Judaism the witness of women mattered very little judicially and socially. Thus no ancient Jewish author would have made up such a story with a woman being the first witness to this important event.

Further undermining Mary's testimony was her being from Magdala, a city Jewish rabbis condemned for its wickedness. And she had a history of demon possession (Luke 8:2). Thus even if she seemed cured, her testimony would have been questioned. Consequently, John's account fortifies the historical fact of Jesus' resurrection.

Why didn't the Savior first appear to Peter or John? Jesus' logic isn't the same as that of the prevailing culture. And the testimony of His death and resurrection is still being entrusted centuries later to unlikely candidates who, like Mary, will follow through faithfully.

The major truth to be proclaimed at Easter is that Jesus Christ, our Savior, has risen from the dead. Knowing this makes all the difference in the world. It spells the difference between despair and joy, and between turmoil and peace.

III. UNITED IN CHRIST'S DEATH AND RESURRECTION: ROMANS 6:3-5

A. United in Jesus' Death: vss. 3-4

Or don't you know that all of us who were baptized into Christ Jesus were baptized into his death? We were therefore buried with him through baptism into death in order that, just as Christ was raised from the dead through the glory of the Father, we too may live a new life.

In Paul's Letter to the Romans it becomes progressively clear that God is concerned with more than just our status with Him (namely, justification, or being declared righteous). He is also concerned about our behavior (namely, sanctification, or becoming increasingly holy). Beginning in chapter 6, Paul indicated that God has a plan for dealing with the power of sin in our lives.

The occasion for Paul's opening remarks is related to his earlier statement in 5:20. There the apostle declared that God instituted His law so that all people could see how sinful they are. Then Paul added, "But where sin increased, grace increased all the more." Opponents responded by asking whether believers should keep on sinning so that God can show them more and more of His grace (6:1).

Paul responded with a forceful "By no means!" (vs. 2). Since believers had died to sin, it was unthinkable that they would choose a sinful way of life just to enjoy the benefits of God's kindness and forgiveness. Grace is one of Paul's favorite topics because it is such a blessing to believers. While it is a source of great comfort, it also has the potential of being abused. People can presume upon God's grace in such a way that they take sin less seriously than they should. We must be careful to keep this kind of attitude from creeping into our lives.

In verse 3, Paul raised the issue of being "baptized into Christ Jesus" and "baptized into his death." The apostle's focus here is on the spiritual union of believers with the Savior, and such is illustrated by the Christian rite of baptism. In the church of Paul's day, baptism dramatized the identification of converts with Jesus' death, burial, and resurrection. The performance of the rite declared to all onlookers that the participants had died to their old way of life and adopted a new way of life with Christ.

Our union with Christ is so inseparable that when He died, we died, and when He was buried, we were buried with Him. These are fundamental truths about the tremendous consequences of trusting in Christ for salvation.

The God-intended outcome of our union with Christ is that we "may live a new life" (vs. 4). That's why Paul used Jesus' resurrection to underscore the difference between the old ways of sin and the new ways of righteousness. Because of what Jesus did for us, we are to set our hearts "on things above, where Christ is seated at the right hand of God" (Col. 3:1). Clearly, the Lord is summoning us to live for Him and His glory.

B. United in Jesus' Resurrection: vs. 5

If we have been united with him like this in his death, we will certainly also be united with him in his resurrection.

Paul spoke triumphantly about the power of Christ's resurrection (Rom. 6:5). The wonderful Easter news is that believers are united with Christ in His resurrection power. Paul did not just have in view our future glory but also our present situation. He wanted Christians to know their new identity in Christ had ramifications for their life here on earth.

In his letters, Paul often described believers as being "in Christ." Bible experts struggle with the exact meaning of this concept. Some say we are "incorporate" with Christ, while others assert we are "one with Him." Regardless of how we say it, the main point is that we enjoy a vital personal relationship with the Savior. It's like the union of a tree and its branches or of shepherds and their sheep. Because Jesus rose from the grave, we have the power to overcome sin and obey the Lord.

IV. CRUCIFIED WITH CHRIST: ROMANS 6:6-8

A. Freed from Sin: vss. 6-7

For we know that our old self was crucified with him so that the body of sin might be done away with, that we should no longer be slaves to sin—because anyone who has died has been freed from sin.

Paul rejected the notion that believers could take God's kindness for granted. Having been saved by God's grace, they were to live holy lives. This was possible because their "old self" (Rom. 6:6) was crucified with Christ. The "old self" refers to everything a person was before trusting in Jesus for salvation. It's the state of being still enslaved to sin, being ungodly, and being an enemy of God.

The tragedy is that, in our unredeemed state, we are slaves to sin and powerless to stop sinning. In fact, all people are either held in sin's clutches, like helpless slaves, or they have been set free by the power of Christ's death and resurrection. When we realize how desperately needy we are, we flee to Christ for help.

Paul made a profound observation in verse 7. Dead people have no problems with sin! After all, a corpse can't be tempted. In other words, because our sinful selves were crucified with Christ, sin has lost its power in our lives. This is because our union with Jesus' death has liberated us from the controlling grip of sin. Now that we're unfettered from sin's chains, we are free to serve the Lord.

B. Alive with Christ: vs. 8

Now if we died with Christ, we believe that we will also live with him.

226

Skeptics say that believers serve a dead hero, not a risen Savior. The New Testament, of course, refutes such notions. In fact, Paul declared that Jesus' rising from the dead is the key to our new life in Him (Rom. 6:8). Without His resurrection, there is no hope of forgiveness, eternal life, justification, and righteous living. Because He lives, we have the supernatural ability to walk in newness of life.

Our sinful nature is like an old military commander who has been stripped of authority but still goes around barking orders, trying to get someone to obey. We are no longer slaves to this tyrant, and thus need not obey it. Instead, we must appropriate what God has provided and choose to live as free people.

Discussion Questions

1. How do you think Mary Magdalene initially felt on Easter morning? What happened to change her feelings?
2. Why do you think Mary at first did not recognize Jesus?
3. What did Jesus tell Mary not to do? Why?
4. How is it possible to consider ourselves dead to sin and alive with Christ?
5. Based on Paul's teaching, what advice would you give to a fellow believer who is being tempted to sin?

Contemporary Application

People today find it no easier to believe in Jesus' resurrection than did the disciples when they first heard the news. In our experience, people who are dead do not come back to life. So perhaps we should not be surprised when our non-Christian friends view the Resurrection message as interesting but not at all convincing.

As Christians we need to recognize the importance of affirming that Jesus' resurrection actually took place. But how do we do it? We do it by cultivating a personal relationship with the risen Lord in our daily life. When we pursue a personal relationship with our Savior, we show that we truly believe He is alive, having been raised from the dead.

Although we cannot see, hear, or touch Jesus physically now, we can draw near to Him spiritually and devotionally. Furthermore, those who want to know Christ intimately are wise to set aside a definite time each day to spend concentrating upon the risen Lord and His Word. For some believers, prayer and silence in the Lord's presence come easier. Whatever we decide to do, we need to begin to do it, for when we do, we enlarge the scope and richness of our time with the risen Lord.

God's Glory Revealed

Scripture

Background Scripture: *Romans 8*
Scripture Lesson: *Romans 8:18-27, 31-34, 38-39*
Key Verse: *I consider that our present sufferings are not worth comparing with the glory that will be revealed in us.* Romans 8:18.
Scripture Lesson for Children: *Romans 8:26-27; Luke 11:5-13*
Key Verse for Children: *"Call to me and I will answer you."* Jeremiah 33:3.

Lesson Aim

To claim the hope of future glory in light of Christ's enduring love.

Lesson Setting

Time: *A.D. 57*
Place: *From Corinth to the church in Rome*

Lesson Outline

God's Glory Revealed

I.   Present Suffering and Future Glory: Romans 8:18-27
   A. *Glory Surpasses Suffering: vs. 18*
   B. *Glory Means a New Body in a New World: vss. 19-23*
   C. *Hope Undergirds Salvation: vss. 24-25*
   D. *The Spirit's Help: vss. 26-27*

II. The Foundation of Glory: Romans 8:31-34
   A. *God's Gracious Gift: vss. 31-32*
   B. *Our Justification: vs. 33*
   C. *Christ's Intercession: vs. 34*

III. The Guarantee of Glory: Romans 8:38-39

Introduction for Adults
Topic: *Is There Hope?*

When the newly-appointed physician began his practice at a hospital, he was struck by the number of patients who had to be treated because they had tried to commit suicide. What disturbed him even more was that many of them were relatively young. Somehow, it had never occurred to him that attempted suicide was a major medical malady.

There are numerous complex factors that cause people to attempt suicide. We can be sure that a major one is a loss of hope. It is especially appalling when teenagers and college students seek to end their lives because they think there is no hope for the future.

Part of the answer for people like this is an understanding of God's love in Christ, especially as it pertains to the future. The Gospel does not deliver us from dark days, but it does deliver us from succumbing to hopelessness. Christians boldly apply God's unfailing love to all of their circumstances. When life seems like it is falling apart, we remember the cross, the resurrection, and the intercession of God the Son and God the Holy Spirit. "Through him who loved us" (Rom. 8:37), we can conquer the worst that life can throw at us. Clearly, the future is ours in Christ!

Introduction for Youths
Topic: *Does Anybody Care?*

The legless beggar pulled himself along the crowded city street. Who cared for him? The prosperous businessman had suffered a stroke and could no longer speak. Who cared about him?

We cannot avoid people who are seemingly devoid of hope. The Gospel does not promise a life free of pain and disappointment. But Jesus does promise us that, when we look beyond present pain, we can find future heavenly glory. We who are Christians know that our eternal future is safe with God. We also know that heavenly glory awaits us.

We moreover know that, because God gave us His Son, He will provide all we need in Christ to live for Him. The Lord cares supremely, even when we feel cast off and forsaken. We understand that, no matter what life brings, nothing will ever cut us off from God's love for us in Christ.

Concepts for Children
Topic: *Tell God Your Needs*

1. Jesus gives us His Spirit to help us when we pray.
2. Jesus taught His followers to pray as much as possible.
3. When we pray to God about our needs, He will answer our requests.
4. God is like a good parent who gives us the things we need to obey Him.
5. As we grow in our faith, we learn to trust God's love and wisdom.
6. God is more eager to bless us than we can imagine.

The Lesson Commentary

I. PRESENT SUFFERING AND FUTURE GLORY: ROMANS 8:18-27

A. Glory Surpasses Suffering: vs. 18

I consider that our present sufferings are not worth comparing with the glory that will be revealed in us.

The Gospel brings an entirely new dimension to human experience: a confident assurance of future glory with God. This hope empowered the believers in the early church to endure persecution. And their hope prevented the enemies of the faith from extinguishing the spreading fires of Christianity.

Paul wrote about future glory in the context of facing contemporary hardships and tribulations. For instance, in Romans the apostle discussed future glory in the context of God's eternal plan of redemption. His plan includes believers living in a godly manner. Note that chapters 6 and 7 describe the principles and practices of loving and serving the Lord. Next, in 8:1-17, we learn that the power to be holy rests in the rule of the Spirit in our lives.

Then, beginning with verse 18, we find a new theme in Paul's letter: the glorification of believers. When the apostle thought about his tough experiences, he saw them in the light of God's plan for the future—"the glory that will be revealed in us." This promised glory is the foundation of our Christian hope.

Believers face their present sufferings in the strength that Jesus gives to them. He told His disciples that they would be persecuted (John 15:20). And Paul said that part of our Christian calling is to suffer for the Lord (Phil. 1:29). We can do so, for we know that the joy of our future glory far surpasses the horror of our present suffering. After all, "our light and momentary troubles are achieving for us an eternal glory that far outweighs them all" (2 Cor. 4:17).

B. Glory Means a New Body in a New World: vss. 19-23

The creation waits in eager expectation for the sons of God to be revealed. For the creation was subjected to frustration, not by its own choice, but by the will of the one who subjected it, in hope that the creation itself will be liberated from its bondage to decay and brought into the glorious freedom of the children of God. We know that the whole creation has been groaning as in the pains of childbirth right up to the present time. Not only so, but we ourselves, who have the firstfruits of the Spirit, groan inwardly as we wait eagerly for our adoption as sons, the redemption of our bodies.

Christians have been blessed in Christ "with every spiritual blessing" (Eph. 1:3). Jesus gives us abundant life here and now (John 10:10). He enables us to "participate in the divine nature" (2 Pet. 1:4). And as redeemed members of God's family, we have been set free from sin's power and penalty (Rom. 6:1-11).

In addition, there is future glory to come. What is this glory like? Among other things, it will mean freedom from physical decay and receiving a glorified, resurrection body (8:19-23). In these verses Paul gives us a preview of what the future holds. First comes the revealing of the "sons of God" (vs. 19) and then the redemption of our bodies (vs. 23). Apparently, both occur simultaneously, related as they are to the release of the whole created universe "from its bondage to decay" (vs. 21). In the meantime, "creation waits in eager expectation" (vs. 19) and Christians "groan inwardly" (vs. 23).

Paul explained what he meant by these statements. Right now creation is subject to incompleteness and is in bondage to decay. Creation "was subjected to frustration" (vs. 20), not by its own choice, but because of human sin. The consequences of sin included both humankind's banishment from God's presence and also the degradation of the created world.

All is not lost, however, for there is the hope of future liberation (vs. 21). Paul personified creation as longing with hope, despite frustration, decay, and death. Deliverance will come when believers share in Christ's future glory. At that time all creation will join God's children in "glorious freedom" from death and decay.

Right up to the present time, all creation has been groaning as if it were a mother in the pains of giving birth to a child (vs. 22). Frustration and decay appear to reign now, but one day all the damage of sin will be wiped out. When God's children are set free, the creation will also be set free from the ravages of sin. In that future day of blessing, Christians will receive glorified, resurrection bodies (vs. 23).

In the meantime, we wait for our adoption. We already are full-fledged members of God's family (vss. 15-17), but there is more to come in terms of eternal blessing. What we experience now as God's children Paul called "the firstfruits of the Spirit" (vs. 23). "Firstfruits" is a word used of Old Testament offerings. The first of the crops and herds were given to the Lord. This was the Israelites' way of thanking God for the promise of a bountiful harvest to come.

In a similar way, the Spirit within us is a foretaste of future glory to come. He takes up residence in us when we put our faith in Christ. The Spirit is the divine resource we need to live for God. At the same time, we anticipate God's glory. In this regard, the Spirit is the first down payment, or guarantee, of God's magnificent blessings to come.

Spirit as first fruit in us.

C. Hope Undergirds Salvation: vss. 24-25

For in this hope we were saved. But hope that is seen is no hope at all. Who hopes for what he already has? But if we hope for what we do not yet have, we wait for it patiently.

Paul related the future day of redemption to the present hope of the believer. Hope is what sustains us as we endure our present sufferings (Rom. 8:24-25). Our hope looks to that day when we will finally be delivered from the body of sin, decay, and death.

Of course, the redemption of our physical bodies has not yet occurred. The fact that we continue to grow old is ample testimony to that. Our hope is for a future redemption, something we have not as yet seen. On that day hope will become a reality. In the meantime we are told to wait patiently for that which is still to come.

It's natural for children to trust their parents, even though parents sometimes fail to keep their promises. Our heavenly Father, however, never makes promises

He won't keep. Perhaps at times His plan of redemption seems to be taking more time than we expect. Rather than becoming impatient with Him, we should wait for God's will to unfold. We can do this for we know that God's timing and wisdom are perfect.

D. The Spirit's Help: vss. 26-27

In the same way, the Spirit helps us in our weakness. We do not know what we ought to pray for, but the Spirit himself intercedes for us with groans that words cannot express. And he who searches our hearts knows the mind of the Spirit, because the Spirit intercedes for the saints in accordance with God's will.

Paul recognized the weakness of our faith and hope in the midst of circumstances beyond our control. The apostle therefore noted that one of the Holy Spirit's responsibilities is to help us in our weakness and frailty. He does so by interceding for us when we pray (Rom. 8:26).

The Spirit perpetually intercedes on our behalf with "groans that words cannot express." In addition, the Father—"he who searches our hearts" (vs. 27)—knows the mind of the Spirit. Thus, the groanings of the Spirit do not need to be put into words, for God is intimately familiar with the Spirit's heart.

Paul was saying that the Lord matches our needs with the Spirit's prayers. This is a remarkable teaching of how God takes care of us in our present state of physical decay. We don't even know what the really important prayer issues are, so the Spirit intercedes on our behalf in the presence of the Father. With the Spirit helping us to pray, we don't need to be afraid to come before the Lord with our requests.

II. THE FOUNDATION OF GLORY: ROMANS 8:31-34

A. God's Gracious Gift: vss. 31-32

What, then, shall we say in response to this? If God is for us, who can be against us? He who did not spare his own Son, but gave him up for us all—how will he not also, along with him, graciously give us all things?

These verses follow Paul's profound teaching about our place in God's plan of redemption. First, the apostle reminded us that, whatever our circumstances are as we wait patiently for the future revelation of God's glory, the Lord controls everything for our good (Rom. 8:28). Second, believers are called to faith according to God's wise and loving purposes. Ultimately, all who have trusted in Christ are on the way to be conformed to His likeness (vs. 29). This helps us to put our present circumstances in the proper context.

Third, having stated what's in store for believers, Paul focused the attention of his readers on the implications of these truths. The apostle began by asking, "If God is for us, who can be against us?" (vs. 31). Certainly human beings stand against us from time to time. And Satan and his demons stand against us as our adversaries. But God is the King of the universe and the one who is ultimately in control. Because He is for us, no one can successfully stand against us. Therefore, we anticipate eternal glory with full confidence that God is by our side in all things.

Fourth, Paul noted that our hope rests in the Father's gracious gift of His own Son. Scripture reveals to us that God gave Jesus for our salvation and future glory. Since the Father did not spare His Son, we can trust Him to take care of all our needs, especially while we live in this interim period between bondage and freedom, between decay and new life (vs. 32).

This truth should undergird us when it seems like everything is going against us. Yes, life is filled with sorrow. But the reality of God's gift of salvation gives us courage, steadfastness, and hope even in the midst of nerve-racking circumstances.

B. Our Justification: vs. 33

Who will bring any charge against those whom God has chosen? It is God who justifies.

Paul raised three hypothetical questions: (1) Who will accuse us of wrongdoing? (2) Who will condemn us for our transgressions? and (3) Who will separate us from Christ's love? The word rendered "charge" (Rom. 8:33) carries the idea of "formal accusation." Certainly Satan—the "accuser of our brothers" (Rev. 12:10)—denounces us because of our sin. But because we have trusted in Christ, God declares us to be forgiven (completely cleared of guilt). Thus, all charges are dismissed for those who put their faith in the Savior.

C. Christ's Intercession: vs. 34

Who is he that condemns? Christ Jesus, who died—more than that, who was raised to life—is at the right hand of God and is also interceding for us.

Paul asked, "Who is he that condemns?" (Rom. 8:34). It's true that Jesus has been appointed by the Father to judge the world (Acts 17:31); but it's also true that Jesus champions our cause. After all, He died for us, was raised to life for us, and is sitting at the place of highest honor next to the Father to plead our case.

Paul then asked, "Who shall separate us from the love of Christ?" (Rom. 8:35). The apostle mentioned seven things that might seem to have the power to separate us from the love of Christ. The wonderful truth, though, is that none of these things can undo the Savior's great love for and commitment to us.

Paul quoted from Psalm 44:22 to emphasize that the believer, while in the world, would face affliction—perhaps even martyrdom (Rom. 8:36). In all such adversities, they are more than conquerors through Christ (vs. 37). Believers not only win their spiritual battles, but in the end they enjoy the Lord's presence.

III. THE GUARANTEE OF GLORY: ROMANS 8:38-39

For I am convinced that neither death nor life, neither angels nor demons, neither the present nor the future, nor any powers, neither height nor depth, nor anything else in all creation, will be able to separate us from the love of God that is in Christ Jesus our Lord.

Paul exulted in the fact that nothing can separate His own from the love of God that is in Jesus (Rom. 8:38-39). The apostle provided a series of items to illustrate his point. Most of these are in pairs—the extremes of existence (death, life), spiritual armies (angels, demons), time (present, future), and space (height, depth). None of these things—at either extreme—can separate us from God's love.

Thus, no matter how dark the days, no matter how grim the future looks, we can claim God's love in Christ. We are called to affirm it as Paul did—even when our feelings and plans seem shattered by unforeseen developments. Our faith grows in the midst of tears, pain, suffering, and disappointment. Such adversities force us to drive our stakes ever deeper into the heart of God's unfailing love.

Discussion Questions

1. How does the promise of future glory help us to endure present sufferings?
2. Why was the creation subjected to death and decay?
3. What does it mean for believers to have "the firstfruits of the Spirit" (Rom. 8:23)?
4. How does the Spirit help us in our times of prayer?
5. In what ways has God's unfailing love encouraged you during difficult circumstances?

Contemporary Application

"Cast all your cares on God; that anchor holds," wrote the English poet Alfred, Lord Tennyson. When personal hardships seem unbearable, God is there to steady us because He cares for us. God is the source of every mercy. His consolation is evident when we are lonely, under stress, or fatigued. He helps us deal with financial problems, family tensions, and difficulties at work.

There is no trial we may experience where God's consolation is not available. If we were to list all the times He has comforted us, the list would be practically endless. In fact, it is hard to imagine all the ways that God has shown us His mercy and love. There are numerous examples throughout the Bible of how God has comforted His people, and these accounts can encourage us as well as those around us who are hurting.

Just as the Lord comforts us in our times of hurting, so too He wants us to be as caring to others. He wants to work through us to bring sympathy and encouragement to others. The more we experience God's comfort and encouragement, the more we should be a source of consolation to others. God can use what we have learned from our personal experiences to tenderly comfort those who are going through similar trials.

Proclaim the Gospel

DEVOTIONAL READING

Romans 11:1-16

DAILY BIBLE READINGS

Monday April 15
*James 1:19-27 Be Doers of
the Word*

Tuesday April 16
*James 2:1-13 Love Does Not
Discriminate*

Wednesday April 17
*James 3:1-12 Control Your
Tongue*

Thursday April 18
*James 3:13-18 Wisdom from
Above*

Friday April 19
*James 5:7-12 Patience and
Endurance*

Saturday April 20
*Romans 12:1-8 Not
Conformed, but Transformed*

Sunday April 21
*Romans 12:9-21 Marks of
Christian Living*

Scripture

Background Scripture: *Romans 10:1-17*
Scripture Lesson: *Romans 10:1, 3-10, 12-17*
Key Verse: *And how can they hear without someone preaching to them? And how can they preach unless they are sent?*
Romans 10:14-15.
Scripture Lesson for Children: *Romans 10:12-13; Luke
10:1-10*
Key Verse for Children: *"Everyone who calls on the name of
the Lord will be saved."* Romans 10:13.

Lesson Aim

To reflect on the importance of proclaiming the
Gospel to the lost.

Lesson Setting

Time: *A.D. 57*
Place: *From Corinth to the church in Rome*

Lesson Outline

Proclaim the Gospel
   I. Paul's Desire: Romans 10:1
  II. Two Ways of Righteousness: Romans 10:3-7
       A. *By Faith: vss. 3-4*
       B. *By Law: vss. 5-7*
 III. The Believer's Confession: Romans 10:8-10, 12-13
       A. *Jesus Is Lord: vss. 8-9*
       B. *The How of Saving Faith: vs. 10*
       C. *Salvation for All: vss. 12-13*
  IV. The Gospel's Proclamation: Romans 10:14-15
   V. Hearing the Message: Romans 10:16-17

Introduction for Adults

Topic: *How Are They to Hear?*

The question posed by our topic is often answered in this way—if we invite people to church, they will hear the Gospel. In some cases, the lost are saved as a result of attending church. But often when we ask people how they came to faith in Christ, they give a wide variety of answers that don't involve initially going to a worship service. It's amazing how many ways God uses to bring people to Himself.

This observation should encourage us to keep learning as much as we can about how people actually come to faith in Christ. As we grow in our understanding, we will not be content to assume that an invitation to church is the only way to bring about the conversion of the lost. Therefore, our task as proclaimers of the Gospel is first to find an opening somewhere in a friend's life story. Then with patient love and prayer, we can introduce him or her to Jesus and the salvation He offers.

Introduction for Youths

Topic: *Is There an Answer?*

A Christian magazine once asked 12 theologians from different denominations to describe the Gospel in about 350 words. They all said much the same thing, but they said it with a lot of big words and long sentences. How could the average person possibly understand what the "experts" had to say?

Our friends want simple and direct answers to life's biggest question—how can people be saved and go to heaven? Sometimes the question is expressed indirectly—how can people find meaning in life? or, how can people get out of the mess that they have made of their life?

Whatever the actual words, we know the lost are looking for a clear and meaningful answer. That's why we should be as straightforward as Paul when he gave the heart of the Gospel. He declared that Jesus is the risen Lord and that all who trust in Him will be saved.

Concepts for Children

Topic: *Tell Others about Jesus*

1. God uses believers to tell those who aren't saved about Jesus.
2. Those who put their faith in Jesus are saved.
3. When Jesus was on earth, He initially chose 70 followers to tell others about Him.
4. Jesus warned His followers that some people would not want to hear the Good News.
5. We can trust Jesus to lead us to those who want to hear the Gospel.

The Lesson Commentary

I.   PAUL'S DESIRE: ROMANS 10:1

Brothers, my heart's desire and prayer to God for the Israelites is that they may be saved.

When we read Paul's triumphant declaration of God's unshakable love for us in Christ (Rom. 8:31-39), we might initially feel as if we have reached the climax of his letter. However, we soon discover that the apostle had much to say about the practical effects of the Gospel in our lives.

Part of Paul's desire was for the conversion of his Jewish contemporaries. What would happen to them, especially in light of the truth that people are saved by trusting in Christ, not by keeping the law? Paul knew that many Gentiles were receiving the Gospel with joy, but that many Jews were rejecting the Good News.

In light of this, what did the future hold for the Jews in God's eternal plan? In response, Paul revealed that God is neither unfaithful in His promises nor unrighteous in His dealings (9:1-24). The apostle also noted that God was just to include believing Gentiles in His kingdom and reject unbelieving Jews (9:25-29). The tragedy is that some of the Jews of Paul's day tried to get right with God by keeping the law, rather than believing in Christ (9:30—10:13). Ultimately they are without excuse for rejecting Him as their Savior (10:14-21).

An examination of 11:25-32 indicates that the unbelief of the Jews and their rejection of their Savior will not last forever. Paul declared that one day there will be a believing remnant. It's true that they presently have rebelled against God, but one day they will be the recipients of His mercy. The realization of this truth caused Paul to burst forth in praise to God for His great wisdom (vss. 33-36).

Reminiscent of Paul's concern for Israel described in 9:1-4, the apostle expressed his heart's desire that Israel be saved (10:1). Undoubtedly, Paul said many things in his letter that were objectionable to his fellow Jews. Nevertheless, his motive was sincere and proper. He expressed "tough love" by confronting unsaved Jews with their failure to attain righteousness by their own efforts. He understood how they thought because he had once been like them.

II.   TWO WAYS OF RIGHTEOUSNESS: ROMANS 10:3-7

A. By Faith: vss. 3-4

Since they did not know the righteousness that comes from God and sought to establish their own, they did not submit to God's righteousness. Christ is the end of the law so that there may be righteousness for everyone who believes.

Paul noted that the unsaved Jews exhibited a zeal for God, but that it was misguided (Rom. 10:2). Their basic mistake was to substitute their own righteousness for God's righteousness (vs. 3). Of course, this flawed thinking was not limited to the Jews. Down through the centuries, everyone has to decide whether to try to please God by self-effort or accept His gift of righteousness by faith in Christ.

The coming of the Messiah made it clear that no one can earn salvation by keeping the Mosaic law. In fact, Jesus is "the end of the law" (vs. 4). Some think Paul was saying that Christ has terminated the law or caused it to cease altogether. Another possibility is that Jesus fulfilled the requirements of the law, having accomplished all that it requires (Matt. 5:17). In either case it's clear that believers are no longer under the law's condemnation (Rom. 6:15). Of course, the law still serves the useful purpose of reminding us of God's perfect moral standards.

B. By Law: vss. 5-7

Moses describes in this way the righteousness that is by the law: "The man who does these things will live by them." But the righteousness that is by faith says: "Do not say in your heart, 'Who will ascend into heaven?'" (that is, to bring Christ down) "or 'Who will descend into the deep?'" (that is, to bring Christ up from the dead).

Since Paul was addressing Jewish issues, there was no greater authority he could appeal to than Moses. Thus the apostle quoted Moses to emphasize that, if a person managed to obey *all* the law's commands and likewise never break any of them, he or she would enjoy a certain measure of righteousness (Lev. 18:5; Rom. 10:5). Such an accomplishment, however, is unattainable, for keeping the law perfectly is impossible for human beings.

Paul then quoted from Deuteronomy 30:12-13 to point out that one does not need to bring Christ down from heaven or up from the grave in order to attain God's righteousness, for God's righteousness is received through faith (Rom. 10:6-7). Paul's underlying theme was that one need not go through heroic efforts to attain such righteousness, for God gives it freely and graciously to believers.

In a sense, then, the salvation that God provides is immediately available to us. He will come to us in saving grace wherever we are. All we need to do is respond in faith and accept God's gift of redemption and forgiveness in Christ.

III. THE BELIEVER'S CONFESSION: ROMANS 10:8-10, 12-13

A. Jesus Is Lord: vss. 8-9

But what does it say? "The word is near you; it is in your mouth and in your heart," that is, the word of faith we are proclaiming: That if you confess with your mouth, "Jesus is Lord," and believe in your heart that God raised him from the dead, you will be saved.

In Romans 10:8, Paul quoted from Deuteronomy 30:14 to stress that the message of truth (namely, the Gospel) is close at hand. Salvation is as close as our own lips and heart. Some have made the truth about being saved a complicated process, but it's not. It's simply a matter of believing and accepting the truth about Jesus.

It's helpful to observe the original context of Moses' words in Deuteronomy 30. Here we find his final charge to the Israelites as they were to enter into Canaan. Moses promised blessing for obedience and punishment for disobedience. Since the Israelites of Moses' day had God's message, they did not need to request that it be brought down from Mount Sinai again or that someone descend and cross the sea to get it. Moses emphasized that the generation of Israelites to whom he was speaking indeed had God's message—it was near them and it was in their mouths (vss. 13-14).

Paul applied the same truth to the Jews of his generation. They didn't need to bring Christ down from heaven or up from the grave, because they already had God's message of faith-righteousness. Keep in mind that Christ had already come from heaven to deliver His message, and that He had already been resurrected, thereby validating the message. Hence, the truth about salvation was near. All the people needed to do was exercise faith in their hearts and obey the word, that is, the Gospel (Rom. 10:8).

Many in our day tend to look for God in dramatic experiences. Some feel they have to live in a certain location or be near some well-known Christian personality in order to experience God's fullest blessing. This verse indicates that God is right next to us; He's right where we are.

Paul elaborated on the message of the Gospel by declaring that "Jesus is Lord" (vs. 9). This was a common confession in the first-century church and was probably spoken aloud when a new convert was baptized. This confession affirmed that Jesus is God and reigns supreme. Another part of the message is Jesus' resurrection from the dead—a truth that lies at the heart of Christianity. Apart from Jesus' rising from the dead, Christianity has no real meaning.

To some, Jesus is just another religious teacher or revolutionary hero. But to those who believe, He is the Messiah and the Son of God. Christians affirm that Jesus died on the cross and rose from the dead so that all who believe might have new life in Him. They also affirm that Jesus is unsurpassed in His lordship. This is the glorious Good News we proclaim to a dying world full of hopeless, despairing people.

B. The How of Saving Faith: vs. 10

For it is with your heart that you believe and are justified, and it is with your mouth that you confess and are saved.

How does saving faith work? Paul cited two aspects, inward assurance and outward profession. First, we believe in our hearts. In other words, we have the full assurance that God's message to us in the Gospel is true. Our minds are convinced and our wills are surrendered. When we joyfully give ourselves to Jesus, we receive God's justification, that is, His declaration that we stand righteous before Him by faith (Rom. 10:10).

Second, we give evidence of our salvation by confessing the truth with our lips. It's one thing, of course, to mouth the truths of the Gospel and another thing to live them out. Nevertheless, Paul made it clear that those who are genuinely saved will give evidence of this to others. And doing so makes it clear where they have placed their confidence. They are not relying on themselves or others for eternal deliverance but rather on the Son of God.

C. Salvation for All: vss. 12-13

For there is no difference between Jew and Gentile—the same Lord is Lord of all and richly blesses all who call on him, for, "Everyone who calls on the name of the Lord will be saved."

Those who fail to trust in Christ face a state of eternal gloom. In contrast, those who believe in Christ will "never be put to shame" (Rom. 10:11). (Paul quoted Isaiah 28:16 to validate his point.) The apostle was not saying that believers will never be disappointed. In fact, there will be times when circumstances take a turn for the worse or when people will let us down. Despite such hardships, God will remain faithful in redeeming those who put their faith in His Son.

It doesn't matter whether one is Jew or Gentile, for God is impartial. Jesus is not the Lord of one group only, but rather the "Lord of all" (Rom. 10:12). Both Jews and Gentiles who call upon Him find themselves receiving rich blessings from Him (for example, righteousness, forgiveness, and eternal life).

In verse 13, Paul quoted from Joel 2:32 to stress that all who call on the name of the Lord "will be saved." To the ancients, a person's name was a reflection of his or her personality and character. In Jesus' case, His name points to His deity and His messiahship. Thus to call on the Lord's name is to pray in faith for salvation.

IV. THE GOSPEL'S PROCLAMATION: ROMANS 10:14-15

How, then, can they call on the one they have not believed in? And how can they believe in the one of whom they have not heard? And how can they hear without someone preaching to them? And how can they preach unless they are sent? As it is written, "How beautiful are the feet of those who bring good news!"

Some of Paul's Jewish readers might have tried to argue that the Jews never had a fair chance to hear and respond to God's message of salvation. To answer such a challenge, Paul asked a series of rhetorical questions that point to the necessity of hearing the message of Christ and responding to it in faith (Rom. 10:14-15).

Paul's point was that God first sends a preacher. The herald proclaims the message; the people hear the message; and some believe. The apostle made it clear that God indeed has sent His word through His messengers, but sadly not all the Jewish people have responded favorably.

Paul emphasized his point by quoting from Isaiah 52:7: "How beautiful are the feet of those who bring good news!" (Rom. 10:15). In its context during Isaiah's day, the words described the welcomed message of imminent release from captivity in Babylon. Those who brought such good news would be held in high regard. Paul used the words in reference to those who proclaimed the Gospel. They came with a message of release from the oppressive captivity of sin.

The rhetorical questions Paul asked are relevant to Christians, for how will our loved ones, neighbors, and associates hear the good news of Christ unless we tell them about it? Each of us has a sphere of influence in which God can use us to communicate His message of reconciliation and peace.

V. HEARING THE MESSAGE: ROMANS 10:16-17

But not all the Israelites accepted the good news. For Isaiah says, "Lord, who has believed our message?"
Consequently, faith comes from hearing the message, and the message is heard through the word of
Christ.

Though God's message was provided to the Jewish people, not all of them accepted it (Rom. 10:16). The Jewish people may have been aware of the message, but they didn't respond positively and they certainly didn't obey it. This is why Paul quoted Isaiah, "Lord, who has believed our message?" (Isa. 53:1).

Paul affirmed that faith comes from hearing the message, and the message is heard through the spoken Gospel (Rom. 10:17). Certainly the Jewish people had heard this message, for the "voice" of God's evangelists had gone out into all the earth (Rom. 10:18, where Paul quoted Ps. 19:4). Hence, the Jewish people could have responded in faith, but sadly they chose not to.

The Gospel must be proclaimed and heard. This is the fundamental communication process. Christians are called to spread the good news of Jesus' death and resurrection for sinners. But until people hear and believe, they will not be saved.

Discussion Questions

1. Why was Paul so desirous for the salvation of his fellow Jews?
2. How had the Jewish people sought to establish their own righteousness?
3. How does the righteousness that is by faith contrast with the righteousness that is by the law?
4. Why does God not make any distinction between Jews and Gentiles when it comes to salvation?
5. What are some ways that God can use you to herald His saving message?

Contemporary Application

How do we make the Gospel available to all people? We can use radio, television, films, and books (to name a few things). We have more means available to us than ever before. At the same time we should not forget the important role that each of us serves in proclaiming the Good News. Believers are critical to the success of evangelism because people want to see our love and passion for them as individuals, not just as part of the mass audience. They want to see Jesus in us. They want to ask why our faith works for us. This reminds us that our personal witness for Christ can be just as effective as any other means of spreading the Gospel.

We should be careful not to assume that everyone has heard the message of salvation, despite the media we may use to disseminate the Gospel. We have to think about people from different backgrounds who may be bypassed by the media and by our churches. We dare not give the impression that the Gospel is anyone's private property. Paul made it clear that everyone who calls on the Lord will be saved and that part of the process includes their hearing and understanding the truth. That's where we come in. May we shoulder this awesome responsibility with joy!

Live the Gospel

DEVOTIONAL READING

Romans 12:4-8

DAILY BIBLE READINGS

Monday April 22
Romans 14:1-8 Act to Honor the Lord

Tuesday April 23
Romans 14:9-18 We Must Give an Account to Him

Wednesday April 24
Romans 14:19-23 Do Not Cause Others to Stumble

Thursday April 25
Romans 15:1-6 Build Up Your Neighbor

Friday April 26
Romans 15:7-13 The Gospel Is for Both Jews and Gentiles

Saturday April 27
Romans 15:14-22 Paul: A Minister of Christ to the Gentiles

Sunday April 28
Romans 15:23-33 Paul's Plan to Visit Rome

Scripture

Background Scripture: *Romans 12*
Scripture Lesson: *Romans 12:1-3, 9-21*
Key Verse: *Do not conform any longer to the pattern of this world, but be transformed by the renewing of your mind. Then you will be able to test and approve what God's will is—his good, pleasing and perfect will.* Romans 12:2.
Scripture Lesson for Children: *Romans 12:9-13; Acts 4:32-37*
Key Verse for Children: *Love must be sincere.* Romans 12:9.

Lesson Aim

To understand how salvation in Christ transforms all our relationships, associations, and dealings with others.

Lesson Setting

Time: *A.D. 57*
Place: *From Corinth to the church in Rome*

Lesson Outline

Live the Gospel

   I. Devoted to God: Romans 12:1-3
     A. *A Living and Holy Sacrifice: vss. 1-2*
     B. *A Humble Assessment: vs. 3*
  II. Dedicated in Service: Romans 12:9-21
     A. *Excelling in Love: vss. 9-13*
     B. *Overcoming Evil with Good: vss. 14-21*

Introduction for Adults
Topic: *How Are We to Live?*

Knowing how to live out the truth of the Gospel means that we not only need the right information but also the right spiritual attributes. In this regard, what we learn from Romans 12 may not be new to us who are seasoned Christians. But we have to admit that often we fail to live up to the divine standard for upright behavior advocated by Paul. For instance, we know that we shouldn't be proud and that we should be patient in affliction. We also know that we should bless our enemies and not seek revenge when they wrong us. Regrettably, though, doing what is right and avoiding doing what is wrong eludes our grasp.

It's wise, therefore, for us to remain accountable to God and our fellow believers. Accountability to God can be maintained by means of practicing such spiritual disciplines as prayer and Scripture study. And accountability to our fellow believers can be maintained by corporate worship and one-on-one times of fellowship. Our mutual goal should be to develop proper attitudes and habits. Through the grace of God, the ministry of the Word, and the encouragement of other believers, we will be able to forsake sin and grow in Christlikeness.

Introduction for Youths
Topic: *What Is It All About?*

From our earliest years in school we bump against people who delight in demeaning Christian values. If, for example, we refuse to fight and turn the other cheek, we are ridiculed as wimps. If we don't try to get even for some wrong done to us, we are said to be fools. And if we refuse to participate in sin, we are scorned. In light of the above, it's not hard to understand why the temptation to sin is so great.

God is pleased when we hold to the moral values taught in His Word. He wants us to exercise the courage and faith that is needed to follow the Gospel's high standards. Because Jesus lives in us as believers, we can be strong in the face of adversity and temptation. He enables us to take a stand for truth and goodness. Perhaps unknown to us, many of our peers will respect us because we have chosen to follow the Lord rather than the corrupt ways of the world.

Concepts for Children
Topic: *Love One Another*

1. Paul said that love should be shown through what we do.
2. The Christians in the early church showed their love by sharing what they had with one another.
3. The believers also showed their love by caring for the needy among them.
4. A believer named Joseph (or Barnabas) sold a field and gave the money he received to the leaders of the church so that they could help the needy.
5. God has given us many things, and He is pleased when we share what we have with others.

The Lesson Commentary

I. DEVOTED TO GOD: ROMANS 12:1-3

A. A Living and Holy Sacrifice: vss. 1-2

Therefore, I urge you, brothers, in view of God's mercy, to offer your bodies as living sacrifices, holy and pleasing to God—this is your spiritual act of worship. Do not conform any longer to the pattern of this world, but be transformed by the renewing of your mind. Then you will be able to test and approve what God's will is—his good, pleasing and perfect will.

Paul often divided his letters into two major sections—one dealing with doctrine and the other with practical matters. In this case, Romans 1—11 focuses mostly on theological matters such as sin and salvation, while chapters 12—16 deal with practical aspects of Christian living. Paul's exhortations concern the believer's conduct toward the church, society, and the state. The lordship of Christ in every area of life is emphasized throughout this section.

Paul began this practical discussion by stressing the importance of obedient service to God. Throughout the Book of Romans, the apostle talked about God's great mercy in providing salvation for those who believe. In view of this undeserved kindness, Christians were to offer their bodies as living sacrifices to the Lord (12:1). Paul was talking about dedicating one's heart, mind, and will in unwavering service to God. Such a spiritual act of worship was to be morally pure and pleasing to Him. The desire to serve God wholeheartedly was entirely reasonable and legitimate.

Paul's discussion about living sacrifices should not be confused with the offerings that were made in Old Testament times. In ancient Israel, animals were killed and burned on an altar. This is not required of Christians, however. They offer themselves, including their bodies, in loyal service to God. The body is the vehicle through which we do all things (whether good and bad). When we dedicate ourselves to the Lord, we are unconditionally surrendering to His purpose and will.

An animal sacrificed in Old Testament times was forced to take part in the ceremony being conducted. In contrast, believers are willing participants in serving God. They cannot just do God's will once in a while, however. They should be ready and yield every day to obey Him.

The priests of ancient Israel worshiped God by performing various rites and rituals. Believers in Christ worship the Lord by devoting their lives in service to Him. When they help others and share their possessions, it is a spiritual offering that greatly pleases God (Heb. 13:16). In view of the magnificent things the Lord has done for us through Christ, we ought to be eager to perform this spiritual act of worship.

The work Christians do for God will be displeasing if they act consistently like the unsaved people of the world. Fallen human society is characterized by evil (Gal. 1:4) and ruled by Satan (Eph. 2:2). As believers yield themselves to the Lord, they will no longer model their behavior after the mores of this wicked age. There ultimately must be a change in lifestyle (Rom. 12:2).

God wants to mentally and morally transform His people. His intent is to radically alter their desires and actions so that they are characterized by virtue rather than vice. As they renounce the things of the world, their thinking will be renewed. This is significant because the mind is the control center of one's thoughts, attitudes, and emotions (Eph. 4:22-23).

The spiritual transformation being referred to in Romans 12:2 does not take place in a single event. Instead, it is a lifelong process. It is also not a mere option for the Christian. Rather, God's people must submit to His renewing work in their lives. He brings about change through a variety of means, including prayer, the study of His Word, and Christian fellowship.

As God renews the thinking of believers, they will be able to discern and recognize His will for them in the present. The Lord's desires for His people are never partial. Rather, His will is always beneficial, eternally satisfying, and flawless. When Christians submit to God's plan for them, they will mature as believers and lead spiritually productive lives.

B. A Humble Assessment: vs. 3

For by the grace given me I say to every one of you: Do not think of yourself more highly than you ought, but rather think of yourself with sober judgment, in accordance with the measure of faith God has given you.

Some think the believers at Rome struggled with pride as they appropriated and used their spiritual gifts. If so, this explains the comments Paul made in Romans 12:3. By the authority of the grace that the Lord had given Paul, the apostle directed the believers at Rome not to have an overly inflated opinion of themselves or their importance in the church. Instead, they were to form a sober and sensible estimate of their abilities based on the amount of faith God had given them. Like all Christians, the Roman believers were saved by the mercy of God. Similarly, the Lord had given them the ability to serve Him. Acknowledging this would undercut any tendency they had to be haughty.

A human body is made up of many parts, and each of them has its own function (vs. 4). Similarly, Christ's spiritual body has many members. Nevertheless, they are all united in Him as well as part of one another (vs. 5). Each member contributes in a different way to the common good of the whole body (vss. 6-8). Despite the diversity within the group, there is still unity (1 Cor. 12:12-31).

II. DEDICATED IN SERVICE: ROMANS 12:9-21

A. Excelling in Love: vss. 9-13

Love must be sincere. Hate what is evil; cling to what is good. Be devoted to one another in brotherly love. Honor one another above yourselves. Never be lacking in zeal, but keep your spiritual fervor, serving the Lord. Be joyful in hope, patient in affliction, faithful in prayer. Share with God's people who are in need. Practice hospitality.

The remainder of Romans 12 contains a series of short exhortations dealing with the believer's conduct toward fellow Christians and those in society at large. Paul first mentioned love, which suggests it is a prime virtue to cultivate. If one's compassion for others is filled with pretense, it does not come from the Lord. Christlike love is sincere, not hypocritical, in nature (vs. 9). It is not merely expressed in words or feelings. Genuine love seeks to help those in need (1 John 3:17-18).

The love God has for us is always real, never fake. This is seen in the fact that, out of compassion for us, God sent His Son to die for our sins (John 3:16). As our mind is renewed after Christ's image, God's unpretentious love will be evident in our relationships with others.

Christlike love is active and dynamic, not passive and self-centered. For example, godly compassion is not afraid to perform specific acts of benevolence. In fact, it is visible in all areas of a believer's life. Clearly, this love should govern the use of the spiritual gifts Paul mentioned in Romans 12:6-8.

Love rejoices in the truth, but hates what is evil (1 Cor. 13:6). This suggests that genuine love is characterized by purity. On the one hand, it holds tight to all that is good. On the other hand, Christlike compassion loathes whatever is depraved (Rom. 12:9). When we are completely submissive to the love of God, we will have neither time nor desire for what is evil. We should not be surprised by this, for God Himself is good. This is revealed in His abhorrence of wickedness (Hab. 1:13).

One way the love of God can be displayed is through our affection for our fellow Christians. Since believers are members of God's family, they should show the same kind of devotion for one another that family members naturally exhibit. Such love puts the interests of others above its own. It also honors others more than itself by showing appreciation and recognition whenever possible (Rom. 12:10)

Over time a believer's devotion to the Savior can weaken. That is why Paul urged the Christians in Rome to combat the presence of halfhearted zeal. They were to be fervent in spirit and diligent in their service for the Lord. Scholars have noted that verse 11 could either refer to the Holy Spirit or one's inner spirit. Perhaps both are meant. This would imply that the Spirit enables us to obey God enthusiastically, rather than ambivalently.

Verse 12 contains three exhortations that are vital to one's walk with Christ. First, our hope of redemption should keep us joyful despite the hardships we experience. The source of our hope, of course, is Christ. Second, we are to remain patient when we experience hardship. All of us encounter afflictions from time to time. Because of our relationship with Christ, we can victoriously persevere through different trials. Third, we should keep praying regularly and persistently. During times of affliction, we naturally desire to do so. Nevertheless, even in times of relative ease we should faithfully commune with God.

When we feel overwhelmed by hardship, it is easy to forget the needs of others. Verse 13 reminds us that, regardless of the situation, we should do what we can to take care of God's hurting people. We should also extend hospitality to traveling Christians. This should not be a one-time event but rather a lifelong practice. By welcoming believers into our home and meeting their temporal needs, we show God's love in tangible ways. Ultimately, the hospitality we display to our fellow believers is likewise being shown to Christ, whom they represent (Matt. 10:40).

B. Overcoming Evil with Good: vss. 14-21

Bless those who persecute you; bless and do not curse. Rejoice with those who rejoice; mourn with those who mourn. Live in harmony with one another. Do not be proud, but be willing to associate with people of low position. Do not be conceited. Do not repay anyone evil for evil. Be careful to do what is right in the eyes of everybody. If it is possible, as far as it depends on you, live at peace with everyone. Do not take revenge, my friends, but leave room for God's wrath, for it is written: "It is mine to avenge; I will repay," says the Lord. On the contrary: "If your enemy is hungry, feed him; if he is thirsty, give him something to drink. In doing this, you will heap burning coals on his head." Do not be overcome by evil, but overcome evil with good.

In Romans 12:14-16, Paul told his readers how they should respond to friends, neighbors, and enemies of the Gospel. In times of suffering, it is natural for believers to pray that God would afflict their persecutors with misfortune. Paul said that Christians should ask the Lord to bless those who mistreated them. This reflects what Jesus taught and practiced.

When others rejoice over the good things happening in their life, we should rejoice with them rather than be envious of them. Likewise, when others grieve over some tragedy they have experienced, we should grieve with them rather than gloat over their affliction (vs. 15). Regardless of whether it is the saved or the unsaved, people will see Christ in us when we respond with genuine empathy. In trying times it is easy for believers to argue with one another. Paul said God's people should promote harmony and unity, not discord and division (vs. 16).

The apostle also taught that believers should not be swayed by one's social standing. Rather, Christians should willingly associate with others, regardless of their economic status. Believers should also freely give themselves to humble, or menial, tasks. Paul's comments are aptly summed up in Leviticus 19:18.

Paul's exhortations in Romans 12:17-21 concern how believers should relate to those who are hostile to them. The Old Testament followed a principle of justice called the law of retaliation in which the punishment was limited to fit the offense (Lev. 24:19-21). Equitable justice, not revenge, was the main concern. This was so misunderstood that Christ talked about the law of love (Matt. 5:38-42). Paul advocated this same principle when he said that believers should never mistreat someone who has mistreated them.

The Christians at Rome were to consider what was noble and virtuous in the sight of all people and focus on doing that (Rom. 12:17). They were also to do their best at all times and in every circumstance to live at peace (vs. 18). This means they should use whatever means were at their disposal to promote harmony. There are times, however, when even their best efforts would fail to produce peace.

Paul urged his dear friends at Rome not to try to get even when others abused and exploited them. Retaliation was not the answer. Instead, Christians were to patiently wait for God to right all injustices in His time (vs. 19). Paul's statement agreed with Deuteronomy 32:35, which said that God would repay all wrongs and vindicate the cause of His people.

In view of the fact that it is the Lord who takes vengeance and not His people, Christians should heed what is written in Proverbs 25:21-22, which Paul quoted in Romans 12:20. Believers should give their hungry and thirsty enemies food to eat and liquid to drink. By doing this, God's people would heap burning coals on the heads of their opponents.

There are two primary ways of understanding Proverbs 25:22. Some think it is a metaphorical reference to some act of kindness being done, which causes the abuser to feel guilt, shame, and regret. Others think the verse is referring to an ancient Egyptian custom in which guilty people put a container of hot charcoal on their head as a way of showing their repentance. In this case, the act of kindness to one's enemies would cause them to repent of their evil deeds.

Paul exhorted his readers not to be defeated by evil. In other words, they were to resist the desire to counterattack their opponents. Instead, the believers at Rome were to defeat evil by doing good (Rom. 12:21). By showing love and kindness rather than hatred and vengeance, believers might win the unsaved to Christ.

Discussion Questions

1. What do you think Paul meant when he urged us to offer our bodies to God "as living sacrifices" (Rom. 12:1)?
2. How can we experience the renewing of our minds spoken of in verse 2?
3. How is it possible for us to "hate what is evil" (vs. 9) and "cling to what is good"?
4. What are some concrete ways we can "practice hospitality" (vs. 13)?
5. Why is it important to "overcome evil with good" (vs. 21)?

Contemporary Application

Exactly how radical Gospel living is becomes clear in this week's lesson. This is revolutionary stuff because it flies in the face of contemporary culture. The world tells us to get even with our enemies and stomp on them if you can, but the Gospel tells us to love our enemies, live at peace with everyone, and nourish our enemies with food and water. The world says it's up to us to get satisfaction, while the Gospel says it is up to God to even the scales of justice. That's why Christians live by faith in God's power, love, and righteousness. This relieves us of the awful burden of trying to set things right.

Paul saw Christians engaged in battles between good and evil. He also knew how easy it was to be overcome by evil. That's why the apostle stressed that the way to defeat evil is to do good. He understood that Gospel living is triumphant living, for it rejects the world's values and methods and instead adopts the ways of Christ. This is only possible when we devote ourselves to God. He gives us new minds and transforms us into agents of good in our churches and communities.

We Are the Lord's

Scripture

Background Scripture: *Romans 14:1—15:13*
Scripture Lesson: *Romans 14:1-13*
Key Verse: *Therefore let us stop passing judgment on one another. Instead, make up your mind not to put any stumbling block or obstacle in your brother's way.* Romans 14:13.
Scripture Lesson for Children: *Romans 14:1-4; Luke 14:7-14*
Key Verse for Children: *"Do to others as you would have them do to you."* Luke 6:31.

Lesson Aim

To consider how our actions affect the well-being of other Christians.

Lesson Setting

Time: A.D. *57*
Place: *From Corinth to the church in Rome*

Lesson Outline

We Are the Lord's

I. Disputes over Dietary Regulations: Romans 14:1-4
   A. *Mutual Acceptance: vss. 1-2*
   B. *Mutual Respect: vss. 3-4*
II. Disputes over Special Days: Romans 14:5-9
   A. *Observance versus Nonobservance: vss. 5-6*
   B. *Christ's Lordship: vss. 7-9*
III. Accountability to God: Romans 14:10-13
   A. *God's Evaluation of Believers: vss. 10-12*
   B. *Believers' Mutual Concern: vs. 13*

Introduction for Adults

Topic: *Who Can Judge?*

At a church meeting one night an elderly man challenged the pastor's position on Sunday baseball. When the pastor admitted that the issue was a matter of some indifference to him, the elderly man assailed the minister for his lack of moral and spiritual conviction.

Down through the years churches have split over such nonessentials of the faith. People sharing the same faith in Christ and the Gospel somehow draw up lists of things they think are worth fighting for. Where one draws the line becomes a matter of considerable importance.

Paul's Letter to the Romans shows how much we need to work at mutual trust, respect, and acceptance. There comes a time when, for the sake of Christ, we have to agree to disagree on matters that are peripheral to the faith.

Introduction for Youths

Topic: *Who Can Belong?*

One day a campus student minister walked down the street with a Christian student. The student looked across the way and with a scowl pointed to another student doing something he didn't think was very funny. The irritated student remarked, "He can't be one of us because of what he's doing."

In addition to the irritated student's faulty theology, he had fallen into the trap of judging who belongs and who doesn't belong to Christ. To the upset young man only those who passed moral standards acceptable to him could be approved. Sometimes we make the standards so high that very few seem eligible for membership in God's kingdom.

It's true that we should not condone activities that Scripture labels as immoral or unjust. Nevertheless, we should also be careful not to exclude others who are still learning the ways of Christian discipleship. They need our encouragement and support, not our rejection.

Concepts for Children

Topic: *Respect Others*

1. Paul warned against passing judgment on others.
2. Jesus told a story about humility.
3. Jesus warned against trying to seek out undue honor for oneself.
4. Jesus urged His followers to act humbly toward others.
5. The way of Christian love is to respect one another.
6. When it's hard to respect those who treat us unkindly, we can turn to Jesus for help.

The Lesson Commentary

I. DISPUTES OVER DIETARY REGULATIONS: ROMANS 14:1-4

A. Mutual Acceptance: vss. 1-2

Accept him whose faith is weak, without passing judgment on disputable matters. One man's faith allows him to eat everything, but another man, whose faith is weak, eats only vegetables.

In Romans 14 and 15, Paul stressed the importance of weak and strong Christians treating each other with sensitivity and love. The weak believers were Jewish converts at Rome who abided by certain Old Testament dietary restrictions and observed specific holy days. The strong were Gentile Christians whose faith was more mature and who enjoyed their spiritual freedom to a greater extent.

Tension existed in the church at Rome over what Christians were permitted to do. The weak felt compelled to observe various aspects of the Mosaic law while the strong felt no obligation to do so. As a result, the weak criticized the strong for what appeared to be morally lax behavior. In contrast, the strong looked down on the weak for their overly cautious behavior.

Paul stressed to his readers that Christians could legitimately differ over certain marginal issues and still associate with one another. Therefore, those who recognized their full liberty in Christ should not put down other believers who were more exacting in their behavior. Instead, the strong should unconditionally welcome their weaker brothers and sisters in the faith (14:1).

Paul explained that some believers were confident enough in Christ to eat anything. They realized that the truth of the Gospel liberated them from having to observe the Old Testament dietary restrictions (1 Tim. 4:3-5). There were other believers, however, who did not have the same level of assurance. They thus limited their diet to only vegetables (Rom. 14:2).

Paul knew the strong temptation we face to set people straight who do not see things the way we do. This effort comes to no good and only fuels the fires of controversy. While the subjects of dispute have changed over the centuries, the Christian principles of mutual love and respect have not. Because all believers belong to the Lord, He alone is our judge. We thus must find mutually agreeable and God-honoring ways to solve disputes among our fellow Christians.

B. Mutual Respect: vss. 3-4

The man who eats everything must not look down on him who does not, and the man who does not eat everything must not condemn the man who does, for God has accepted him. Who are you to judge someone else's servant? To his own master he stands or falls. And he will stand, for the Lord is able to make him stand.

Paul, who apparently identified himself with the strong (Rom. 15:1), told them to accept the weak and not despise them for their dietary convictions. By accepting the weaker ones the apostle meant much more than just tolerating them. He had in mind giving them a full, hearty welcome. Likewise, those whose consciences favored a restricted diet were not to condemn their fellow believers who ate anything without any qualms of conscience (14:3).

Such respect grows from the belief that God welcomes everyone into His kingdom. Regardless of what we eat, God accepts us through our faith in Christ. This simple statement once again reminds us that salvation is by grace through faith, not by keeping legalistic traditions (Eph. 2:8-9). Thus the decision whether to eat or not eat certain kinds of foods is not critical from an eternal perspective, as Jesus Himself pointed out (Mark 7:17-23).

It was clear to Paul that the believers in Rome were struggling with controversy and criticism when they should have been known for their mutual love and respect. He dealt with the problem by referring to the common slave-master relationship. They all knew about such matters, for many of the believers in the capital city of the empire were slaves.

The point was clear that only masters had the authority to censure their servants. That right was not given to anyone else. Christ is the Lord of all believers; thus they were not supposed to go around condemning each other. At the end of the age, Jesus will not evaluate believers' actions according to their diets, but rather according to their faith and obedience. And in the final analysis, Christ accepts and approves all believers, and His power will help them act as they should (Rom. 14:4). Therefore, mutual acceptance in His spiritual family is expected and required.

II. DISPUTES OVER SPECIAL DAYS: ROMANS 14:5-9

A. Observance versus Nonobservance: vss. 5-6

One man considers one day more sacred than another; another man considers every day alike. Each one should be fully convinced in his own mind. He who regards one day as special, does so to the Lord. He who eats meat, eats to the Lord, for he gives thanks to God; and he who abstains, does so to the Lord and gives thanks to God.

Another controversial issue among the believers in Rome was the observance of certain holy days, such as the Sabbath as well as times of fasting and feasting. There were some Christians who genuinely felt that one day was more special than others. In contrast, there were other believers who did not hold to such distinctions among the days of the week. Instead, they viewed every day as being equally sacred. In their minds each day was to be dedicated in wholehearted service to God (Rom. 14:5).

Paul said each group should act in accordance with its personal convictions. For example, the believers who were convinced that one day was more important than another did so to honor and serve the Lord. Likewise, Christians who were assured that it was proper to eat meat did so to glorify God, for they consumed the food with a heart of gratitude. Those who, out of personal conviction, refrained from eating meat also sought to honor God with a thankful attitude (vs. 6).

In every situation Paul wanted to see believers acting according to their consciences, but their honest convictions were not to be made into rules for the church. It's true that some issues are central to the faith and worth fighting for with integrity, but many other issues are based on individual preferences and should not be mandated. The underlying principle could be expressed in this way (as others have put it)—in essentials, unity; in nonessentials, liberty; and in everything, love.

B. Christ's Lordship: vss. 7-9

For none of us lives to himself alone and none of us dies to himself alone. If we live, we live to the Lord; and if we die, we die to the Lord. So, whether we live or die, we belong to the Lord. For this very reason, Christ died and returned to life so that he might be the Lord of both the dead and the living.

When people trust in Christ, they experience freedom in three primary areas. First, they are freed from the condemnation of the law. Being justified by faith, they are no longer under God's law; rather, they are under His grace (Rom. 6:14). Second, believers have been freed from the dominion of sin (John 8:34-36). They now desire to serve God and live in an upright manner. Third, believers have been freed from worldly superstitions and demonic doctrines. They have embraced the truth of the Gospel and allow it to be the rule and guide of their life (2 Tim. 3:14-17).

In light of the above, it's clear that issues of whether to eat certain foods or observe certain holy days were not worth battling over. Perhaps that's why Paul sought to shift the argument away from diets and days and remind his fellow believers that they all belonged to God. The apostle explained that Christians did not live only for themselves. Likewise, they did not die with only themselves in mind (Rom. 14:7). God created them, and thus their foremost goal was to please Him in everything they did.

Despite the differences that existed among the groups of believers in Rome, they jointly were to honor and serve the Lord both in life and death. Regardless of whether they lived or died, Jesus' disciples belonged to Him and thus existed to do His will (vs. 8). Even beyond the grave, believers would eternally live to worship and praise God. This means that Christ was to occupy the place of preeminence in the church for time and eternity (Eph. 1:22-23).

The supreme lordship of Christ was a key issue for Paul. He stated that Jesus died and rose again from the dead so that He might reign supreme over all people, regardless of whether they lived or died (Rom. 14:9). As the beginning and end of all things (Rev. 1:8), Christ is the absolute ruler of time, history, and people.

Clearly, then, petty arguments only get us to think about ourselves and our personal agendas. Since we all belong to the Lord, we must build each other up as members of His glorious body.

III. ACCOUNTABILITY TO GOD: ROMANS 14:10-13

A. God's Evaluation of Believers: vss. 10-12

You, then, why do you judge your brother? Or why do you look down on your brother? For we will all stand before God's judgment seat. It is written: "'As surely as I live,' says the Lord, 'every knee will bow before me; every tongue will confess to God.'" So then, each of us will give an account of himself to God.

Apparently some believers were making the church into a courtroom. People were on trial, as it were, and others in the church were judging them. Paul got to the heart of the matter by asking the weak Christians of Rome why they censured their stronger associates in the faith. Similarly, the apostle wanted to know why the strong Christians depreciated others who scrupulously observed certain requirements of the law (Rom. 14:10).

Both types of behavior were unacceptable because every Christian would one day stand before God's judgment seat. When Christ returned, He would evaluate all that believers did. Only that which passed the test of His penetrating scrutiny would yield eternal rewards. Of course, a true believer's salvation in Christ was not jeopardized in any way (1 Cor. 3:10-15; 2 Cor. 5:10).

In Romans 14:11, Paul quoted from Isaiah 45:23 to support his point. The Lord solemnly vowed that everyone would bow before Him in submission and praise His name. (That this verse about God is cited in reference to Christ is a strong proof of His deity.) Thus, every person would one day give an account to God for their actions (Rom. 14:12). Believers, therefore, had no business trying to usurp God's authority as judge (Jas. 4:12).

Paul, of course, would affirm that the church must be uncompromising in its stand against activities that are expressly forbidden in Scripture (such as murder, theft, and sexual immorality). Many times, however, Christians base their moral judgments on opinion, personal preferences, or cultural bias rather than the Bible. This, in turn, leads to the creation of additional rules and regulations that supposedly have equal standing with God's Word.

Paul wanted to cleanse the church of backbiting, gossip, and cliques. He wanted to see a congregation where people could worship in harmony and fellowship. This was possible when Jesus was the central focus, not differences of opinion over irrelevant matters.

B. Believers' Mutual Concern: vs. 13

Therefore let us stop passing judgment on one another. Instead, make up your mind not to put any stumbling block or obstacle in your brother's way.

Paul urged his fellow believers in Rome to stop condemning one another (Rom. 14:13). What each Christian did was the more important issue. That's why Paul told his readers to live in such a way that they would not be putting an obstacle in the path of another believer. In other words, they were not to upset or impede the faith of another believer by their actions. Instead, Christians were to act in love (vs. 15).

Paul was not saying that sin is a negotiable matter. There are certain actions that Scripture declares to be wrong. Other practices, however, are not specifically condemned, and Christians will have valid differences of opinion regarding them. In these instances, believers should respect the convictions of their fellow Christians on disputable matters.

Discussion Questions

1. What did Paul mean by the phrase "him whose faith is weak" (Rom. 14:1)?
2. What were the major controversies that Paul was trying to resolve among the believers in Rome?
3. Why do you think Paul thought it was important to emphasize the lordship of Christ?
4. When will believers give an account of themselves to God?
5. How does the fact that we all belong to the Lord help us to stifle the temptation to judge our fellow believers?

Contemporary Application

Knowing theological facts is important, but fellowship and love are also critical to the life of the church. Being right should not be cause for tearing down relationships. When we feel we are right about an issue, we must see our rights as responsibilities. God expects more from those who have been entrusted with more. Our Christian freedom must be exercised responsibly.

If we truly love God, we will show it by the way we relate to others. Moreover, to love, we need God's love in our hearts. Because weak Christians are vulnerable to temptation, love compels us not to put them in harm's way by what we do. This does not mean that weak Christians are to be pampered. Those who are easily offended need not remain in their immature condition. To edify them means to build them up, to help them handle bigger things. Patience and gentle teaching can help baby Christians to grow.

Christians can be trained to outgrow their immature thinking as they gain a fuller understanding of the truths of God's Word and experience God's grace daily. As they deepen their relationship with Christ through prayer, they will grasp more of the significance of their own freedom in Christ. Moreover, if a believer is to move from being weak to being strong, he or she will need the love and support of the rest of the church. By responding with love, we'll be careful not to flaunt our freedom before weak believers. When we change our behavior, we'll show we're concerned for others.

255

Faith and Works

DEVOTIONAL READING

Acts 13:26-39

DAILY BIBLE READINGS

Monday May 6
1 Corinthians 10:14-22 One Body, One Bread

Tuesday May 7
Galatians 3:1-9 The Gentiles Are Justified through Faith

Wednesday May 8
Galatians 3:10-18 Receive the Promise through Faith

Thursday May 9
Galatians 3:19-29 Heirs according to the Promise

Friday May 10
Galatians 4:1-7 No Longer Slaves, but Heirs

Saturday May 11
Galatians 4:8-20 Do Not Turn Back

Sunday May 12
Galatians 4:21—5:1 Freedom in Christ

Scripture

Background Scripture: *Galatians 1—2*

Scripture Lesson: *Galatians 1:1-2, 6-9; 2:15-21*

Key Verse: *"We, too, have put our faith in Christ Jesus that we may be justified by faith in Christ and not by observing the law."* Galatians 2:16.

Scripture Lesson for Children: *Galatians 1:1; 2:11-14, 20*

Key Verse for Children: *"I live by faith in the Son of God, who loved me and gave himself for me."* Galatians 2:20.

Lesson Aim

To appreciate our call to faith and freedom in Christ.

Lesson Setting

Time: *Either A.D. 48–49 (the South Galatian theory) or A.D. 53–57 (the North Galatian theory)*

Place: *Either the churches in a geographic area called Galatia that was located in central Asia Minor (now Turkey; the North Galatian theory) or the churches in the southern part of the Roman province of Galatia (the South Galatian theory)*

Lesson Outline

Faith and Works

   I. Perverting the Gospel: Galatians 1:1-2, 6-9
      A. *Paul's Pedigree: vss. 1-2*
      B. *Paul's Charge: vss. 6-7*
      C. *Paul's Judgment: vss. 8-9*
  II. Preserving the Gospel: Galatians 2:15-21
      A. *Justification by Faith: vss. 15-16*
      B. *The End of the Law: vss. 17-19*
      C. *Living by Faith: vss. 20-21*

Introduction for Adults

Topic: *Living by the Truth*

Jesus told His disciples that they were truly His followers if they obeyed His teachings. And as they sought to serve God, Jesus' perfect truth would free them to be all that God meant them to be (John 8:31-32). Additionally, Christ would free them from the consequences of sin, from self-deception, and from deception by Satan.

This does not mean that Jesus gives us the freedom to do what we want (for example, wallow in iniquity). Rather, Christ has freed us to love and serve God and His people. This is a lofty goal, one that is impossible to achieve on our own. Because all forms of do-it-yourself religion are bound to fail, we need to rely on Christ and the truths that He taught to live in a way that is pleasing to God.

A young man told his counselor that he was sure God would accept him if he were 99 percent pure and good. He wasn't 99 percent virtuous and he knew it. But he expressed the futile hopes of many people. With God, 99 percent righteousness is not good enough. In fact, only Jesus is perfectly good. He alone is the way to God, the truth about God, and the life of God (John 14:6).

Introduction for Youths

Topic: *The Only Way to Go*

All of us function best under a set of rules. It's true that some children entering school for the first time find it hard to live by the rules, but they eventually learn to adjust their behavior. This is important, for society would dissolve into chaos without rules and laws.

God has given us the best rules by which to live. And when we obey His rules, we find that the world runs smoother and that we are happier and more satisfied. Nevertheless, no matter how many rules we seek to keep, we cannot become good enough to merit God's love and acceptance. Scripture reveals that there is only one answer for us—salvation by faith. Thank God for the gift of life through faith in His Son. It is the only way to go!

Concepts for Children

Topic: *Living What We Believe*

1. Paul said that he was a Christian leader and that he did what Jesus wanted.
2. While Peter was in a city called Antioch, he decided to not eat with people who weren't like him.
3. Paul said that Peter was not living according to the Gospel, which says that Jesus died for all people.
4. Paul said that all Christians should live by faith in Jesus, who loved them so much that He gave His life for them.
5. God wants us to show His love to other people and to accept them just as they are.

The Lesson Commentary

I. PERVERTING THE GOSPEL: GALATIANS 1:1-2, 6-9

A. Paul's Pedigree: vss. 1-2

Paul, an apostle—sent not from men nor by man, but by Jesus Christ and God the Father, who raised him from the dead—and all the brothers with me, To the churches in Galatia.

Paul apparently had founded the churches in Galatia to which he wrote. But during his absence from the Galatians, some Jews who professed to be Christians had come among them and had begun calling into question Paul's authority and began spreading false doctrine. Today these false teachers are called Judaizers [JOO-dee-eye-zuhrs].

From what we can surmise, the legalists taught that faith in Christ is not adequate for acceptance by God. Obedience to the Old Testament law, or at least to parts of it, is also necessary. So they were trying to enforce the law among the Gentile Galatians. The legalists, however, drew a fierce reaction from Paul. In his mind, to make the law mandatory for salvation is, in effect, to nullify the Gospel. Salvation is by grace, apart from the works of the law. Christians are not bound by the law but are free in Christ.

The Letter to the Galatians, then, is a ringing declaration of spiritual liberty. Christians are free from seeking righteousness in rules or religious practices. We are also free from having to do as our sinful nature dictates. Because we live by the Spirit through faith in Christ, we are free to serve and be served in love.

Paul started his letter by following the traditional pattern of his day: he named himself (1:1), he named his readers (vs. 2), and he pronounced a blessing upon them (vs. 3). We can tell from what Paul wrote that he was pained to learn that many people who had come to faith through his ministry were now doubting his authority as an apostle. He knew that if his authority was not respected, his ministry could not be effective. Thus Paul declared himself an apostle, or ambassador, sent by God.

Paul revealed that he had been appointed an apostle neither by "men" (vs. 1, meaning a group of church leaders, such as those in Jerusalem) nor by "man" (meaning any single church leader, such as James, Peter, or John). Instead, Paul had been appointed an apostle by God the Father and God the Son. Paul mentioned the Resurrection not just because it showed the link between the Father and the Son, but also because it showed the link between Christ and Paul. The risen Lord had appeared to Paul on the road to Damascus, and Paul considered his vision of the resurrected Savior to be a factor qualifying him for apostleship.

Paul's greeting to the Galatians came not only from himself, but also from some "brothers" (vs. 2). These may have been the apostle's co-workers and the members of the church with whom he happened to be ministering at the time he wrote the Letter to the Galatians. It's likely that these people had little or nothing to do with the letter's contents. Yet by mentioning others, Paul implied that they stood behind him and the counsel he was going to give to the Galatians.

B. Paul's Charge: vss. 6-7

I am astonished that you are so quickly deserting the one who called you by the grace of Christ and are turning to a different gospel—which is really no gospel at all. Evidently some people are throwing you into confusion and are trying to pervert the gospel of Christ.

In the opening of his letter, Paul hinted at his concerns about the Galatians. Now he got to the point. He admitted to being "astonished" (Gal. 1:6) that the Galatians were allowing themselves to fall into the Judaizers' errors. The apostle hadn't expected it of them. They had been saved only a few months or years before, and their experience of grace was still fresh. And now, already, they were allowing themselves to be bound by the law.

From other New Testament books we know that Paul could be tolerant about matters of secondary importance (Acts 21:20-26). But this was not such a matter. The teaching that the Galatians had accepted was nothing less than "a different gospel" (Gal. 1:6), which was really "no gospel" (vs. 7). In other words, this teaching was a perversion of the true Gospel. By accepting this teaching, the Galatians were "deserting" (vs. 6) God, who had called them to belief.

Paul had learned from personal experience the truth that salvation comes by grace through faith alone, apart from works of the law. The Judaizers, by saying that faith was not enough, were actually contradicting the Gospel they claimed to believe. False gospels always mix truth with error. This makes them seem safe, but even partial error can be deadly. Mature and discerning Christians need to confront each error and purge the church of it.

C. Paul's Judgment: vss. 8-9

But even if we or an angel from heaven should preach a gospel other than the one we preached to you, let him be eternally condemned! As we have already said, so now I say again: If anybody is preaching to you a gospel other than what you accepted, let him be eternally condemned!

Paul did not mince any words when he declared his disgust with those who misrepresented the Good News and troubled God's people. The apostle prayed that the Lord would eternally condemn anyone who heralded an unbiblical message of salvation. The Greek word translated "condemned" (Gal. 1:8) is *anathema.* Originally this word referred to anything dedicated or consecrated to God. But eventually it came to mean something delivered over to God for destruction.

Paul felt so strongly about the matter that he repeated his terse rebuke. It was his hope that God would punish anyone who preached anything different from the Gospel the Christians at Galatia had already believed (vs. 9). The apostle was saying that those who added any additional requirements to the Good News were under the Lord's condemnation. Regardless of their credentials, they did not have the authority to twist the clear message of salvation through faith in Christ.

Paul included himself among those who had no right to preach any other Gospel. Thus no one could level the charge that Paul was merely jealous of the legalists who had won the hearts of some of the Galatians. Paul was not motivated by jealously when he called for exclusive acceptance of the Gospel that he preached; rather, it was because the Good News made no provision for any other message.

II. PRESERVING THE GOSPEL: GALATIANS 2:15-21

A. Justification by Faith: vss. 15-16

"We who are Jews by birth and not 'Gentile sinners' know that a man is not justified by observing the law, but by faith in Jesus Christ. So we, too, have put our faith in Christ Jesus that we may be justified by faith in Christ and not by observing the law, because by observing the law no one will be justified."

In Galatians 1:11-24, Paul related that the message of salvation he proclaimed came from the Lord. Then in 2:1-10, Paul recounted how the other apostles had accepted him. Verses 11-13 introduce a later episode involving Peter in the church at Syrian Antioch. Paul charged Peter with hypocrisy for withdrawing from the Gentile converts, perhaps as a result of receiving criticism from the Jewish legalists. Paul accused Peter of forcing Jewish laws on the Gentile converts (vs. 14).

Peter was not alone in hypocrisy. The other Jewish Christians in the Antioch church, except Paul, were hypocrites in their actions. So Paul broadened his speech to address all those who were "Jews by birth" (vs. 15) and not "Gentile sinners." The second phrase was the way Jews slurringly referred to non-Jews.

For centuries legalistic Jews had believed they could make themselves acceptable to God by obeying the law. But they were mistaken. No one can perfectly keep the law, so no one can be justified by it. In fact, that was never the law's purpose. The Jewish Christians at Antioch had learned this lesson. In addition, they had learned that sinners can be declared righteous only through faith in Christ. Paul reminded them of these truths (vs. 16). The implication is clear. It was not just Gentiles who needed Christ; Jews needed Him, too.

It would be wrong to conclude that Paul was condemning God's laws. In fact, he wrote in Romans 7:12 that God's law was holy, righteous, and good. The apostle was deploring the improper application of the law. It would also be wrong to conclude that justification is based on a believer's faith. Paul was saying that faith is the means through which believers receive God's grace.

B. The End of the Law: vss. 17-19

"If, while we seek to be justified in Christ, it becomes evident that we ourselves are sinners, does that mean that Christ promotes sin? Absolutely not! If I rebuild what I destroyed, I prove that I am a lawbreaker. For through the law I died to the law so that I might live for God."

Paul's teaching that we are justified by faith, and not by works, led some critics to charge that he was encouraging Jews to become sinners (namely, breakers of the law). For example, when Paul encouraged Jewish believers to have fellowship with Gentile believers, he was said to be going against Jewish laws.

Paul was concerned, because at first glance one might conclude that his teaching promoted sin (Gal. 2:17). The critics also claimed that Paul's teaching not only degraded the value of the law but also disgraced Christ. "Absolutely not!" was Paul's response. Jesus did not further any Jewish believer's sinning simply because the new convert abandoned law-keeping as the way to salvation.

For Christians to revert to the Jewish law is really to break the law (vs. 18). Paul may have been thinking of Peter's attempt to rebuild the wall between Jew and Gentile that had been torn down by the Gospel. Peter's efforts reinstated the condemnation of the law. Paul argued that the lawbreaker was not the one who looked to Christ for justification. Instead, it was the one who looked to the law for justification.

Paul declared that he had stopped living for the law, for the law had put him to death. Through the law, he realized how spiritually dead he was and how much he needed Christ. When Paul trusted in Christ for salvation, he was identified with His death, burial, and resurrection. Through spiritual union with Christ, Paul died to the law so that he could live for God (vs. 19).

C. Living by Faith: vss. 20-21

"I have been crucified with Christ and I no longer live, but Christ lives in me. The life I live in the body, I live by faith in the Son of God, who loved me and gave himself for me. I do not set aside the grace of God, for if righteousness could be gained through the law, Christ died for nothing!"

God established the Mosaic law to show people their need for a fuller relationship with Him—a relationship made available through faith in Christ. In a sense, we have been nailed to the cross with Christ and have spiritually died there with Him. We also have been united with Him in His resurrection. Now that we have been saved, Jesus lives within us and we look to Him for direction in life (Gal. 2:20).

Paul was insisting that a person who trusted in Christ was changed. To think about going back to the former way of life was absurd to one who had become a new creation. Although the possibility of sinning remained, Christ gave the believer the power to resist the temptation to sin, something the law could never do.

Apparently the Judaizers claimed that Paul nullified God's grace in giving Israel the law when the apostle taught that Gentiles did not have to obey all the law. Far from it, said Paul. He did not set aside the grace of God. Instead, he established God's grace by teaching that justification and right behavior are possible through Christ rather than through the law (vs. 21).

In Paul's speech to the mistaken Jewish believers, we see the centrality of Christ in the apostle's thought and life. And in this way Paul becomes a good model for us. Do we trust in anything other than Christ to make ourselves pleasing to God? At every point of decision, do we ask ourselves what Christ would have us do?

Discussion Questions

1. Why was it important for Paul to emphasize the uniqueness and integrity of his apostolic commission?
2. How can the grace and peace of God transform our lives?

3. Why do you think some of the Galatians abandoned the true Gospel for a false one?

4. If good works cannot justify people, why do some continue to spurn the justification that Christ offers?

5. Why did Paul stress that he had died with Christ?

6. What does it mean to be justified by faith and to live by faith?

Contemporary Application

Christians who are knowledgeable about the modern religious scene know that teachers with seemingly new spiritual insights combine ideas that sound reasonable with a smattering of Bible verses. These insights are not really new but actually echo ancient lies. When skilled speakers preach these lies through the modern electronic and print media, these ideas can come across sounding fresh and exciting.

It's even more tragic when a gifted speaker with questionable motives and dubious biblical views wins a following and gradually substitutes his or her own authority for that of Scripture. That's how most religious cults gain a toehold in society. Thus, Christians need to evaluate the teaching they hear, making certain that it is grounded in God's Word and honors Christ.

It is not enough to disregard false teachers, but Christians should also listen to godly ones. These are believers who reject the notion of being saved by good works and affirm the truth of being declared righteous through faith in Christ. In addition to remaining true to the Gospel, they teach Jesus' followers how to remain faithful to God, how to be more like Christ, and how to serve Him. Good teachers will help believers comprehend these things about God. That's why, in today's supermarket of religious ideas, Christians should beware. They should accept only what conforms to the Gospel of Christ.

Heirs with Christ

Scripture

Background Scripture: *Galatians 3—4*
Scripture Lesson: *Galatians 3:6-9, 23—4:7*
Key Verse: *You are all sons of God through faith in Christ Jesus.* Galatians 3:26.
Scripture Lesson for Children: *Galatians 3:25-29; John 4:3-9, 27-30*

Lesson Aim

To understand that God's provision of His blessings are linked to faith in Christ, not keeping the Mosaic law.

Lesson Setting

Time: *Either* A.D. *48—49 (the South Galatian theory) or* A.D. *53—57 (the North Galatian theory)*
Place: *Either the churches in a geographic area called Galatia that was located in central Asia Minor (now Turkey; the North Galatian theory) or the churches in the southern part of the Roman province of Galatia (the South Galatian theory)*

Lesson Outline

Heirs with Christ

   I. The Blessing of Abraham: Galatians 3:6-9
      A. *Righteousness by Faith: vss. 6-7*
      B. *Worldwide Blessing through Abraham: vss. 8-9*
  II. The Intent of the Law: Galatians 3:23-29
      A. *Guardianship under the Law: vss. 23-25*
      B. *Union with Christ: vss. 26-29*
 III. The Inheritance of Believers: Galatians 4:1-7
      A. *The Plight of Those under the Law: vss. 1-3*
      B. *The Privileges of Those in Christ: vss. 4-7*

Introduction for Adults

Topic: *God's Blended Family*

"I just don't know who I am anymore," the recently widowed woman said. "Before Bill died, my identity revolved around him. Even in church, I felt my identity was linked with his." Many people struggle with feelings like this. Some people cover up their fears with hard work, some with harmful indulgences, and others with money and possessions. None of these options, however, provide a satisfying solution.

The wonderful truth about the Gospel is that Jesus frees us from the shackles of doubt and discouragement and replaces these with joy and hope. We also have the confidence of knowing that we are complete in Christ. For instance, we are full members of His spiritual family. This enables us to enjoy all the rights and privileges associated with being children of God. These truths apply to every believer, regardless of our race, gender, or socio-economic status. How wonderful it is to be in God's blended family!

Introduction for Youths

Topic: *God's Blended Family*

More and more children live in blended families, mostly because of marital breakups. Some youth adjust well, but many do not. The strugglers tend to develop poor self-images, and they often blame themselves for what happened to their parents. A few even try to commit suicide as a way out of their problems.

The Gospel offers hurting people opportunities to make fresh starts. No matter how deep the wounds might be, the Spirit can heal us. The way to healing begins with understanding what God has done for us in Christ. Others may fail or disappointment us, but not Jesus. He remains faithful through the worst that life has to offer.

We gain peace and self-confidence when we learn that God is a loving Father. He knows all our needs and He has met them fully in His Son. We can know God intimately because of the saving work of Christ.

Concepts for Children

Topic: *Live as God's Children*

1. When we believe in Jesus, we become part of God's family.
2. As Jesus and His followers traveled through a place called Samaria [suh-MAIR-ee-yuh], Jesus stopped at a well to rest.
3. A woman from that area was surprised when Jesus asked her for a drink of water (because their people didn't like each other).
4. After the woman and Jesus had talked for a while, the woman quickly went back to her village to tell others about Him.
5. Many of the people in the village came out to meet and hear Jesus.
6. God wants us to tell others—even if they are different from us—about Jesus and His love for them.

The Lesson Commentary

I.   THE BLESSING OF ABRAHAM: GALATIANS 3:6-9

A.   Righteousness by Faith: vss. 6-7

Consider Abraham: "He believed God, and it was credited to him as righteousness." Understand, then, that those who believe are children of Abraham.

At this point in his letter, Paul began a more systematic argument against the Judaizers. Carefully, line by line, he presented reasons and proofs why the Galatians should not depend upon the law to earn God's favor (chapters 3—4). To set the stage for his argument, Paul asked the Galatian believers a series of pointed questions (3:1-5). Then, after calling on the Galatians to remember their own experiences with Christ, Paul proceeded to strengthen his argument for the superiority of grace over the law by appealing to Scripture (vss. 6-14).

Paul's first scriptural teachings were grouped around the figure of Abraham. The Judaizers had evidently taught the Galatians that male Gentile believers needed to be circumcised, as Abraham had been. Supposedly the absence of circumcision meant one was not part of the community of faith and thus could not participate in God's blessings on Abraham.

In discussing Abraham, Paul may have used the same Bible passages the Judaizers had used, only interpreting them differently. First the apostle quoted Genesis 15:6, "He believed God, and it was credited to him as righteousness" (Gal. 3:6). Though Abraham and his wife were childless and past the age of having children, Abraham believed God's promise that he would have a son and, through the son, many descendants. God accepted Abraham's faith and declared that he was in a right relationship with Him because of it.

In a sense, Paul said, all who believe are children of Abraham (vs. 7). Even Gentiles—who are neither physically descended from the patriarch nor necessarily circumcised—can become spiritual children of Abraham through faith in Christ. Abraham's justification by faith is an example for us. We believe God's promise concerning Christ, and God credits His righteousness to us by faith.

Evidently some of the legalists claimed that Paul's emphasis on grace undercut the covenant God had made with Abraham. By referring to Genesis 15:6, the apostle set the record straight. It did not matter whether someone was physically descended from Abraham. The true children of the patriarch have a faith like his. Only those who trust in the Lord, as Abraham did, share in God's blessings upon him.

Every person must make the same choice Abraham did. We receive righteousness as a gift. There is nothing we can do to earn it. Of course, exercising faith implies that we are guilty of disobeying God and in need His forgiveness. Once we appreciate the consequences of our sins, we understand why we need God's righteousness in Christ.

B. Worldwide Blessing through Abraham: vss. 8-9

The Scripture foresaw that God would justify the Gentiles by faith, and announced the gospel in advance to Abraham: "All nations will be blessed through you." So those who have faith are blessed along with Abraham, the man of faith.

The inclusion of Gentiles in Abraham's family was part of God's plan from the beginning. Paul personified the Scripture, saying it foresaw God's justification of Gentiles and declared the Gospel to Abraham (Gal. 3:8). This means that God, represented by His Word, proclaimed the Gospel of grace for Gentiles even as early as Abraham's day. This is especially true when God told Abraham, "All nations will be blessed through you" (compare Gen. 12:3; 18:18; 22:18).

Christ is a descendant of Abraham. Through Jesus, God's grace is available to people of all nations. Thus, through Christ, the blessings the Lord promised to Abraham are distributed worldwide in the form of salvation and life in the Spirit (Gal. 3:9). In light of this truth, it's tragic that many people mistakenly view the Old Testament as having little more than historical value for Christians. We should be thrilled to realize that many promises of the Old Testament are applicable to believers of all time.

II.   THE INTENT OF THE LAW: GALATIANS 3:23-29

A. Guardianship under the Law: vss. 23-25

Before this faith came, we were held prisoners by the law, locked up until faith should be revealed. So the law was put in charge to lead us to Christ that we might be justified by faith. Now that faith has come, we are no longer under the supervision of the law.

In light of what Paul said in Galatians 3:10-18, the apostle asked and answered two questions that might naturally have arisen in his readers' minds. The first question is this: "What, then, was the purpose of the law?" (vs. 19). To summarize Paul's answer, God added the law to bring about a knowledge of sin and also to place all humanity under its curse. Thus the law prepared people for faith in Christ, who was the fulfillment of God's promises in Scripture (vs. 22).

The second question is this: "Is the law, therefore, opposed to the promises of God?" (vs. 21). The answer was *no*, though they did operate on different levels. The law had been practiced over a period of centuries, yet it had made no one righteous. Since only God's grace could do that, Paul concluded that the law could not produce righteousness.

Wealthy families in the Roman world often would have a servant who supervised the conduct of the family's sons. Paul compared the law to this servant. In other words, the law controlled us and kept us under its power until the time when we would have faith in Christ (vs. 23). Paul had already noted that all are prisoners of sin (vs. 22). Being a prisoner of the law is not much different, except that the law reveals sin in us and provokes it to action.

Before the time of Christ's coming, the law was our tutor "to lead us to Christ" (vs. 24). In Bible times, a tutor was a slave who trained his master's children. For example, the tutor might be responsible for pointing out and punishing improper behavior. The law functioned as a tutor by revealing sin and condemning it.

Now that God has established faith in Christ as the way to be saved or justified, people no longer need to be under the guardianship of the law (vs. 25). Just as a child's guardian is no longer needed when the child grows up and becomes an adult, so the law was superseded when the Gospel came. Thus the law prepared people for faith in Christ, who was the fulfillment of God's promises to Abraham.

B. Union with Christ: vss. 26-29

You are all sons of God through faith in Christ Jesus, for all of you who were baptized into Christ have clothed yourselves with Christ. There is neither Jew nor Greek, slave nor free, male nor female, for you are all one in Christ Jesus. If you belong to Christ, then you are Abraham's seed, and heirs according to the promise.

Jewish Christians could have been said to have grown up (in terms of their relationship to the law) and reached spiritual adulthood (in terms of their relationship to the Gospel). Although the Gentile believers in Galatia had not been raised according to the law, they had become spiritual adults too. Their faith in Christ demonstrated their spiritual adulthood.

To emphasize this truth, Paul called the Galatians "sons of God" (Gal. 3:26). The Greek word rendered "sons" refers to those who have reached adulthood. The point Paul was making is that God's children reach adulthood, not by keeping the law, but by trusting in Christ. Faith effects the passage from life under the law, which condemns all sinners, to life under God's grace, which declares as righteous those who believe in Christ.

Paul described salvation not only as becoming adults in God's family but also as being "baptized into Christ" (vs. 27) and "clothed . . . with Christ." Use of the word "baptized," of course, reminded the Galatians of their baptismal ceremonies. Thus the phrase "baptized into Christ" revealed their close identification with and participation in Christ. Furthermore, the Galatian believers wore Christ like they wore clothing. In other words, they took on His righteousness by faith.

For believers to realize that they have entered this unique relationship with Christ upon their conversion is both wonderful and awesome. To be one with Jesus by the grace of God is an experience that defies expression and description. But to realize the responsibility this places upon us as believers is sobering indeed.

Christ's coming into the world made it possible for people to become children of God. And through faith, they are baptized into and clothed with Christ. Jesus' coming also broke down worldly divisions, such as those based on distinctions of race, social status, and gender (vs. 28). This means that such distinctions have no bearing on who can become a follower of Christ. It also means that all people in society should be seen as persons of worth.

The three social distinctions Paul mentioned were significant ones in his day. Prejudice existed between Jews and non-Jews over religious, political, and cultural issues. Hundreds of thousands of people in the Roman Empire were enslaved by others. Women had limited legal rights and were often looked down upon by men. Thankfully through the valid influence of Christian principles, many of these social divisions have been abolished.

After describing Christians as children of God baptized into and clothed with Christ, Paul repeated his teaching that believers are Abraham's children and heirs (vs. 29). The law of Moses did not make people children of God and Abraham's heirs. That happens by a promise fulfilled in Christ. It also happens by grace through faith in Christ.

III. The Inheritance of Believers: Galatians 4:1-7

A. The Plight of Those under the Law: vss. 1-3

What I am saying is that as long as the heir is a child, he is no different from a slave, although he owns the whole estate. He is subject to guardians and trustees until the time set by his father. So also, when we were children, we were in slavery under the basic principles of the world.

In order to drive home his point concerning the status of the believer in Christ, Paul used one more illustration based on the customs of his day. The apostle established a hypothetical situation in which a father apparently had died, leaving behind a young son, a minor, as the heir of his father's estate. The estate actually belonged to the child, but he could not control it until he reached the age specified by the father in the trust (Gal. 4:1).

The child was subject to "guardians and trustees" (vs. 2), or tutors and managers, who were in complete control of the child. As far as having freedom to act and decide on his own, the child was no different from a slave. Paul took the child's "slavery" (so to speak) as symbolic of our spiritual slavery before coming to faith in Christ. We were enslaved to the "basic principles of the world" (vs. 3).

Much debate has centered on what Paul meant here. To list just three suggestions by Bible scholars, Paul may have been referring to the law, to angels and demons, or to the superstitions of pagan religions. Whatever the apostle meant by this, he was underscoring the enslaved status of a person before receiving the Gospel of grace concerning Christ.

B. The Privileges of Those in Christ: vss. 4-7

But when the time had fully come, God sent his Son, born of a woman, born under law, to redeem those under law, that we might receive the full rights of sons. Because you are sons, God sent the Spirit of his Son into our hearts, the Spirit who calls out, "Abba, Father." So you are no longer a slave, but a son; and since you are a son, God has made you also an heir.

Onto the dark and dreary scene of slavery, Paul shone the glorious light of freedom in Christ. With great care, Paul gave his statement about Jesus' coming (Gal. 4:4). In God's exercise of His will, He chose the moment for His Son's birth. It was the climax toward which the divine plan had been moving throughout the ages. All that happened in the coming of Christ, in His earthly ministry, and in His death was under the most precise scrutiny of the Father.

Paul affirmed Jesus' virgin birth ("born of a woman," not of man) and His obedience to the law ("born under law"). In the fullest sense of the word, God became sinless man in the person of His Son so that He might identify with us. In Christ's death on the cross, He accomplished His purpose in providing redemption for all those "under law" (vs. 5). He shared the curse of the law with all of us (3:13) and became the permanent sacrifice for our sins. The word translated "redeem" (4:5) literally refers to a ransom or payment. Jesus brought us out of our slavery.

Paul brought his earlier illustration to a climax by describing those who have received Christ as having received their full inheritance. This is more than just a legal maneuver in which repenting sinners are adopted into God's family as children. We receive "the Spirit of his Son" (vs. 6). We actually share the life of God in our daily experience.

This new relationship revolutionizes our prayer lives. We approach the Father, not as slaves—apologetic and fearful. Rather, we who have experienced this new freedom in Christ come as children of the King. "Abba, Father" is an address of love and intimacy reserved for children who are fully aware of their standing with their father.

Verse 7 sums up Paul's argument. The Galatians were no longer slaves to the basic principles of the world, but now were children of God and heirs of God. The same is true of all believers. We are entitled to all the benefits and privileges of being spiritual members of God's family. Because God loves us as His children, He will give us all good things.

Discussion Questions

1. Why did Paul stress that faith was an essential characteristic of being "children of Abraham" (Gal. 3:7)?
2. In what sense were we "held prisoners by the law" (vs. 23)?
3. How can we become "sons of God" (vs. 26)?
4. What does it mean to be an heir of God (4:7)?
5. What kind of spiritual slavery binds people today? How can they be freed?

Contemporary Application

For many people, winning the lottery is the best thing they can think of that could happen to them. If not that, then it would be inheriting lots of money from a parent or relative. Sadly, though, these dreams are a kind of slavery, for they keep us from facing reality. They also keep us from enjoying the fullness of God's blessings in Christ.

The good news is that, through faith in Christ, we can enter God's family and enjoy our eternal inheritance. Jesus offers us heavenly riches we could never earn and can't possibly live without. As followers of Christ, we should encourage the lost to focus on where their true riches lie. They need to know that Christ offers them not only freedom from sin, but also the privileges of heaven.

Called to Freedom

DEVOTIONAL READING

1 John 2:7-17

DAILY BIBLE READINGS

Monday May 20
Ephesians 3:1-13 The Mystery Proclaimed by the Spirit

Tuesday May 21
Ephesians 3:14-21 Be Filled with the Fullness of God

Wednesday May 22
Ephesians 4:1-13 One Body and One Spirit

Thursday May 23
2 Corinthians 5:1-10 Longing for Our Heavenly Dwelling

Friday May 24
2 Corinthians 6:1-13 Now Is the Acceptable Time

Saturday May 25
Galatians 5:16-26 The Fruit of the Spirit

Sunday May 26
Galatians 6 You Reap What You Sow

Scripture

Background Scripture: *Galatians 5:1-15*
Scripture Lesson: *Galatians 5:1-15*
Key Verse: *You, my brothers, were called to be free. But do not use your freedom to indulge the sinful nature; rather, serve one another in love.* Galatians 5:13.
Scripture Lesson for Children: *Galatians 5:13-15; John 13:2-9, 12-15*
Key Verse for Children: *"Love your neighbor as yourself."* Galatians 5:14.

Lesson Aim

To realize the importance of holding on to Christian liberty and using it properly.

Lesson Setting

Time: *Either A.D. 48–49 (the South Galatian theory) or A.D. 53–57 (the North Galatian theory)*
Place: *Either the churches in a geographic area called Galatia that was located in central Asia Minor (now Turkey; the North Galatian theory) or the churches in the southern part of the Roman province of Galatia (the South Galatian theory)*

Lesson Outline

Called to Freedom

  I. Refusing to Turn Back to Slavery: Galatians 5:1-6
      A. *Freedom in Christ: vs. 1*
      B. *Slavery in Legalism: vss. 2-6*
  II. Recognizing the Teachers of Truth: Galatians 5:7-12
      A. *Ignoring the Truth: vss. 7-9*
      B. *Condemning the False Teachers: vss. 10-12*
  III. Properly Using Christian Freedom: Galatians 5:13-15
      A. *Service through Love: vss. 13-14*
      B. *Destruction through Self-centeredness: vs. 15*

Introduction for Adults

Topic: *The Point of Freedom*

When Paul wrote about freedom, many of his readers were slaves. In fact, freedom in the Roman Empire was reserved for the privileged few. Within the kingdom of God, however, these restrictions need not determine our importance. All who trust in Christ can enjoy freedom of the heart, soul, and spirit. Jesus also makes available freedom from sin's guilt and power. These kinds of freedom transcend time and place and are enjoyed by countless believers today.

Contemporary people typically think of freedom and slavery in political and economic terms. If we tell them that they are in bondage, they will scoff at the idea. But ironically when something terrible happens, they claim they cannot remedy the situation because of their being in bondage to something. Only the Gospel of Christ can bring true freedom. That's why the Spirit uses the message of grace to help people understand their basic need and how to meet it. In this way they come to a true point of freedom.

Introduction for Youths

Topic: *We've Been Set Free!*

Do you remember what it was like when the school day ended? As kids we typically shouted, "We're free!" Young people today tend to feel the same way. They can't wait to be released from the routine and rules of the classroom to pursue a host of more "desirable" activities.

Our society gives many wonderful freedoms to youth. Consequently, there are many tough choices they have to make about how to spend their time and money. Such unparalleled freedom brings huge risks. They need to be careful lest they needlessly expose themselves to danger.

As responsible Christians, we should encourage our youth to be responsible in the exercise of their freedoms. They can be told that God has set wise limits on their conduct for their benefit and safety. Even the spiritual freedoms they have through faith in Christ must be used wisely. For example, God is pleased when they say *no* to sin and *yes* to virtuous living.

Concepts for Children

Topic: *Learning to Serve*

1. God wants us to serve one another in a loving and kind way.
2. After Jesus had eaten supper with His followers, He served them by washing their feet.
3. At first Peter didn't want Jesus to do this; but then after listening to Jesus' explanation, Peter went along with the idea.
4. Jesus told His followers that He had given them an example about serving one another.
5. As Jesus' followers, we should be willing to serve others, especially by helping those in need.

The Lesson Commentary

I. REFUSING TO TURN BACK TO SLAVERY: GALATIANS 5:1-6

A. Freedom in Christ: vs. 1

It is for freedom that Christ has set us free. Stand firm, then, and do not let yourselves be burdened again by a yoke of slavery.

Thus far in Paul's Letter to the Galatians, he defended grace on personal and theological grounds. In the remainder of the letter his emphasis falls on the practical implications of the Gospel. For instance, Paul began Galatians 5 with a powerful pronouncement of liberty: "Christ has set us free" (vs. 1). The apostle meant by this that the Savior purchased our freedom from sin and condemnation when He died on the cross. His intent was not that we would allow ourselves to become enslaved again. Rather, He liberated us so that we would remain permanently free.

With spiritual liberty comes personal responsibility. While the Galatians could not have set themselves free (Christ did that for them), Paul said they had the duty to resist being enslaved again. The Judaizers were trying to place on their shoulders the yoke of obedience to the law. But Christians should stand firm as free people, and not allow themselves to be weighed down under legalistic burdens, like oxen.

Bible students often wonder why Paul called his readers' subjection to the law being burdened "again." Perhaps the apostle had in mind their former bondage to the "basic principles of the world" (4:3). In Paul's mind, unbelieving Jews and Gentiles were all under the domination of legalistic ways of thinking and acting. Thus for former pagans to turn from Christianity to a works-based righteousness was, in effect, to become enslaved once again.

B. Slavery in Legalism: vss. 2-6

Mark my words! I, Paul, tell you that if you let yourselves be circumcised, Christ will be of no value to you at all. Again I declare to every man who lets himself be circumcised that he is obligated to obey the whole law. You who are trying to be justified by law have been alienated from Christ; you have fallen away from grace. But by faith we eagerly await through the Spirit the righteousness for which we hope. For in Christ Jesus neither circumcision nor uncircumcision has any value. The only thing that counts is faith expressing itself through love.

Circumcision figures predominantly in Galatians 5:2-6. God instituted this practice as a sign of the covenant between Him and Abraham's descendants. Circumcision was intended to mark their entry into the community of faith in Lord. In ancient Israel circumcision was done on the eighth day after the son's birth, usually by the father. Several non-Jewish groups also practiced the rite. Later, rabbis performed the ceremony for the Jews. Modern medicine has confirmed that the eighth day is the optimum time for this procedure.

Over time, some Jews began to see circumcision, not as a *sign of* a relationship with God, but rather as the *means to* a relationship with Him. This overvaluation of circumcision carried over into the early church. Paul's opinion was that, while Jews were free to decide whether to circumcise themselves and their sons, no one should try to force Gentile Christians to be circumcised.

Although the Galatians had begun observing the Jewish religious holidays and perhaps had assumed other aspects of the law at the instigation of the Judaizers, they apparently had not yet submitted to circumcision. However, they were contemplating this move. Paul was aware of this and thus tried to convince them not to accept circumcision. The apostle did this by warning them about two negative consequences of the step.

First, Paul assured the Galatians that if they got circumcised, Christ would not do them any good (vs. 2). Circumcision was a symbol of submission to the law. If the apostle's readers looked to the law for righteousness in their lives, they could not be looking to Christ for righteousness.

Second, the Galatians would be a debtor to the law and obligated to obey every aspect of it (vs. 3). The rigorous demands of the law formed a single unit, and one could not choose what he or she wanted to heed. This means that circumcision was not the only precondition for being accepted by God. The sinful person had to observe all the law perfectly. Of course, this was impossible to do outside of Christ.

Although the Galatians had not yet submitted to circumcision, they had already begun looking to the law for righteousness. That is why Paul said they had alienated themselves from Christ and had abandoned the grace of God (vs. 4). By their insistence on keeping the law, they had denied the sufficiency of Christ's sacrifice and righteousness. Since He is the source of God's grace, they had moved away from it when they turned away from the Savior.

Believers are justified through faith in Christ. As the Spirit works in their lives, they become increasingly devoted to God. The Spirit helps them to anticipate the day when God will make their justification complete and final (vs. 5). Right now the Spirit is the foretaste of what God promises to do for His people in Christ.

Paul made no mention of circumcision with respect to righteousness. This is because the presence or absence of circumcision did not matter when it came to being justified. The apostle declared that it is not the act of circumcision that mattered, but rather faith in Christ demonstrating itself in genuine acts of love (vs. 6). Paul neither condemned circumcision nor saw it as being inherently evil. In reality, he was indifferent to the practice. But he strongly opposed circumcision being performed out of a misguided idea that it was a means to attain righteousness.

II. RECOGNIZING THE TEACHERS OF TRUTH: GALATIANS 5:7-12

A. Ignoring the Truth: vss. 7-9

You were running a good race. Who cut in on you and kept you from obeying the truth? That kind of persuasion does not come from the one who calls you. "A little yeast works through the whole batch of dough."

In ancient times track-and-field events drew huge crowds. Most cities in the Roman Empire had a large, oval stadium where footraces and other athletic events were held. Paul's awareness of this prompted him to often refer to the Christian life in athletic terms, and he did so again in the Letter to the Galatians. He compared his readers to runners in a race, and he compared the Judaizers to unfair competitors who had cut in on them, causing them to break their stride (5:7).

Paul was saying that the Judaizers had hindered his readers from obeying the truth of the Gospel. Undoubtedly, the legalists claimed their message came from God. But Paul denied this (vs. 8). His true Gospel, not their false but persuasive message, originated with God.

Verse 9 quotes a popular proverb of Paul's day: "A little yeast works through the whole batch of dough." This maxim fits the Galatian situation perfectly. False teaching, like yeast (or leaven), spreads and affects everything it touches. Consequently, all the Christians of Galatia were in danger because of the Judaizers' doctrine.

B. Condemning the False Teachers: vss. 10-12

I am confident in the Lord that you will take no other view. The one who is throwing you into confusion will pay the penalty, whoever he may be. Brothers, if I am still preaching circumcision, why am I still being persecuted? In that case the offense of the cross has been abolished. As for those agitators, I wish they would go the whole way and emasculate themselves!

Though the situation looked grim, Paul was convinced the Galatians belonged to the Lord. That is why the apostle was certain his readers would hear and heed what he said and reject what the Judaizers had been telling them. Furthermore, Paul believed that those who had confused the Galatians with their false ideas would suffer God's judgment (Gal. 5:10).

Apparently the Judaizers had claimed that Paul himself preached the necessity of circumcision. They may have based this claim on the fact that Paul did not object to Jews living according to the law. But the apostle responded to their claim by indicating that, though once before his conversion he had advocated circumcision for all, he no longer did (vs. 11).

Paul substantiated his counterclaim by pointing to his persecution by the Judaizers. It should have been clear that if he truly agreed with them, they would not be harassing him. The apostle explained that he did not insist on the necessity of circumcision anymore because that would nullify Christ's work on the cross. The cross is an offense to Jewish law, yet it is the source of life for all who believe (1 Cor. 1:18).

Paul brought closure to this section with a sarcastic and even crude statement, which revealed just how he felt about the Judaizers: "As for those agitators, I wish they would go the whole way and emasculate themselves!" (Gal. 5:12). Yet crude as it is, this statement came out of the apostle's belief that circumcision had no religious significance for Christians and that when it was forced on Gentile converts, it amounted to bodily damage.

III. PROPERLY USING CHRISTIAN FREEDOM: GALATIANS 5:13-15

A. Service through Love: vss. 13-14

You, my brothers, were called to be free. But do not use your freedom to indulge the sinful nature; rather, serve one another in love. The entire law is summed up in a single command: "Love your neighbor as yourself."

The threat of the Judaizers was not the only problem facing the Galatians. They also had a problem with immorality. Presumably this had been a problem for them much longer than the problem caused by the Judaizers. We should not be surprised by this, for many of Paul's churches had a problem with immorality. Coming out of pagan cultures, converts had a difficult time adjusting to Christian morality. The Galatians seem to have been particularly troubled by selfishness and disregard for one another.

Having stressed Christian freedom strongly, Paul sensed he had better make sure the Galatians understood this liberty was not a license to sin. They were not to use their freedom to gratify their unspiritual nature but rather to serve one another with love (Gal. 5:13). Note the irony in Paul's argument. He had urged the Galatians not to become slaves to the law. They were now free in Christ to become slaves of one another.

The word rendered "serve" is a strong term often used for slavery. Slavery was widespread in the Roman Empire by Paul's day. Slaves back then were often treated well. Most were well fed and clothed. They had the right to have families, control their own money, and defend themselves in court. Many were educated at their owners' expense and some held posts of importance. Because of their security, slaves were often better off than poor free people.

Most owners set their slaves free after a few years. The reason for such an action might be to show gratitude, or to save money, or to make the slaves available for military service. Frequently, masters established their freedmen in business, and then became partners in the business.

Paul stated that when Christians love and serve others, they are actually fulfilling the essence of the law. In other words, God's people are closest to pleasing Him and keeping His commandments when they love and serve others as much as they love and serve themselves (vs. 14). From this we see that Paul was not against the law, just its misapplication. He argued that certain aspects of the law, such as its dietary requirements, were no longer binding. Nevertheless, the ethical directives in the law continued to represent God's will for Christian behavior.

B. Destruction through Self-centeredness: vs. 15

If you keep on biting and devouring each other, watch out or you will be destroyed by each other.

The Galatians needed to be reminded of the importance of love because they were biting and devouring one another like wild animals. In other words, their legalistic mentality had produced a critical, self-righteous spirit among them, and it threatened to destroy their fellowship if they did not put a stop to it quickly (Gal. 5:15). Disputes within a church fellowship, if not resolved in love, can seriously damage the spiritual welfare of the church members. Admittedly, it's not easy to go from fighting one another to loving one another. But that is possible if we live by the Spirit (vs. 16).

Discussion Questions

1. What would you say are some of the devastating effects of looking to the law for righteousness?
2. How could Paul be so confident that the Galatians would accept what he had said?
3. In what sense is the cross of Christ an offense, and what eternal good can come from it?
4. What principles can we find in Galatians 5:13-15 to guide us in the proper use of Christian liberty?
5. How would you evaluate Paul's attitude toward the false teachers? What is the best way to refute false teachers today?

Contemporary Application

Christ died to set us free from sin and from a long list of laws and regulations. This does not mean we are free to do whatever we want, for that way of thinking would lead us back into slavery to our selfish desires. Rather, Jesus liberates us to do what was impossible before—to show Christlike love.

When we are not motivated by love, we become critical of others. We stop looking for good in them and see only their faults. Soon the unity of believers is broken. Those who appeal to their freedom so that they can have their own way or indulge their own desires are falling back into sin.

Of course, it is also wrong to put a burden of lawkeeping on Christians. Paul urged us to take a stand against those who would enslave us to rules, methods, or special conditions for being saved or growing in Christ. If we choose legalism, we fool ourselves into thinking we can make it on our own. This in turn boosts our pride. However, if we choose Christ, we humbly acknowledge that we cannot live without Him. Coming to this realization is the first step in seeing victory over sin and experiencing spiritual growth in our lives.

Live by the Spirit

Scripture

Background Scripture: *Galatians 5:16—6:18*
Scripture Lesson: *Galatians 5:16—6:5, 7-9*
Key Verse: *Live by the Spirit, and you will not gratify the
desires of the sinful nature.* Galatians 5:16.
Scripture Lesson for Children: *Galatians 6:10; Esther
3:1-2, 5, 8-9; 4:9-11, 14-16*
Key Verse for Children: *As we have opportunity, let us do
good to all people.* Galatians 6:10.

Lesson Aim

To understand the importance of relying on the Spirit
to be productive, godly Christians.

Lesson Setting

Time: *Either* A.D. *48–49 (the South Galatian theory) or* A.D.
53–57 (the North Galatian theory)
Place: *Either the churches in a geographic area called Galatia
that was located in central Asia Minor (now Turkey; the
North Galatian theory) or the churches in the southern part of
the Roman province of Galatia (the South Galatian theory)*

Lesson Outline

Live by the Spirit

I. The Spirit versus the Sinful Nature:
Galatians 5:16-26
   A. *Conflict between the Spirit and the Sinful Nature:
   vss. 16-18*
   B. *The Acts of the Sinful Nature: vss. 19-21*
   C. *The Fruit of the Spirit: vss. 22-23*
   D. *The Rejection of the Sinful Nature: vss. 24-26*
II. The Call for Mutual Help: Galatians 6:1-5, 7-9
   A. *Sharing Each Other's Troubles: vss. 1-5*
   B. *Reaping What One Sows: vss. 7-9*

Introduction for Adults

Topic: *Choices and Consequences*

Of the multiplication of choices there is no end. Each year seems to bring something new on the scene that requires us to vote *yes* or *no* with our feet, time, money, and strength. Consequently, Christians are pulled in many directions. Because the future is murky, we do not always see the consequences ahead. We're tempted to straddle the fence in some cases because we lack wisdom. We know that every *yes* to one option is a *no* to another option.

That's why Paul's counsel is sorely needed. We must learn how to live in obedience to the Spirit. We also must learn how to make use of His guidance, wisdom, and strength. With the Spirit's help, we can focus on what is supremely important—our Christian character—and not settle for second best.

Introduction for Youths

Topic: *Which Way Do You Choose?*

The young man was desperate to discover God's will. In fact, the teen felt so confused that he looked for a sign from heaven. He concluded that if he received a letter with a certain stamp on it, he would be sure of God's will. This sort of thinking has more superstition to it than faith.

God confronts us with choices so that we can learn to trust Him for the answers. The basic principle is that we live by faith, not by sight. Choosing to live that way means we are open to learning from our mistakes, from our foolishness, and from our violations of God's will.

We are not alone in this difficult but important venture. God sent the Spirit to be our guide and helper. We can be confident that when we develop a keen sense of the Spirit's leading, He will guide us in the path of truth and virtue. He will also uphold us in the most difficult circumstances of life. Of this we can be certain.

Concepts for Children

Topic: *Live for the Good of All*

1. Whenever we have the opportunity, we should work for the good of others.
2. When a person named Mordecai [MORR-dih-keye] refused to bow down to a person named Haman [HAH-mun], Haman became very angry.
3. When Haman ordered that the Jewish people be put to death, a queen named Esther (who was Jewish) planned to ask the king (who was her husband) to help the Jewish people.
4. Esther asked the Jewish people to fast and pray; then she would make her request to the king for help.
5. God wants us to pray for wisdom and courage to know how best to help others.

The Lesson Commentary

I. THE SPIRIT VERSUS THE SINFUL NATURE: GALATIANS 5:16-26

A. Conflict between the Spirit and the Sinful Nature: vss. 16-18

So I say, live by the Spirit, and you will not gratify the desires of the sinful nature. For the sinful nature desires what is contrary to the Spirit, and the Spirit what is contrary to the sinful nature. They are in conflict with each other, so that you do not do what you want. But if you are led by the Spirit, you are not under law.

It's not easy to go from fighting one another to loving one another. But that is possible if we "live by the Spirit" (Gal. 5:16). By this Paul meant we are to allow the Spirit to control our lives. This is the same as saying He is to direct our thinking and guide our actions. As Paul wrote to the Galatians, he wanted to see them yielded to the power and promptings of the Spirit on a continual basis. The Spirit would make it possible for them to resist their "sinful nature," which had led them to cause strife and commit sins.

One of the most frequently used words in Paul's Greek vocabulary was *sarx*, literally "flesh." Paul used the word to refer to a number of things, such as the human body (2:20) and human striving (3:3). But its seven occurrences between 5:13 and 6:8 are all in an ethical context. In each case the term refers to our unspiritual nature. By giving *sarx* an ethical meaning, Paul was not implying that the physical flesh of the body is inherently evil. Instead, he meant that ever since the Fall, human nature is corrupt, or sinful.

Paul noted in 5:17 that the sinful nature is in opposition to Spirit. That is because when the Spirit comes into a person's life, He begins transforming the person's nature from one that is dominated by sin to one that desires to please God. In our hearts we may want to do good, but if we obey the wishes of our sinful nature, we will not do good. We can only do good if we live by the Spirit.

When we are led by the Spirit , we do not do the evil prompted by our sinful nature, and neither are we under the law (vs. 18). Presumably the Judaizers had told the Galatians that if they did not obey the law, the only other option was to obey their own sinful nature. Paul said there was a third option. We can obey the Spirit.

B. The Acts of the Sinful Nature: vss. 19-21

The acts of the sinful nature are obvious: sexual immorality, impurity and debauchery; idolatry and witchcraft; hatred, discord, jealousy, fits of rage, selfish ambition, dissensions, factions and envy; drunkenness, orgies, and the like. I warn you, as I did before, that those who live like this will not inherit the kingdom of God.

Until now, Paul had talked generally about how wrong it was to indulge one's sinful nature and how right it was to yield to the Spirit's control. The apostle got down to specifics when he described in detail the negative consequences of allowing the flesh to control one's life.

According to Paul, the evil deeds the unspiritual nature performs are clear (Gal. 5:19). By this he meant it is plain to see that these acts are wrong, even without the aid of the Old Testament law. Also, it is obvious that these iniquities spring from the flesh.

In verses 19-21, Paul listed 15 sinful acts to reflect all the ways people do evil. The representative nature of the catalog is made clear by his addition of "and the like" at the end. Many sinful acts did not make Paul's list, but that makes them no less reprehensible.

Paul may not have intended to list the 15 sinful acts in any particular order, but they seem to fall into four categories. The list includes three vices of sensuality (sexual immorality, impurity, and debauchery), two vices associated with pagan religions (idolatry and witchcraft), eight vices of interpersonal conflict (hatred, discord, jealously, fits of rage, selfish ambition, dissensions, factions, and envy), and two vices related to the misuse of alcohol (drunkenness and orgies).

The acts of the flesh that Paul listed are highly varied; yet they are all alike in arousing God's indignation. So Paul warned his readers about the consequences of these acts. As the apostle had told the Galatians earlier when he was with them, no one who did these evil acts would share in the blessings of God's kingdom (vs. 21).

Paul did not mean that every believer who commits a sin is prevented from inheriting God's kingdom. Rather, the apostle meant that people who continually or habitually commit these wrongful acts thereby reveal that they are not following Christ and have no place in His kingdom. Nevertheless, believers can learn from Paul's warning how seriously God views human sin.

C. The Fruit of the Spirit: vss. 22-23

But the fruit of the Spirit is love, joy, peace, patience, kindness, goodness, faithfulness, gentleness and self-control. Against such things there is no law.

To balance the list of acts of the sinful nature, Paul presented a list of godly virtues produced by those who yield their life to the Spirit. This list, too, is representative rather than exhaustive. The items mentioned are some of the effects appearing in the lives of those in whom the Spirit of God dwells.

Paul used a singular word for "fruit" (Gal. 5:22). He could have said "fruits," but he did not. He may have wanted to suggest that the aspects of the fruit of the Spirit develop and grow together like a bunch of grapes. They are not separate pieces of fruit existing independently of each other. All the elements of the fruit of the Spirit should be found in all believers.

Love is at the top of Paul's list of spiritual fruit because all the other virtues develop from it. Love is the opposite of the selfishness of the flesh. Joy and peace follow. Paul then listed patience, gentleness, goodness, faithfulness, meekness, and self-control.

The law contained a curse against those who failed to keep it. But that curse does not apply to those who are bearing the fruit of the Spirit, because they are thereby fulfilling what the law intended (vs. 23).

D. The Rejection of the Sinful Nature: vss. 24-26

Those who belong to Christ Jesus have crucified the sinful nature with its passions and desires. Since we live by the Spirit, let us keep in step with the Spirit. Let us not become conceited, provoking and envying each other.

Non-Christians are not able to bear the fruit of the Spirit because they do not have the Spirit. Though they may have respectable qualities, they are still ruled by their flesh and act in keeping with that nature by seeking to satisfy their passions and desires.

Believers, however, can bear the fruit of the Spirit. They receive the Spirit when they trust in Christ. At the moment of salvation, their sinful nature (in one sense) is crucified, or put to death (Gal. 5:24). This is because Jesus earned the right to break sin's grip of control over believers when He hung on the cross, and He sets them free from it when they believe in Him.

In another sense, of course, the Christian life is a daily process of believers putting their sinful nature to death. We cooperate with God by letting go of our past sinful ways and taking up a holy way of living.

Although believers already have the Spirit living in them, they are not automatically under His control. They need to consciously yield to Him as He leads and empowers them. Because the Spirit is the source of every believer's life, they should also allow Him to direct its course (vs. 25).

Paul gave a few specific examples of what he did not mean by keeping in step with the Spirit: being conceited, provoking others to anger, and envying others (vs. 26). Most likely, these were particular problems among the Galatian believers. They are also some specific kinds of unspirituality that we should avoid.

II. THE CALL FOR MUTUAL HELP: GALATIANS 6:1-5, 7-9

A. Sharing Each Other's Troubles: vss. 1-5

Brothers, if someone is caught in a sin, you who are spiritual should restore him gently. But watch yourself, or you also may be tempted. Carry each other's burdens, and in this way you will fulfill the law of Christ. If anyone thinks he is something when he is nothing, he deceives himself. Each one should test his own actions. Then he can take pride in himself, without comparing himself to somebody else, for each one should carry his own load.

In this section we find a number of specific instructions about Christian living, combined with warnings and encouragements. Probably Paul chose these instructions because they related to specific problems in the church at Galatia. The instructions do not spell out all that is expected of those who live by the Spirit. But they do provide some representative examples that can serve as models for us as we make our own decisions.

Paul began by dealing with situations in which believers are "caught in a sin" (Gal. 6:1). The idea behind this phrase is not that others have found out someone's sinning, but rather that the sinner has allowed himself or herself to be trapped or enticed by sin. Once the person's sinning has become public knowledge, Paul said those who were spiritual should help restore the transgressor; that is, other Christians should support and guide the struggling believer as he or she recovers from the sinning.

Next, Paul broadened the area of Christians' concern for each other to include those who suffer all kinds of burdens (vs. 2). These may include grief, illness, and persecution—anything that may hurt or hinder believers. By helping carry others' burdens, we fulfill "the law of Christ" (namely, His teachings). This includes not only loving our neighbor but also our enemy, with God's love being the model.

If there was a problem in the Galatian churches with believers not helping one another, it was probably due to the arrogance of those who considered themselves free of such burdens. That would explain why Paul warned against prideful self-deception (vs. 3). Paul supplied a defense against pride—self-testing (vs. 4). The idea is to measure ourselves against God's will as revealed in Scripture. From this we can gain a proper perspective on our failings as well as take satisfaction in what we have achieved by His grace.

Paul urged us to carry our own load (vs. 5). By this he meant we are each individually responsible to God for the way we conduct our lives. Thus if we are wise, we will be realistic about where we stand with Him.

B. Reaping What One Sows: vss. 7-9

Do not be deceived: God cannot be mocked. A man reaps what he sows. The one who sows to please his sinful nature, from that nature will reap destruction; the one who sows to please the Spirit, from the Spirit will reap eternal life. Let us not become weary in doing good, for at the proper time we will reap a harvest if we do not give up.

Serving others requires unselfishness and dependence on God's Spirit. But those who do not do the hard work of Christian living had better not kid themselves that God will bless them (Gal. 6:7). People who perform the acts of the sinful nature rather than bear the fruit of the Spirit will not be rewarded, for God will not be mocked. Unlike people, He cannot be fooled, and His justice is perfect.

Paul said there is a simple relationship between how people live and how God judges and rewards them (vs. 8). For instance, a farmer who sows barley cannot expect to harvest wheat. And no more so can those who obey the callings of the flesh (and thereby give evidence of their unregenerate state) expect to receive eternal life from God. Instead, they will earn eternal destruction. Happily, though, the opposite of this truth is that if we live by the Spirit, we will enjoy eternal life.

Paul feared that the Galatians, who had started well in their faith, were losing enthusiasm for Christian living. The Judaizers' false teachings and the Galatians' own unethical living had weakened their spiritual vitality. Thus Paul portrayed the reward awaiting the faithful—namely, an intimate relationship with God—as an incentive to renew their efforts at doing good (vs. 9).

God provides strategic opportunities for us to do good to others (vs. 10). We should try to discern these opportunities and eagerly act on them. Helping unbelievers is an excellent way to witness wordlessly to God's goodness. But if anything, we should be more eager to help other Christians, since we are all part of God's family.

Discussion Questions

1. Practically speaking, how can believers live by the Spirit?
2. Why does so much conflict have to exist between the sinful nature and the Spirit?
3. Why is walking in step with the Spirit a good way to describe the Christian life?
4. Why is it important for us to financially support those in the ministry?
5. Have you ever felt weary of doing good? What encouraged you to continue doing good?

Contemporary Application

Sin versus the Holy Spirit seems like a battle that will never end. Once we think we have licked sin, it pops up somewhere and we fall prey to it. Sounds rather discouraging, doesn't it? But in this battle we never fight alone. With the Holy Spirit living in us, and with the encouragement and prayers of fellow Christians, we can win the battle.

Perhaps we are most vulnerable when we think we don't need other people. And possibly that's why Paul envisaged a fellowship of believers together fighting the battle against sin, rather than fighting against each other. He talked about our being individually responsible, but he also called us to be responsible for one another.

Our individualistic society militates against our receiving help, prayer, counsel, and admonitions from one another. But as we keep in step with the Spirit, we will also be much more inclined to depend on our fellow believers and strengthen them in their faith. They in turn will minister to us, and together we will glorify God through the spiritual victories that He brings about in our lives.

Worship and Wisdom for Living

The Way of the Righteous

DEVOTIONAL READING

Psalm 19:1-6

DAILY BIBLE READINGS

Monday June 3
  Psalm 42 Hope in Distress

Tuesday June 4
  Psalm 56:1-6 In God I Trust

Wednesday June 5
  Psalm 56:7-13 I Am Not Afraid

Thursday June 6
  Psalm 62 My Hope Is from God

Friday June 7
  Psalm 71:1-11 You Are My Hope

Saturday June 8
  Psalm 71:12-24 I Will Hope Continually

Sunday June 9
  Psalm 43 God Is My Hope and Help

Scripture

Background Scripture: *Psalms 1; 19*
Scripture Lesson: *Psalms 1:1-6; 19:7-10*
Key Verse: *For the LORD watches over the way of the righteous, but the way of the wicked will perish.* Psalm 1:6.
Scripture Lesson for Children: *Psalms 1:1-3; 19:7-10*
Key Verse for Children: *The law of the LORD is perfect.* Psalm 19:7.

Lesson Aim

To distinguish God's way of righteousness from the world's way of wickedness.

Lesson Setting

Time: *Psalm 1: date unknown, though possibly written during the reign of either David (1010–970 B.C.) or Solomon (970–930 B.C.); Psalm 19: written sometime during the reign of David (1010–970 B.C.)*
Place: *Israel*

Lesson Outline

The Way of the Righteous

I. Life's Two Roads: Psalm 1:1-6
  A. *The Path of Uprightness: vss. 1-3*
  B. *The Path of Evil: vss. 4-6*
II. Divine Revelation's Virtues: Psalm 19:7-10
  A. *Trustworthy and Upright: vss. 7-9*
  B. *Inestimable in Value: vs. 10*

Introduction for Adults

Topic: *The Right Way*

All of us have our favorite sweets. If we were writing Psalm 19 today, we might say that God's Word is sweeter than a chocolate bar. In fact, many people are "chocoholics." They like chocolate bars and chocolate syrup on their ice cream. They love rich chocolate ice cream and devil's food cake with fudge frosting. They think nothing of spending money for imported chocolate truffles from Europe.

Whatever our passions, as Christians we realize they must take second place to our love for Scripture. Sometimes Christians get slack in their time with God in His Word and prayer. As a result, their spiritual lives decline. Sometimes they fall for lesser loves and their love for Christ grows cold.

These possibilities underscore the reason why the truths recorded in Psalms 1 and 19 (the focus of this week's lesson) are important to study and apply. They serve as vital checkpoints of our spiritual vitality.

Introduction for Youths

Topic: *The Right Way*

Youth reflect the character of individuals they admire but never have met. Adolescents also exemplify the behavior, dress, and habits of family members, friends, neighbors, and co-workers. Imitating others can be a good thing if those who serve as role models are upright people.

This week's lesson will challenge Christian teens to consider the way of the Lord the best path to take in life. They will also be encouraged to become godly examples for others to follow. The more class members focus their attention on the Lord and His Word and behave in ways that are characteristic of Him, the more they will set a godly example in their words and deeds.

Concepts for Children

Topic: *Living by God's Rules*

1. Believers experience the most joy when they study the Bible and do what it says.
2. When believers live this way, they are like well-watered, fruitful trees.
3. The Word of God is perfect and able to give us wisdom and understanding about life.
4. The laws of God are true and more valuable than anything else people experience.
5. God wants us to obey the truths He has recorded in the Bible.

The Lesson Commentary

I. LIFE'S TWO ROADS: PSALM 1:1-6

A. The Path of Uprightness: vss. 1-3

Blessed is the man who does not walk in the counsel of the wicked or stand in the way of sinners or sit in the seat of mockers. But his delight is in the law of the LORD, and on his law he meditates day and night. He is like a tree planted by streams of water, which yields its fruit in season and whose leaf does not wither. Whatever he does prospers.

This quarter's lessons take us through Psalms and Proverbs, the so-called wisdom literature of the Old Testament. The lessons are grouped under three major themes: "Songs for Faithful Living," "Praise the Creator and Redeemer," and "Words for the Wise."

In the first unit, the subjects include following God's laws, expressing pain in the midst of suffering, relying on God in times of trouble, being instruments of justice, and establishing family relationships. The second unit focuses on our relationship to God as our Creator, being founded on His blessings, enjoying His providential care, and benefiting from His forgiveness. In the third unit, selected Proverbs help us consider how to find God's wisdom, reject evil, speak carefully, and care for the poor.

The Psalms are songs and prayers capturing, in Alexander Maclaren's words, "the heart's echo to the speech of God." Perhaps more than any other part of Scripture, the Psalms tell us what it feels like to walk in the way of the Lord. Old Testament scholars, having noted the similarity of forms and themes among many of the Psalms, have tried to classify them according to type. For instance, Psalms 1 and 19 are called wisdom psalms, for they provide instruction about living as the people of God. In these portions of Scripture we are admonished to abandon the way of evil and follow the way of the Lord.

Psalm 1 is an appropriate introduction to the Psalter, for it is a map showing two roads—the way of righteousness and the way of wickedness. The psalmist did not use the word "righteous" to describe godly behavior, though it is clear this is what he had in mind. Rather, the writer used the Hebrew word translated "blessed," which could more literally be rendered "blessedness[es]." The word is not found in the singular in the Hebrew text because there is no such thing as a single blessing. Instead, wherever there is one blessing from God there is another from Him, too.

The Psalms arose from a long tradition of Hebrew poetry. We can observe this because most books of the Old Testament, beginning with Genesis, contain at least some fragments of poetry. Hebrew poetry is flexible in form and rhythm. However, most Hebrew poetry exhibits a distinguishing characteristic called *parallelism*. This term simply means that two (or sometimes three) lines of poetry are, in one way or another, parallel in meaning.

Consider Psalm 1:1. The writer used a dramatic three-fold parallelism to note what divinely blessed people avoid doing. They shun the thinking, practices, and fellowship of ungodly people. Notice that the progression—walk, stand, and sit—denotes successive downward steps in evil activities. There is also a threefold collection of wicked contemplations: counsel, way, and seat. Finally, three words describe the character of the ungodly: wicked, sinners, and mockers.

The three clauses emphasize that godly people completely avoid all association with wickedness and evildoers. They do not adopt the principles of the wicked as a rule of life. They do not persist in the practices of notorious offenders. And they do not associate with those who openly mock God, His Word, or His people.

The psalmist next focused attention on the "law of the LORD" (vs. 2), and said it is to be the believer's rule of conduct. God's law is not an irksome restriction, but rather the object of the upright's love and constant study. Virtuous people find true happiness in the revealed will of God as recorded in His Word.

The phrase "the law of the LORD" can refer to either teaching or instruction. It is also used of a body of laws, especially the laws of Moses recorded in the first five books of the Old Testament. In Psalm 1:2, the writer made the phrase synonymous with the Word of the Lord and stressed that it served as the believers' guide for life.

Believers relate to God's Word in two ways. First, they delight in it. "Delight" does not refer to a mere external formalism, but rather to an obedient heart (37:31). Second, believers meditate on Scripture constantly. The psalmist was referring to thoughtful reflection and study in an attitude of prayer and worship.

Psalm 1:3 contains a powerful simile to describe godly people. They are like flourishing, fruitful trees nourished by constant supplies of water. The writer might have had in mind the desert palm tree because of its love of water, its stately growth, its evergreen foliage, and its valuable fruit. "Streams of water" could mean either natural streams or irrigation channels. Without this supply of water, a desert tree would die under the burning sun. The biblical truth being communicated is that the upright are sustained by bountiful supplies of God's grace. Such is drawn from their fellowship with Him through worship, prayer, and fellowship (Pss. 52:8; 92:12).

Not only is the righteous person happy and able to stand up under hardship, but also "whatever he does prospers" (Ps. 1:3). Believers regularly produce fruit, like a well-watered tree. The psalmist probably had in mind such material benefits as a large family, influence in the community, and a good income.

The ancient Israelites, living before Christ, did not have a complete understanding of eternal life. Thus, they tended to think that rewards and punishments are always given in this life. But from our perspective, we can see that sometimes justice has to wait until the next life. Nevertheless, it remains true that the righteous will prosper—if not now, then eventually.

B. The Path of Evil: vss. 4-6

Not so the wicked! They are like chaff that the wind blows away. Therefore the wicked will not stand in the judgment, nor sinners in the assembly of the righteous. For the LORD watches over the way of the righteous, but the way of the wicked will perish.

The psalmist offered a sharp contrast between the godly and ungodly. The former are like firmly rooted, flourishing, and fruitful trees. However, the latter are like the chaff on a threshing floor, which is worthless and liable to be swept away by every passing breeze (Ps. 1:4). The scattering of chaff by the wind is a common Old Testament figure for the sudden destruction of the wicked (Job 21:17-18; Ps. 35:5). It describes both the character and the end of the ungodly.

The real character of the wicked will be revealed in the judgment (Ps. 1:5). Since they are worthless and unstable, the wicked will not hold their ground when God separates them from the upright. The psalmist was not just referring to God's final judgment, but also included all acts of divine justice against the wicked.

The wicked would have no weight, or influence, in the proceedings of the community ("the assembly of the righteous"). They would not be able to gather at the city gate with the community leaders to decide issues of justice. Neither could they worship in the temple with the people of God. Their wicked behavior would become known, making them outsiders.

When we put our faith in Christ, we begin a new life in Him. And after death this life in Christ continues, but on a higher plane. We who believe in Christ will remain forever in God's presence. In contrast, those who reject God's offer of love may travel down their own road of earthly life as long as believers do on theirs. But after that, the wicked will receive a sentence of terrible finality (vs. 6).

II. DIVINE REVELATION'S VIRTUES: PSALM 19:7-10

A. Trustworthy and Upright: vss. 7-9

The law of the LORD is perfect, reviving the soul. The statutes of the LORD are trustworthy, making wise the simple. The precepts of the LORD are right, giving joy to the heart. The commands of the LORD are radiant, giving light to the eyes. The fear of the LORD is pure, enduring forever. The ordinances of the LORD are sure and altogether righteous.

In Psalm 19, David depicted the Lord as the author of both His world and His Word. For instance, God has revealed Himself to humankind through the Creation (vss. 1-6). Though the universe gives clear witness to the existence and power of God, sinful humanity has consistently rejected this testimony (Rom. 1:18-32). That's why the knowledge of salvation can only come through the Word of God. (10:17). As Paul related in 1:16, the Gospel is "the power of God for the salvation of everyone who believes."

The "law of the LORD" (Ps. 19:7) is part of God's revealed Word. The Hebrew noun translated "law" might also be rendered "teaching," "direction," or "instruction." Like the rest of Scripture, the Mosaic law bears witness to its divine author, the Lord. It's no wonder, then, that David said the "law is perfect," which suggests that it is complete and not lacking in any way.

God's Word revives our souls and gives us wisdom. It does so by telling us to repent and confess our sins, and also to trust in the Lord for salvation. The law of the Lord never fails, being completely reliable. Thus, we can trust it implicitly to be a perfect source of guidance for us.

God's Word shows us the right way to live (vs. 8). We not only find truth about God and His salvation, but also about moral values and standards. The law of the Lord is radiant in the sense that it is pure, being free from corruption. Scripture is like a crystal clear stream with no pollution, and like a windowpane without dirty streaks.

God's Word clearly shines its truth and power into our lives. It's no wonder, then, that when we heed Scripture, we experience joy and spiritual enlightenment. Through faith in the Lord, we have the joy of forgiveness, eternal life, and ever-lasting hope. Also, we are given insight into life and what makes it genuinely meaningful.

The Bible opens our eyes to see God as He is and ourselves as we are. Scripture helps us to think in an upright way. We learn how to discern the times, to see the truth behind human events, and to recognize the unfolding of God's eternal plan of redemption. Only in Scripture can we see the end from the beginning. And only in the Bible do we learn who we are, why we are here, and what our destiny is.

"Fear" refers to a reverence for the Lord, not a cringing terror of Him. Such reverence is pure, not sullied, and has a lasting quality (vs. 9). Our devotion to the Lord is grounded in His ordinances. Such confidence in God's decrees is based on the awareness that what He has said is true and upright. We are certain that Scripture is completely reliable and worthy of our undivided allegiance.

From the above we see that God's law is not something that keeps us from having fun. Rather, it gives us insight, warns us, and rewards us. The Word of God lights our path rather than chains our hands and feet. Scripture points at danger to caution us, and then points at success to guide us.

B. Inestimable in Value: vs. 10

They are more precious than gold, than much pure gold; they are sweeter than honey, than honey from the comb.

David had a clear understanding of human nature. For instance, he knew that people value precious metals such as gold and devoted large amounts of time and energy to acquire it. The psalmist declared that the law of the Lord was "more precious than gold" (Ps. 19:10). In fact, God's Word was beyond valuing.

In a parallel thought, David declared that Scripture was sweeter than honey. Even the dripping from the comb of honey could not compare with the joy and satisfaction to be found in heeding the Bible. In contrast, those who spurned the law of the Lord experienced bitterness, frustration, and disillusionment. If we want our soul nourished, our spirit invigorated, and our hope strengthened, we will focus our attention on what God has revealed in His Word.

Discussion Questions

1. In what do the upright find delight?
2. Why do you think the psalmist compared the wicked to chaff (Ps. 1:4)?

3. In what way do the destinies of the righteous and wicked contrast?
4. In what way is the Word of God perfect? How does it provide spiritual nourishment for our soul?
5. How has God's Word proven to be a source of wisdom, clarity, and truth for you?

Contemporary Application

People want meaning and satisfaction in their lives. They also want their lives to count for something. The Bible tells us how to achieve those goals. We obtain direction and value to our lives through God's Word.

We are discerning when we heed the teaching of Scripture. The reasons are clear. Like the powerful beacon of a lighthouse guiding seagoing vessels away from a rocky shoreline, the Bible steers us away from moral dangers. Scripture reminds us of God's judgment and tells us about the consequences of our disobedience.

There is great reward in heeding God's Word. For instance, there is forgiveness of sins and the promise of eternal life with the Lord. There is also the fellowship of the Father, the love of the Son, and the abiding presence of the Spirit. We have peace with God and hope for the future. It is for these reasons that we should call one another to a disciplined study and conscientious application of Scripture. In God's Word we find a joy that transcends our earthly circumstances. It's no wonder that the Bible is "more precious than gold" (Ps. 19:10).

Hope in God

Scripture

Background Scripture: *Psalms 42—43*
Scripture Lesson: *Psalm 42:1-6a, 7-11*
Key Verse: *Put your hope in God, for I will yet praise him,
my Savior and my God.* Psalm 42:11.
Scripture Lesson for Children: *Psalm 42:1-6a, 8, 11*

Lesson Aim

To remember to meditate on God's kindness and love
when feelings of loneliness or depression occur.

Lesson Setting

Time: *Date unknown, though possibly written toward the end
of Joash's reign (835–796 B.C.)*
Place: *Israel*

Lesson Outline

Hope in God
  I.   Thirsting for God: Psalm 42:1-3
  II. Worshiping God: Psalm 42:4
  III. Finding God in Trouble: Psalm 42:5-6a, 7-11
       A. *The Question and Answer: vss. 5-6a, 7*
       B. *The Assurance: vs. 8*
       C. *The Oppression: vss. 9-10*
       D. *The Refrain: vs. 11*

Introduction for Adults

Topic: *Live in Hope*

A middle-aged man, along with his wife, went to Florida to recover from cancer treatments. The couple hoped to walk along the beach and soak up the sun's rays, and in this way help the man to regain his strength. But sadly, the man's health did not improve. As a result, his wife had to push him to the beach in a wheelchair, for he was not strong enough to walk the beach on his own.

Despite these difficulties, this couple continued to be people of faith. They did not give up their trust in the living God. Rather, their experience drove them to a deeper level of commitment. They came to know God in ways they had not known Him before.

The testimony of this couple illustrates the power of the hope we have in God. None of us has any guarantees of long life and perfect health. But we do have the assurance of God's love and care, and of His wisdom and power. As Psalm 42 reminds us, even when life seems dismal, putting our hope in God is the wisest thing we can do.

Introduction for Youths

Topic: *Don't Lose Hope*

The young fellow had his heart set on going with a group to see a major league baseball game. But on the day of the event, it rained and the trip had to be canceled. The lad's hopes were shattered.

Most of us can relate to how this teen felt. Yes, life is filled with disappointments, but we somehow get over most of them and move on to other things. For instance, the young fellow I mentioned above got to see many baseball games later in his life.

It's helpful to admit, though, that when life gets tougher, and the issues loom larger, we're tempted to give up on God. We might begin thinking of Him as a cosmic Scrooge who wants to cheat us out of fun. However, we know from Scripture that this is a flawed way to view the Lord. We learn that hoping in God never brings disappointment. As Ephesians 3:20 reminds us, God "is able to do immeasurably more than all we ask or imagine."

Concepts for Children

Topic: *Living with Hope in God*

1. The person who wrote Psalm 42 said that he especially longed for God when he felt sad.
2. The writer said he remembered leading a group of joyous people to the house of God.
3. Despite the sadness he felt, the writer said his hope in God remained strong.
4. The writer said God's love for him was present both day and night.
5. God cares how we feel and can help us when we are lonely or sad.

293

The Lesson Commentary

I. Thirsting for God: Psalm 42:1-3

As the deer pants for streams of water, so my soul pants for you, O God. My soul thirsts for God, for the living God. When can I go and meet with God? My tears have been my food day and night, while men say to me all day long, "Where is your God?"

From ancient times Psalms has been divided into five "books" of unequal length. Each of these books closes with a doxology, or passage praising God. The last psalm serves as a concluding doxology to the whole Book of Psalms.

Many commentators see a relationship between the five "books" of Psalms and the five books of Moses (Genesis-Deuteronomy). For instance, Book I (Pss. 1—41) is said to correspond to Genesis. Generally speaking, this section of the Psalter begins by showing humanity in a state of blessedness, then traces human rebellion and restoration. Book II (Pss. 42—72) is said to correspond to Exodus, with this section of the Psalter opening with a cry of distress and ending with the portrait of a righteous ruler.

Book III (Pss. 73—89) is said to correspond to Leviticus, with this section of the Psalter showing the counsel of God in relation to the temple sanctuary. Book IV (Pss. 90—106) is said to correspond to Numbers, with this section of the Psalter starting with a prayer about Israel's unfaithfulness in the wilderness, and then providing the contrast of the Messiah's faithfulness. Book V (Pss. 107—150) is said to correspond to Deuteronomy, with the last portion of the Psalter focusing on God's Word and ways.

From what has been said, it is clear that Psalm 42 (the focus of this week's lesson) appears at the beginning of Book II of the Psalter. Some have labeled Psalm 42 as an individual lament in which the writer expressed a thirst for God. The title says the psalm was "for the director of music," which is a notice that this song is from an early collection of hymns used in temple worship. It's also possible that when the psalm was used in the Hebrew liturgy, the leader of the Levitical choir spoke it before the assembly of worshipers.

The term rendered "maskil" may indicate that the psalm was intended to inspire contemplation, facilitate teaching, or foster greater skill in living uprightly. The writer (and possibly main speaker of the song) was a descendant of Korah and perhaps a leading member of that Levitical priestly group, which held positions of responsibility within the temple.

Many experts think that Psalms 42 and 43 originally formed a single unit because of their similar structure and themes. If so, they possibly were separated in the Psalter for liturgical reasons. The reference in 43:1 to an "ungodly nation" might provide a clue concerning the historical context. Some suggest raiders had invaded Judah and taken the author captive to a foreign land.

Though we cannot be dogmatic on these points, it is clear that the psalmist was enduring a time of distress and yearning for God. The writer longed to worship in the Jerusalem temple, but could not. He thus poured out his desires to God.

The imagery of verses 1 and 2 is that of a deer being relentlessly pursued by hunters and longing for a refreshing drink from a stream. As the life of the deer depended upon water, so too the life of the author depended on God. The psalmist experienced oppression from his foes and evidently felt separated from the Lord. Yet he wouldn't give up until he restored his relationship with God.

Verse 2 suggests the psalmist was discouraged because he was exiled to a place far from Jerusalem and its temple. He yearned to be in the presence of the living God, to come to His temple and stand before Him in reverential worship. The author exclaimed that day and night tears had been the only "food" (vs. 3) he ate, so desperate was his situation.

The psalmist's oppressors arrogantly spoke as if God neither existed nor cared for His afflicted people. In fact, these enemies of the faith constantly taunted the writer by asking, "Where is your God?" The idea is that if the Lord of Israel had been truly present, He would not have abandoned the psalmist to his enemies.

God was the center of the psalmist's basic spiritual drive, and he would not settle for anything less. His desire was so intense that he wanted to plumb the depths of God's riches moment by moment. He wanted a direct, personal encounter with God, not something secondhand. Relatively few people talk about God and their feelings for Him so deeply. Until we value God more than anything else, we cannot share this experience. In fact, when we try to satisfy our hopes and longings with material things and human relationships, we cannot begin this intense spiritual search.

II. WORSHIPING GOD: PSALM 42:4

These things I remember as I pour out my soul: how I used to go with the multitude, leading the procession to the house of God, with shouts of joy and thanksgiving among the festive throng.

The psalmist, being in exile far from the Jerusalem temple, lamented how his heart felt broken, especially as he remembered how things used to be (Ps. 42:4). He recalled walking among the crowds of worshipers and leading a procession to the "house of God." It was a time of great celebration that was characterized by singing for joy and giving thanks.

All that changed, however, for the psalmist now that he was in exile far from the temple and the worshiping community. For the believer who lived in Old Testament times, there was only one place where he felt the true worship of the Lord was possible—the temple in Jerusalem. That's why the psalmist felt distant from God's presence among His people and longed for intimacy with the Lord.

From this verse we learn the value of corporate worship. When our souls thirst for the living God, we cry out to Him with our tears. Relief comes when we seek comfort, peace, and hope in the presence of other believers. This is as it should be, for God has made us so that we need each other. There thus is great strength in gathering together to praise the Lord, no matter how dark our circumstances may seem.

III. Finding God in Trouble: Psalm 42:5-6a, 7-11

A. The Question and Answer: vss. 5-6a, 7

Why are you downcast, O my soul? Why so disturbed within me? Put your hope in God, for I will yet praise him, my Savior and my God. . . . Deep calls to deep in the roar of your waterfalls; all your waves and breakers have swept over me.

The psalmist was in touch with his emotions. Though he admitted feeling sad, he did not wallow in self-pity. Instead, the writer redirected his attention to the Lord (Ps. 42:5). The author realized that by putting his hope in God, he would be able to once again offer up praises to Him. The psalmist could do so for he knew that one day he would experience again the presence of his Savior and God (vs. 6).

None of us is immune to feelings of discouragement from time to time. One remedy is to think about how God has been good to us. When we reflect on the many ways the Lord has been kind to His people, it will shift our focus off the present situation and onto God's ability to do what seems impossible.

In verse 7, the author talked about hearing the tumult of the raging seas, as if God's vicious waves had swept over him like an angry ocean or a roaring waterfall. Some think the psalmist was referring to the mighty waters of the upper Jordan River surging down from Mount Hermon. Another possibility is that the writer was talking about a deluge from the sky dumping large quantities of water, which then filled the rivers and streams that eventually flowed into the seas.

In either case, the author's intent behind the imagery is much the same. He sensed that God was ultimately responsible for the oceans of trial in which he seemed to be drowning. It was as if God was sending one trouble after another upon him, like the relentless pounding of the surf, and causing him great distress.

We should not fault the psalmist for taking such a candid look at his situation. When we are troubled, it is appropriate for us to think honestly about our circumstances. This helps us to be realistic and to anchor our hope in God, rather than in people or possessions.

B. The Assurance: vs. 8

By day the Lord directs his love, at night his song is with me—a prayer to the God of my life.

Psalm 42:8 forms the thematic center for the entire song and interrupts the laments coming before and after it. Though the psalmist's situation seemed bleak, he could still say that through each day the Lord poured out His unfailing love upon him. This helped the author sing songs of praise to God "at night." This was the writer's way of praying to God, whom he knew was the ultimate source of life.

We are reminded of a similar refrain appearing in Lamentations 3:22-24. Jeremiah believed that an understanding of God's faithfulness in dealing with His people was reason for hope rather than despair. Even in his afflictions, the prophet remembered God's unfailing love and kindness, and he found reason for hope and godly self-discipline.

C. The Oppression: vss. 9-10

I say to God my Rock, "Why have you forgotten me? Why must I go about mourning, oppressed by the enemy?" My bones suffer mortal agony as my foes taunt me, saying to me all day long, "Where is your God?"

Having recalled God's unfailing love and kindness, the psalmist once again lamented that he felt the Lord had forgotten and possibly forsaken him (Ps. 42:9). The writer also wondered why God would permit him to wander in a seemingly dark situation, all the while "oppressed by the enemy."

In asking these questions, the psalmist was not so much looking for answers from God. Rather, the questions reflected his own sense of loss and confusion. He simply wanted to tell God how he felt. The questions show us why he was despondent and longing for the Lord. Perhaps some of us are taken aback by the tone of the writer's remarks. It's helpful to remember that despite his anguish, he remained full of faith and hope. After all, he referred to God as his "Rock," that is, his protector and foundation.

The psalmist needed this eternal perspective as he endured terrible circumstances. His enemies mistreated him, and he felt distressed when they again asked him, "Where is your God?" (vs. 10). Such taunts pierced the psalmist like a fatal wound. In his affliction, he envisioned his bones being in great pain. (In Hebrew poetry the bones stood for the whole body, being the framework for it.)

Clearly, the writer was not playing games with God. Instead, he was transparently honest. He knew the living God in such a way that he could do this. This suggests that he was a mature believer and seasoned worshiper. He could not have spoken as he did on the spur of the moment.

D. The Refrain: vs. 11

Why are you downcast, O my soul? Why so disturbed within me? Put your hope in God, for I will yet praise him, my Savior and my God.

Having rehearsed his troubles, the psalmist once again redirected his attention to the Lord. The writer could be candid enough with God that he did not need to gloss over his discouragement and restless spirit (Ps. 42:11). Such openness before the Lord can be solid tonic for our troubled souls.

The author admonished himself (and perhaps those who might hear his psalm being read in the temple) to place his hope in the Lord. After all, He is the living God and Savior of His people. Because of this, He was worthy of unending praise. This closing verse reminds us of 1 Peter 5:10-11. The apostle told his readers—who were going through a time of intense suffering for their faith—that God would one day restore and strengthen them. Thus to Him belonged "the power for ever and ever."

Discussion Questions

1. What do you think were the circumstances being experienced by the psalmist?
2. Why did the writer express a deep longing for God?
3. How did the author encourage himself in the midst of his despair?
4. How did the psalmist's enemies taunt him?
5. How can a knowledge of God's goodness and grace benefit us in trying circumstances?

Contemporary Application

Hunger and thirst are two of our basic physical drives. The Bible uses these to picture our spiritual appetites and desires. However, it is hard to convince people to give the satisfaction of their spiritual yearnings even greater priority than the meeting of their physical needs.

Too often, many people we know try to suppress the spiritual desires God has placed within them. They go through life dissatisfied, unfulfilled, and devoid of hope. In this regard, Psalm 42 reveals one person's deepest longings and his hope in God. If all of us were as honest as the psalmist, we would admit to having the same kind of ache in our hearts.

Why are people ashamed to admit this void in their lives? Why do they try to cover it up? Why can't they be as open and frank about their spiritual needs as they are about their physical needs? People spend a lot of time talking about their health, food, clothing, homes, and retirement plans. But rare are the times when they share intimately their deepest spiritual needs.

This week's lesson urges us to take a different approach to life. May we have the wisdom and courage to do so with the Lord's grace. After all, He is our Savior and God (vs. 11).

The Lord, Our Keeper

Scripture

Background Scripture: *Psalms 23; 80; 121*

Scripture Lesson: *Psalms 23; 121*

Key Verse: *I lift up my eyes to the hills—where does my help come from? My help comes from the LORD, the Maker of heaven and earth.* Psalm 121:1-2.

Scripture Lesson for Children: *Psalm 23*

Lesson Aim

To learn to depend more upon God for help, guidance, and protection throughout life.

Lesson Setting

Time: *Psalm 23: written sometime during David's reign (1010–970 B.C.); Psalm 121: date unknown, though possibly written during or after the Babylonian captivity (about 550–450 B.C.)*

Place: *Israel*

Lesson Outline

The Lord, Our Keeper

I. The Lord Is My Shepherd: Psalm 23
  A. *The Shepherd's Provision: vss. 1-3*
  B. *The Shepherd's Protection: vss. 4-5*
  C. *The Shepherd's Promise: vs. 6*
II. The Lord Is My Protector: Psalm 121
  A. *The Protector's Power: vss. 1-2*
  B. *The Protector's Watchfulness: vss. 3-4*
  C. *The Protector's Constant Care: vss. 5-6*
  D. *The Protector's Assurance: vss. 7-8*

Introduction for Adults

Topic: *Don't Be Afraid*

It's easy to tell someone not to be afraid when everything seems to be going well, but when a friend comes down with a serious illness that's a different matter. Automatically, it seems, fear kicks in. Fear has positive value when it keeps us from taking risky chances. However, fear has negative value when it begins to undermine our faith.

When the trials of life seem overwhelming, we should fortify our souls, not with wishful thinking, but with truths about God revealed in His Word. We can't promise people that everything will be all right. But we can reassure them that God's love and care will be there when they need it.

Our prayers and our counsel must be rooted in the strong affirmations found in Scripture, such as Psalms 23 and 121. In these two beloved passages we learn that God will never forsake His own. In fact, nothing can separate us from His love that is found in Jesus Christ (Rom. 8:39).

Introduction for Youths

Topic: *Someone to Watch Over Me*

What an encouragement it is to read accounts of God's care. In this regard, the psalms of the Bible function as recitals of how God has helped and protected His people. We all can benefit from the spiritual reinforcement these memorable passages offer.

That's why it's valuable to take time to recall what the Lord has done down through the centuries. Such accounts need not focus just on hair-raising rescues. Even what seems to be unimportant can help us recognize the hand of God at work in the lives of His people.

When we reflect on these things, we quickly come to understand that God watches over all we do. He will uphold us when we feel spiritually weak and He will guide us when we feel morally confused. We never need to feel alone when the great God of the universe is ever present to lead and strengthen us in the pilgrim way.

Concepts for Children

Topic: *Living in God's Care*

1. The Lord is like a shepherd who supplies all our needs.
2. When we go through difficult times, we do not need to be afraid, for God brings us safety and comfort.
3. The Lord is like a gracious host who protects us and provides for us.
4. The Lord's care lasts forever.
5. The Lord is pleased when we tell others about His goodness.

The Lesson Commentary

I. The Lord Is My Shepherd: Psalm 23

A. The Shepherd's Provision: vss. 1-3

The Lord is my shepherd, I shall not be in want. He makes me lie down in green pastures, he leads me beside quiet waters, he restores my soul. He guides me in paths of righteousness for his name's sake.

Psalm 23 is undoubtedly one of the most favorite of all the psalms. David's confession of faith, hope, and trust in the Lord as the good Shepherd-King has inspired and comforted millions of believers down through the ages. Its timeless truths continue to be the bulwark of Christian living in times of travail.

David was himself a shepherd in Israel, and his familiarity with the shepherd's life permeates this psalm. He compared himself to a sheep on the mountains of Israel tenderly cared for and kept by his Shepherd (vs. 1). While we may not have experienced the same kind of outdoor life that David did, his imagery still moves us to reflect on our own relationship with God. We feel the intensity of David's emotions toward the Lord. His psalm invites believers from all walks of life to examine how they relate to God.

In David's opening confession, he acknowledged that the God of the universe can be known in a warm, personal relationship. In ancient times, shepherds were responsible for the total care of their sheep. That theme emerges in Psalm 23. Because David knew God as his Shepherd, he had everything he needed to be an effective servant for the Lord.

The implications of David's shepherding imagery are profound, for sheep in Bible days typically were at the mercy of the elements and wild beasts. The safety of sheep had to be maintained on a day by day and moment by moment basis. Like a sheep exposed to the perils of life, David had tasted danger when various enemies threatened his life. Despite these difficult circumstances, David knew that his Shepherd, the King of Israel, would provide everything he needed. David had complete confidence in God's protection, guidance, and provision.

The psalmist described with vivid poetic imagery what it was like to be fed and watered by his Shepherd. The Lord allowed David to rest in green, fertile pastures, having grazed to his fill. Israel's God led David to quiet pools of fresh water so that his thirst could be satisfied (vs. 2). The image is one of total satisfaction, contentment, and peace.

An able shepherd would lead his flock along the paths where they needed to go. David knew firsthand about being restored in his soul and about turning to paths of righteousness (vs. 3). After the prophet Nathan confronted David with his sin of adultery (2 Sam. 12:1-14), David repented and entered on a course of moral restoration. Such restoration brought honor to God.

When we allow God, our Shepherd, to guide us, we have contentment. This is because He knows the "green pastures" (Ps. 23:2) and "quiet waters" that will restore us. We can reach these places only by following Him obediently. Otherwise, if we rebel against the leading of our Shepherd, we will bring frustration, dissatisfaction, and sadness into our lives. It's only by heeding the Lord that we can have "the peace of God, which transcends all understanding" (Phil. 4:7).

B. The Shepherd's Protection: vss. 4-5

Even though I walk through the valley of the shadow of death, I will fear no evil, for you are with me; your rod and your staff, they comfort me. You prepare a table before me in the presence of my enemies. You anoint my head with oil; my cup overflows.

Psalm 23:4 is the thematic center of this song of trust. Here we find David referring to God in a direct, reverent manner, and declaring his confidence in the Shepherd-King's abiding presence. David knew that, while he trusted in the Lord, he was not immune from the trials of life. The psalmist referred to these as "the valley of the shadow of death." This was a vivid way of referring to a life-threatening situation.

There are times when a shepherd in ancient Israel might have to lead the flock through a narrow gorge. Such could be a dangerous place, especially as the evening shadows hid bandits or fierce beasts. David's own experiences matched this imagery, for he often had to flee for his life to the mountains and caves of Judah. Yet even in those dark times, when it seemed as if his life would be snuffed out, God protected David. Because he knew his Shepherd, David did not experience paralyzing fear.

David compared his experiences to the sheep's being comforted by the shepherd's rod and staff. A typical Israelite shepherd would carry a "rod," or club, to defend against enemies. He would also be equipped with a "staff," or crook, to control the sheep. For these reasons his presence would comfort his sheep, just as God's powerful and disciplining presence comforted David.

David's faith in the Lord's protection sustained him throughout each harrowing incident. The same should also be true of us. What could be more encouraging than the realization that we have the Lord as our Shepherd? When we face any trial—even death—He is there by our side to help us.

At verse 5 the figure of the Lord changes from a shepherd with his sheep to a host of a banquet. This host entertained David lavishly. David's head was anointed with perfumed oil in the traditional way of showing honor to a guest. The table was spread with food, and David's cup was kept filled with wine. Meanwhile, David's enemies were present to look with envy upon his happiness, in the way captive enemies would be forced by ancient kings to observe their victory celebrations.

God's lavish treatment of David is indicative of the loving care that the Lord provides for His people. Jesus echoed this theme when He urged His followers to live for God and make His kingdom their primary concern, for the Lord would give them all they needed from day to day to serve Him (Matt. 6:33). Paul voiced a similar sentiment in Philippians 4:19, "My God will meet all your needs according to his glorious riches in Christ Jesus."

C. The Shepherd's Promise: vs. 6

Surely goodness and love will follow me all the days of my life, and I will dwell in the house of the LORD *forever.*

Throughout David's life, he had to endure pain, suffering, and threats to his life. God enabled him to overcome these with strength and courage. Death, however, was a different matter. It could not be overcome by conventional human means. Only the God of life, Israel's Shepherd-King, could enable David to face death with the assurance of eternal comfort in God's presence.

David poetically expressed these thoughts when he declared that God's goodness and unfailing love would "follow" (Ps. 23:6, literally "pursue") him throughout his life. David would not have to beg the Lord for evidences of His care. God would be eager to give them. Knowing this enabled David to entrust his eternal future with the Lord.

The feast David described earlier was more than a victory celebration. It was also the seal of his alliance with God. David realized that he had not come to the Lord's house for one meal only. He had come to live "forever." This does not mean that David expected to take up residence in the tabernacle. Rather, it means he looked forward to eternal communion with God.

In the final verse of this psalm, we see that believers dwell with God in eternity. Their perfect Shepherd-King promises to guide and protect them throughout their life and to bring them to His heavenly home forever.

II. THE LORD IS MY PROTECTOR: PSALM 121

A. The Protector's Power: vss. 1-2

I lift up my eyes to the hills—where does my help come from? My help comes from the LORD, *the Maker of heaven and earth.*

Each of Psalms 120—134 is entitled "A song of ascents." The most likely explanation for this title is that pilgrims sang these psalms as they made their way from the countryside to the capital for major religious festivals. Jerusalem occupies a hilltop, so one must ascend to it.

The songs of ascent have various themes. For instance, Psalm 121 is about protection. Travelers to Jerusalem must have found it heartening to think of God as their Guardian, which is how the psalm portrays Him. The psalm is a dialogue made up of four two-verse sections. Apparently, the first section is one person's statement of trust in God, while the remaining three sections are someone else's confirmation of God's protection. Another possibility is that several sections of this brief poem were recited back and forth by small groups of pilgrims in a caravan, for there is liturgical quality to these verses.

Central Israel, the location of Jerusalem, is hilly country. But why, as verse 1 indicates, would a pilgrim, when approaching the city, look to the hills? Perhaps this verse describes a traveler's impulse to take refuge in the hills when danger occurred. Or perhaps the verse describes a pilgrim keeping a lookout for robbers who might descend from the hills.

Regardless of what verse 1 may have intended, it's clear where the psalm's first speaker envisioned finding protection. His help came neither from hiding nor from vigilance, but from the Lord. As the "Maker of heaven and earth" (vs. 2), God has more than enough power to take care of His people.

These opening verses remind us of the nature of spiritual warfare in ancient Israel. Pagans looked to the hills for protection, for this is where they had built shrines to false deities such as Baal. The godly people in Judah, however, knew there was no protection in such a worthless idol. Not even the city walls and temple of Jerusalem could protect the people of faith. Rather, their hope was in the one true God, the King of all creation. The upright knew that since He had made everything, He was quite capable of protecting them, too.

B. The Protector's Watchfulness: vss. 3-4

He will not let your foot slip—he who watches over you will not slumber; indeed, he who watches over Israel will neither slumber nor sleep.

The psalm's second speaker (whose speeches are recorded in 121:3-8) described how thoroughly God protects His people. For instance, verses 3 and 4 teach that God watches over His people intimately and wakefully. God was so concerned about the pilgrims that He would even keep them from slipping and falling during their journey.

On the long trek to Jerusalem, the people would have to stop and sleep. In contrast, God's alertness never faltered. The language of confidence in this psalm indicates that it is about the speaker's trust in the living Lord. And the statements made in verses 3 and 4 were, in part, meant as a snub to the false Canaanite gods, whose followers excused them for allowing crops to fail by saying they were asleep.

C. The Protector's Constant Care: vss. 5-6

The LORD watches over you—the LORD is your shade at your right hand; the sun will not harm you by day, nor the moon by night.

Like Psalm 121:3-4, verses 5 and 6 teach that God is near and ever vigilant. But these verses use different terms. "Shade" (vs. 5) was a conventional symbol for protection in the sun-baked Near East. God's protection is "at your right hand." This means it is always nearby, ready for use. In verse 6, "the sun" represents dangers found in the daytime and "the moon" represents nighttime dangers. At no time was God "off duty" (so to speak). The Keeper of Israel was always present to protect His people in every circumstance.

These statements remind us of where we should place our confidence. We must never trust in a lesser power than God Himself. In addition to being all-powerful, the Lord also watches over us. Nothing can distract or deter Him, which means that we are safe in His care.

D. The Protector's Assurance: vss. 7-8

The LORD *will keep you from all harm—he will watch over your life; the* LORD *will watch over your coming and going both now and forevermore.*

Ancient Judaism had a single focus for its religious activities. That focus was the sanctuary, which for much of the nation's history was the temple in Jerusalem. Able-bodied Israelites who lived all over were expected to make the trip to the sanctuary for at least three annual religious festivals: Passover, Weeks, and Tabernacles.

In addition to worship, pilgrimages afforded the opportunity to meet new people and to enjoy new experiences. But pilgrims also faced dangers, including sandstorms, robbers, and wild beasts. In Psalm 121:7, the speaker plainly declared that the Lord would keep His pilgrims "from all harm." In fact, almighty God would preserve their lives.

All activities are covered by the words "your coming and going" (vs. 8). From journey's start to journey's end, the pilgrims would be protected by God. Likewise, from life's start to life's end, believers in all ages are protected by God. Though we don't make religious pilgrimages like those the ancient Israelites made, we too need and receive God's protection.

Discussion Questions

1. What ideas come to mind when you read that "the LORD is my shepherd" (Ps. 23:1)?
2. What was the basis for David saying, "I will fear no evil" (vs. 4)?
3. According to Psalm 121:2, from where does the believer's help ultimately come?
4. In what sense does the Lord watch over His people (vs. 5)?
5. How do Psalms 23 and 121 prompt you to trust God implicitly in all circumstances?

Contemporary Application

Psalms 23 and 121 do not promise that believers will avoid all accidents and illness. But they do teach that no trouble can destroy our relationship with God or render His power inoperative. Each step we take, each breath we breathe, we can know that God is with us and that we are under His care.

This climactic affirmation of faith rests on what we know about the Lord. God the Creator watches over every detail of our lives. The Protector's assurance is that He will continue to do this, regardless of whatever threats might emerge against us in the future. Of course, harm might arise from enemies at home and abroad, or even from within our own families. But because we are people of faith, we have put our trust in God's all-knowing, all-loving care.

Much more than physical protection is in view here. The assaults of the world, the flesh, and the devil are made against our souls, and thus we need God's protection in each of these arenas. It's reassuring to know that nothing escapes the attention of our loving Guardian and Keeper.

God of Justice

DEVOTIONAL READING

Psalm 72:11-19

DAILY BIBLE READINGS

Monday June 24
Psalm 89:1-8 Proclaim His Love to All Generations

Tuesday June 25
Psalm 89:9-18 God Rules Heaven and Earth

Wednesday June 26
Psalm 90:1-6 From Everlasting to Everlasting

Thursday June 27
Psalm 102:12-22 God's Name Endures for Generations

Friday June 28
Psalm 77:11-20 Remember God's Wonders of Old

Saturday June 29
Psalm 78:1-8 Teach His Statutes from Generation to Generation

Sunday June 30
Psalm 135:1-7 The Lord Is Above All Other Gods

Scripture

Background Scripture: *Psalms 72; 82; 113*
Scripture Lesson: *Psalms 82; 113:5-9*
Key Verse: *Rise up, O God, judge the earth, for all the nations are your inheritance.* Psalm 82:8.
Scripture Lesson for Children: *Psalms 82; 113:5-9*
Key Verse for Children: *Teach me your way, O LORD.* Psalm 27:11.

Lesson Aim

To evaluate our spiritual walk in light of God's concern for social issues.

Lesson Setting

Time: *Psalm 82: date unknown, though possibly written during or after the Babylonian captivity (about 550–450 B.C.); Psalm 113: date unknown, though possibly written during the reign of either David (1010–1090 B.C.) or Solomon (970–930 B.C.)*
Place: *Israel*

Lesson Outline

God of Justice

  I. God's Judgment of the Wicked: Psalm 82:1-8
      A. *Judgment on the Judges: vss. 1-2*
      B. *Exhortation to Judge Fairly: vss. 3-4*
      C. *Condemnation of the Wicked: vss. 5-8*
 II. God's Kindness to the Upright: Psalm 113:5-9
      A. *The Greatness of God: vs. 5*
      B. *The Compassion of God: vss. 6-9*

Introduction for Adults

Topic: *Where Is Justice?*

"There isn't any justice" is the common refrain of people who think they have been cheated by the "system." No doubt such complaints seem reasonable in some cases, being caused by what we call a miscarriage of justice. However, we must be careful not to jump to premature conclusions, for often we do not know all the facts.

When considering the issue of justice, our own integrity is important to safeguard. For instance, we should avoid all appearances of unseemly behavior, even when others have wronged us. We should also avoid wallowing in bitterness, for an angry, resentful heart brings no pleasure to God, and it can destroy our spiritual vitality. The Lord is honored and pleased when we leave the issue of justice in His hands.

Introduction for Youths

Topic: *God Is the Judge*

The teenager complained to his father about the family rules. The father explained that he was trying as best he could to establish Christian values within the home. His desire was not to make his son miserable, but rather to please God. The father explained, "I am answerable to God for how I run my family. One day I will stand before the Lord and He will evaluate how I exercised my responsibilities as your father."

That was a new thought for the teenager. He knew he lived under his father's authority, but he had not considered that his father was accountable to an even higher authority. God is the Judge, not just of teenagers, but also of their parents and everyone else (for example, pastors and teachers).

These observations remind us that God wants us to help one another do the best we can to carry out His will for our lives. We should strive to be fair and honest in all our relationships, rather than taking advantage of one another or showing favoritism of any kind.

Concepts for Children

Topic: *Living with Fairness*

1. God cares about how we treat others, especially people in need.
2. There are wicked people who try to disobey God, but He will not let them succeed in their plans.
3. The psalmist prayed for God to punish those who are wicked.
4. God comes to the aid of those who need help and gives them reasons to be joyful.
5. God wants us to be kind and fair to other people.

The Lesson Commentary

I. GOD'S JUDGMENT OF THE WICKED: PSALM 82:1-8

A. Judgment on the Judges: vss. 1-2

God presides in the great assembly; he gives judgment among the "gods": "How long will you defend the unjust and show partiality to the wicked?"

The title line of Psalm 82 mentions Asaph. He was a Levite and the son of Berekiah (1 Chron. 15:17). Asaph was one of the musicians who sounded the cymbals before the ark of the covenant when it was moved from the house of Obed-Edom to Jerusalem (vss. 16-19).

Asaph's family became one of the three families given responsibility for music and song in the temple (25:1-9). Following the Jews' return from Babylonian captivity, 128 members from the family of Asaph conducted the singing when the foundations of Zerubbabel's temple were laid (Ezra 2:41; 3:10). In all, 12 psalms (50, 73—83) are attributed to the family of Asaph.

Psalm 82 is a wisdom song. As such, it provides instruction about living for the people of God. The writer pictured God standing in the assembly of earthly leaders, to whom He had delegated authority, and condemning their injustices. Verse 8 especially envisions the Lord Himself taking direct control of the affairs of the world.

In this drama, God is pictured as presiding over a "great assembly" (vs. 1), namely, the court of heaven. In this somber setting, the Lord pronounces judgment against the "gods." There are several ways to understand this reference. Some say the psalmist was referring to the unjust rulers and judges of Israel, while others say the verse is talking about demons or false pagan gods.

Perhaps the best interpretation is that "gods" is a sarcastic reference to the world's evil human leaders (such as judges and kings). In ancient times, it was common for the nation's rulers to be honored as divine beings, or to take upon themselves the title of some pagan deity. Some think these leaders issued their decrees in the names of certain false gods in order to claim more authority for themselves.

The point of verse 1 is that ultimately all authorities are accountable to God. He measures the integrity of those to whom He has delegated power according to their treatment of the poor, the orphaned, the afflicted, and the needy. Sadly, as verse 2 makes clear, many of the rulers of the nations surrounding Israel were guilty of handing down unjust decisions. They showered special favors on the wicked, rather than punishing them for their crimes.

The truth about God's rule is also affirmed in other parts of Scripture. For example, Daniel 4:17 says that the Lord controls all kingdoms and establishes those who rule in positions of power. Verses 25, 34, and 35 likewise indicate that God is sovereign over earthly rulers.

B.　Exhortation to Judge Fairly: vss. 3-4

"Defend the cause of the weak and fatherless; maintain the rights of the poor and oppressed. Rescue the weak and needy; deliver them from the hand of the wicked."

God had accused the rulers of the nations of the earth with a variety of social injustices. For instance, they had failed to "defend the cause" (Ps. 82:3), or give fair judgment, to the disadvantaged in society, such as the destitute and the oppressed, as well as widows and orphans. God had appointed earthly leaders to rescue the "weak and needy" (vs. 4) from the grasp of evil people. Tragically, the opposite happened.

These verses summarize the teaching of the Mosaic law and indicate God's basic desire that the defenseless would find a haven of justice in the law courts of the nation in which they lived. Instead of judging fairly, the rulers had misjudged, and instead of coming to the aid of the disadvantaged, the leaders had exploited them. By showing favoritism to the wicked (vs. 2), the wicked kings and judges had trampled the cause of the righteous.

C.　Condemnation of the Wicked: vss. 5-8

"They know nothing, they understand nothing. They walk about in darkness; all the foundations of the earth are shaken. I said, 'You are "gods"; you are all sons of the Most High.' But you will die like mere men; you will fall like every other ruler." Rise up, O God, judge the earth, for all the nations are your inheritance.

In the Lord's condemnation of the wicked rulers surrounding Israel, He declared that "they know nothing" (Ps. 82:5). In other words, the oppressors of the disadvantaged were spiritually ignorant and morally deficient, even though they claimed otherwise. This sentiment is echoed by the statement, "they walk about in darkness."

The evil rulers acted as if they did not care about their official responsibility or the judgment from God they would receive for abusing their power. Because of the profound wickedness of the world's leaders, the situation was unstable. In fact, "the foundations of the earth are shaken." When officials rule unjustly, the divinely established moral order upon which human existence operates is eroded.

The statement in verse 6, "You are 'gods,'" literally means "You are 'mighty ones.'" The idea is that all earthly leaders are set up ultimately by the decree of the Lord, the true God. These rulers could loosely be called "sons of the Most High," for God, in effect, invested His authority in them for the stability of the world. Thus, these human rulers operated as the Lord's representatives, regardless of whether they affirmed this truth. Despite such power on their part, God could revoke it at any time.

In John 10:34, Jesus quoted the phrase "you are gods" appearing in Psalm 82:6. The Savior did this as He responded to the religious authorities, who wanted to stone Him for declaring Himself to be the Son of God. Jesus' statement supports the view that "gods" refers to earthly rulers. In a play on words, the Savior reasoned that if human leaders can be called "gods" (even though they are not), certainly the Messiah can be called God (especially when He is).

God had created these monarchs and judges for a life of service to Him. Tragically, however, they had spurned this responsibility and lived for themselves. As a result, they would die like the mere mortals they were (vs. 7). Though they might have claimed to be invincible, they would "fall like every other ruler." Perhaps the idea here is that these rulers, though made in God's image and entrusted with great power, would become vulnerable to the violent deaths that often accompanied the tyranny they promoted.

The psalmist could see the end in store for the wicked rulers of the world. He thus prayed that God, the supreme Judge of the earth, would "rise up" (vs. 8). The idea is that the Lord would act to bring the rule of the wicked to a speedy end. God could justly exert such authority, for all the nations belonged to Him. Here we find the psalmist anticipating a future day when the Lord would restore order and perfect justice to a world cursed by sin. The psalmist wanted this perfect reign of God over the entire world to come quickly.

Down through the centuries, wicked rulers have brought overwhelming disaster, especially in their oppression of the poor and their exploitation of the disadvantaged. One day the true Judge, the Lord God, will vindicate the cause of the afflicted. The righteous one will ensure that the cry of the redeemed for justice comes to pass (Pss. 96:13; 98:9).

II. GOD'S KINDNESS TO THE UPRIGHT: PSALM 113:5-9

A. The Greatness of God: vs. 5

Who is like the LORD our God, the One who sits enthroned on high?

Psalm 113 is a song of descriptive praise that begins and ends with the command to "praise the LORD" (vss. 1, 9). It lauds God for His great majesty and compassion to the disadvantaged. This psalm and Psalm 114 are regularly recited at the Passover seder [SAY-duhr], which is a Jewish celebratory meal that comes before the serving of the dinner. Psalms 115—118 are recited after the dinner.

Psalm 113:5 is the thematic center of the song and rhetorically asks "who is like the LORD?" No one, of course, is like Him, for He is high in majesty and awesome in power. These truths are underscored in the refrain "the One who sits enthroned on high." There should be no doubt among the redeemed concerning the praiseworthiness of God.

B. The Compassion of God: vss. 6-9

Who stoops down to look on the heavens and the earth? He raises the poor from the dust and lifts the needy from the ash heap; he seats them with princes, with the princes of their people. He settles the barren woman in her home as a happy mother of children. Praise the LORD.

Although the psalmist pictured God as sitting on His lofty throne in heaven, he knew that God actively looks over His creation. The Almighty "stoops down" (Ps. 113:6) from His throne to consider the heavens and the earth. God is great both in His exaltation and in His condescension. Though He transcends our earthly limitations, He is still present.

Human beings are not irrelevant specks of dust lost in the vast regions of space. Rather, they are important to the Lord. The psalmist reflected on a number of human circumstances to substantiate his point. He considered the poor and needy and saw how God took care of them (vss. 7-8). He remembered barren women who had become happy mothers in Israel (vs. 9). These were token reminders that the universe is monitored by a watchful and loving heavenly Father.

In the world's way of thinking those who are powerful and authoritative should associate only with those like them. But the God of the universe defies such logic. Though He is exalted in His majesty and in supreme control of everything, the Lord chooses to associate with the lowly and afflicted, not with the rich and powerful.

It's tragic, of course, that the poor of the world often have to eke out their existence by clawing and scratching through rubbish heaps just to find a scrap of food to eat. This psalm declares that God cares for them. We are also reminded of our spiritual poverty. While we scrounge around for meaning in life, God's mercy in Christ gives us the opportunity to become citizens of heaven. The Lord not only fills us with significance, but also with joy.

Discussion Questions

1. What were some of the wrongs being committed by the unjust rulers?
2. What were the unjust rulers supposed to be doing?
3. What end awaited the unjust rulers?
4. What is God's attitude toward those who are disadvantaged?
5. What are some things we can do as believers to help the poor and oppressed in our society?

Contemporary Application

The tragic scenes depicted in this week's lesson result when people become engrossed in their own interests and disregard how they're treating others. When we become preoccupied with ourselves and our concerns, our focus on God's concerns is lost. Who will fix the fence in the backyard? Is my retirement secure? Will I get the promotion I want? These concerns are not wrong, but it's inappropriate to let them encroach upon the moments in which God is likely to alert us to His concern for others in need.

Instead of spending so much time on our wants and even our needs, we should evaluate our walk with Christ and determine whether we are aware of God's concerns for social issues. If we don't, we may find ourselves living in a way that is displeasing to the Lord. Our devotion to God can become formal and lifeless when we merely go through the motions of being a Christian. Rather than love the Lord and the people He created, we busy ourselves in a flurry of activity (even religious activity).

The solution is to unclutter our minds of everyday concerns and chores and refocus our attention on God's concern for social issues. He is pleased when we seek to be more alert and responsive to the needs of others. For instance, we can take time to see how others are doing and volunteer to help them resolve their problems. We can also cultivate an attitude of humility and love. Just as arrogance and hate foster unjust practices, so humility and love promote fairness and sensitivity to others.

Teach the Wonders of God

DEVOTIONAL READING

Psalm 135:1-7

DAILY BIBLE READINGS

Monday July 1
  Psalm 136:1-9 The Creator's Steadfast Love

Tuesday July 2
  Psalm 147:1-11 The Sustainer of Land and People

Wednesday July 3
  Psalm 103:15-22 An Eternal God Sustains His Perishable People

Thursday July 4
  Psalm 93 God Has Established the World

Friday July 5
  Psalm 104:1-18 God Set the Earth's Foundation

Saturday July 6
  Psalm 78:1-8 Teach Generation to Generation

Sunday July 7
  Psalm 65 God Creates and Sustains

Scripture

Background Scripture: *Psalm 78:1-8*
Scripture Lesson: *Psalm 78:1-8*
Key Verse: *We will not hide them from their children; we will tell the next generation the praiseworthy deeds of the LORD, his power, and the wonders he has done.* Psalm 78:4.

Lesson Aim

To recognize the importance of trusting in the Lord and obeying His commands.

Lesson Setting

Time: *Date unknown, though possibly written about the time of the prophet Hosea (750–715 B.C.)*
Place: *Judah*

Lesson Outline

Teach the Wonders of God

  I. God's Purpose: Psalm 78:1-4
      A. *The Summons: vss. 1-3*
      B. *The Message: vs. 4*
  II. God's Program: Psalm 78:5-8
      A. *God's Commands: vs. 5a*
      B. *Parents' Responsibility: vss. 5b-6*
      C. *Children's Commitment: vs. 7*
      D. *Ancestors' Failure: vs. 8*

Introduction for Adults

Topic: *Tell the Story*

The leader of a men's retreat asked a Christian friend to tell the audience the message of the Gospel. But the leader added an important qualification. "Don't use the typical Christian vocabulary," he said. "I want you to explain the Gospel in everyday words, not theological terms. Try to avoid religious language, if you can. Many people today just don't understand our Christian jargon." That proved to be a challenge, and the Christian friend revised what he was going to say several times before the leader of the men's retreat gave his approval.

Can a person with no church background really understand the Gospel? The answer is *yes*! One of the beauties of telling others about the Lord is that we can use everyday language. If our message is fresh and clear, it can make a great impact for the cause of Christ. Regardless of what we say, we want people to learn that God is real and that following Him is the most important decision they could ever make.

Introduction for Youths

Topic: *Pass It On*

The college chaplain asked a well-known football player who was a Christian to speak on campus. The player could not make it on a specific day, so the chaplain asked him to recommend another player who was a Christian. The first player refused, not because he was critical of his teammate, but because the other person was terrible at public speaking.

Giving our personal testimony requires both courage and skill. God doesn't expect all of us to be able to stand in front of a crowd of college students and speak eloquently. But He is pleased when we maintain a fresh supply of personal accounts that we can tell our friends. God desires us to be ready at all times to answer questions others might ask about our faith in Christ.

Admittedly, it's hard work to give our personal testimony on the spur of the moment. One reason is that it's easy to forget important details of how God has cared for us. Nevertheless, the effort we put forth to be prepared is well worth the investment of our time, for God is glorified through the sharing of the Gospel.

Concepts for Children

Topic: *Passing On God's Teaching*

1. The psalmist asked people everywhere to hear all the wonderful things God had done.
2. The psalmist asked people to tell their children what they had learned about God.
3. God wants parents and grandparents to tell their children and grandchildren about His commands, which are written in His Word.
4. Learning about God helps us to put our trust in Him and obey His commands.
5. God wants us to tell others about the wonderful things He has done for us.

The Lesson Commentary

I. GOD'S PURPOSE: PSALM 78:1-4

A. The Summons: vss. 1-3

O my people, hear my teaching; listen to the words of my mouth. I will open my mouth in parables, I will utter hidden things, things from of old—what we have heard and known, what our fathers have told us.

In Psalm 77 the writer recalled God's wonderful works in the past to encourage faith in times of distress. In Psalm 78 the writer urged the people of God to learn from the nation's history. Too often the Israelites had forgotten God's great works. Their short memories and ingratitude led to unbelief and rebellion. The psalmist painted this picture so that his contemporaries would not repeat the sins of their ancestors.

While a significant portion of the psalm concerns periodic outbreaks of stubbornness and disobedience among God's people, this week's lesson will focus specifically on the faithfulness of the Lord. Asaph, who clearly had a strong command of Scripture, noted that had the Israelites been faithful to follow God's decrees in the Mosaic law, they would not have fallen into apostasy and despair. This is the main point we must take home from our study.

The psalmist began with a summons for God's people to listen to his teaching (vs. 1). He wanted them to pay attention because he was about to set forth the lessons to be learned from Israel's past. In ancient times, God's people were to respect the authority of His Word. And those who taught from Scripture (such as the prophets of God) were to reflect upon the past as well as discuss the future.

The psalmist explained that he would teach "parables" (vs. 2) and "hidden things . . . from of old." The Hebrew word rendered "parable" is used here in the broader sense of a story with a moral and spiritual application. "Hidden things" refers to obscure sayings or riddles. The idea is that the lessons of history are not easily or correctly discerned. The specific enigma concerning Israel's history is the people's rebellious attitude despite the grace of God.

Such words as "my people" (vs. 1) and "we" (vs. 3) shows that the psalmist regarded himself to be part of the Israelite community even though he related to them as their teacher. The writer wanted to share stories that had been heard and known. These were accounts their ancestors handed down to them and that were important to recall and heed. They are also important for us to consider so that we can avoid the same errors.

B. The Message: vs. 4

We will not hide them from their children; we will tell the next generation the praiseworthy deeds of the LORD, his power, and the wonders he has done.

The psalmist was clear about the content of the message that he wanted to teach the present generation of God's people. They, in turn, were to convey these truths to "their children" (Ps. 78:4). The general theme was "the praiseworthy deeds of the LORD." Specifically, the message concerned God's power and wonderful works in the lives of His people.

In the following history of Israel as recorded in this psalm, we get a sense of what the writer had in mind: the rebellion of the people of Ephraim (vss. 9-11), God's marvelous deliverance of Israel in the Exodus (vss. 12-16), the people's complaints (vss. 17-20), God's anger against the ungrateful people (vss. 21-25), God's judgment through the quail (vss. 26-31), the continuing unbelief of the people (vss. 32-33), the people's remembrance of God's true character and His remembrance of the people's weaknesses (vss. 34-39), God's faithfulness and the people's unfaithfulness (vss. 40-55), Israel's sins during the period of the judges (vss. 56-64), God's victory over Israel's enemies (vss. 65-66), and God's choice of Judah, Jerusalem, and David (vss. 67-72).

God's covenant statutes and saving acts throughout Israel's history should have moved the people to be faithful in worshiping, obeying, and serving Him. The incidents recounted by the psalmist were a rich and varied heritage, one that provided the foundation for the nation's walk with the Lord. If only the present generation of God's people would heed the past as they lived in the present, they would have a bright future.

Tragically, however, this did not occur. The people of Israel rebelled and were unfaithful to God (vs. 8). They ignored and forgot the miracles the Lord had performed (vss. 11-12). In fact, they put God to the test by making demands of Him (vs. 18). They lied to Him, tried to flatter Him (vs. 36), and continued to turn away from Him even after He had done great things on their behalf (vss. 42-56). In 1 Corinthians 10:1-12, Paul used the account of Israel's unfaithfulness to warn believers about the tragedy of unbelief and disobedience and to urge them to be devoted followers of Christ.

The church today grows strong by feasting on the wonderful things God has done. That's why God's mighty acts should be rehearsed both individually and corporately. The New Testament, of course, spotlights God's saving work in Christ. But Christians can also learn much from the accounts recorded in the Old Testament. The intent is not merely to memorize the details of episodes of what God has done in the past for His people. More importantly, it is to encourage us to trust in God and heed His commands.

II. GOD'S PROGRAM: PSALM 78:5-8

A. God's Commands: vs. 5a

He decreed statutes for Jacob and established the law in Israel.

The psalmist made it clear that the glorious deeds of the Lord were to be told from generation to generation. The writer also stressed that God's covenant statutes were to taught and obeyed. These were the decrees and ordinances the Lord had conveyed to Israel through Moses. God gave these laws and commandments to keep Israel loyal to Him and to indicate how His people were to live in an upright, virtuous manner (Ps. 78:5).

The Mosaic laws and Israel's covenant relationship with God set apart the people from the surrounding pagan nations. Part of their rich heritage included God's choice of Abraham and his descendants to be His people. It also included the deliverance of Israel from Egypt. Because the statutes and ordinances were given within this context, the laws and the history surrounding them could not be separated. Together they became the basis for Israel's faith and obedience down through the centuries.

B. Parents' Responsibility: vss. 5b-6

Which he commanded our forefathers to teach their children, so the next generation would know them, even the children yet to be born, and they in turn would tell their children.

All along it was God's desire that the parents and grandparents of Israelite children would tell them the accounts of His saving acts (Ps. 78:5-6). For instance, in Exodus 10:2 we learn that each successive generation of Israelites was to learn how God "dealt harshly with the Egyptians and how [He] performed [His] signs among them." The goal was that God's people would know that He is "the LORD."

This admonition was reiterated in 12:24-27 concerning the Passover celebration. Moses noted that when Israelite children asked about the significance of the ceremony, their parents were to explain the historical basis for observing it. Likewise, during the dedication of the firstborn sons of Israel, Moses directed the parents to explain to their children why they were doing this (13:8, 14).

Deuteronomy 6:7-8 perhaps summarizes best the way in which the instruction of future generations of Israelite children was supposed to take place. Parents were to talk with their children about the Lord's commandments when at home and while on a journey, as well as when lying down or getting up again. In other words, religious instruction was to be life-oriented, not information-oriented, and be woven into the context of daily activities.

C. Children's Commitment: vs. 7

Then they would put their trust in God and would not forget his deeds but would keep his commands.

In God's program, the outcome of faithful religious instruction by Israelite parents would be their children's unbroken commitment to the Lord. The psalmist noted three aspects of this commitment: the children putting their trust in God, remembering His deeds, and keeping His commands (Ps. 78:7).

These were the fundamental responsibilities for all the people of Israel, for this was at the heart of what it meant to be a true follower of God. These basics of the faith could not be handed down physically from one generation to the next. In other words, simply being born an Israelite did not guarantee a person would trust in God and obey His commands. Parents had to teach their children, and each child had to make a personal commitment to heed the Mosaic law.

This verse reminds us that religious faith is not something that happens automatically. Rather, each person is responsible to God and must decide to trust in Him and heed His Word. The strong temptation, of course, is to forget the Lord and His saving acts. If children are to make the right choices, God's deeds, character, will, and commands must be constantly taught and lived out by believing parents.

D. Ancestors' Failure: vs. 8

They would not be like their forefathers—a stubborn and rebellious generation, whose hearts were not loyal to God, whose spirits were not faithful to him.

The goal of religious instruction was to help each generation obey God and set its hope on Him (Ps. 78:8). Otherwise, a group of younger Israelites might forget the commands and saving acts of the Lord and slip into a rebellious state of unbelief. They would then be prone to repeat, rather than avoid, the same mistakes made by their wayward ancestors.

In this verse, the psalmist envisioned each generation having a certain group of general characteristics. For example, the exodus generation was known for being "stubborn and rebellious." Likewise, they refused to give their hearts to the Lord. In other words, their emotions, thoughts, motivations, and actions were focused on gratifying their sinful passions, not on glorifying God.

In contrast, the succeeding generation of Israelites entering the land of promise affirmed the statement that Joshua made: "But as for me and my household, we will serve the LORD" (Josh. 24:15). In fact, that entire generation remained loyal to God (vs. 31). Tragically, however, the situation reversed itself for the succeeding generation. As Judges 21:25 says, "everyone did as he saw fit." Rather than follow the Mosaic law, the people made up their own rules and lived by them.

The writer of Hebrews discussed the failure in Israel in order to challenge Christians to be faithful. "Do not harden your hearts" (Heb. 3:8, 15; 4:7), he repeated. A stubborn, rebellious mind-set is caused by the deceitfulness of sin (vs. 13). It is like a predator "crouching at [the] door" (Gen. 4:7) of a building so that it might attack an unsuspecting victim. That's why we need to be spiritually vigilant against sin.

Religious instruction is a key tool that godly parents have to help pass on the baton of faith to their children. By telling the accounts of God's saving acts, explaining His commands, and emphasizing the grace of God in Christ, parents are more likely to see their children turn their hearts to the Lord.

Discussion Questions

1. What was the main point of the writer's teaching in Psalm 78:1-8?
2. Why did the psalmist want to focus the attention of his readers on particular events from Israel's past?
3. Why did the writer emphasize the importance of religious instruction to children?

4. What were some of the "praiseworthy deeds of the Lord" (vs. 4) that the psalmist had in mind?

5. How can we keep from forgetting the wonderful deeds of God?

Contemporary Application

What shall we choose for our children? Will it be faith in God and obedience to His commands, or unbelief and rebellion against Him? Clearly, we would prefer the first option. Since that is true, why don't we spend more time trying to achieve it?

God has given us many wonderful opportunities for religious education. Our churches train teachers and use sound curricula. We also have other community resources that are available to reinforce our Christian teachings and values. These include youth programs and summer camps for spiritual enrichment.

The psalmist's generation had few, if any, of these resources. He primarily focused on one approach for fostering faith in children and grandchildren—teaching them spiritual truths and values throughout the course of their daily life. Have we overlooked this part of God's program for us, perhaps because we have so many other things competing for our time and attention?

Because parents are pressured, they often hand off the teaching of their children to other parties. Yes, parents should take advantage of the resources in their churches and schools. But these should not take the place of personalized religious instruction. This reflects Paul's directive to parents in Ephesians 6:4. They are responsible for bringing up their children "in the training and instruction of the Lord."

Creator and Sustainer

Scripture

Background Scripture: *Psalms 65; 104*
Scripture Lesson: *Psalm 104:24-35*
Key Verse: *How many are your works, O LORD! In wisdom you made them all; the earth is full of your creatures.* Psalm 104:24.
Key Verse for Children: *I will sing to the LORD all my life; I will sing praise to my God as long as I live.* Psalm 104:33.

Lesson Aim

To learn to appreciate God more through His creation.

Lesson Setting

Time: *Date unknown, though possibly written sometime before the fall of Jerusalem in 586 B.C.*
Place: *Judah*

Lesson Outline

Creator and Sustainer

I.   The Scope of God's Creation: Psalm 104:24-26
   A. *The Earth: vs. 24*
   B. *The Sea: vss. 25-26*
II. The Creation's Dependence on God: Psalm 104:27-30
   A. *For Food: vss. 27-28*
   B. *For Renewal: vss. 29-30*
III. The Glory of Creation: Psalm 104:31-35
   A. *God's Rejoicing: vss. 31-32*
   B. *Our Praise: vss. 33-35*

Introduction for Adults

Topic: *Let Praise Continue*

World-renowned French chemist and microbiologist Louis Pasteur (1822–1895) once said, "Posterity will some day laugh at the foolishness of modern materialistic philosophy. The more I study nature, the more I am amazed at the Creator." Imagine what Pasteur would have said had he been party to all of the discoveries of the past century.

With each new discovery of the intricacies of Creation, Christians declare, "Let the praise of God continue." That's because we believe God's handiwork in the world will continue to be unfolded, giving further evidence of His wisdom and power. At the same time, it's our hope that those who do scientific research will be open to the idea that they can know the Creator of all things through faith in His Son, Jesus Christ. We also hope for the proper application of new scientific discoveries so that they will be used for good, not evil, purposes. Praise and prayer go hand in hand as we walk down the path of increased knowledge and understanding of our world.

Introduction for Youths

Topic: *A Reason to Sing*

When we look at the psalms recorded in Scripture, we find magnificent prayers to God. These hymns, which give us reasons to praise, arise from the lives of people who knew what it meant to worship the Lord. The psalmists recorded their thoughts because they were deeply devoted to God.

Such devotion makes all the difference, whether it is in creating a memorable song, putting it to music, or performing it before a congregation of believers. God is pleased when our worship of Him is sincere, enthusiastic, and reverent. Such expressions of praise seek to glorify the Lord and edify His people.

Our worship of God, of course, is more than just a simple display of emotion. It is grounded in the truth of Scripture and welcomes believers from all walks of life to participate. The focus is on the great things God has done for us, not on what we imagine we can do for Him. Our desire is to be united in spirit and a credible witness for our Lord to the world.

Concepts for Children

Topic: *Praise God: The Creator of All Things*

1. God, in His great wisdom, created all things.
2. All creation depends on God for life and food.
3. We should respond to these truths by singing praises to God.
4. We should also respond by thanking God for what He has done for us.
5. We should take some time to tell others about our wonderful God.

The Lesson Commentary

I.   THE SCOPE OF GOD'S CREATION: PSALM 104:24-26

A.   The Earth: vs. 24

How many are your works, O LORD! In wisdom you made them all; the earth is full of your creatures.

Psalm 104 emphasizes God's great act of Creation and reflects the teaching and vocabulary of Genesis 1. The poetry of the psalmists and prophets often reflected upon God's work in Creation (Pss. 8, 19). But unlike pagan hymns, Scripture affirms that God, the Creator, alone brought the world and celestial bodies into existence and that only He should be worshiped.

The arrangement of material in Psalm 104 is as follows: praise for God's great creation (vss. 1-2); the creation of the heavens (vss. 3-4); the creation of the earth (vss. 5-9); the waters of blessing (vss. 10-13); the fullness of the earth (vss. 14-18); the patterns of life (vss. 19-23); praise for God's great creation (vss. 24-26); an acknowledgement that all life is dependent upon the Lord (vss. 27-30); a prayer for God's glory (vss. 31-32); and a personal response to God (vss. 33-35).

As the psalmist sang of the glory of the Lord's creation, he exclaimed at "how many are [God's] works" (vs. 24). Whether it be the lights in the sky, the heavens and the waters, the land and vegetation, the sun, moon, and stars, the fish and birds, or the animals, people, and food to sustain them, the Lord in His wisdom made them all. This sentiment reflects the mind-set of the Hebrew wisdom writers. They looked at the world with reverence because it reflected the glory of its Creator.

Psalm 8 is a good example of this way of thinking. David extolled God for His enormous skill, care, and precision in giving shape to the world and populating it with plant and animal life. The one who made the heavens, moon, and stars (vs. 3) also crowned humankind with glory and honor (vs. 5). The Lord gave men and women dominion over His wonderful works. He graciously put them in charge of His expansive and marvelous creation (vs. 6), which includes tame and wild animals (vs. 7), birds, and sea creatures (vs. 8).

These truths reminds us how important it is for us to consider God's power and wisdom in His created universe. The earth is built on the Lord's foundations, and He guarantees its permanence. Though one day the present heavens and the earth will be destroyed (2 Pet. 3:10), God will create new heavens and a new earth that will last forever (Isa. 65:17; Rev. 21:1). The same power that upholds the world also provides a firm foundation for believers. Such a great God is worthy of devotion and praise from His people (Ps. 8:9).

B.   The Sea: vss. 25-26

There is the sea, vast and spacious, teeming with creatures beyond number—living things both large and small. There the ships go to and fro, and the leviathan, which you formed to frolic there.

As we noted earlier, the Creation account of Genesis 1 forms the backdrop for Psalm 104. During the first three days of God's creative activity He brought order out of the original formlessness specified in Genesis 1:2. He created light where there had been only darkness and filled what had been empty with the first signs of life.

During the final three days of His creative activity, the Lord established and filled the earth with all forms of life, including fish in the sea, birds in the air, and animals on the dry ground. In Psalm 104:25-26, the writer specifically focused on the immense seas with their many forms of aquatic life. The rich variety of the world's oceans stood as a testimony to the enormity of God's wisdom.

The Lord's wisdom is especially evident in humankind. People have abilities and aptitudes that far exceed those of other creatures. For instance, humankind has made abundant use of the world's seas. People and nations have built all kinds of sailing vessels to travel over the oceans. The psalmist also noted the presence of "leviathan, which you formed to frolic there" (vs. 26). This is a reference to one of God's large sea creatures that harmlessly played in the oceans of the world.

II. THE CREATION'S DEPENDENCE ON GOD: PSALM 104:27-30

A. For Food: vss. 27-28

These all look to you to give them their food at the proper time. When you give it to them, they gather it up; when you open your hand, they are satisfied with good things.

The psalmist noted that every living thing is absolutely dependent on God for life, health, and vigor. The Lord provides sunshine, rain, and oxygen so that the creatures He so wondrously created might continue to exist and thrive. His benevolent provision of food occurs at the right times and in the proper seasons (Ps. 104:27).

God graciously enables people to plant crops and harvest an ample supply of food from it. He generously opens His hand to supply the inhabitants of the earth with other good things (such as minerals, precious metals, building materials, and so forth) for their need and benefit (vs. 28). Clearly, this is not the work of impersonal, mechanical forces, but rather the provision of our heavenly Father. This awesome Creator and bountiful Sustainer is worthy of unending praise.

B. For Renewal: vss. 29-30

When you hide your face, they are terrified; when you take away their breath, they die and return to the dust. When you send your Spirit, they are created, and you renew the face of the earth.

In Psalm 104:29, the writer described what life was like when the Lord hid His face, or withheld His gracious care. When God allowed severe drought or devastating storms to occur, humankind was "terrified." This means being more than upset. People were overwhelmed by the disastrous turn of events. Eventually they turned to their Creator and implored Him to bring them relief from their calamity.

Both death and life are in the hands of almighty God. The breath of life that the Lord graciously imparts to every person is eventually taken away by Him. When it is removed, people die and "return to the dust." This is a sobering reminder of how mortal humankind truly is and how utterly dependent they are on the Creator and

Sustainer of the entire universe.

God is not only the master of death but also the one who creates life. The psalmist depicted the Lord as breathing the spirit of life into every creature, which implies that all entities are brought into existence by His supreme act (vs. 30). He also sustains life; if it were not for the nurturing hand of the Lord, all living things would wither and die. With each passing season and each successive generation He renews the face of the earth. None of this happens haphazardly or in its own strength, but is the result of God's gracious intervention.

III. THE GLORY OF CREATION: PSALM 104:31-35

A. God's Rejoicing: vss. 31-32

May the glory of the LORD endure forever; may the LORD rejoice in his works—he who looks at the earth, and it trembles, who touches the mountains, and they smoke.

As the poet considered the marvelous works of God's creation, he expressed his desire that the Lord's glory would "endure forever" (Ps. 104:31). God's guardianship of everything He made would bring Him eternal honor and splendor. Just as the Lord took great delight in the things He originally created (Gen. 1:31), the psalmist prayed that God would continue to enjoy and rejoice in everything He made.

The poet noted that God is so powerful that one direct glance at the earth causes it to tremble, or quake, in fear (Ps. 104:32). He is so awesome that one slight touch of some grand hill or lofty mountain causes it to spew out smoke. These facts serve as a reminder of God's infinite majesty and His unmatched ability to blot out whatever He graciously brings into existence.

This verse reminds us that God did not have to make the world and all the life within it. He was not lonely, bored, or in need of a challenge. He created all things because of His great love. He sustains life on earth so that all creatures might be the recipients of His benevolent care. He especially wants people to take notice of His abundant provisions and timely help. As they reflect on all the things the Lord does for them, they should be filled with awe and be eager to give Him praise.

B. Our Praise: vss. 33-35

I will sing to the LORD all my life; I will sing praise to my God as long as I live. May my meditation be pleasing to him, as I rejoice in the LORD. But may sinners vanish from the earth and the wicked be no more. Praise the LORD, O my soul. Praise the LORD.

The psalmist arrived at the apex of his praise, based on his contemplation of God's work in nature. The writer declared that as long as he lived he would sing in exultation to the Lord (Ps. 104:33). But the poet also realized how easy it is to use the mind God had given him for corrupt and evil undertakings.

This concern remains true even today. Tragically, some people are unimpressed by what they see in creation. Their sinful hearts make it impossible for them to recognize the Lord's eternal power and divine nature as it is unveiled in Creation

(Rom. 1:18-25). Believers, however, look at nature through eyes that have been opened by God's grace in Christ.

The poet wanted to honor the Lord by meditating on those things that were "pleasing" (Ps. 104:34), or acceptable, to Him. One of the things that pleased God was people's taking delight in Him. The Lord was honored when humankind rejoiced in His goodness and greatness. It would be one humble way they could express their infinite debt of gratitude to Him.

Clearly, God has been merciful to let His fallen human creation live on. Yet the psalmist longed for the day when the wicked were removed from the earth and the curse of sin was erased forever (vs. 35). In the meantime, he would continue to praise the Lord with every aspect of his being. This also should be true of us.

Praising the Lord gives us the opportunity to honor Him for the way He graciously takes care of us. We also have the opportunity to express our gratitude to Him for what He has done and continues to do for us. Recalling how God gave us life and what He does to sustain it helps us realize that we are His mortal, dependent creatures who exist to serve and worship Him.

When we neglect to praise God for His goodness, we indicate that we do not appreciate what He has done for us. We take for granted His abundant provision of food, clothing, and shelter. We trivialize the value of His supreme care of the world. In our arrogance we communicate to God that we do not need, nor want Him, and that we can survive and prosper by ourselves. We know, however, from this week's Scripture passage that the smallest details of our lives are in His hands.

Discussion Questions

1. How is God's wisdom evident in the many things He has created?
2. What would life be like if God withdrew His sustaining hand?
3. Why is it important to regularly praise our Creator and Sustainer?
4. What are we saying to God when we neglect to praise Him for His goodness?
5. What impact does our praising God have on the unsaved?

Contemporary Application

Praise is often stimulated by awe. The more we can explain and rationalize the facts we see around us, the less likely we are to praise God or other people for making them happen. If our response to an event is "That's no big deal," then obviously praise is not likely to follow. However, when we see or hear something that causes us to exclaim, "How did they do that?"—then praise is a natural response. We praise out of wonderment.

This week's lesson seeks to draw us to praise God for that which goes beyond our human explanation. When we are astonished at the wonder of creation, we are more likely to praise God than when we attempt to explain it rationally. For example, to realize that a single tongue of a solar flare is more than 40 times the diameter of the earth causes amazement. And even rapidly counting nonstop, it would take us thousands of years to number the stars in just one galaxy. The universe contains untold numbers of galaxies.

We should praise God not only for His wonderful works but also for the way He sustains everything He made. Without God's sustaining hand, life would become intolerable. Also, it would be impossible to find adequate food, water, or clothing. Such information helps us to better appreciate the grandeur, diversity, and power of the world that God has made and our dependence on Him. He truly is worthy of our highest praise!

The Crown of Creation

DEVOTIONAL READING

Psalm 100

DAILY BIBLE READINGS

Monday July 15
   Psalm 106:1-12 Our Ancestors' Sins and Ours

Tuesday July 16
   Psalm 103:1-14 The Lord Heals and Forgives

Wednesday July 17
   Psalm 85 Restore Us Again, O God

Thursday July 18
   Psalm 130 With God There Is Forgiveness

Friday July 19
   Psalm 51:1-9 Blot Out My Transgressions

Saturday July 20
   Psalm 51:10-19 Give Me a New and Right Spirit

Sunday July 21
   Psalm 32 Happy Are Those Who Are Forgiven

Scripture

Background Scripture: *Psalms 8; 100*
Scripture Lesson: *Psalm 8*
Key Verse: *What is man that you are mindful of him, the son of man that you care for him?* Psalm 8:4.
Key Verse for Children: *O LORD, our Lord, how majestic is your name in all the earth!* Psalm 8:1

Lesson Aim

To recognize that God, the all-powerful Creator, cares for His most valuable creation—people.

Lesson Setting

Time: *Written sometime during the reign of David (1010–970 B.C.)*
Place: *Israel*

Lesson Outline

The Crown of Creation
   I.   The Prelude: Psalm 8:1
   II. Fitting Worship: Psalm 8:2
   III. Humanity's Place: Psalm 8:3-5
   IV. Humanity's Responsibilities: Psalm 8:6-8
   V.   The Postlude: Psalm 8:9

Introduction for Adults

Topic: *Responsible to Care*

Each generation discovers new wealth in God's creation. These discoveries show how prolific are the mighty acts of God. But each discovery brings new challenges and responsibilities. The more God gives to us, the greater our responsibility to exercise wise stewardship according to His commands recorded in Scripture.

Our greatest failure seems to be our lack of gratitude. Simply put, we take God's gifts for granted. Many times we do not even acknowledge His daily provision of our needs. This is sad, for we could not survive very long without the air we breathe, the food we eat, or the water we drink, all of which come from God.

Psalm 8 reminds us that God is supremely praiseworthy. Wherever we look, we find reasons to praise Him. Most of all, when we consider what He has done for us in Christ, we should submit to Him as our Lord. After all, He's the author of life, whether physical or spiritual in nature.

Introduction for Youths

Topic: *Truly Awesome!*

Advertisers pandering to youth outdo themselves to make their products more attractive than their competitors'. For example, when we consider teen fashions, we can see how important it is for adolescents to stand out in a crowd. Yet no matter how impressive our clothes, computers, and cars might be, they are nothing compared to the magnificence of God's creation. We need to be careful, lest we lose sight of God's glory in the welter of things that are supposed to make us happy.

The world has a way of dominating our time, and it tries to shape our desires and values. But as Christians, we are wise to step back and ask why God made us. What does He desire of us? Also, how can we strengthen our faith in Him and not be stunted by the world's values? Meditating on God our Creator, as David did, is a step in the right direction.

Concepts for Children

Topic: *Praise God: The Creator of People*

1. There is no name more wonderful than that of God.
2. God is pleased when we take time to praise Him.
3. Even though God is very great, He still takes time to care for us.
4. God loves us so much that He gives us important things to do.
5. Let us show our love for God by doing what He wants.

The Lesson Commentary

I. THE PRELUDE: PSALM 8:1

O Lord, our Lord, how majestic is your name in all the earth! You have set your glory above the heavens.

According to the title of Psalm 8, it was written by David. The phrase "for the director of music" suggests that this song is from an early collection of hymns used in temple worship. It's also possible that when the psalm was used in the Hebrew liturgy, the leader of the Levitical choir spoke it before the assembly of worshipers. The word rendered "gittith" was probably a musical term and may have referred to a stringed instrument. One suggestion is that it was a guitar-like harp associated with Gath in Philistia.

The beginning and ending of this song suggests that it was a hymn of praise. The interior of the psalm, however, focuses on the Lord's sovereign ordering of the creation. It's for this reason that some classify this hymn as a nature psalm (or psalm of creation).

We don't know the original circumstances leading up to David's writing of this song, but it's not hard to imagine. Many of us can recall times out in the country when we gazed up into the sky on a clear night and saw countless stars extending from one end of the horizon to the other. If such was the case for David, we can only infer how puny he must have felt against the immense expanse of the heavens above which God had set His glory (vs. 1).

Two different Hebrew words are rendered "Lord" in this verse. The first term is *Yahweh,* and underscores the everlasting quality of His self-existence (Exod. 3:14-15). The second term is *Adonai,* and places emphasis on God's supreme and unchallenged authority. It's no wonder that David declared that the name of the all-glorious one was "majestic . . . in all the earth!" (Ps. 8:1). (In Scripture, the name of the Lord was considered a reflection of His character, encompassing all His attributes.)

This psalm ends with the same words it begins with. These words of praise to the name of God form a frame for it's central subject—praise from humankind, whom God has made to reflect His majesty. Here we see that people count for something in God's eyes. We are important and valuable to Him—not just because He created us, but also because He sent His Son to redeem us and give us eternal life.

When we visibly give thanks to God for His goodness, we declare to the unsaved that He is our Creator and Sustainer. We bear witness to the truth that every person needs God for present life and future hope. Our words of praise and gratitude to God (such as those recorded in verse 1) might encourage the unsaved to consider the truths of Christ and turn to Him in faith for new life and eternal joy.

II. FITTING WORSHIP: PSALM 8:2

From the lips of children and infants you have ordained praise because of your enemies, to silence the foe and the avenger.

David recognized that whenever God reveals Himself, whether above the heavens or upon the earth, He is majestic. His praise is chanted on high and echoed from cradle and nursery. This praise is a sufficient answer to God's opponents.

What is sweeter than the songs of children? Our hearts are lifted when we hear them singing the Lord's praises. He is worthy of such adoration, and He sees to it that even helpless "children and infants" (Ps. 8:2) draw the world's attention to Him. The unbelieving world rejects the rule of God, but the forces of darkness cannot silence His praise.

The Savior quoted verse 2 when the Jewish religious authorities complained that some children in the temple courts were singing praise to Jesus as the Son of David. The chief priests and scribes were enraged over what they perceived to be inappropriate conduct and asked the Messiah whether He heard the children's praises (Matt. 21:15-16). The implication is that He was wrong for not stopping them. Jesus, admitting that He did hear the praises, referred His critics to Psalm 8:2 and in this way defended the children against the religious leaders. The boys and girls had spoken more wisely about our Lord than did the chief priests and scribes.

III. HUMANITY'S PLACE: PSALM 8:3-5

When I consider your heavens, the work of your fingers, the moon and the stars, which you have set in place, what is man that you are mindful of him, the son of man that you care for him? You made him a little lower than the heavenly beings and crowned him with glory and honor.

David gazed into the heavens once again and considered his place in the grand scheme of creation. Did he matter to God? Was he important and valuable compared to the heavenly bodies? He recognized that what he could see in the sky was the work of God's "fingers" (Ps. 8:3). Of course, David knew that God did not have literal fingers, but in lavish poetic style he used a powerful figure of speech to describe God's creative power.

Verse 4 indicates that the heavens belonged to God, for He had made them. We also learn that He set all the solar bodies in exactly the right place for our benefit. Ultimately, it takes faith to acknowledge that even the universe with its infinite distances is the work of God. As Hebrews 11:3 says, "By faith we understand that the universe was formed at God's command, so that what is seen was not made out of what was visible."

To respect God's majesty, we must compare ourselves to His greatness. That's what David did when he asked, "What is man that you are mindful of him?" (Ps. 8:4). Here "man" refers to all human beings regardless of gender. David's use of the phrase "son of man" looks upon people as insignificant and transitory. If the entire universe appears microscopic in the sight of the Creator, how much less must be the significance of humanity?

To feel small like this is a healthy way to get back to reality. Of course, God does not want us to become transfixed on our smallness. Rather, He wants us to humbly turn our gaze to Him. David seemed to do this in verse 5 when he noted that God made human beings "a little lower than the heavenly beings." The phrase can be translated "a little lower than God." This would ascribe even more dignity to us than being compared with angels (Heb. 2:7). Also, the phrase translated "a little" (Ps. 8:5) could read "for a little while." This might mean that believers, when glorified in heaven, are somehow "higher" than the angels.

Whichever interpretations are taken, it's clear that God has crowned humankind with "glory and honor." This insight could not be obtained by looking at the sky or by any other part of nature. The writer wrote under the inspiration of the Holy Spirit. David knew that, despite our apparent unimportance in the universe, we humans are in fact highly valued by God.

Our dignity stems from our creation in the image of God (Gen. 1:26-27). Despite Adam's sin, all people bear vestiges of God's image (5:1). Followers of Christ are in the process of having the image of God restored in them (2 Cor. 5:17; Col. 3:10). Therefore, Psalm 8:5 not only applied to Adam and Eve when they were created, but also applies to us. Hebrews 2 also applies it to Christ.

IV. HUMANITY'S RESPONSIBILITIES: PSALM 8:6-8

You made him ruler over the works of your hands; you put everything under his feet: all flocks and herds, and the beasts of the field, the birds of the air, and the fish of the sea, all that swim the paths of the seas.

Because humans are the only creatures on earth made in God's image, God put us in charge of the rest of creation (Gen. 1:28-30). As Psalm 8:6-8 reminds us, we have dominion over the animal world. We have the right to use nature to meet our needs, while at the same time fulfilling our responsibility to take care of nature.

When we candidly take this into account, we sense a great opportunity to honor and please God. The Lord has given us everything to bless us and provide for all our needs. We of course need great wisdom in being responsible stewards over God's creation. It is His creation and we are not at liberty to despoil it for selfish ends.

Some people claim that humans are no more valuable than any other form of life. But Psalm 8 plainly contradicts that opinion. God has bestowed on us more significance than any other part of the visible creation. Because of our sin, none of us has perfectly achieved the dignity God wanted us to have. That's why God sent Jesus to put things right and to restore His creation to glory and honor. In fact, as Hebrews 2:6-8 reminds us, Psalm 8:4-6 finds ultimate fulfillment in Christ. It is because of Him that redeemed humanity will be able to fully realize its appointed destiny over the creation.

V. THE POSTLUDE: PSALM 8:9

O LORD, our Lord, how majestic is your name in all the earth!

David concluded his psalm with another powerful affirmation of God's glory. The writer's prelude put him in the proper frame of mind to consider God's creation works. And his postlude moved him to exclaim "how majestic" (Ps. 8:9) God's name was "in all the earth." This psalm emphasizes how blessed we are. If we do not take the time to think about God and His work, we will not be moved to praise Him. But when we contemplate the universe that God created, we will want to humbly worship Him.

Discussion Questions

1. In what way had God set His "glory above the heavens" (Ps. 8:1)?
2. Why would God ordain praise from "the lips of children and infants" (vs. 2)?
3. In light of God's greatness, why does He care for humankind?
4. How has God crowned humanity "with glory and honor" (vs. 5)?
5. How can we, as God's stewards over His creation, conduct ourselves responsibly?

Contemporary Application

Psalm 8 reminds us that God is worthy of our praise because He both created and sustains us. This truth is also taught in the New Testament. In Matthew 6:25-33, Jesus urged His disciples not to worry about where they would get food to eat, water to drink, or clothes to wear. The Savior indicated that their heavenly Father would graciously provide what they needed, just as He supplied the birds of the air and the lilies that carpeted the fields of Palestine. He would do even more for His people, who were of immeasurably greater value to Him.

As Paul addressed the philosophers of Athens, he declared that God made the world and everything in it and that He gives life and breath to every creature (Acts 17:24-25). The apostle made it clear that this powerful Creator determines the various eras of history and the limits of each nation's territory (vs. 26). Paul also said that this great God gives people the ability to live, move about, and become responsible citizens in their communities (vs. 28).

Finally, James 1:17 reveals that every good thing, every generous action, and every perfect gift comes from the Father who created the lights of heaven. Every aspect of our lives is under God's loving care. This one who is all-powerful, all-wise, and all-knowing deserves nothing less than our highest adoration.

Joy in Forgiveness

DEVOTIONAL READING

Psalm 51:1-12

DAILY BIBLE READINGS

Scripture

Background Scripture: *Psalms 32; 51*
Scripture Lesson: *Psalm 32*
Key Verse: *Blessed is he whose transgressions are forgiven, whose sins are covered.* Psalm 32:1.
Scripture Lesson for Children: *Psalm 32:1-2, 5-11*
Key Verse for Children: *Blessed is he whose transgressions are forgiven.* Psalm 32:1.

Lesson Aim

To show our gratitude for God's forgiveness by becoming more forgiving of others.

Lesson Setting

Time: *Written sometime during the reign of David (1010–970 B.C.)*
Place: *Israel*

Lesson Outline

Joy in Forgiveness

  I. Relief from Guilt: Psalm 32:1-5
      A. *An Exclamation of Joy: vss. 1-2*
      B. *God's Hand of Discipline: vss. 3-4*
      C. *Confession and Forgiveness: vs. 5*
  II. Admonitions to the Upright: Psalm 32:6-11
      A. *An Exhortation to Confess Sin: vss. 6-7*
      B. *A Word of Godly Instruction: vss. 8-9*
      C. *A Call to Praise God: vss. 10-11*

Introduction for Adults

Topic: *Joy in Forgiveness*

When we think about King David's notorious sins of adultery and murder, we may be surprised to learn that he wrote songs about this terrible time in his life. Even more astounding is that, through the marvels of God's grace and mercy, David found forgiveness, and this prompted him to rejoice in the Lord.

David's experience stands as a strong corrective to those who think that God could not possibly forgive them for all the awful things they have done. Tragically, many people are caught in the deadly snare of believing they are beyond redemption. The account of David's pardon and restoration can give them sorely needed hope.

Christians have the immense responsibility to point the way to God's forgiveness. And as pardoned sinners, we never outgrow the need to give our testimony to others who want to know the way to salvation and forgiveness.

Introduction for Youths

Topic: *Forgiven!*

One afternoon after school, Joe decided to do some target shooting with his father's shotgun. The lad had been allowed to use the gun for hunting game, but not for anything else. His father and mother were not at home, and so Joe felt it would not matter if he blasted away at some old metal cans along a tree line at the back of their lot. No sooner had he fired the weapon than his parents pulled into the driveway.

Joe became rigid. What should he do? Should he say he was hunting rabbits, for example? The lad decided to tell the truth. He admitted that he had been shooting at some metal cans. With this admission, Joe anticipated that he would lose his hunting privileges. But instead, his parents forgave him and asked him not to be irresponsible again.

To be forgiven is a wonderful feeling. It's one of the reasons for experiencing joy in the Christian life. When we sin, we should confess our wrongdoing to our loving and wise heavenly Father. God promises to forgive us and restore us to fellowship with Him. He can do this because of what Jesus did for us on the cross.

Concepts for Children

Topic: *Praise God: The One Who Forgives*

1. There are times when we disobey God.
2. We usually feel sad when we don't do what God wants.
3. When we tell God that we have disobeyed Him, He forgives us.
4. We are happier when we admit to God what we have done wrong.
5. We can tell God about our sins when we pray to Him.

The Lesson Commentary

I. RELIEF FROM GUILT: PSALM 32:1-5

A. An Exclamation of Joy: vss. 1-2

Blessed is he whose transgressions are forgiven, whose sins are covered. Blessed is the man whose sin the LORD does not count against him and in whose spirit is no deceit.

Psalm 32 is an analysis of sin and forgiveness, willfulness and repentance. It is generally believed that this penitential (or repentance) song—like Psalm 51—has its origin in David's response to God following his infamous affair with Bathsheba and murder of her husband, Uriah the Hittite (2 Sam. 11:1—12:13). It is one of the marks of the integrity of Scripture that the low points as well as the triumphs of a prominent character such as David are described.

Though Psalm 32 records David's confession of his sin, it reads as if it was to be performed during a worship service at the temple. For example, the wording of verses 1, 2, and 11 suggest that the song leader read these to the congregation. Next, while in the hearing of the same assembly, the leader spoke directly to the Lord (vss. 3-7). Then a priestly representative gave a word of exhortation, both to the main speaker and those in attendance (vss. 8-10).

The hymn opens with an expression of joy at God's mercy (vss. 1-2). It says the forgiven are "blessed," or happy. It is appropriate that this term is used of both the righteous person of the first psalm and the confessed sinner of this psalm. God wants to pardon sinners. In fact, forgiveness has always been part of His loving nature. The Lord announced this to Moses (Exod. 34:6-7), He revealed it to David, and He dramatically showed it to the world through Jesus Christ.

The notion of forgiveness presumes the reality of sin. Likewise, the concept of sin presumes a holy standard that has been broken. When we disobey God, we offend His holiness. David used three Hebrew words to describe sin. The word rendered "transgressions" (Ps. 32:1) referred to rebellion against God. "Sins" stood for offenses that constituted a swerving from the path of obedience. And "sin" (vs. 2) indicated distortion, illegality, or a lack of respect for God's will.

Matching the three words for human evil are three terms for divine forgiveness. The term rendered "forgiven" (vs. 1) meant "lifted" or "removed." "Covered" suggested that God conceals sin from His own eyes. And "does not count against" (vs. 2) referred to the cancellation of a debt. The joy of forgiveness rests on the fact that our holy God has pardoned us. Of course, our confession of sin must be sincere, for forgiveness comes only to those "in whose spirit is no deceit."

B. God's Hand of Discipline: vss. 3-4

When I kept silent, my bones wasted away through my groaning all day long. For day and night your hand was heavy upon me; my strength was sapped as in the heat of summer.

David knew how to value the happiness of the forgiven. Previously his stubborn refusal to confess his sin had brought him nothing but misery. He evidently hoped that in time the sin and its penalty would go away. But this didn't happen.

The psalmist related that, when he tried to stifle his conscience, he grew progressively weaker and groaned in discomfort "all day long" (Ps. 32:3). This was due in part to the fact that he felt God's hand of discipline "day and night" (vs. 4). In contrast to the righteous, who are like trees that flourish even during a drought (1:3), David had been like a plant whose strength withered in the summer heat.

Psychologists have long known that bottling up feelings of guilt triggers harmful reactions in both the mind and body. At the heart of the psalmist's discomfort was the conviction of sin that was sent by God. This weight of David's feelings of guilt must have felt relentless and unbearable. Not all physical illness and mental distress can be traced to specific sins, but some can be. If the Spirit convicts suffering believers about a wrong action or attitude, their proper response is to agree with God and ask for His cleansing.

C. Confession and Forgiveness: vs. 5

Then I acknowledged my sin to you and did not cover up my iniquity. I said, "I will confess my transgressions to the LORD"—and you forgave the guilt of my sin.

Sometime after David's intense physical and spiritual suffering, he decided to confess his sins. To confess our sin is to agree with God, to acknowledge that He is right to declare that what we have done is wrong. No matter who else is hurt, the principal offense of any sin is always against "the LORD" (Ps. 32:5). Confession is to affirm our intention of forsaking our sin in order to follow God more faithfully.

The step David took brought immediate relief. His confession had been complete, as shown by his repeating all three words for sin. Though this verse uses just one word for God's forgiveness, we can be sure it was complete as well. The consequences of David's sin with Bathsheba remained despite God's pardon (2 Sam. 12:13-20). Nevertheless, God had forgiven David and restored His relationship with the king of Israel.

The Gospel assures us that Jesus died on the cross to atone for our sins. The Savior also rose again to defeat sin and death. Because of what Jesus did, God is able to cancel the "written code, with its regulations, that was against us and that stood opposed to us" (Col. 2:14). It was as if the Lord took our guilt and nailed it to the cross of Christ.

Over the centuries, many believers, overcome by an awareness of their own sins, have found in the words of Psalm 32:5 a ray of hope. David shared with God the depth of his sorrow and repentance, as well as the height of his joy at being forgiven. We too, when we confess our sin, can rejoice in the knowledge that God responds with complete forgiveness. As 1 John 1:9 says, "if we confess our sins, [God] is faithful and just and will forgive us our sins and purify us from all unrighteousness."

II. ADMONITIONS TO THE UPRIGHT: PSALM 32:6-11

A. An Exhortation to Confess Sin: vss. 6-7

Therefore let everyone who is godly pray to you while you may be found; surely when the mighty waters rise, they will not reach him. You are my hiding place; you will protect me from trouble and surround me with songs of deliverance.

On the basis of his own experience, David instructed the congregation. He urged them not to repeat his error (Ps. 32:6). Rather than trying to hide our wrongdoing, we should confess it to God while He "may be found." A similar admonition is found in Isaiah 55:6, "Seek the LORD while he may be found; call on him while he is near." The idea is that there will come a time (after death) when sinners will no longer have the opportunity to seek forgiveness.

David noted that those who repent receive God's help in escaping troubles. When "the mighty waters rise" (Ps. 32:6), we can flee to high ground, and when trials come, we can flee to God. The creation myths of many Near Eastern peoples told of deities who subdued a chaotic ocean and formed the world from it. These peoples viewed large bodies of water as evil. While Israelite religion denied the reality of such myths, the people of God were familiar with them. Thus it was natural for David to compare encroaching evil with water that seems to engulf the land.

Verse 7 reveals a quick and dramatic shift from addressing the congregation to speaking directly to God. David declared that the Lord was his "hiding place." The king of Israel could find refuge in the all-powerful and ever-living God. He would protect David from trouble and surround him "with songs of deliverance." The idea seems to be that, as David brought his offerings of thanks to God, the congregation of worshipers in the sanctuary would also affirm the Lord's deliverance by singing loudly in unison.

B. A Word of Godly Instruction: vss. 8-9

I will instruct you and teach you in the way you should go; I will counsel you and watch over you. Do not be like the horse or the mule, which have no understanding but must be controlled by bit and bridle or they will not come to you.

At this point in the psalm, the speaker changes. The Lord (perhaps through a priestly spokesperson) instructed David and those assembled in the sanctuary. God's intent was to guide His people along the best pathway for life. He wanted not only to advise them but also to "watch over" (Ps. 32:8) them.

God described some people as being like senseless horses or mules that had to be controlled "by bit and bridle" (vs. 9). Rather than letting the Lord lead them step-by-step, they stubbornly left Him only one option. In order to keep them useful for Him, God had to discipline them.

Those of us who hear the message of this psalm have a responsibility. God is willing to guide and keep His watchful eye on us, but we need to have teachable spirits. We thus should not be ornery, like a horse or mule that needs a strong hand from its rider before it will go where it should. Instead, we should heed the advice written in God's Word.

C. A Call to Praise God: vss. 10-11

Many are the woes of the wicked, but the LORD's unfailing love surrounds the man who trusts in him. Rejoice in the LORD and be glad, you righteous; sing, all you who are upright in heart!

David resumed his song by drawing a contrast between the ungodly and the faithful. The "woes of the wicked" (Ps. 32:10) are various calamities and chastisements. However, those who trust in God will be enfolded by His "unfailing love." Though they may encounter trouble, believers will be upheld by God's comfort and peace. They need not be afraid, for the Lord "will never leave [them] nor forsake [them]" (Deut. 31:6).

The word translated "surrounds" in Psalm 32:10 is the same term used in verse 7 regarding songs of deliverance. It's as if David was calling for all the righteous in the sanctuary to join him in public praise of the wonder of God's mercy. To be encompassed by the Lord and by His saints declaring His praise is reason enough to "rejoice" (vs. 11) and "be glad."

Discussion Questions

1. What "transgressions" (Ps. 32:1) do you think David was referring to?
2. How is it possible for God to put our sins out of His sight?
3. What effect did David's unconfessed sin have on him?
4. How did God respond when David acknowledged his sin?
5. What real difference does it make for us to confess our sins to the Lord?

Contemporary Application

An unfaithful spouse, a rebellious child, an abusive parent, a traitorous friend—no doubt any one of these can cause inexpressible pain. When these kinds of people devastate our hopes and expectations, we wrestle with deep anger and sorrow that threaten to become bitter. How can we possibly forgive?

It's possible—even necessary—for us to forgive because God has forgiven us in Christ (2 Cor. 5:21). The offended holiness of God is no light matter. Though we can hardly imagine the greatness of our offense against Him, we can get an idea of it when we consider what it cost Him to forgive us: a bleeding, suffocating Jesus crying out from a cross, forsaken by His Father, to whom He had been unswervingly faithful. This is the picture of the pain of an offended God, deeply wounded by our sin yet willing to bear that pain for the sake of reconciling us to Himself.

Because God is absolutely holy and righteous, all forms of disobedience bear a penalty. In order for us to be forgiven, we would have to somehow pay the debt we owe to God. Our liability, however, is too great for us to bear. Only Christ, through His sacrifice on the cross, could pay the penalty associated with our sin. Because Jesus is both fully divine and fully human, His sacrifice on the cross is infinite in its saving value and a legitimate atonement for the sins of all humanity. God has declared that He will pardon all who have put their trust in Christ.

In light of this, our question "How can we possibly forgive?" becomes "How can we possibly not forgive?" No one—not even Jesus—said it would be easy. God forgave us by way of the Cross, and we dare not deceive ourselves by thinking we will escape the pain of having to forgive the offenses committed against us in this life. But as our gratefulness for God's forgiveness grows, our willingness to forgive others will grow as well.

Let All the Peoples Praise God

DEVOTIONAL READING

Psalm 97:6-12

DAILY BIBLE READINGS

Monday July 29
Proverbs 1:1-7 Learning about Wisdom

Tuesday July 30
Proverbs 1:20-33 Listen to Wisdom for Security

Wednesday July 31
Proverbs 2:1-15 Accept God's Word

Thursday August 1
Proverbs 3:1-12 Trust God, Not Your Own Insight

Friday August 2
Proverbs 3:13-26 Keep Sound Wisdom and Prudence

Saturday August 3
Proverbs 4:1-17 Hold on to Instruction

Sunday August 4
Proverbs 8:1-11 Choose Knowledge over Gold

Scripture

Background Scripture: *Psalms 67; 96*
Scripture Lesson: *Psalms 67:1-5; 96:1-9*
Key Verse: *May the peoples praise you, O God; may all the peoples praise you.* Psalm 67:3.

Lesson Aim

To rejoice in God's unique authority and glory.

Lesson Setting

Time: *Dates unknown, though both psalms were possibly written sometime before the fall of Jerusalem in 586 B.C.*
Place: *Israel*

Lesson Outline

Let All the Peoples Praise God

I. A Prayer for Divine Mercy: Psalm 67:1-2
II. A Plea for Universal Worship: Psalm 67:3-5
III. A New Song: Psalm 96:1-3
IV. Above All Gods: Psalm 96:4-6
V. Worthy of Glory: Psalm 96:7-9

Introduction for Adults
Topic: *Sing a New Song*

The men's rooming and boarding house had a weekly meeting convened by the owner. The residents were expected to attend. More than that, they were expected to tell about something that God had done in their lives. Of course, a few attendees were not too keen about this idea. But something always happened after those meetings. The stories about fresh encounters with God were like blood transfusions. The accounts injected spiritual vitality into those who were just going through the same old religious routines.

Every convocation of believers can benefit from testimonies of how God has been powerfully at work among His people. That's why Psalms 67 and 96 (the focus of this week's lesson)—which are hymns of worship and praise—are so invigorating and life-changing. We all need to contemplate "new songs" such as these, for they help to keep our love for Christ from growing cold.

Introduction for Youths
Topic: *A New Song*

"Declare his glory among the nations" has been the theme of student missionary conventions. Thousands of students have responded to the command. They have given their lives to serve Christ where His name is not known, loved, and obeyed. These dedicated young people have changed countless communities and brought hope to innumerable people.

When we sing a new song of praise to God for what He has done for us, we should also think about people locally and around the world who have no reason to sing. Some have never heard the good news of Jesus, while others have rejected it. In either case, we should continue filling our hearts with the praises of Psalms 67 and 96 (the focus of this week's lesson). Doing this will keep us from hardening our hearts to the needs of the lost around us.

Concepts for Children
Topic: *God Deserves Praise*

1. The psalmist asked God for His favor and presence so that His truth could be told to others.
2. The psalmist asked God to let the people offer praise to Him for His fairness and guidance.
3. The psalmist declared the greatness of God and told others that salvation is found only in Him.
4. The psalmist invited all the people of the world to worship the Lord.
5. We should praise God for all of the wonderful things He has done for us.

The Lesson Commentary

I. A PRAYER FOR DIVINE MERCY: PSALM 67:1-2

May God be gracious to us and bless us and make his face shine upon us, that your ways may be known on earth, your salvation among all nations.

Psalm 67 is a hymn of praise that served as either an invocation or doxology in worship. Because of its reference to a "harvest" in verse 6, this psalm seems to have been designed for use in Israel's harvest festival. Yet the poem's scope extends far beyond national interests. The unknown writer repeatedly referred to "nations" and "peoples," expressing his hope that the blessing bestowed on Israel might spread around the world.

A blessing must be received before it can be passed on to others. That is why the psalmist began his song by asking God to bless "us" (vs. 1), meaning the Israelites. The first verse echoes the benediction with which the priests blessed the nation (Num. 6:24-26). By borrowing these words, the writer sought prosperity for his people, for if Israel fared poorly, other nations would fail to appreciate the greatness of Israel's God. On the other hand, if God blessed the Israelites, saving knowledge of Him would spread near and far (Ps. 67:2).

Verses 1 and 2 teach us that it is proper to ask God for material and spiritual blessings. But once the blessings are given, we should share them with others as freely as God has shared them with us.

II. A PLEA FOR UNIVERSAL WORSHIP: PSALM 67:3-5

May the peoples praise you, O God; may all the peoples praise you. May the nations be glad and sing for joy, for you rule the peoples justly and guide the nations of the earth. May the peoples praise you, O God; may all the peoples praise you.

The refrain of verses 3 and 5 is a prayer that all peoples will praise God. These verses frame verse 4, which tells why the peoples should praise Him. God's reign over the world brings joy to His subjects, for He rules justly like a good judge and He guides tenderly like a good shepherd.

The final two verses of the psalm express confidence that God's blessings will come and that everyone will recognize God for giving them. A good harvest was just the beginning of the blessings. The greatest blessing will be that "the ends of the earth [meaning people everywhere] will fear him" (vs. 7). The God of Israel— "our God" (vs. 6)—will be recognized as the God of the world.

In ancient cultures each nation had its own religion with its own deities. One unique aspect of the Hebrew religion was the belief that its God, the living Lord, reigns everywhere, and that one day everyone will know it. This theme is evident in Psalm 67, for it anticipates the rule of God over Jews and Gentiles.

This vision for the worldwide spread of God's knowledge, rule, and worship appears early and often in the Old Testament. God told Abraham, the founder of the Hebrew race, that "all peoples on earth will be blessed through you" (Gen.

12:3). Old Testament law provided a way for aliens to enter the covenant community. Prophets kept the vision before the people through such words as these: "I will beckon to the Gentiles, I will lift up my banner to the peoples" (Isa. 49:22).

In the Old Testament, God's worldwide worship remained a vision of the future. But when Jesus came, it was time to begin making that vision a reality. While the predictions of Psalm 67 are nearer fulfillment than ever before, millions living today still have not heard about Jesus. They need someone to tell them. It's our privilege and responsibility to help spread the Good News to people all over the world who have grown accustomed to bad news.

III. A New Song: Psalm 96:1-3

Sing to the LORD a new song; sing to the LORD, all the earth. Sing to the LORD, praise his name; proclaim his salvation day after day. Declare his glory among the nations, his marvelous deeds among all peoples.

Psalm 96 seems to have been composed for use in public worship, most likely in the temple. The fact that it is quoted almost entirely in 1 Chronicles 16 suggests that David could have written it. However, the psalm's strong resemblance to the latter part of Isaiah has led others to suggest a later date for its composition.

The presence of a "new song" (Ps. 96:1) indicates that something has changed; things are no longer the same in the world. There is a new order in place—the Lord reigns over all the earth (vs. 10). This speaks of a new world order where God exercises His supreme control.

Because of God's rule, all the people of the earth are called upon to sing the Lord's praises as thoughts of His greatness come to mind (vs. 1). The exuberance of the passage suggests that the adoration could not be restrained or held back, even if the people were to try. How could they keep quiet in light of the Lord's great salvation? As verse 2 makes clear, God's people were to make known the Lord's deliverance among those who did not know Him.

The word rendered "nations" (vs. 3) refers to the idolatrous Gentiles of the world. All the nations were to hear about the Lord's salvation, and Israel was to be God's witness to the world. When we truly understand the greatness of our Lord and what He has done for us, we cannot help but become a witness of His wonderful work!

IV. Above All Gods: Psalm 96:4-6

For great is the LORD and most worthy of praise; he is to be feared above all gods. For all the gods of the nations are idols, but the LORD made the heavens. Splendor and majesty are before him; strength and glory are in his sanctuary.

The primary consideration behind the psalmist's call to sing the Lord's praise is that of His surpassing greatness. No other being compared to Him. The Lord is to be revered above all territorial or national gods, for He is the one and only true God (Ps. 96:4).

The term rendered "idols" (vs. 5) indicates the nothingness of these so-called gods in contrast to the Lord, who created the heavens. "Idols" can either mean that these pagan deities have no existence or that they are totally powerless. Either way, it emphasizes their complete impotence in contrast to the Lord, who controls them.

The idolatrous world considered the heavens to be the dwelling place of their gods. The fact that the living and true God made their residence emphasizes His authority over these supposed deities. Compared with the all-powerful Lord, these so-called gods were utterly powerless. Everything about them was created by the God of Israel.

The latter part of Isaiah contains many passages contrasting the magnificence of God with the worthlessness of idols (40:18-20; 44:9-20; 46:5-7). Isaiah 46:9 sums up the superiority of the Lord in contrast to other gods: "I am God, and there is no other; I am God, and there is none like me." Isaiah 42:17 shows the future despair of those who hope in idols: "But those who trust in idols, who say to images, 'You are our gods,' will be turned back in utter shame." Contrast that with the singing that accompanies the realization of the Lord's salvation (Ps. 96:13). Only the true God can bring such joy to His people.

Verse 6 describes God's glory in a poetic way. The pairs of divine qualities, "splendor and majesty" and "strength and glory," are personified as attendants before the Lord. What other god can match the magnificence and splendor of the Lord?

While we might not be tempted to worship pagan gods (though the worship of statues is becoming more and more common in the Western World), we do struggle with putting the things of the world before the Lord. Just as with the Israelites, we need to be brought back to reality by acknowledging the true place of God in contrast to the other things that compete for our devotion.

V. WORTHY OF GLORY: PSALM 96:7-9

Ascribe to the LORD, O families of nations, ascribe to the LORD glory and strength. Ascribe to the LORD the glory due his name; bring an offering and come into his courts. Worship the LORD in the splendor of his holiness; tremble before him, all the earth.

The Lord's infinite superiority to all supposed gods prompted the writer to invite all nations to join in worshiping the one true and living God (Ps. 96:7). Just as the blessing of the Lord's salvation includes all the nations (vss. 2-3), so also does the obligation to give God the recognition He deserves.

What is worship? It is the ascribing of worth, respect, or praise to the Lord. In ancient times the Israelites worshiped God in a variety of ways. Their expressions of praise were formal and informal, structured and unstructured, solemn and joyous. They would glorify God through song, prayer, and the study of Scripture.

Even in the Old Testament, God was concerned that all the nations would hear about His salvation and respond by worshiping Him alone. The Lord never intended for His good news to be hidden; Israel was to be a witness to God's unique authority and power (Isa. 43:10, 12). For instance, it was the Lord who sent Jonah to Nineveh so the people of that city could hear God's warning and repent.

God's sovereignty is not limited to just one race, one continent, or one hemisphere. The Lord's rule touches every nation, making everyone on earth ultimately accountable to Him. Because there is no other true deity, He alone is deserving of the worship of all people everywhere.

There is a critical point to be made relating to the theme of Psalm 96. God used Israel as the means of revealing Himself to the world. Because of the universal reign of the Lord taught in this hymn, Christianity should never be considered as a Western faith limited to a group of cultures. God's reign over all the world means that every person on earth is responsible to Him for his or her life and worship.

Over the years critics have accused Christian missionaries of spreading Western culture. The universal nature of God's rule, however, means that we are responsible to be witnesses to the entire world. It demands that the church be involved in a mission to reach the entire earth with the Gospel, while validating what is worthwhile and distinctive in each culture.

In ancient times, acts of worship were usually expressed with a sacrifice. The Israelites were required to bring a variety of offerings into the temple courts that showed their gratitude as well as their desire to walk in fellowship with God (vs. 8). Worshiping the Lord in the "splendor of his holiness" (vs. 9) means coming before Him in garments that are suitable for those who recognize God's glory. At first it might be easy to think that this specifies proper worship attire. However, this actually refers to our behavior and attitude. We are to be attired in holiness (Col. 3:12).

In one sense we can never be holy enough to stand before the Father apart from the righteousness we possess in Christ. Because of what He did on the cross, believers are dressed in His righteousness. But in another sense, the glory of God demands that we approach Him showing appropriate reverence as people in the presence of a mighty and holy God.

To "tremble before [God]" (Ps. 96:9) means to recognize that He is the Lord of all the earth. He has full control of everything, even the daily details of our lives. True worshipers of God recognize not only His purity but also His power. They submit to Him fully and proclaim His truth everywhere they can.

Discussion Questions

1. Why do you think the writer of Psalm 67 wanted the ways of God to be known throughout the earth (vs. 2)?
2. What will be the reason for the nations giving praise to God (vs. 5)?
3. Why do you think the writer of Psalm 96 encouraged us to sing God's praise (vss. 1-3)?
4. What do you think is the importance of rejoicing in God's superiority to all other "gods"?
5. Why is it important that our rejoicing be based on a clear understanding of God's character?

Contemporary Application

One athletic shoe company uses the slogan "Just Do It" to promote its product. In many ways, that is also true of praising God. It is often just a matter of doing it, of taking the time to praise Him with other believers or even by ourselves. Adoration is not difficult. All it requires is that we be able to think—to meditate on revealed truth and turn that into great thoughts about God. And we can do this anywhere, at any time. We do it alone, in a crowd of people, or while we are worshiping together with other believers.

While formal worship of God with other Christians is a necessary part of our walk, we are also encouraged to rejoice in our faith at all times. Philippians 4:4 says, "Rejoice in the Lord always. I will say it again: Rejoice!" It doesn't just have to be while we are having devotions or are in church. We can also praise God while driving our car, at work, at home, or anytime we are reminded of His glory.

One example of giving glory to the Lord (whether corporately or individually) is by giving Him the credit for all our talents and accomplishments. It means that we recognize our dependence on God as our strength and sustainer. Rather than boast about our abilities, we should point others to God as the one who made us what we are.

Embrace Wisdom

Scripture

Background Scripture: *Proverbs 3—4*
Scripture Lesson: *Proverbs 3:13-18; 4:1-9*
Key Verse: *Blessed is the man who finds wisdom, the man who gains understanding.* Proverbs 3:13.
Scripture Lesson for Children: *Proverbs 3:5-7, 13-15; 4:1-7*

Lesson Aim

To recognize the supreme value of wisdom and heed its instructions.

Lesson Setting

Time: *Sometime during the reign of Solomon (970–930 B.C.)*
Place: *Israel*

Lesson Outline

Embrace Wisdom

I. The Search for Wisdom: Proverbs 3:13-18
   A. *Wisdom's Value: vss. 13-15*
   B. *Wisdom's Promises: vss. 16-18*
II. The Supremacy of Wisdom: Proverbs 4:1-9
   A. *How Wisdom Is Taught: vss. 1-4*
   B. *Why Wisdom Is Important: vss. 5-9*

Introduction for Adults

Topic: *Wisdom Brings Happiness*

During a church missionary conference, someone asked one of the missionaries why they thought their children turned out so well. The mother explained that every day she read to them from the Book of Proverbs. "We simply wanted them to understand the difference between wise and foolish behavior," she said.

Many adults have yet to learn this lesson. Their lives show the bitter consequences of having failed to take heed to the teachings of Proverbs. Tragically, many people think they can escape the damages caused by foolish behavior. That's why society needs to see the difference it makes when we live according to God's rules. The testimonies of Christians are valuable assets in helping others to find happiness through God's wisdom.

Introduction for Youths

Topic: *Get Smart*

Academic excellence is a worthy goal, and in the long run it's better to study hard than to loaf. However, if we get straight A's in school but flunk the lessons that God wants us to learn about wisdom, we haven't really accomplished anything of eternal importance. God's course in how to live is expertly taught in the Book of Proverbs.

The Hebrew people knew all too well the perils of breaking God's laws and the blessings of keeping them. The pithy sayings recorded in Proverbs reflect this ancient wisdom. In this book we find godly counsel on how to deal with a wide variety of situations. If we neglect the truths of Proverbs, we are planting the seeds of our own destruction. But if we seek the book's divine wisdom above everything else, we will reap rich eternal dividends.

Concepts for Children

Topic: *Choose to Be Wise*

1. The Book of Proverbs encourages us to trust in God and turn away from wrongdoing.
2. Wisdom is more valuable than silver, gold, and jewels.
3. Wisdom brings happiness to those who find it.
4. When we do what God wants, we are living in a wise way.
5. We should show by the way we act that God's wisdom is the best way to live.

The Lesson Commentary

I. THE SEARCH FOR WISDOM: PROVERBS 3:13-18

A. Wisdom's Value: vss. 13-15

Blessed is the man who finds wisdom, the man who gains understanding, for she is more profitable than silver and yields better returns than gold. She is more precious than rubies; nothing you desire can compare with her.

We end the quarter with a series of four lessons based on the Book of Proverbs. Our overall goal is to explore the place of wisdom in Christian living. Selected texts from Proverbs deal with seeking God's wisdom, rejecting evil, speaking carefully, and caring for the poor. Those who are able to do these things demonstrate an understanding of the true wisdom that comes from God.

Solomon is a principal author of Proverbs (1:1; 10:1; 25:1). There were also other writers of Proverbs, such as Agur (chap. 30) and Lemuel (31:1-9). According to 25:1, a group of assistants to King Hezekiah compiled and added the proverbs of Solomon contained in chapters 25—29. Thus, while many of the wise sayings were penned during Solomon's reign in the tenth century B.C, others were not completed until the time of Hezekiah, whose reign ended in 686 B.C.

The structure of Proverbs includes a prologue (1:1-7) and an epilogue (31:10-31). At the beginning and end of the book are sections of extended instruction (1:8—9:18; 30:1—31:9). The heart of Proverbs contains a large collection of wisdom sayings with no particular organization (10:1—29:27). Despite the vast diversity in the subjects covered in this material, it does not touch on several of the more prominent religious themes in the Old Testament. But through dealing with what are often considered the more mundane areas of life, Proverbs teaches us that all of life is to be lived to the glory of the Lord. There is a moral order to all of creation, and violations of that order only lead to adverse consequences.

Proverbs gives a course of instruction in divine wisdom so that believers might know how to live in such a way that their thoughts, actions, and desires are pleasing to God. The "fear of the LORD" (1:7) is the central truth around which the entire book revolves. The wise person displays a loving reverence for God, which includes submission to His will and obedience to His Word. One's reverence for the Lord is evident in the way one handles riches, success, and social relations.

The Hebrew word commonly rendered "proverb" literally means "a comparison." Through time and usage, the term came to stand for any wise saying or observation, or even a sermon or doctrinal teaching. The major form of proverbs was one-sentence pithy sayings. These are frequently given in parallel form, in which the second line makes a direct contrast with the first, or in which the second line carries forward the idea contained in the first. The contrasting parallel is usually to compare wisdom with folly, or righteousness with wickedness.

As we study Proverbs, we learn that wisdom is to be found in God's Word. Thus, the search for wisdom is not based on random human speculation. Instead, the

349

learner must treasure and explore the teachings of God and seek to penetrate His principles of godly living. The short, compact statements recorded in Proverbs express general truths about human behavior. This means that, while they are often valid, there are always possible exceptions (due to the uncertainty of life and the unpredictable behavior of fallen people). For example, the wise (namely, those who trust and obey God) tend to prosper. But there are times when the wicked prosper and the righteous suffer.

In the first nine chapters of Proverbs, Solomon instructed the young people of his day like a father giving advice to his child. While many of these proverbs are directed toward young people, the principles supporting them are helpful to all believers, regardless of gender or age. Thus, for example, we find in 3:1-2 the exhortation to remember what Solomon has already taught. In fact, heeding his instruction is said to be the key to a long and satisfying life.

Solomon knew how easy it would be for people of faith to forget the guiding principles recorded in Scripture. That's why his approach throughout this chapter of Proverbs is intimate and personal. His concern for the welfare of his readers prompted him to give counsel from the heart, not just the head.

The supreme value of divine wisdom is the focus of verses 13-15. Solomon noted that those who found wisdom and gained understanding were truly "blessed" (vs. 13). This term in the original means to be happy, prosperous, or satisfied. It is the opposite of the stressful pursuit of wealth and importance. Such blessing comes from God alone and is only found in His Word (Josh. 1:7-9; Ps. 1). Divine wisdom leads to practical understanding, which in turn enables believers to make the right decisions in life.

In ancient times silver and gold were highly valued, and people would go to inordinate lengths to obtain them. Solomon declared that the profit of wisdom far outstripped these precious metals (Prov. 3:14). In fact, divine wisdom was worth more than "rubies" (vs. 15), a reddish stone that the ancients highly prized. Solomon plainly stated that nothing we desire "can compare" with wisdom, so great is its value.

Here, then, is a workable philosophy for life. We might strive to do our best in our chosen vocations and careers. But our highest priority, our supreme desire, is to know God and His wisdom. All other goals pale in comparison.

B. Wisdom's Promises: vss. 16-18

Long life is in her right hand; in her left hand are riches and honor. Her ways are pleasant ways, and all her paths are peace. She is a tree of life to those who embrace her; those who lay hold of her will be blessed.

Why is obtaining and heeding God's wisdom incomparable as a life goal? Consider what Solomon said in Proverbs 3:16-18. Wisdom promises long life, riches, and honor. She brings enjoyment, peace, and stability. She is a "tree of life" (vs. 18) for those who follow her. The image here is one of abundance, fruitfulness, and contentment in the Lord.

The world defines wisdom in terms of information acquired from the study of science and philosophy. Wisdom is also associated with having good sense, insight into human relationships, and the ability to take a moderating course of action. Tragically, such notions do not necessarily acknowledge the value of righteousness, holiness, and redemption (1 Cor. 1:30). And yet, from an eternal perspective, these three concerns are of greater eternal value than all the knowledge one could gain from the study of science and philosophy.

Paul noted this vast difference in perspective when he talked about the cross of Christ. From the world's perspective, the idea that the Messiah had to atone for humanity's sin is absurd. Yet it is the supreme expression of God's wisdom (vss. 18-23). Jesus is "the power of God and the wisdom of God" (vs. 24). In fact, "the foolishness of God is wiser than man's wisdom, and the weakness of God is stronger than man's strength" (vs. 25).

The choice is clear. People can opt for either life or death. If they disregard God's wisdom and His way of salvation through Christ, they will reap eternal ruin. However, if they choose to trust in Christ, they will prove themselves to be truly wise, for in Him they will find the "righteousness, holiness and redemption" (vs. 30) that they long for deep down inside.

II. THE SUPREMACY OF WISDOM: PROVERBS 4:1-9

A. How Wisdom Is Taught: vss. 1-4

Listen, my sons, to a father's instruction; pay attention and gain understanding. I give you sound learning, so do not forsake my teaching. When I was a boy in my father's house, still tender, and an only child of my mother, he taught me and said, "Lay hold of my words with all your heart; keep my commands and you will live."

One of the greatest responsibilities of godly parents is to encourage their children to become wise. In Proverbs 4:1-4, we find Solomon doing just that with the young people to whom he originally wrote. This meshed well with earlier admonitions found in Scripture. For instance, Deuteronomy 6:4-8 urged Israelite parents to pass on to their children truths about God they had learned.

The value of this counsel has never been replaced or superseded. It is the key to spiritual growth and development in our families. In this regard, it's interesting to note that Solomon addressed his counsel to children, not to their parents. He evidently felt the parents would be faithful to their calling as wise instructors in the principles of godly living.

Solomon believed that the guidance he offered was "sound" (Prov. 4:2). This refers to healthy, wholesome, and spiritually enriching instruction. Such teaching was practical and unequivocal. It made God's commands clear and spelled out both the benefits of obedience and the disasters of disobedience. Thus, it would be foolish to disregard Solomon's instruction. That's why he repeatedly urged his readers to pay attention to what he had to say, for in so doing they would "gain understanding" (vs. 1).

In verses 3 and 4, Solomon related how his father, David, encouraged him when he was a lad to seek wisdom (1 Kings 2:1-9). Like the people to whom he originally wrote, Solomon said that he too was once naive and inexperienced. Because his parents loved him, they urged him to take their godly instruction to heart. Solomon learned that if he followed David's counsel, his life would be pleasing to God.

Thankfully, Solomon did not give his readers one lecture and then forget them. Rather, he kept at it by repeating the principles of God's Word. And Solomon did so with a compelling sense of urgency. He did not give his readers the option of picking and choosing what suited them. Rather, he implored them to "lay hold of my words with all your heart" (Prov. 4:4). This meant not just hearing what he had said, but also integrating his teaching into their lives.

B. Why Wisdom Is Important: vss. 5-9

"Get wisdom, get understanding; do not forget my words or swerve from them. Do not forsake wisdom, and she will protect you; love her, and she will watch over you. Wisdom is supreme; therefore get wisdom. Though it cost all you have, get understanding. Esteem her, and she will exalt you; embrace her, and she will honor you. She will set a garland of grace on your head and present you with a crown of splendor."

Life these days seems overflowing with different things to experience. But when all is said and done, there are only two crystal clear and very different options—the path of wisdom and the road of folly. The first choice leads to life, while the second option leads to death.

This perspective is evident in Jesus' teaching recorded in Matthew 7:13-14. He declared that the highway to hell is broad; also, its gate is wide for the many who choose to walk down its easy, gliding path. In contrast, the gateway to life is small; also, the road is narrow with only a few ever finding it. By this Jesus did not mean that it is difficult to become a Christian. Rather, He was teaching that there is only one way to eternal life with God. The way of wisdom is to trust in Christ. Living His way may not be popular, but it is nevertheless true and right.

Such a stark contrast between choosing right over wrong, life over death, and wisdom over folly can be found in Proverbs 4:5-9. Solomon was conveying to his readers what his father, David, had told him. His father urged him to develop good judgment by heeding the wise counsel he received. Solomon learned that, if he truly loved wisdom, he would never reject its teachings. Wisdom (here personified as a faithful guardian) would respond by protecting him.

Wisdom could do this because it was "supreme" (vs. 7); this means it was superlative in value. Solomon, reflecting the teaching of his father, declared that if his readers wanted wisdom, they had to decide to go after it. No matter how difficult the road of life might become, they must not abandon their efforts to acquire and apply sound judgment. If the righteous valued wisdom and held tightly to it, they would enjoy great honor (vs. 8).

Solomon was not necessarily referring to worldly accolades. Rather, he had in mind personal integrity and a good reputation. Solomon compared the experience of choosing wisdom over folly to wearing on one's head a "garland of grace" (vs. 9) and a "crown of splendor." In ancient times, people at weddings and religious festivals typically wore wreaths to symbolize their joy. Such illustrated the eternal delight that surrounded those who chose the path of virtue over vice.

Today we enjoy the benefits of God's Word revealed in holy Scripture. Therefore, we know essentially what the Lord desires of us. We are to learn and heed His teachings. We are also to point people to His truths. Such is not a waste of time, for "the holy Scriptures . . . are able to make you wise for salvation through faith in Christ Jesus" (2 Tim. 3:15).

Discussion Questions

1. Why do you think those who find wisdom are "blessed" (Prov. 3:13)?
2. What sorts of riches and honor was Solomon referring to in verse 16?
3. Why would Solomon urge his readers not to "forsake my teaching" (4:2)?
4. What eternal dividends does one reap from heeding godly wisdom?
5. What steps can parents take to ensure the faithful teaching of God's wisdom to their children?

Contemporary Application

Thanks to modern computer technology, we can benefit from what are called search engines on the Internet. These powerful services can answer just about any questions we might have. We now have greater access to more facts than we've ever had in history. But the search engines cannot lead us to God, the fountain of life and the source of all true wisdom.

This week's Scripture passages remind us that the wisest people have not necessarily accumulated the most facts. We all know there's a difference between gaining more and more knowledge and finding redemption in Christ. We can have our heads filled with facts and still miss out on the eternal life that God offers through faith in Christ.

We have noted that modern life is filled with choices. The Book of Proverbs tells us to choose the best way, namely, God's wisdom. If we fail in this regard, we will lose everything. All our intellectual achievements and academic credentials will count for nothing if we reject the truth of Scripture.

As believers, we have a wonderful opportunity to show what we value most in life. When we make knowing Jesus our highest priority, we are truly prudent, for He alone is our wisdom. And only He can make us wise enough to handle whatever life may bring. Therefore, let us point others to Him so that they might have eternal life.

Run from Evil

DEVOTIONAL READING

Proverbs 6:6-15

DAILY BIBLE READINGS

Monday August 12
*Proverbs 11:9-14 Our
Mouths Can Destroy
Neighbors*

Tuesday August 13
*Proverbs 12:13-22
Transgressions of the Lips*

Wednesday August 14
*Proverbs 15:1-14, 23-30
Foolish and Gracious Words*

Thursday August 15
*Proverbs 16:21-29 Pleasant
Words Are Like a
Honeycomb*

Friday August 16
*Proverbs 17:4-20 Stop before
Quarreling Begins*

Saturday August 17
*Proverbs 18:6-8, 19-21 The
Tongue's Power Is Life and
Death*

Sunday August 18
*Proverbs 20:15-22 Lips
Informed by Knowledge*

Scripture

Background Scripture: *Proverbs 6:16-35*
Scripture Lesson: *Proverbs 6:16-28*
Key Verse: *My son, keep your father's commands and do not forsake your mother's teaching. Bind them upon your heart forever; fasten them around your neck.* Proverbs 6:20-21.
Scripture Lesson for Children: *Proverbs 6:16-23*
Key Verse for Children: *My son, keep your father's commands and do not forsake your mother's teaching.* Proverbs 6:20.

Lesson Aim

To recognize the wisdom of pursing virtue and shunning vice.

Lesson Setting

Time: *Sometime during the reign of Solomon (970–930 B.C.)*
Place: *Israel*

Lesson Outline

Run from Evil
   I. What God Hates: Proverbs 6:16-19
  II. What God Requires: Proverbs 6:20-28
     A. *Obedience to Parents: vss. 20-24*
     B. *Chastity: vss. 25-28*

Introduction for Adults

Topic: *Do the Right Thing*

Sin is so seductive that even with the best of intentions we find ourselves breaking God's commands. That's why we need constant reminders of what pleases God and what He detests. Perhaps if we looked at our choices in the light of what meets with the Lord's approval, we would make different decisions.

Our decisions often depend on the information and guidance we receive. For instance, we know the devil—as well as people who have no desire to please God—feeds us false information. "Surely doing such and such is not so bad. After all, you won't hurt anybody," is the standard argument made by the enemy of our faith.

We have to face temptation the way Jesus did, by heeding the truth of Scripture. That's why this week's lesson from the Book of Proverbs is so important. We can't do the right things unless we know and believe the right things.

Introduction for Youths

Topic: *Who Knows What's Right or Wrong?*

Public opinion polls regularly reflect the fact that people cannot agree on what's right and wrong. Therefore, we should not be surprised when young people do not make wise moral choices. There's always somebody else either doing what's immoral or advocating what's immoral.

As Christians, we have to start with God and His Word. Much else is a matter of opinion. When we profess to follow Christ, we accept that He is the way, the truth, and the life (John 14:6). He does not lead us down blind alleys like the leaders of public opinion often do.

Even casual observers without any particular religious bias admit that society suffers from a severe lack of moral guidance. But they cannot agree on what to do about it. It is therefore imperative that Christians stand firmly on the teaching of God's Word, for He clearly tells us what is right and wrong.

Concepts for Children

Topic: *Choose to Do Good*

1. The writer of the Book of Proverbs mentioned seven ways of thinking and acting that God does not like.
2. God wants us to listen to and obey the wise teaching of our parents.
3. What our parents tell us to do and not do can help us avoid acting in ways that are harmful.
4. God is pleased when we seek to do what is right.
5. We show that we love God when we treat others in a kind manner.

The Lesson Commentary

I. WHAT GOD HATES: PROVERBS 6:16-19

There are six things the LORD hates, seven that are detestable to him: haughty eyes, a lying tongue, hands that shed innocent blood, a heart that devises wicked schemes, feet that are quick to rush into evil, a false witness who pours out lies and a man who stirs up dissension among brothers.

The Book of Proverbs tells us the difference between prudent and reckless behavior. It also discusses the difference between wisdom and folly. In very clear, practical terms, Proverbs reveals the way of virtue and the path of vice, and urges us to choose the first and shun the second. Many aspects of daily life are covered so that we need not speculate on matters of morality and ethics.

Job, Proverbs, and Ecclesiastes make up the wisdom literature of the Bible. These books can be distinguished from the rest of the Old Testament in the way in which they present divine truth. Though the wisdom writers relied on observation and study, they made greater use of introspection and meditation than other Hebrew authors. The sages commented little about Israel's history, politics, geography, kings, and laws. Instead, the wisdom writers focused on the enduring aspects of the human condition. The sages examined the world around them and, under the guidance of the Spirit, drew conclusions about human nature and living in a way that is pleasing to God.

A consistent characteristic of wisdom literature is its practical advice and teaching on how to navigate skillfully through the twists and turns of life. From beginning to end, biblical wisdom is sourced in God for its ideas, methods, and morals. In His revelation through the sages, the Spirit ranged from direct and down-to-earth proverbs, to the puzzling, often difficult words of Ecclesiastes, to the mysterious and sublime words of Job. Though the wisdom writings are practical, they are not superficial or external, for they contain moral and ethical elements that stress upright living that flows out of a right relationship with God.

In Proverbs 6:12-15, Solomon offered a description of those who are wicked. They are constant liars who signal their true intentions to their friends by making signs with their eyes, feet, and fingers. They plot evil with their perverted hearts, and they're constantly stirring up trouble. Utter ruin, though, is the end for them.

In verses 16 though 19 we learn exactly what kinds of behavior displease the Lord. These verses remind us that our conduct affects not only our neighbors but also God. Because He created us, He has the right to dictate how we should live. By saying that certain behaviors are detestable to God, Solomon accepted the truth that God is holy and pure and that His holiness can be offended by sinful human activities. Unlike whimsical human hatred, God's hatred of evil arises from His holiness and justice.

God is the supreme Lord and we are accountable to Him. Thus, it does make a difference how we live. The road to eternal peace and joy begins with an understanding of God's attitude toward sin. Until we confess that our sins are detestable to Him, we are not prepared to accept the forgiveness He offers through faith in Christ.

The use of numerical progression in verses 16 through 19 is a rhetorical device that embellishes the poetry, provides a memory aid, and builds to a climax. It gives the impression that there is more to be said about the topic. The progression in these verses involves not just numbers but also words. Note that the term "hates" (vs. 16) intensifies to "detestable," with the latter term being the Bible's strongest expression of hatred for wickedness. In this way, Solomon made it clear that he did not intend to make this an exhaustive list of evil behaviors that displease the Lord. Nevertheless, it is a sufficient starting point to give us a true understanding of the evil that God despises.

Verse 15 says that disaster will overtake the wicked person "in an instant." The reason is given in verse 16—the Lord abhors evil attitudes and actions. At the top of the list are "haughty eyes," which reflects an arrogant attitude. Such pride indicates that we do not need the Lord, and certainly will not worship, love, and obey Him. Sobering is the reminder found in Psalm 18:27, "You save the humble, but bring low those whose eyes are haughty." A similar thought is expressed in 101:5, "whoever has haughty eyes and a proud heart, him will I not endure."

Jesus said that haughtiness comes from our hearts. He associated it with evil thoughts, sexual immorality, theft, murder, adultery, and other vices (Mark 7:20-23). Paul included arrogance in his list of sins that bring God's wrath (Rom. 1:30). Other New Testament writers similarly declared that God resists the proud (Jas. 4:6; 1 Pet. 5:5).

Proverbs 6:17 next mentions "a lying tongue." Lying is one of two abominations of speech in this list (the second being "a false witness," vs. 19). Since the Lord is a God of truth, He also expects people to be truthful. Truthfulness in social relationships is the foundation of community and family life. It undergirds not only our legal system but also the business world.

Proverbs is packed with sound advice about the perils of lying and the benefits of telling the truth. Consider the following verses. "Truthful lips endure forever, but a lying tongue lasts only a moment" (12:19). "The LORD detests lying lips, but he delights in men who are truthful" (vs. 22). From these admonitions we see that wise people tell the truth, while the foolish engage in deception. Perhaps that's why Paul wrote, "Therefore each of you must put off falsehood and speak truthfully to his neighbor" (Eph. 4:25). The apostle's command shows that, even as Christians, we often battle against telling lies.

"Hands that shed innocent blood" (Prov. 6:17) comes next on Solomon's list of vices. The Ten Commandments strictly prohibit murder. It is an abomination to the Lord because we are made in His image. And our lives are sacred to Him because He made us for His glory.

Pride and lying often lead to the folly of murder. Many people have been killed because others have been unable to take the path of humility and truth. In many cases the innocent are the weak and powerless. They are the victims of people who refuse to abandon their evil ways.

Verse 18 begins by mentioning "a heart that devises wicked schemes." The inner world of the human heart is often veiled to others, but not to God. He knows our thoughts and desires. He also knows what ideas we have toward Him and toward others. Sadly, knowing this truth has not stopped people from expending much time and energy thinking about how to dupe others through fraudulent schemes. And if they have been offended, they plot how they will get even.

God detests such schemers because their plans violate His laws and the laws of society. Incredible amounts of money are spent trying to thwart and catch wicked plotters. Human efforts in this regard might fail from time to time, but from an eternal perspective, unholy plans ultimately lead to disaster for those who hatch them.

Solomon's mention of "feet that are quick to rush into evil" suggests that wicked plans often lead to evil deeds. Not all evil schemes succeed, but many do, for the schemers are quick to carry out their plans. God hates those who perpetrate such deeds, for they violate His holy will and hurt many innocent people.

Verse 19 begins with the mention of "a false witness who pours out lies." The Ten Commandments prohibited bearing false witness, yet people in Israel suffered incredibly because of this sin. If witnesses were not credible, just verdicts could not be rendered. That's why Israel's prophets constantly inveighed against this sin. They knew that God expected truth to prevail among His people. Though He gave laws regarding how witnesses were to be called to testify, perjury remained a serious offense.

Solomon next mentioned those who stir up "dissension among brothers." Usually we don't think of sowing discord as being as detestable as perjury. But then we realize that deceit is often the cause of quarrels, which in turn can lead to murder and other unsavory deeds. Dissension can also arise from gossip, slander, and malice, and it breeds in the soil of mutual distrust and hatred. Tragically, such divisive forces are not absent from the church (1 Cor. 1:10-17).

II. What God Requires: Proverbs 6:20-28

A. Obedience to Parents: vss. 20-24

My son, keep your father's commands and do not forsake your mother's teaching. Bind them upon your heart forever; fasten them around your neck. When you walk, they will guide you; when you sleep, they will watch over you; when you awake, they will speak to you. For these commands are a lamp, this teaching is a light, and the corrections of discipline are the way to life, keeping you from the immoral woman, from the smooth tongue of the wayward wife.

In Colossians 3:20, Paul admonished children to "obey your parents in everything, for this pleases the Lord." The philosophical basis for this command is found in Proverbs 6:20-24. Solomon understood that a good home life—one in which the parents responsibly rear their children to love and serve the Lord—went a long way to help young people from falling prey to the seductive snare of immorality.

This passage links the teaching of the father with that of the mother (vs. 20). Wise, responsible youth were to adorn their lives with such godly instruction. This is the idea behind Solomon's picturesque command to tie moral teaching around one's neck and keep it always in one's heart (vs. 21). In this way the truth of Scripture would never be absent from one's life. Wherever one might walk, there godly counsel would be to provide guidance. Moral instruction would be with the upright to protect them when they slept and to advise them when they woke up (vs. 22).

Solomon explained that when young people heeded godly parental teaching, the instruction would be like a lamp to light the way ahead of them (vs. 23). This statement reminds us of Psalm 119:105, "Your word is a lamp to my feet and a light for my path." Such adolescents would accept "the corrections of discipline" (Prov. 6:23) as the way to prompt wholesome living. By this is meant attitudes and actions, dreams and goals, that are pleasing to God.

In the natural scheme of things, children eventually grow to adulthood and become increasingly independent of their parents. If godly parents have done their jobs properly, they will have prepared their children for the challenges of life. Young adults, in turn, are wise to heed (rather than ignore) the wise counsel and virtuous instruction of their parents, especially when it is needed the most. A parent's many years of experience can give young adults the discernment they need to navigate skillfully through the moral pitfalls of life.

B. Chastity: vss. 25-28

Do not lust in your heart after her beauty or let her captivate you with her eyes, for the prostitute reduces you to a loaf of bread, and the adulteress preys upon your very life. Can a man scoop fire into his lap without his clothes being burned? Can a man walk on hot coals without his feet being scorched?

Solomon envisioned young adults being totally immersed in their parents' wise instruction (rather than giving halfhearted or grudging obedience to it), for it would strengthen them against the strong attraction of sexual sin. There was no doubt in the writer's mind that such temptation would come. It was a matter of *when*, not *if*, it would happen.

Solomon narrowed his focus to "the immoral woman" (Prov. 6:24). In the original the harlot is literally referred to as "foreign" or "strange," perhaps because her immoral ways were alien to the path of virtue advocated in Scripture. The seduction of the adulteress began with a "smooth tongue," that is, deceptive flattery. In 5:3 we learn that the lips of a harlot are sweet as honey, and her mouth is smoother than oil. However, as verse 4 makes clear, "in the end she is bitter as gall, sharp as a double-edged sword." She drags her victims along with herself "straight to the grave" (vs. 5).

It's no wonder that Solomon admonished young adults not to lust for the beauty of the adulteress, and not to let her coyness seduce them (6:25). The reason is given in verse 26. A prostitute would reduce her victims to poverty. In fact, sexual sin can ruin one's life, if not physically, then certainly spiritually (vs. 26). We can understand why Paul admonished, "Flee the evil desires of youth, and pursue righteousness, faith, love and peace" (2 Tim. 2:22).

In Proverbs 6:27-28, Solomon asked a series of rhetorical questions to underscore the inevitability of disaster striking those who embrace immorality. Scooping fire into one's lap will lead to severe burns. Also, walking on hot coals is bound to blister one's feet. Similarly, those who commit adultery will not escape the ruinous consequences of this sin.

The world says that it's all right to mess around with others as long as nobody gets hurt. The truth, however, is that all parties involved (and many others, too) get hurt. For instance, the sin of adultery can leave the jilted spouse feeling devastated and the children emotionally scarred. And even those engaging in immorality may discover that they can no longer make fulfilling commitments or be entirely open with another person.

Discussion Questions

1. What do you think the Lord finds the most detestable about "haughty eyes" (Prov. 6:17)?
2. Why is it so undesirable to stir up "dissension among brothers" (vs. 19)?
3. What are some ways young adults can cling tightly to their parents' godly instruction?
4. What are some of the damaging consequences of sexual sin?
5. How do you think believers can successfully resist the temptation to commit adultery?

Contemporary Application

Christians who are thoroughly biblical in their theology and determined to please God in their lifestyles face temptations just as anyone else. Godly living is no more a matter of knowledge and willpower than is salvation. In fact, Satan probably takes particular delight in tripping up Christians who think they are impervious to temptation. Thus we not only need to become more aware of the temptations we face, but even more importantly, we need to seek God's help in overcoming them. Mere knowledge of how we are being tempted will only make the enticement to sin more desirable and us less resistant.

God's help can come to us in many ways. For example, we may be tempted to hate someone who has mistreated us. One way God might help us overcome this temptation is by getting us to assimilate His Word about Jesus' loving attitude toward His enemies. Or we may be tempted to behave immorally. One way God might help us overcome this enticement is by getting us involved in Christian work so that we are too busy to be tempted.

Reliance on the Lord reveals many ways of resisting temptations (1 Cor. 10:13). This does not mean, however, that conquering enticements to sin will be easy. Breaking patterns of ungodly behavior developed over long periods of time may require the intervention of pastors and counselors. But God promises that it can be done.

Watch What You Say

Scripture

Background Scripture: *Proverbs 15—17*
Scripture Lesson: *Proverbs 15:1-4, 7-8; 17:4-10*
Key Verse: *A gentle answer turns away wrath, but a harsh
word stirs up anger.* Proverbs 15:1.
Scripture Lesson for Children: *Proverbs 15:1-3; 17:4-6*

Lesson Aim

To consider how to tame our tongues and use them as
instruments of blessing.

Lesson Setting

Time: *Sometime during the reign of Solomon (970–930 B.C.)*
Place: *Israel*

Lesson Outline

Watch What You Say

  I. Self-Discipline in Speech: Proverbs 15:1-4, 7-8
     A. *What Is Said: vss. 1-4*
     B. *What Results: vss. 7-8*
 II. Wise Versus Foolish Speech: Proverbs 17:4-10
     A. *Foolish Speech: vss. 4-5*
     B. *An Enduring Heritage: vs. 6*
     C. *Virtue, Not Vice: vss. 7-10*

Introduction for Adults

Topic: *Say the Right Thing*

Many times we wish we could retract things we have said in the heat of an argument. But we all know that once our words have been uttered they cannot be recalled. It's in those moments that we learn how constructive or destructive our words have been to others.

That's why Proverbs has so much to say about our speech. Yet rarely do we take seminars in how to control our tongues. We're too embarrassed, perhaps, to admit the damage we have done. And it's hard for us to confess that something we said has injured another person.

We should not dismiss our lapses in speech as just another bad habit. The truth is, our lips betray what's in our hearts (Matt. 15:18-20). That's where we must begin to apply the remedies advocated in this week's Scripture passages, all the while asking the Lord to forgive us and to give us clean hearts.

Introduction for Youths

Topic: *Watch What You Say*

The proliferation of profane, obscene language has overwhelmed our culture. We hear it everywhere we turn, not just in secret conversations in back alleys. Children grow up surrounded by this abusive speech. For instance, they hear music, movies, television, and the radio spew a daily diet of the worst kind of language. Christian youth are often embarrassed by filthy speech. And when they do not use it themselves, they are ridiculed by their peers.

The Book of Proverbs directs us to ways we can use our speech for positive values and outcomes. While Solomon did not directly address the problem of bad language itself, he did provide instruction on how to avoid destructive words, lying, gossip, slander, and evil reports about others. He made it clear that, as people of faith in varying roles and relationships, we have many opportunities to demonstrate the quality of our commitment to Christ through what we say.

Concepts for Children

Topic: *Choose to Speak Kind Words*

1. God wants us to avoid mean answers and give gentle responses.
2. God is concerned as much by what we say as He is with what we do.
3. The Bible is filled with good advice on how we can speak words of wisdom.
4. We should use words to build up people, not to tear them down.
5. We are wise to avoid lying, spreading rumors, or feeling happy when other people suffer.

The Lesson Commentary

I. SELF-DISCIPLINE IN SPEECH: PROVERBS 15:1-4, 7-8

A. What Is Said: vss. 1-4

A gentle answer turns away wrath, but a harsh word stirs up anger. The tongue of the wise commends knowledge, but the mouth of the fool gushes folly. The eyes of the LORD are everywhere, keeping watch on the wicked and the good. The tongue that brings healing is a tree of life, but a deceitful tongue crushes the spirit.

The Book of Proverbs is loaded with both warnings about the sins of the tongue and blessings arising from proper speech. Society in ancient Israel suffered from bad speech, as does the church today. Yet we often fail to guard our lips, making lame excuses for our bad habits of speech.

James gave us ample reasons to purify our lips. He wrote, "The tongue also is a fire, a world of evil among the parts of the body. It corrupts the whole person, sets the whole course of his life on fire, and is itself set on fire by hell" (Jas. 3:6). Therefore, we cannot easily dismiss the sins of our tongues, as if they don't really matter. We need the wise teachings of Solomon to remind us to clean up our speech. And we should follow the example of Christ, whose speech was full of grace and truth (John 1:17).

The comparison in Proverbs 15:1 reveals the way of God's wisdom. In our conversations, two kinds of answers are possible, either gentle or harsh. The situation here involves an accusation and how godly people should respond. One of the severest tests of our commitment to wise living is how we stand up under such a provocation.

Solomon's guidance was full of practical wisdom. The gentle, soft, nondefensive, loving, and nonaggressive reply will turn away conflict. In contrast, the harsh, judgmental, and critical answer will stir up trouble. "Gentle" does not mean we should hide our true convictions or avoid moral issues. Rather, we must speak "the truth in love" (Eph. 4:15). When we do so, we avoid the harsh words that hurt others and spark anger.

There are two kinds of speech: wise and foolish (Prov. 15:2). The wisdom people claim to have will be revealed in their choice of words. Much clever rhetoric is not necessarily wise. Rather than tearing people down, a wise speech will contribute to their overall well-being. In this regard, the Word of God is the standard by which all our speaking is measured. What is consistent with Scripture is wise, and what violates Scripture is foolishness.

God's observation of what we do and say is all-inclusive (vs. 3). The implication of this verse is that God hears everything we utter. Of course, all our behavior is subject to His scrutiny and judgment, but the context here refers to what we say and how we say it. The tongue can produce both evil and good, or, as James wrote, "praise and cursing" (Jas. 3:10). We can avoid a lot of trouble if we consider how God views our speech, including such sins as gossip and slander.

363

There are two kinds of words, life-giving and death-dealing (Prov. 15:4). The Bible leaves us in no doubt about the tongue's potential, both for us and for others. Scripture depicts the tongue as both the bearer of life and the destroyer of the spirit. A healing tongue speaks wholesome, uplifting words, and brings life and encouragement to others. Thus the goal of our speech is both to avoid trouble and bring healing.

In contrast, our tongues can be "deceitful," or perverse, in the sense of promoting treachery. By this Solomon meant that we can twist the truth as well as tell outright lies. In this verse, the harmful effect seems to be on the listener's morale, though wicked tongues can also cause greater destruction than that.

B. What Results: vss. 7-8

The lips of the wise spread knowledge; not so the hearts of fools. The LORD detests the sacrifice of the wicked, but the prayer of the upright pleases him.

The fruit of wise lips is the diffusion of knowledge (Prov. 15:7). In contrast, out of the hearts of fools comes folly. This kind of certainty characterizes the teaching of Proverbs. There is no possibility of keeping one foot in wisdom and the other in foolishness.

"Knowledge" here refers to godly wisdom and understanding. It includes both a theoretical and practical awareness of morals. The tongue is the main way we teach knowledge about God and His truth from one generation to the next. Of course, we now have access to all kinds of technology to transmit knowledge, but the main idea in Proverbs is that we both live and teach the truth personally.

God made us for His pleasure. Our worship and fellowship please Him when what we say and do are characterized by virtue, not vice. He gave us tongues to utter His praises and to honor Him above everything else. Prayer is one of the most fruitful uses of our tongues (vs. 8).

The context of this verse, of course, was Israel's corporate worship. God detested hypocrisy among His people (namely, "the sacrifice of the wicked"). In contrast, the Lord delighted in the prayers of the upright. When we gather as His people, worshiping God in spirit and truth (John 4:24), we use our tongues in prayer and singing. We bless the Lord with our lips, and our tongues become instruments of righteousness that bring glory to His name (Eph. 5:19-20).

II. WISE VERSUS FOOLISH SPEECH: PROVERBS 17:4-10

A. Foolish Speech: vss. 4-5

A wicked man listens to evil lips; a liar pays attention to a malicious tongue. He who mocks the poor shows contempt for their Maker; whoever gloats over disaster will not go unpunished.

In Proverbs 17:4-5, we find wise sayings about our speech as well as about other behaviors. All of these wise sayings merit our careful consideration, for they help us to live righteously in line with our profession of faith in Christ.

One of our toughest temptations is to listen to "evil lips" (vs. 4) that spread malicious rumors. Many people feast on gossip and slander, and they love to believe the worst. Sadly, they do not trouble themselves with the facts. As a result, countless people have suffered grievously because of character assassination. The liars who spread such false reports are guilty of malice. That's because reputations are tarnished, jobs are lost, and marriages are smashed. Instead of believing rumors about other people, we should make every effort to verify the facts.

How quick some people are to mock the poor and gloat over the misfortune of others (vs. 5). We should resist the temptation to believe the worst news about others and impulsively conclude that they "deserved it." Otherwise, we assume the role of God in knowing why people experience hardship. This verse reminds us what Paul said in 1 Corinthians 13:6-7, "Love does not delight in evil but rejoices with the truth. It always protects, always trusts, always hopes, always perseveres."

B. An Enduring Heritage: vs. 6

Children's children are a crown to the aged, and parents are the pride of their children.

God blesses us with children and grandchildren who are proud of their parents (Prov. 17:6). Such a situation doesn't just haphazardly happen. Rather, stable family and community life depends on God's Word being taught, respected, and obeyed. Occasionally, our speech gets out of hand in our families, and we injure those we love the most with hasty words. The fruit of wise, godly, and loving lips can go a long way toward healing such wounds and developing stronger family bonds.

C. Virtue, Not Vice: vss. 7-10

Arrogant lips are unsuited to a fool—how much worse lying lips to a ruler! A bribe is a charm to the one who gives it; wherever he turns, he succeeds. He who covers over an offense promotes love, but whoever repeats the matter separates close friends. A rebuke impresses a man of discernment more than a hundred lashes a fool.

The Hebrew word rendered "arrogant" (Prov. 17:7) has been variously translated as "excellent," "eloquent," or "fine." Moral excess is the main idea behind the NIV rendering. We might say that Solomon meant talking boastfully. This nicely describes what the Book of Proverbs meant by a "fool." The fool is characterized by overbearing, crude, and ungodly speech and behavior.

In mentioning the "lying lips [of] a ruler," Solomon did not just have in mind monarchs. He was also referring to anyone in positions of power or prominence. When the leaders of a nation resort to falsehoods, trust is destroyed and rivalries develop. Throughout Israel's history, such divisive forces often led to bloodshed and the overthrow of many rulers.

In verse 8, Solomon noted that a bribe seems to work like magic for those who give it, for they succeed in whatever they do. In saying this, Solomon was simply underscoring the deplorable state of human behavior. Later (vs. 23) he censured the acceptance of bribes. This is another unequivocal statement about the negative use of our tongues. Our speech should be devoted to promoting justice, not perverting it.

In 17:9, the idea of covering an offense does not mean we should ignore sin, excuse it, hide it, or pretend that we haven't been hurt by it. Rather than telling tales behind someone's back, we should speak directly to them about how they have harmed us.

Once we have done this, we should not endlessly talk about what the other party did wrong, for harping on the matter simply breeds suspicion and discontent. Before long, friends become estranged and resentment and bitterness take over. This proverb warns us that even close friends can become alienated by the wrong use of our tongues. It's no wonder the Gospel enjoins us to forgive those who have sinned against us.

We have a lot to learn about giving and receiving rebukes (vs. 10). Often we show by what we say that our tongues are not skilled in proper, wise, and godly confrontations. For instance, our tempers are prone to rise when someone rebukes us. Yet the wisdom of Scripture reminds us that we are much better off if we seriously consider the correction of our friends.

We all struggle with sin in many and varied ways. But without a doubt, the part of our body that most reveals our sinfulness is the tongue. The tongue is the gateway from the inner to the outer world; it reveals to others what is inside of us. James says that if people can control their tongue, they can control their entire body and are perfectly self-controlled individuals (Jas. 3:2). Of course, some talk more than others, but James is not considering how much we speak, but rather what comes out when we do.

James offered two illustrations to demonstrate how a small device can control a much larger vehicle (vss. 3-4). First, a bit in a horse's mouth allows the rider to dictate to the large animal where it will go, and when it will start and stop. Second, a ship's rudder determines the course of its many-times-larger vessel. The one steering the boat needs only to change the direction of the rudder and, despite strong winds, can keep the ship on course. So it is with the tongue (vs. 5). It is small, but it can do a great deal of good or harm, and we are ultimately responsible for the direction it takes.

Discussion Questions

1. Why are our tongues often so difficult to control?
2. Why do we sometimes not take the sins committed by what we say as seriously as other forms of wrongdoing?
3. What are some things we can learn about the perils of foolish speech?
4. What virtues and blessings can come from wise speech?
5. What spiritual disciplines can help us control our tongues?

Contemporary Application

Thankfully, godly wisdom isn't just for life-and-death situations. It can be part of everyday living. For instance, imagine that a neighbor storms up to your front door. He's hopping mad because he's certain that your dog is responsible for tearing up his vegetable garden last night, and he's letting you know exactly what he thinks about you and your pet.

There is some mistake, however, because only two weeks earlier, you had to take your dog to the vet to be put to sleep. The dog had been like a part of the family, and you're still sad about the loss. Your first impulse is to blast your rude, insensitive neighbor with some sharp retorts to his accusations that would humiliate him and send him packing. But should you follow your impulse? Your neighbor has finished his tirade, and now you have an opportunity to respond. What will you say?

On the surface, this situation may seem relatively insignificant. But what if this neighbor is not a Christian and knows that you are one? Our lives are filled with situations that offer opportunities to demonstrate our faith to others by what we say and do. But those opportunities can come and go quickly. We never know how one of our responses might impact someone. A good or bad word at a critical time in someone's life may leave an indelible impression in his or her thinking about believers and ultimately about Christ. As God's ambassadors we need His wisdom daily to guide our words and actions.

Care for the Poor

DEVOTIONAL READING

Proverbs 19:1-8

DAILY BIBLE READINGS

Monday August 26
  2 Chronicles 29:1-11
  Hezekiah Calls for Renewal

Tuesday August 27
  2 Chronicles 29:15-24
  Purification and
  Consecration

Wednesday August 28
  2 Chronicles 29:25-30 The
  People Worship

Thursday August 29
  Psalm 149 Sing to the Lord

Friday August 30
  2 Chronicles 29:31-36 The
  People Bring Thank
  Offerings

Saturday August 31
  2 Chronicles 30:1-12 The
  People Celebrate Passover

Sunday September 1
  2 Chronicles 30:21-27 God
  Hears the People's Prayer

Scripture

Background Scripture: *Proverbs 19:17; 22:1-4, 8-9, 16, 22-23; 23:10-11*

Scripture Lesson: *Proverbs 19:17; 22:1-4, 8-9, 16, 22-23; 23:10-11*

Key Verse: *He who is kind to the poor lends to the LORD, and he will reward him for what he has done.* Proverbs 19:17.

Scripture Lesson for Children: *Proverbs 19:17; 22:1-2, 8-9, 16, 22-23*

Lesson Aim

To see the importance of sharing with those in need, both through kind words and generous actions.

Lesson Setting

Time: *Sometime during the reign of Solomon (970–930 B.C.)*
Place: *Israel*

Lesson Outline

Care for the Poor

  I. Preserving Integrity: Proverbs 19:17
  II. Making Wise Choices: Proverbs 22:1-4,
    8-9, 16, 22-23; 23:10-11
    A. *Choosing a Good Reputation: vs. 1*
    B. *Choosing Prudence: vss. 2-4*
    C. *Choosing Justice over Injustice: vs. 8*
    D. *Choosing to Help the Poor: vss. 9, 16, 22-23*
    E. *Choosing to Aid the Defenseless: 23:10-11*

Introduction for Adults
Topic: *Who Cares for the Poor?*

Who cares for the poor? God does, and Christians should, too. During Jesus' earthly ministry, He stood against oppression, and the poor and helpless flocked to Him. Knowing that our Lord cares for the poor does not relieve us of our duty to give time, wisdom, and money to help them. Rather, we who belong to Christ by faith are to be His instruments of goodness and grace to the disadvantaged in society.

We admit that there are risks in being so generous. People who offer help to the poor have sometimes suffered for their efforts. We might worry about channeling our material resources in the wrong direction. We may also be concerned that our benevolent programs are not well managed. While these shortcomings do exist, they should not prevent us from reaching out to people in need. If we wait until all conditions are perfect, we will never find the right time to do anything.

Introduction for Youths
Topic: *Why Should I Care?*

Christians care for the poor for a number of reasons. First, it is the Lord's command. Second, Jesus gave us His example. Third, our communities need our help. Fourth, Christians are obligated to love and serve one another. Fifth, those who have the means should come to the aid of those who lack. Sixth, God promised to bless us spiritually when we seek to help the disadvantaged. Seventh, we feel better about ourselves when we give to others in need.

Perhaps our biggest obstacle to caring for the poor is our consuming self-interest. The world tells us to put ourselves first, to look out for number one. We know, though, that God hates such pride. When we care for others, we strip ourselves of the desire to be first. We affirm the teaching of Jesus that "it is more blessed to give than to receive" (Acts 20:35). That's a spiritual principle we dare not ignore, especially if we want to enjoy the eternal delight of God.

Concepts for Children
Topic: *Choose to Help*

1. Acts of kindness that we do for the poor are pleasing to the Lord.
2. God cares about the poor and wants us to do what we can to help them.
3. God judges those who try to harm others, and He blesses those who try to help others.
4. We lose more than we gain when we try to take what belongs to others.
5. God can give us the desire and ability to help those in need.

The Lesson Commentary

I. Preserving Integrity: Proverbs 19:17

He who is kind to the poor lends to the LORD, and he will reward him for what he has done

The Book of Proverbs is jam-packed with wise counsel about how to treat the poor. This reflects the sentiment of the Mosaic law, which gave clear guidelines to the Israelites on taking care of the poor, both their own people and the foreigners living among them. We learn from Scripture that when the faith community helped the poor, they honored both the Creator and His creation. The Lord accepted such help as if the benefactors had offered it directly to Him.

A variety of Hebrew words stand behind our English words in Scripture for "poor" and "poverty." The most frequently used term refers to the lower class of people who lacked the wealth of the upper class. A second word stresses the oppression and pain of poor people who were powerless in society. A third term describes the critical needs of the poor for food and clothing, thus making them dependent on others. This word appears frequently in the Psalms and pictures destitute people who were righteous but who suffered at the hands of the wicked.

More than physical deprivation was included in the concept of poverty. Because of their low social status, the poor were vulnerable to abuses from the rich and powerful. Because the disadvantaged were defenseless, they were likely to be treated unfairly in the courts. When defrauded, they had no recourse but to appeal to God. Their ongoing state of poverty stripped them of their rights, respect, and a place in society.

In Proverbs we find divine counsel that was intended to keep people from falling into poverty (10:4; 20:13; 21:17; 23:21). But we also find repeated condemnation of the unjust practices of those who misappropriated resources and land. God acknowledged that the victims of such abuse had no control over these atrocities. He held responsible the religious, civil, and military leaders for Israel's failure to protect the poor. In this regard Isaiah 58:6-7 and Zechariah 7:9-12 are typical of God's admonitions to the rich and powerful among His people.

Each of the proverbs we will study in this week's lesson reveals a practical aspect of Christian living. The first one, which appears in Proverbs 19:17, is astonishing because it tells us that when we help the poor we really are lending to the Lord. Jesus had the same principle in mind when He said that what we do for people in need is really being done for Him (Matt. 25:37-40). Keeping this truth in mind can help us to open our hearts and our resources willingly and not grudgingly to the poor.

When we are generous to those in need, we receive a "reward" (Prov. 19:17) for our kind deeds. The reward is not specified, but we should not assume that it means we will get our money back. Also, the prospect of getting a reward should not be our primary reason for helping the poor. From an eternal perspective, the Lord blesses the generous with His favor and heavenly graces.

Being kind to the poor goes far beyond the occasional offering in the church's benevolent fund. The poor need other kinds of help, too. For example, they frequently need transportation to medical appointments, assistance in financial planning and legal affairs, tutoring, job training, and so on. Many churches have developed extensive assistance programs for the poor that do not result in long-term dependencies, but rather help the disadvantaged to make it on their own.

II. MAKING WISE CHOICES: PROVERBS 22:1-4, 8-9, 16, 22-23; 23:10-11

A. Choosing a Good Reputation: vs. 1

A good name is more desirable than great riches; to be esteemed is better than silver or gold.

Proverbs 22:1 does not directly address helping the poor, but rather counsels us to put material wealth in the right perspective. The verse teaches us not to worry if we are not rich, for our reputations are far more important than our possessions. "To be esteemed" by others does not depend on our wealth or position. We are esteemed according to our character and good deeds. Those held in highest honor are people who love the most, give the most, and devote themselves to helping others.

Jesus urged His disciples not to covet positions of greatness and power. Rather, He said that the truly great in the kingdom of God are those who serve others. In fact, those who seek to be first will be last. Jesus also said that He came to serve, not to be served (Mark 10:41-45). Because He went to the cross to die for our sins, Jesus has a name that is above all other names (Phil. 2:5-11).

B. Choosing Prudence: vss. 2-4

Rich and poor have this in common: The LORD is the Maker of them all. A prudent man sees danger and takes refuge, but the simple keep going and suffer for it. Humility and the fear of the LORD bring wealth and honor and life.

According to Proverbs 22:2, the rich have no right to abuse the poor, for both were created by God. Thus they are equally precious in His sight. God does not slant His favors toward the rich, for He is completely impartial. This profound truth, when properly understood, has the potential of wiping out social distinctions, levels the pride of the rich, and exalts the poor. It is a powerful safeguard against neglecting the needs of the disadvantaged.

The ways of the wise and foolish often are revealed by their attitudes toward danger and risks (vs. 3). Wise people are able to recognize danger when it appears and they take appropriate steps to avoid it. Foolish people, however, do not see the trouble coming and suffer the consequences.

This truth may easily be applied to how we care for the poor. When we are able to help them avoid costly mistakes, it is important that we do so. Of course, the poor are not impoverished necessarily because they are foolish, but in some circumstances our wise counsel can help them out of tight spots, whether economically, educationally, spiritually, or socially. Thus, if we see trouble coming, we have a moral obligation to warn them.

If we see an opportunity to help the disadvantaged and refuse to do so, we have sinned against the Lord (1 John 3:17-18). We have disregarded Jesus' statement that we should love our neighbors as ourselves (Matt. 22:39). This surely includes the poor.

Proverbs 22:4 reveals that wealth and pride go hand in hand. This is why Moses warned the Israelites against becoming proud when they became rich in the land of promise (Deut. 8:10-14, 17-18). Rather than gaining wealth and honor—often at the expense of the poor and powerless—the people of God were to be humble and fear the Lord. Humility is the proper attitude to inspire care for the poor. That's why God promised that when we walk humbly before Him, we will gain wealth, honor, and life (Prov. 22:4). This does not necessarily mean material riches, but rather something far more important—a right standing with the Lord and our neighbors.

C. Choosing Justice over Injustice: vs. 8

He who sows wickedness reaps trouble, and the rod of his fury will be destroyed.

In ancient times, the poor often suffered at the hands of the wicked rich (Prov. 22:7). That's why verse 8 would be such an encouragement to the disadvantaged. "Wickedness" here refers to ill treatment of the poor and helpless. Jesus' teaching on justice reflects the idea in this verse. People who live by violence are likely to die violently. Likewise, people who live wickedly should not be surprised if they fall victim to crime (Matt. 26:52).

Paul also emphasized the principle of sowing and reaping in Galatians 6. The apostle declared that people who perform the acts of the sinful nature rather than bear the fruit of the Spirit will not be rewarded, for God will not be mocked. And unlike people, He cannot be fooled (vs. 7).

Paul said there is a simple relationship between how people live and how God judges and rewards them (vs. 8). A farmer who sows barley cannot expect to harvest wheat. And no more so can those who obey the callings of the flesh expect to receive eternal life from God. Instead, they will earn eternal destruction. Happily, however, the opposite of this truth is that if we live by the Spirit, we give evidence that we have eternal life.

God provides strategic opportunities for us to do good to others (vs. 10). We should try to discern these opportunities and eagerly act on them. Helping unbelievers is an excellent way to witness wordlessly to God's goodness. But if anything, we should be more eager to help other Christians, since we are all part of God's family.

D. Choosing to Help the Poor: vss. 9, 16, 22-23

A generous man will himself be blessed, for he shares his food with the poor. . . . He who oppresses the poor to increase his wealth and he who gives gifts to the rich—both come to poverty. . . . Do not exploit

lawsuits

the poor because they are poor and do not crush the needy in court, for the LORD will take up their case and will plunder those who plunder them.

The ancient Israelites did not have a formal government welfare program. Thus society depended on the generous sharing of wealth, including basic essentials such as food (Prov. 22:9). Today we are accustomed to welfare programs for the poor, but these programs do not relieve us of our obligations to be generous toward the inpoverished, for many people still need our help.

Job noticed how greatly the poor suffered (Job 24:2-12). Unlike the wicked rich, he determined to bring relief to the disadvantaged. "I rescued the poor who cried for help, and the fatherless who had none to assist him. . . . I was a father to the needy. I took up the case of the stranger" (29:12, 16). Some well-off people do not care to help the needy because they fear losing their long-term financial security. But those who trust and obey the Lord can be sure that He will take care of them spiritually and financially (Deut. 15:9-10; 2 Cor. 9:7-8).

In Bible times, the rich and powerful got their money and privileged positions because they abused the poor and offered bribes. But according to God's Word, such people will become poor themselves (Prov. 22:16). The Lord's judgment may not be readily apparent, but we can trust His promise that righteousness will prevail. For instance, Jesus warned against the terrible perils of wealth, teaching that those who fall prey to acquiring it above everything else will in the end perish (Luke 12:13-21).

Proverbs 22:22-23 contains another stern warning against oppressing the poor. The Hebrew word translated "exploit" (vs. 22) conveys the idea of plundering or ravishing the poor. "Crush" refers to lawsuits against the poor. In both cases, we have a vivid picture of the abuses that prevailed in ancient Israel. Tragically, such crimes continue to exist today in various parts of the world.

In answer to these terrible sins, God promised to be the defender of the poor in courts of law and to plunder the perpetrators of violence (vs. 23). The wicked rich would not escape from the righteous Judge of all the earth. We are therefore wise when we defend the cause of the poor and stand up for their legitimate rights and concerns.

E. Choosing to Aid the Defenseless: 23:10-11

Do not move an ancient boundary stone or encroach on the fields of the fatherless, for their Defender is strong; he will take up their case against you.

In ancient times the wicked rich would transgress the property of the defenseless by removing the stones that marked off the boundary lines of their land (Prov. 23:10). Sadly, the tendency of evil people in all ages is to take advantage of the helpless. Such perpetrators of ungodliness either forget or ignore that the disadvantaged have a "Defender" (vs. 11), and He is "strong" (or mighty).

The Hebrew word translated "Defender" referred to someone who bought back a family member who had fallen into slavery or who accepted the obligation to marry the widow of a family member. In this verse, the term refers to God as the Redeemer of the helpless. He protects their rights and champions their cause. As 15:25 makes clear, even the most desolate, when they receive God's help, possess a more permanent dwelling place than the wicked rich.

Discussion Questions

1. Why do you think wealthy people often find it difficult to be generous to the poor?
2. Why do you think Scripture places more value on the reputation of people than on their material wealth?
3. What are some ways the wicked rich have exploited the poor over the centuries?
4. In what sense is the Lord a defender of the disadvantaged (Prov. 23:11)?
5. What steps can individuals and churches take to care for the poor?

Contemporary Application

People who do evil things to others hate the light of God's truth and do not want to listen to it because it clearly shows what they have done wrong. Despite their repugnance toward God's truth, we are to show them how wrong their injustices are to others. Our aim should be that they will repent and seek God's forgiveness.

The wicked rich often forget that God observes everything that people do. There are no small matters with the Lord. And that is true for us as well. We must not only uncover injustices we see in what others are doing, but more importantly, in what we ourselves are doing. The Lord, who Himself is completely just and fair in His dealings with us, presents Himself as the pattern for our relations with others. He constantly calls us to promote justice in every area of our lives (Amos 5:24).

Do our actions indicate an insensitivity toward the needs and rights of people with whom we deal? Have we in any way developed a focus on ourselves that makes us so indifferent to others that we treat them unfairly? Since God measures us by His own standards of justice, we ought to measure ourselves by the same rule. For example, God wants us to do what is right to other people and to treat them kindly (Mic. 6:8).

In a selfish age like ours, we should search our own hearts to prevent ourselves from slipping into a posture of injustice. We should also cultivate an attitude of humility and love. Just as arrogance and hate foster unjust practices, so humility and love promote fairness and sensitivity to others.